Art School

SELF-TAUGHT

Head of Apollo, by Van Bree, an illustration of the qualities of expression through variety of line as well as fine classical draftsmanship.

Art School

SELF-TAUGHT

by

Matlack Price

and

A. Thornton Bishop

GREENBERG · PUBLISHER · NEW YORK

Contents

Part I—Fine Arts

Part II—Professional Arts

In a subject as broad as the field of art it would be uncommon to find two experienced teachers in full agreement on every detail of the profession. Their different careers would naturally foster this result.

In this regard Mr. Price and Mr. Bishop are no exceptions. However, there are two factors which make their collaboration on this book of great benefit to a student. First, they are in full agreement on the need of a thorough training for anyone endeavoring to make art a life work and, second, both men are fundamentalists in the belief that beauty is comprised of harmonies, and that certain principles governing these harmonies were discovered years ago and have been bequeathed by masters to future generations.

While Mr. Price and Mr. Bishop present their views differently at times, it is the student's good fortune that their varied viewpoints toward similar objectives give a broader exposition of the subject matter.

The Publishers

Introduction

by JOSEPH CUMMINGS CHASE

Here is help for the art student—valuable and dependable help.

Art never comes by chance. It is the product of trained intelligence. Shaw gave us the credo of his Dr. Dubidot: "I believe in Michelangelo, Velasquez, and Rembrandt; in the might of design, the mystery of color, the redemption of all things by Beauty everlasting, and the message of Art which has made these hands blessed. Amen. Amen!"

This trained intelligence is achieved in many ways and derived from a large variety of sources. Nowadays art schools provide the usual foundation. However, many noted artists never attended an art school, from Tintoretto to Grandma Moses. And many of the oddities in art have been products of art schools, for instance—Picasso.

Art is not new; it is artists that are new. For art is not a thing that can be described and defined. It is a life, an existence, a realm in which people called artists labor hour after hour, day after day, year after year, producing works that sometimes are pronounced to be art.

Aptitude and continuous devoted effort certainly are essential to the acquiring of proficiency in art work—in any of the arts.

In one sense, there is no "self-made man" nor "art school self-taught," since all the learning we absorb comes from without. However, in another sense, there is truth in art being self-taught inasmuch as all art education depends upon the individual's own effort, his indefatigable and persistent attempts, his prevailing interest, his insatiable appetite for proficiency, and his dauntless sincerity.

There are certain "know-hows" that can be acquired from readable texts more rapidly, perhaps, than from art school courses if the student combines that reading with "practice."

The "tools of the trade" are draftsmanship, an understanding of perspective, and a workable appreciation of the elements of design—without which there is no art. These can be acquired by diligent trying and by learning what the two authors, experienced craftsmen-artists both, offer in this book.

No small child senses perspective; it has to be learned. And few children have understanding of color values. All of us have to learn to see! And for most of us this is possible.

Besides this learning there is a certain something without which no art is possible. This essential something is a development of the spirit, the sensing of beauty and the appreciation of excellences.

Creating things is exciting; it is "fun"—from mud-pies to tapestries. Making one's creations beautiful and useful adds tremendously to the excitement.

The authors, Matlack Price and A. Thornton Bishop, have grown and prospered in art. Both have the gift of being helpful. They have labored in many art fields with distinguished success. They are inspiring teachers and authors of notable books.

Mr. Price was first trained as an architect, practiced architecture and interior decoration. He is an authority on typography. He was art director for several advertising agencies. He has edited *The Architectural Record, Arts and Decoration,* and *International Studio.* His book *Poster Design* is a standard work. He has taught in the Pratt Institute School of Fine Arts and now teaches in the Rhode Island School of Design.

Mr. Bishop has achieved a reputation as a draftsman and renderer of architectural design. He is at present an art director. His published works include *Renaissance Architecture of England* and the *Complete Guide to Drawing, Illustration, Cartooning and Painting.*

This collaboration for helpfulness is extraordinary. The publishers are to be congratulated, as are the fortunate art students.

The authors wish to acknowledge permission to use material and reproductions granted by the following:

Scholastic Awards, The Metropolitan Museum of Art, American Association of Advertising Agencies, Artists' Technical Supply Company, Arthur Brown, *House Beautiful* Magazine, *Photography* Magazine, Higgins Ink Company, Inc., C. Howard Hunt Pen Company, Eastern Sculpstone Company, American Typefounder's Sales Corporation, National Foundation for Infantile Paralysis, Inc., X-acto Crescent Products Company, Inc., Einson-Freeman Company, Oberly E. Newell Lithograph Corporation, *Design* Magazine, Studio Publications, Ziff-Davis Publishing Company, Jane Zook, William Helburn, Inc., Ben Brown, R. H. Hugman, D. Mac-Donald Brown, and Cora Scovil.

They are particularly indebted to Mr. Walter T. Foster for the use of material from his practical workbooks and to the many students whose work is reproduced in this volume. Names of students have been omitted. Since many of them are now doing professional work in various art fields, they would not wish to appear indefinitely as students.

Part I
Fíne Arts

A detail from the pavement of the Duomo, in Siena, by Domenico Beccafumi, Italian painter and sculptor (1486-1550), depicting the pact between Elias and Achab. The cathedral itself belongs to the thirteenth and fourteenth centuries.

An eighteenth-century French drawing of an artist sketched in the act of making a visual measurement of his model with his crayon. This drawing was made with transparent wash. (A. de Saint-Aubin: "Portrait d' Artist," 1754.)

CHAPTER 1

Let's Talk About Art

When a person chooses a certain profession as a life's work, that choice is likely to be influenced primarily by an expectancy of what the profession is like. A far-off view of it can encourage an illusion, and frequently legends wrap the profession in a cloak of glamor.

What the profession is really like, what aptitudes its practitioners should possess to warrant their choosing it, and an understanding of the fields of study and training necessary to promise a degree of success in it are perhaps the first considerations a new student should give to it.

Therefore, let us begin by discussing first things first so that we can understand what this thing called Art is all about.

What Is Art?

We speak of art as the expression of a people through their work conceived in form which comprises the skill and experience of craftsmen, and which embodies the aesthetic principles and characteristics of the people themselves. Art is that which lifts a thing of sheer utility to an experience rich in feeling. It gives to a song a

rhythm that invites one to sing it. It shapes the phrase with a cadence that pleases the ear. It endows the statue with nobility. In the painting, it typifies life. In all forms of expression, it conveys the aspiration of the artist to a universal audience.

The genesis of art is the urge to express simply the emotions one feels in terms which symbolize this feeling. The earliest utterances of the Anglo-Saxon were made with such rhythmic cadence that our English forebears, whose ears were pleased and whose hearts were stirred by the emotions the phrases activated, adopted the rhythm as a standard for the poetry of their language. This was the recognition of the existence of art in an audible sense.

Symbols have studded the records of the picture-writer from the earliest of times because in a symbol a whole story could be told. Chaldean and Egyptian monuments reveal the civilizations of these nations through the symbol, carefully chosen to convey the expression of the story-teller. It simplified the story-telling and epitomized the expression. Simplification may, therefore, be considered one of the basic attributes of art.

3

Crayon drawing of an artist by the famous nineteenth-century French poster artist Jules Chéret. The rough texture of the paper on which the original was drawn gives a special quality to the drawing.

Aesthetic values of people differ according to the kinds of lives they live and the environments in which they live them. One cannot dwell by the sea, subjected to the constant and rhythmic pounding of the surf, and remain unaffected by this dynamic rhythm. People who live in very colorful surroundings are more likely to express themselves in a vivid and colorful way. If we think for the moment of the contrast in characteristics between the Nordic and the native along the shores of the Mediterranean, we will perceive why the aesthetic expression of people vary and why the art of one people cannot be appraised fairly by the art standards of other people. There are, however, habits of the human mind that respect no nationality, such as a sense of balance and orderliness. But these are more concerned with the organization of elements in art and, accordingly, will be treated later on.

Therefore, we can consider art as the expression of a people which embodies the emotions they feel throughout their daily experience. The form the art takes depends much on the sense in the artist that has been stimulated by the emotional experience. Although, during the later years of his life, Beethoven was deaf to the common noises, his inner ear heard harmonies that resulted from a deep emotional experience. With Turner, the British painter, the emotional experience was conveyed in terms of light and color through his eyes to his brilliant canvasses. The sculptor seeks to express the embodiment of his story in three-dimensional form. It more nearly portrays an actual representation of Nature. The materials he uses seem eternal. This is one reason why sculpture is the form of art chosen most frequently to memorialize a person or an idea.

Other forms of art include architecture, literature and the creative and interpretative forms of the dance. Although this book will confine its scope and limited space to the field of painting and the other representational phases of pictorial and decorative art, it is desirable that the student realize there is a close relationship between all arts. The principles which direct the painter, musician, sculptor, architect, danseuse and poet are essentially the same. In their search for beauty, they seek the same objectives and pursue similar paths. Broad truths about Art as a generally understood human concept apply equally to all the separate arts.

The leaven which works so similarly in these broad creative fields is the influence that Nature, in her many forms, has had on the lives of all of us. Her rhythms, her harmonies, and her variety of forms have become our standards in our interpretation of her beauty. Nature has taught both artist and his audience a common language through which the former creates, and the latter appreciates, beauty.

Plant life with its many forms, the sea and fire with their rhythmic patterns, and the clouds with their varying shapes, all offer impressions which produce emotional reactions with those who observe them. These reactions sponsor the impetus of much art expression, and a closer analysis of these patterns of Nature will be a source of continual inspiration to an artist, be he painter, sculptor or poet. This study will be pursued further in the section of this book devoted to Design.

What Is Fine Art?

When we speak of a work of art as worthy of consideration as "Fine Art," we feel that it expresses the highest quality of the artist's spirit conceived in his search for Beauty through which, because of his human qualities, the work makes its appeal. The very personal and human qualities of the artist are always evident in a work of "Fine Art."

There are many works of art masterfully executed that have been appropriated to a commercial purpose. This need not necessarily condemn them. If the artist has not subjugated his spirit to the ultimate function the work is to perform, and if he has not been deterred in his search for beauty, his effort can attain the quality of "Fine Art."

Most art commonly designated as "Fine Art" was created to serve a definite purpose, and many paintings which hang in the galleries of museums today were the result of direct commissions to the artist. Up to the time of the Renaissance the Church was the artist's principal patron. Consequently, the works contained a spiritual quality.

It may be a coincidence that much of the art classified by museum curators and critics as "Fine Art" was created for an ecclesiastical use. It is possible that this practice has helped form a prejudice in favor of works possessing a "spiritual" quality when referring to "Fine Art." But the spirit of man seeking beauty has a quality no less than was that of the Renaissance artist.

An abstract design composed of unfamiliar characters by a student beginner in lettering. Painted in black and tones of gray, it shows that any material, skilfully organized, may be created into an effective design.

Another abstract design by a student. He used specimens of contemporary lettering to compose an arrangement striking in character. Elements that intersect compel attention.

Beauty as expressed in Nature has long been the quest of the spirited artist, for "the groves were God's first temples," and natural form can stimulate the human qualities in both artist and his audience creating for the picture, the statue or the poem, its unusual appeal.

What Is Abstract Art?

In recent years, there has come upon the modern scene a group of experimenters called abstractionists who seek to create designs without the use of recognizable natural form and who frequently distort the familiar patterns of geometric form. For instance, instead of painting a tree or a still life that conveys intelligently to an observer some idea of what the object looks like, the abstractionist might daub his canvas to produce an effect that would suggest he was cleaning his brushes. Neither in color or form would his painting resemble the tree or the still life. What can this mean if, indeed, it means anything?

Abstractionists regard any interpretation of a subject where it is fashioned to resemble the original object a useless operation. "You have the original, so why waste time producing a counterfeit?" they reason. To produce a facsimile of an article, an artisan must adopt an objective approach which, they say, can be adequately accomplished by a camera. Too little of the creative faculties of an artist are called into play for the effort, according to the argument.

So, abstractionists tell us, they are trying to put on canvas, or in sculptured form, an expression of their emotional reactions at the sight of the original subject. It can be wondered, if this be true, how much these "interpreters" are pained by the world the way they view it. Human form, expressed by both painter and sculptor of this school of thought, is generally distorted to a point where it appears grotesque. It seems they look elsewhere than toward Nature in their search for beauty, and to this extent they express their own frustration.

In the projection of an idea where natural form may be borrowed to help symbolize the thought, these abstractionists sometimes seek to express themselves in a language of curves and angles, attributing to these lines an aesthetic significance. It is possible to suggest the mood one is in by selecting color, as in a dress ensemble.

6

In this, one is successful only because the people they impress react in a similar way to the brightness, drabness, gaiety or reserve, expressed by the color.

Lines can also express thought by the way in which they are drawn. For instance, straight vertical lines suggest dignity, horizontal lines suggest restfulness, oblique, violent action, and the complete circle gives the suggestion of oneness, unity. The application of these line-symbols has appeared in art from the earliest times, and the forces they imply have been stamped on the consciousness of people for so long that they are readily understood whenever they appear in paintings, sculpture, theatrical designs and textiles.

This suggestion of mood can be carried too far, that is, to a point where the lines or forms are not generally understood. Art is a universal language and, when we mumble a jargon that is not understandable to others, we fail to express what is in our hearts and minds, at least in a manner that will merit attention. In the field of pictorial representation, therefore, abstractionists fail to satisfy most of the people to whom they wish to speak, and one can only wonder if much of the interest shown in these unintelligible endeavors is founded on curiosity. As in any language, the meaning of terms must be generally understood.

In the field of decoration, abstract art finds a place. A design for wall paper or textiles need not carry an understandable message. Its function is "background," and its place in the scheme of things is to serve as an undertone, creating a mood, discerned but not competing with the thematic material of the greater composition which in this case would be the room in which the furniture or architectural detail would be featured.

You can, of course, design a textile pattern of recognizable flowers or any other motif, but it could be just as good a design if the motif used were not a recognizable form at all. Repetition of form and color and the flow of line can be made interesting without telling a particular story.

Designs do not have to tell stories but every artist should remember that in all art everything done should have a purpose to be worthy of its being. Art should serve a positive good. It should not be negative, which means that it should contribute something to general use and make the

An abstraction using typography in a montage technique, the effect depending upon the fantastic arrangement of its subject matter. Repetition of the diagonal gained emphasis for the design.

An interesting abstraction, surrealistic in character, made by an art school student as an assignment in which it was required to "dramatize" the classic Roman letter.

world a little bit better for having been created.

A better understanding of abstraction as related to symbolism would be a worthy addition to our philosophy of art, inasmuch as all symbols in art are, actually, a form of abstraction. An instance of this may be seen in Chinese writing in which the characters, having no pictorial significance unless explained, are nevertheless abstractions from definitely pictorial characters and recognizable as pictures in their original forms.

How To Study Art

The study of art is a constant search for beauty. This search takes in a broad world filled with sensations which please the eye and ear, and our goal may be more easily attained if only we know how to recognize beauty from the more commonplace sensations we experience along the way.

Beauty is visible to those only who can appreciate her. "No thing is beautiful," said Robert Henri, "but all things await the sensitive and imaginative mind that may be aroused to pleasurable emotion at sight of them. This is beauty. All is as beautiful as we think it."

This is a pretty broad statement but it directs the search for beauty to within ourselves. We wonder what we must feel and understand to appreciate beauty, and we might reason further to see if that which arouses pleasurable emotions in us will do likewise to our neighbors. There are many instances, such as the enjoyment of a sunset, the satisfying qualities of a vista along the countryside, or the graceful contour of a vase, in which we share pleasurable emotion with others. Therefore, we can expect to find certain elements comprising the sunset, the vista and the vase which have a general appeal.

In the study of art we seek an understanding of these elements which evoke pleasurable sensations so generally. Beauty is apprehended through the emotions, not through the intellect, although we should approach the search with as much analytical intelligence as possible. At this stage of our study we become scientists.

In our search for beauty we should study the elements which create beauty and, in the plastic and representational arts with which we are chiefly concerned, they consist of space, form and color.

Nothing offers us a broader field for study than

Classical sculpture will always remind us of the serene and timeless beauty of true art. This example of the fineness of Greek conception of beauty is known as the Lemnian Athena.

Nature. Here we find the widest variety of material creating beauty, which is to say, producing pleasurable emotion within us. The particular qualities and characteristics in these natural elements that have produced these emotions in us throughout the years have injected themselves so thoroughly into our emotional beings that they have become criteria to prevail in any matters where these basic qualities are recognized.

Nature's patterns have become fundamental standards for our preferences in matters of form and color and also in relationship of various forms and colors to one another. We accept these standards as expressing good design. This is an important stage in our art study because it represents the rudiments of the universal language in which we wish to become eloquent.

In addition to being a student of Nature, the young artist should become interested in the history of social development in various countries and in the biographies of the outstanding thinkers of those countries. All art, including painting, literature and architecture, is the result of trends in thinking directed by the prevailing social forces at the time. For a long period of time the Church dominated the lives of the people in

Europe; later, the personalities of monarchs made their impression, and frequently the course of art expression ebbed and rose with the political crises of the nation affected.

The architecture of a country assumed an important voice in these art trends because it provided the people with a means in which they could express themselves in the building of their homes and churches and in the employment of motifs in their decoration which were significant in their daily lives.

So, quite apart from the practice of architecture, which requires long and thorough training in both school and drafting room, there are two non-technical aspects which hold great value to the art student. These are an appreciation of architectural history which leads to an ability to recognize architectural styles and an understanding of architectural forms which can aid a student working in other fields of design.

This part of a student's training can be gained from any number of books. He will find that "style" in architecture is the outgrowth of (1) the use of the building, (2) the materials, suitable and available, and (3) the methods of construction and craftsmanship understood by the workmen at the time. Style in its purest quality is the natural development of these three conditions, and where historic styles of past eras have been introduced in the buildings of later periods, the chief reason has been the designer's desire to recapture some of the spirit of the original.

The trend in architectural schools at the present time—to consider historic styles as decadent art—is to miss the most important point. Principles of design, or those pleasing relationships of mass to space, of satisfying arrangements in light and shade, and in harmony of colors, which have been carried forward from each preceding age to its successor should be incorporated into a new style to make of it a fine art. Observance of good scale, so important to the earlier builders regardless of the period in which they lived, is a principle time has not changed and one which no designer can afford to ignore.

It is a mistake to think that historic forms have no modern use. New adaptations make a new art, and without a good basic knowledge of the development of architectural form, the modern designer is greatly handicapped in his information and training.

Many forms adapted by early builders to adorn their structures were derived from Nature.

Egyptians made much use of the reeds from the Nile, and of the lotus; Greeks found a use for the acanthus, a plant found in the south of Europe and Asia Minor; Renaissance carvers developed the vine, Della Robbia fashioning borders for his medallions which resemble garlands of fruit.

Textiles throughout the ages display a consistent use of floral, human, and animal forms. Again, the Egyptians' love of flowers showed itself in their weaving as in their stonework. Land lilies, marguerites and tulips bloomed on Cretan fabrics. Animals and flowers furnished motifs for the Babylonians, and the Assyrians leaned toward the use of beasts to express their fondness for war and the hunt. Throughout the ages, Nature has provided the arts with her variety of forms to use as motifs.

Geometric forms have also provided the designer with motifs for patterns used in architectural work and textiles. Many of these forms are symmetrical and present a formal appearance, or static balance. When the forms are used in a continuous arrangement they can serve as a pattern suitable for unlimited areas. Once more records show that the Egyptians created patterns of geometric shape, leaving us examples of their pottery where woven twigs were pressed into clay to make decorative effects and, later, were

Greek amphora, of approximately 550-500 B.C. Simple in design, graceful in contour, and rich in coloring, it offers inspiration to students who seek the secrets of the Greek sense of pattern. (Courtesy of The Metropolitan Museum of Art.)

developed into squares, triangles and zigzag lines alternating with groups of parallel lines.

The Greeks introduced a pattern called a *fret* which consisted of a stripe drawn to produce short straight lines intersecting each other at 90 degrees making an ornamental border of indefinite length. This pattern was used on their garments and buildings in a continuous arrangement.

In a later day, when rooms were panelled in wood, these panels and the ornamental treatment within them frequently followed geometric forms. The character of these forms suggests a state of stability and orderliness and has proven to be satisfying as wall decoration in many periods of historic styles.

Therefore, we might sum up the study of art as a study of the world in which we live. It presents us with many materials which we can use in an expression of our sense of beauty.

Sensationalism in Art

Paintings and wall carvings from the earliest of times have included in their picture material scenes suggesting extreme brutality. Early Christian art stressed heavily the sufferings of Christ, many of which had no foundation in the Scriptures. Aside from religious impulses which probably inspired many examples, there seems to be a morbid streak in human nature that exhibits itself at times in depicting horrifying situations. This is a form of sensationalism in art and seldom inspires the spirit of either the artist or the observer of the work in their search for Beauty.

Cartoonists of the present day must use their talents to drive home some message which must be rendered in a sensational way to be effective. Although in these instances, to seek Beauty is not the prime objective, yet the message will carry more appeal if the elements of the picture have been designed in a way satisfying to the observer. The same principles with which we design in an effort to create Beauty are applicable in pictures of a sensational nature. There should be nothing ugly even in pictures of unpleasant subjects. Ugliness is the absence of Beauty just as darkness is the absence of light, and anything created in a spirit to avoid Beauty is unworthy of the effort to do it.

Bas-reliefs from the south façade of the Cathédrale de Paris. Here beauty is created through relationships of dark and light. The depth of the carving permitted a three-dimensional design. Note how the figures are formed to fit into the curved recesses of frame. Treatment of the folds in the garments was kept simple, and a general effect of balance was obtained

The Lure of Paint

Of the fine arts, painting offers the most fascinating medium for expression of an artist's feeling about the world—an ever-changing panorama of color. People of adult years who have come to feel an urge for self-expression through art most frequently turn to painting. It offers satisfaction through the creating of something with one's hands. It provides a release of tension for business and professional people. Each year the number of amateurs who exhibit their work in local civic centers increases.

Every year, in New York, an art exhibition is staged by a group of prominent doctors who have found painting a highly beneficial recreation to balance their exacting professional responsibilities. And the level of their performance as artists is high. Probably the outstanding example of a man seeking the rewarding pleasure in painting is the great statesman Winston Churchill.

The thrill which comes to the non-professional painter is the discovery of Beauty in Nature. He delights in putting on canvas what he sees with as much knowledge as he can acquire. Sincere students welcome all the help they receive from professional, teacher, or book. To them it is a hobby, but to the student who desires to make art his profession, it is a life work, a vocation to which he will gladly give the best and most that is in him. The urge to create should be fundamental in the art student and the need of skill should spur him on through seemingly endless periods of training.

How an Art Student Prepares

It is natural for many beginners to start by copying various things which strike their fancy. It is not uncommon for them to copy the photograph of a motion picture star. This may or may not be good practice, according to the technique one uses in doing it, but very little is accomplished along the road of becoming an artist. The urge to copy is largely a manual one. One desires the replica of something together with the satisfaction of doing it by one's self. No art judgments are necessary, so little benefit is derived from the exercise.

Any kind of drawing is a form of practice and therefore better than no practice at all, but the student will learn more by copying from good works of art than by laboring over the close imitation of a photograph. A worthwhile approach to portraiture would be the copying of various portrait drawings by Holbein, known as the Windsor prints. Here, a master craftsman created in line a series of personalities of the time of King Henry the Eighth of England, and by the artist's skill each character is made to live again.

After the instinctive impulse to copy comes the urge to imitate. The beginner discovers the work of some artist he admires and sets out to acquire the artist's successful style by attempting to imitate the technique.

Imitation, like copying, has a certain amount of practice value, but should be dropped as soon as possible, since both copying and imitating delay progress toward the development of the student's individuality and creative faculties.

Many students, advanced in their training, can be seen in the galleries of museums copying the works of masters with precise accuracy. This is done for different reasons, two of which are: an exercise in color with emphasis on technique, and the reproducing of a duplicate as a commission.

Studies of masterworks require careful analysis through copying of certain portions, but these copies are made solely as an exercise and are not intended by the student as pictures for public view. There is no real harm in a beginner copying or imitating the works of another so long as he keeps in mind that the only value gained is practice.

Acquiring an Art Library

Anyone choosing art as a career should accumulate a well-rounded library on the subject. When one plans a self-taught program this is almost indispensable. If well chosen, these books should supply advice and sound instruction which, in school, would be provided by the instructor. So important is this phase of our study that a bibliography appears in the Appendix which lists books dealing with the topics of the various chapters.

Aside from books of instruction, the student should try to collect monographs featuring works of artists and illustrating historic periods of art. In addition to these, he should also collect a broad assortment of photographs and drawings which he can classify in an orderly manner, by

"Le Pauvre Pêcheur" (The Poor Fisherman) by Puvis de Chavannes, in the Luxembourg, Paris, is impressive because of simplicity and the variety of pattern created by the elements in the picture.

11

subject, to provide him with illustrative information on many subjects. Somewhat of a scrap-book of facts, this collection is referred to by professionals as a "scrap file," and it is drawn on continuously for accurate detail of subject matter. This "scrap file" saves many dollars and hours of time in searching for necessary information.

The value of any book or any piece of illustrative material is in the way its information can be applied by the student to the problem in hand.

Some books, called "how to" books will give information on the practical approach to the problem. Other books are philosophic, consisting of theories about art, and these can stimulate a student's thinking in the broader aspects of his profession. Both kinds are valuable. In fact, any book which helps to generate in a student's mind the desire to carry forward with increased zeal his search for the attributes of Beauty should be not only in his library but in his heart.

Have You Got What It Takes

In a review of our first discussion about art, the student should put himself through a self-examination to determine how well he understands the basic thinking about art. He should be sure that he has the necessary aptitudes to become a good student and he should be honest with himself in an evaluation of his powers to retain what he studies. He should also question himself as to his natural inclination to be observant and inquiring. All good students should be inquisitive.

Talent, as a gift, is usually little more than a natural inclination to follow a certain bent. Sometimes it is the result of association, as when the son follows in the footsteps of the father. Here he has been exposed to, and made familiar with, many of the practices of the parent. In other cases, the child develops this inclination without any apparent influence.

The inclination to create through drawing or painting is a talent which must be cultivated if it is to flourish. A student having such talent has, indeed, a gift which should aid him toward a successful career, but he cannot take this advantage for granted and so regard his training less seriously.

An Aptitude Test for Any Art Career

Read each question carefully, and think it over. It might help to write down your answers; you might think more carefully about them.

1. Why have you chosen art as your life's work? Because of prospects of wealth? Fame? Because you think it offers a contemplative style of life? The so-called "Bohemian" atmosphere? Or, are you seeking a hobby? Or, possibly, an escape from the tensions of a business world, in which case, of course, the first question will not apply. But the following questions will be significant whether art has been chosen as your vocation or your avocation.

2. Are you observant?

3. Do you possess an inquiring mind?

4. Do you find contentment in Nature? Are you fascinated by the constantly changing colors of a sunset? Do you find pleasure in the stark silhouette of forms against a contrasting background? Are you apt to watch the passing clouds and note with interest as their shapes assimilate more familiar objects?

5. Do you desire to dramatize a situation? Do you want to project personality and character through illustrative processes?

6. Are you interested in other arts, such as music, the theater, literature, architecture, sculpture, and the classic and interpretative forms of the dance?

7. Do you believe that the search for Beauty will be a thrilling experience?

8. Are you willing to work? How much time can you give to develop whatever ability you have? If art is to be your career, it should dominate your life and absorb your energies. If it is to be your hobby, it should be given your constant attention in your spare time.

9. Are you hesitant about beginning this work? Are you waiting for the "perfect opportunity?" Is it just something you would like to do when you get around to it? If so, forget it.

10. Are you happier when doing a piece of art work than when doing anything else? If so, let's go on.

CHAPTER 2

The Background of Art

In our discussion about art we have tried to show the great influence Nature has on the artist's mind in the creation of a work of art. Though the works of Nature are innumerable and different, the effects of them are similar on the artist in an expression of them. What is common to all is the impression of perfectness and harmony—which is Beauty.

To the Italian masters, the standard of beauty was the entire circuit of natural forms. They spoke of it as "il piú nell' uno,"—"the many in one" or all in unity, intimating that what is truly beautiful seems related to all Nature.

A student exploring the background of art will do well to turn first to an intimate study of Nature. As mentioned in the previous chapter, it is a world filled with material for the artist. All things good in. Nature reproduce themselves. With the artist the Beauty of Nature reforms itself in the mind where it finds new creation.

Let us examine Nature's influence in the works of artists throughout the ages. And, as we do so, let us remember that these artists were the modernists of their time and that with each succeeding era Nature's influence remained strong although the manner of the production of art differed with the times. We are no different than they were, in our exposure to Nature's influences, as we strive to succeed them with our "modern" viewpoint toward art.

The museum presents the most accessible field for study of Nature working through the minds of generations of artists. It brings us face to face with the full scale work of our predecessors, far surpassing in satisfaction the viewing of these masterpieces in small book reproductions. The spiritual force of man is shown in his fancy and imagination, and the student who learns to discern the fundamental good in an artist's expression, to recognize the derivatives of its pleasure-giving qualities, will discover that he has come into possession of a broad background in art.

This is not time spent merely with the antique or study devoted to theory; it has a direct application to the everyday work of the modern designer. Many modern designs and productions in art are enriched because of research in the works of early artists and craftsmen. In the pre-industrial era, the designer expressed the tastes, interests and ideas of the society of the time. The market in his day made its demands based on the needs of the people. He succeeded or failed as he worked to satisfy his market.

As we pass in rapid review of the outstanding examples of art through the ages, whether they be paintings, porcelains or textiles, we must feel that the quality of popular taste was high. Therefore, no student need ever fear that the museum places a dead hand on art. It brings one closer not only to the products of artists but to the preferences of society that dictated the standards of art.

Familiarity with the fine works of the past should be part of the education of every artist. For those to whom a museum is not accessible, composite pictures of historic periods in art are reproduced on accompanying pages. Space would not permit an adequate illustration of each of the subjects chosen to represent each period. They are reproduced chiefly to show the *general character* of art as expressed in these periods. The method is a modern technique called "montage" which gives a composite picture of many things at a single glance. Since art expression has had a certain unity in every period, the various images appearing in the montages are closely related. For every image shown there are hundreds, equally significant, which could not be included.

Many things comprise the arts and skills of any period. While these include painting, sculpture and architecture, there are many others just as important. They include costume, furniture, textiles, ceramics, metal crafts, embellishment

13

of manuscripts, and printing. If these montages suggest a source of inspiration sufficient to encourage the student to seek a fuller knowledge and a larger reproduction of the subjects, either in other books or in a museum, they will be serving their purpose splendidly.

Appreciation, Judgment and Taste

From a familiarity with the art of the past springs our appreciation of the quality of standards attained by our predecessors in art. As we appreciate this quality we must recognize the sources of the artist's inspiration. Through this process our judgment grows. We become more discriminating and are regarded as showing Taste.

According to Emerson, love of Beauty is Taste. In a search for Beauty, artists show discriminating Taste because they practice the habits of their minds which were produced by their particular sort of education. Taste is not a gift but a development of one's faculty to appreciate the quality in a work of art and to judge according to high standards.

People regarded as possessing this faculty are sought frequently on matters of "good or bad design," the right or wrong color to be used, or the right thing to wear. Too few people understand why they accord such persons this distinction. It is somewhat of a mystery to them but they will not deny this particular "talent" exists with "art-minded" people.

Taste is possessed not only by artists in search of Beauty but by many others content with their appreciation of Beauty. While this larger audience may not, as artists do, study the elements which comprise Beauty, they are stimulated by the emotional reactions resulting from an experience with Beauty. Discriminating judgment is developed by a repetition of these experiences.

Taste is a positive force, not negative; active, not passive. It works for better things, more pleasing solutions. And, as it is used, it improves.

Taste is not only related to art. It may be practiced in any human activity but its employment in social matters is strangely analogous to its use in art. The love of Beauty is mainly the love of harmony, restraint and good proportion. The person who screams, or uses the superlative degree too generally, or converses with unreasonable agitation can provoke much displeasure.

What makes for good or bad manners has its counterpart in art. Discriminating taste abhors the harsh note, the crude effect, and the inharmonious color. Taste does not mean merely "fashionable," complying with the whims of the "upper classes"; it means agreeing with the appreciative sense which an education gained through a search for Beauty gives to anyone.

Taste has no reference to time. Modes and fashions come and go. Taste may sponsor this fashion or another for a time. There have been periods when the general level of taste was low, particularly in the second half of the 19th century. This was an era of great industrial development, of broadening frontiers, and of scientific research. The objectives were material and the soul in its search for Beauty found little nourishment.

Therefore, we can regard taste as the exercise of discriminating judgment in matters where selection and expression are guided by one's consciousness of the harmonious interrelation of elements in Nature creating Beauty.

In the development of taste, the student should be consistently fastidious, applying knowledge as he acquires it, never compromising with his conscience, for fear his perceptions may become dull. Taste is an artist's professional character. He should guard against a deterioration of its value.

Acquiring an Art Philosophy

In our discussion of a background of art, we have touched on topics for a student's thinking that will aid him in formulating his own philosophy about art. It is a combination of an emotional and an intellectual approach to art matters. It helps bring into orderly arrangement the things one feels and thinks about art. Like a chart to a mariner, a clear, concise pattern of thinking will serve to direct the art student toward the choice of his objectives and the means of attaining them.

No better pattern of orderliness exists than can be found in Nature. It is not sheer poetry to speak of the constancy of the star-lit firmament, the alternate succession of daylight and darkness, and the repetitive seasons with measured consistency in all their phenomena. "Minds which are closely harmonized with Nature possess the power of abstracting Beauty from things, and reproducing it in new forms," wrote Emerson. "This is Art.

"Since Beauty may be considered an abstraction of the harmony and proportion that reigns in all Nature, it can therefore be studied in Nature," continues the poet. It cannot be found in what does not exist.

All artists seek to make this radiance in Nature the focal point of their objectives, and each in his own way works to satisfy the love of Beauty which stimulates him to produce.

The student will find as he proceeds with his studies that they are all related to the world he lives in. With this philosophy he is prepared to go on. A review of the prominent periods of art will show how this philosophy guided the masters.

The Art of Ancient Egypt

It is customary to treat Egyptian history as a series of successive dynasties extending from 3400 B.C. to 30 B.C. Many of these dynasties were named for the conquering nation which established the ruler. The first ten dynasties extended from 3400 to 2160 B.C. and are referred to as the Ancient Empire. The next ten covered the period from 2160 to 1090 B.C. and are known as the Middle Empire. The 21st to 31st dynasties spanned the years to 332 B.C., when the land was conquered by Alexander. This period was known as the New Empire during which Grecian influence rose across the sea. The 32nd and 33rd dynasties, considered by historians as the last two, closed with the death of Cleopatra and the organization of the kingdom as a Roman province.

The monuments extant and dating from the Ancient Empire are almost wholly sepulchral. They consist of the pyramids, the Sphinx and a single temple, called the Temple of the Sphinx. The remains of the Middle Empire are also tombs. It was not until the New Empire dawned that Egypt's great temples were built. These include Karnak and Luxor, the Ramesseum, and the rock-cut temple at Abu-Simbel. The temples at Philae, Kom-Ombo and Edfu were erected during the last dynasties.

Both tombs and temples manifested the religious beliefs and the social organization of the nation, at the head of which stood the king. He was supreme in both ecclesiastical and civil matters. The most powerful absolute monarch history has ever recorded, the king was considered the living incarnation of God. His supreme desire seems to have been to construct a monument which in magnificence and durability should surpass all efforts of his predecessors. His method for obtaining the necessary labor was compulsion.

An important factor in Egyptian art and architecture was the national conception about death and immortality. The Egyptians called that which did not perish with the last breath of a dying man his "double." A duplicate of the mortal body, this double had to be installed in a suitable lodging and sustained by food; and it was the duty of survivors to see that this dependent spirit was not neglected.

The Egyptians also invented a process of embalming which rendered the mummy almost indestructible so long as it remained in the dry soil of Egypt. They also believed the mummy should be preserved from sacrilege; if an enemy entered the sepulchre, the "double" might be made homeless for eternity. This is the reason for much of the art of Egypt being preserved throughout the centuries. Every ingenious artifice was used to conceal the burial chambers.

Around the royal pyramids of Gizeh sprang up the tombs of nobles who chose to be buried near their sovereign, which created a vast cemetery. At the foot of this cemetery rose the great Sphinx, the image of Harmachis, personifying the resurrection. According to one authority, the Sphinx originally was a likeness of King Amenemhet III of the 12th dynasty. In the montage, it may be seen in the lower left corner. The features have been disfigured but we may still admire something of the nobleness in the expression which impressed early writers.

There were undoubtedly many temples built during the Ancient and Middle Empires but no trace of them remains, probably because the buildings were razed to provide materials for the greater edifices erected by later kings. Traces of prehistoric fetishism, such as the ornamental use of various animals—the bull, the ibis, the crocodile—suggest these symbols as surviving totems of early tribes. Egyptian religion also embraced polytheism—a worship of the powers of Nature, especially the sun, moon and the stars—and many of Nature's forms were utilized in wall painting and decoration.

The sculptor was employed not only for wall

carvings, but for the capitals of columns and colossal figures guarding the pylons of the temples, and for sphinxes which lined long avenues approaching the temples. As early as the Ancient Empire Egyptians carved two of their favorite and sacred plants, the lotus and the papyrus, to decorate their columns.

Let us examine the montage. At the upper right is shown the back of the golden coronation throne of King Tut-ankh-amen, overlaid with sheet gold and adorned with polychrome glass, faience and stone. Below, on the right, are the effigies of Ra-Holep and his wife Nefert, of the 13th dynasty. At the bottom of the montage sits a stone image of a royal scribe with his scroll.

In the center, to the left, is seen an entrance on the approach to Karnak. This forms (with the exception of the pyramids) the largest and most imposing ruin in Egypt. The approach was formerly by an avenue nearly two miles long, lined with at least 2,000 sphinxes, crouching side by side.

Other examples illustrated in the montage are fragments of sculpture and other ancient Egyptian artifacts now in possession of prominent museums.

The Arts of Greece and Rome

While the greatest of Egypt's temples were rising along the banks of the Nile, a new civilization was showing signs of life on the islands and along the shores of the Mediterranean. With an ancestry from Central Asia, these people, known first as Pelasgians were followed by the Dorians, the Ionians and the Aeolians, and they mingled in their arts the forms used by Egyptians and Assyrians. However, as a people, they advanced rapidly in culture, and strove for ideals in beauty which surpassed the sources in the lands of their origin.

Spreading from the islands of Crete, Rhodes, and Cyprus to the mainland, Greek civilization reached its full flower between 600 and 400 B.C., a thousand years later than the epoch of the Rameses in Egypt. The Greek temple followed the Egyptian idea of construction—walls of squared stone with the openings bridged by a lintel—with greater simplicity and beauty in detail and execution.

The sculpture comprised magnificent effigies in marble of Greek gods and national heroes. These were not military leaders but the legendary heroes and deities of the people. Refinement replaced the massive grandeur of the Egyptians. Beauty of line and form became the artists' aim instead of mystic symbolism, and nature was studied with greater appreciation.

In addition to religious and historic sculpture, the Greeks memorialized activities of civic and athletic character. These consisted of statues of chariot-racers, discus-throwers, wrestlers, and victors in musical contests and in dramatic and comic poetry contests. Workers in bronze, precious metals, wood-carvers, and potters also contributed to the arts with tables, chairs, chests, vases, lamps, mirrors, and objects of personal adornment.

It was in architecture and sculpture that the Greeks made their most lasting contribution. They made their roofs of gabled form to shed the rain, and arranged the columns that supported the roof with a delicate sense of fitness in the relationships of mass to space and in light and shade. They developed three orders, or styles, of architecture: the severely beautiful Doric, the richer and graceful Ionic with its scroll form at the top of the column, and the still richer Corinthian which united the scroll with the acanthus leaf.

The death of Alexander in 323 B.C. left the Greeks dominating the civilized world without a central government of sufficient strength to maintain an orderly and consistent development in the arts. Separate kingdoms sprang up from Egypt on the east to Syracuse, on the island of Sicily, in the west. The Hellenistic world embraced Asia Minor, the northern part of Africa and, for a while, portions of Spain and France. Wars reduced Greek unity and a new power rose over the Greek states.

Kindred to the Greeks by remote ancestry, the Romans also inherited some of the same traditions. Many elements were melded in the Roman character which directed their development as administrators, soldiers, and organizers, rather than as artists like the Greeks. The Etruscans contributed their engineering skill to the new civilization and, when the Romans overran the disorganized Hellenistic states, they adopted Greek forms but applied them on different structural principles. They faced walls of concrete with brick or stone, and spanned the openings

in their masonry with arches. The truss—a frame of beams and rods that provides continuous support or bridge across an open space between piers or walls—was also developed by these builders. This made it possible to roof a wide space with much lighter materials than used formerly. This development had an important bearing on all future construction, and for a thousand years the churches of Rome were built after the general pattern of the antique basilica-halls.

There were many reasons for the lack of a national Roman art. First, as a people they held the practice of art in contempt, a work fit only for slaves. Then, there was never an employment for art in the service of religion. Portrait busts were an indulgence purely for self-glorification. These were probably the work of Etruscans who emulated their Grecian ancestors to the best of their ability. There was, consequently, a lack of idealism and inspiration.

However, as the Roman conquests of Greek centers continued, their artistic education broadened and refinement of taste and workmanship progressed. The better models of the Greek school were brought to Rome which resulted in a series of decorative works on a large scale, culminating in the arches of Titus and Trajan, the columns of Trajan and Marcus Aurelius and the arch of Constantine.

As we examine the montage we see the better examples of the Greek work at the top, the Roman work at the bottom. In the upper left-hand corner is a part of the porch of the Erechtheum, Athens; in the upper right, part of a Doric cap and entablature; beneath it, a Corinthian capital; left center, an Ionic capital, with a colonnade of Ionic beside it.

At the bottom are shown parts of the Coliseum and the arch of Constantine, both in Rome; an aqueduct; and in the lower right corner, the Composite Order as developed by the Romans from a combination of the Ionic and Corinthian.

The Arts of the Middle Ages

During the 5th century A.D. the Roman Empire crumbled, pressed by the Goths and Vandals of the north, and the Eternal City was devastated by barbaric hordes. The seat of empire was transferred to a new capital on the shores of the Bosphorus, and from here for the next thousand years, Byzantine emperors defended Christendom against the Moslem world.

Architecturally, Constantinople comprised a mixture of Asiatic-Greek and Roman traditions which differed markedly from the developments in Italy and southern Europe following the fall of Rome. In the west, the timber-roofed basilica, previously described, suited large throngs of worshippers adequately throughout the early Middle Ages. In Asia Minor the early Roman vault, suggested by the tombs and round temples, was developed with more variety and ingenuity. This introduced a new principle of construction—a balanced thrust—in which the thrust or pressure of one vault neutralized and counteracted that of another. This idea was carried later by the Gothic builders into their lofty edifices throughout Western Europe.

The decline of classic art can also be attributed in part to the triumph of Christianity in the 4th century when Constantine placed the religion under state protection. Ancient temple architecture was regarded as pagan because it glorified a pantheon of the ancient gods. Ancient sculpture was pagan because it served idolatry, and this prompted a wholesale condemnation of the art. Furthermore, there was the antagonism of the Christian ideal of those days to the Greeks' ideal of beauty and physical well-being as expressed in their sculpture. The Christian idea was to exalt the things of the spirit over those of the body—poverty, humility, and suffering, rather than affluence, grandeur and athletic prowess. Moreover, it was a revolution in the standing of the classes of society. The triumph of Christianity was a defeat of the aristocracies of wealth which did not join the new movement. Philosophers, the learned, and the well-born were the advocates of paganism. Loss of taste and refinement in the arts was the natural result when the Roman culture was overwhelmed by the revolution.

One hundred years had passed after the recognition of Christianity by Constantine before the first Germanic state in western Europe was established, with which event the history of the Middle Ages might appropriately begin. The history of the art of the Middle Ages is a history of the civilization in the Germanic countries of Europe. Many of these German tribes, known as Goths, had served as mercenary legions for the Romans at the far-flung outposts of their empire, and most of them had embraced

the new Christian faith. As in all periods of social unrest, it was one of ceaseless warfare which impoverished the countryside and set up illiterate military leaders as land owners and the new ruling caste of Europe. Learning sought refuge with the church. The clergy were the only power which could cope with the situation.

Under the protection of the monasteries, the arts flourished and men learned to build massively. All effort was dedicated to religion which resulted in abbey churches, hospitals and monastic cloisters. The basilica plan was retained for the churches but massive piers were substituted for the slender Roman columns. To make their churches fireproof, they developed the vaulted stone ceiling which had been so successful in the east, and the style of the building little resembled the earlier Roman.

Throughout this period the Byzantine style of Eastern Europe kept alive certain classic traditions which were mixed with wall painting carried over from the days of the early Christian decorations in the Roman catacombs. It provided a traditional set of designs—pictures of saints, and Bible stories—with little attention given to natural forms. The figures are elongated, and the expressions lifeless, yet they furnished the models for the embellishment of the buildings being erected for church use. The style is referred to as Romanesque or monastic. Many examples are to be found in Italy and southern France.

In borrowing from the basilican Roman style the three-aisled, cruciform plan with apse and transepts, the clerestory and the round arch, the builders had by their own ideas of construction transformed the style of the church. Marble wainscots and timber roofs had given way to massive vaults. But from this beginning in the new Gothic style sprang the glorious cathedrals of the 13th and 14th centuries.

During the 12th century the power of the monasteries waned as control of church affairs passed to the bishops and kings. Cathedrals began to replace the abbey churches and the pointed arch took the place of the round. Other changes included the ribbed vault for the barrel-shaped roof of the Romans and, to support the loftier nave roof, the flying buttress was introduced. Stained glass and window tracery also entered the scheme and carvings, following early Christian traditions, enriched the structure.

In the montage we see in the center the interior of a cathedral with roof of ribbed vaults; in the upper right-hand corner, carvings over a church door. Under this is shown Notre Dame, Paris, dating from the 12th century. Other items show some influence of the East gained by virtue of the crusades, and give some idea of the qualities of intricacy and craftsmanship which characterized the arts of the Middle Ages.

The Arts of the Renaissance

The Renaissance was not merely a revival of the classic tradition in the arts but a stirring of the human mind and spirit. The consolidation of the great nationalities of Europe, the passing of feudalism into centralized autocracies, the invention of gunpowder and of movable type for printing, the discovery of the solar system by Copernicus and Galileo, and the discovery of America, were all part of an awakening of intellectual energy.

We have seen how no intellectual freedom could be enjoyed until the barbaric Goths had run their course, to be absorbed by the peoples they conquered. The abbeys which first befriended the thinker and the artist had narrowed their viewpoint so that "ignorance was made to appear acceptable to God as a proof of faith and submission."

The awakening occurred first in Italy because a common language existed, a greater degree of political freedom was enjoyed, and commercial prosperity was the result of the broadening horizons of trade. First signs of the free spirit appeared in the poetry of Dante and the writings of Petrarch and Boccaccio which showed new consciousness of the beauty of the world and the love of life unterrified by the shadow of death.

The fall of Constantinople in 1453 may be considered as signalizing the change of thought. Men took notice of what the ancients had achieved. They compared the beauty of the ancient sculpture with the frigid reproductions of lifeless form which covered their church walls. They saw that the human body was a thing of beauty worthy of study, and they sought to present the Madonna and the Christ child with a full appreciation of their new sense of beauty and their new love of nature as a manifestation of God's handiwork.

The architects, under the impulse of the revived classic spirit, returned to the old Roman forms but added to them the lofty dome set upon a drum, often surrounded by pillars, the whole crowned by a "lantern." St. Peter's in Rome is the outstanding example. They also created a new architecture of palaces and public buildings in which a horizontal ceiling was made of timber and lavishly decorated. No effort was spared to adorn the walls, embellish the furniture with rich carving, and introduce tiles and marbles into elaborate decorative schemes.

In the field of painting, progress was slow at first, all artists being limited to the Byzantine patterns on which they practiced improvements toward more natural effects. No one painter began the movement. Craftsmen throughout Italy sought new ideas at the same source, and as the schools in the various localities developed the differences at first were hardly noticeable. The major schools were the Florentine and Sienese, the former distinguished by Cimabue (1240–1302) and his pupil Giotto (1276–1337), the latter by Lorenzetti (1330–?). From their early beginnings which showed definite traces of Byzantine influence, the schools developed and multiplied, and the painting showed increased technical knowledge and greater freedom from the former religious sentiment. The Church still retained its patronage of art but the artist painted the religious subjects in a more beautiful world.

The Florentine school soon became the leader and drew to it artists from neighboring communities. They became proficient in draftsmanship, a quality in which the school's most prominent exponent, Michelangelo, excelled. In Venice, the situation was a bit different. While Venetians accepted Christianity, they did so with less enthusiasm than it aroused elsewhere. Consequently, the contrast in thinking occasioned by the Renaissance was less marked. Venetians were merchants, not scholars, and though they harbored the Greek teachers after the fall of Constantinople they did not turn from their commerce that was winning them great wealth to engage in the intellectual movement that was crystallizing in Florence. Venetian artists memorialized the lavishness of the Republic and the sensuousness of its nature.

Another factor in the development of Renaissance art was the political situation in Italy wherein many of the cities were ruled by wealthy noblemen who patronized the arts throughout the 15th and 16th centuries. Among these families were the Visconti and Sforza at Milan, the Gonzaga at Mantua, the Montefeltro at Urbino, the Malatesta at Rimini, the Este at Ferrara, and the Medici at Florence. Their patronage nourished the goldsmiths and sculptors, and made possible many of the finest examples of art, regardless of period, that we are privileged to study today. The statues of Donatello, the bronze doors on the baptistery at Florence by Ghiberti, and the tombs of the Medici by Michelangelo, are outstanding examples of the highest period in Italian art.

The montage presents a variety of objects, all suggesting the richness in detail which characterized the decorative arts of the period. Particular notice should be given the examples of printing because in this era the Renaissance moved rapidly over the printed page. Virgil was printed in 1470, Homer in 1488, Aristotle in 1498, and Plato in 1513. And two years later, far to the north in Germany Martin Luther nailed his famous thesis on the cathedral door which started the intellectual movement in the north of Europe.

The Arts of the Orient

Appreciation of Oriental art depends upon recognition of the principle that great art need not be an imitation of nature, but may be a generalization of forms representing man, nature, and the spiritual forces which dominate the two. Western art most nearly approached the Oriental ideal in certain Byzantine mosaics and in the paintings of Botticelli. The difference lay in that the West emphasized the visual representation; the East, an abstract expression of the relative values of man's existence in an eternal program.

The essence of this philosophy was contained in a Japanese poem:

"The morning glory blooms but for an hour, and yet it differs not at heart from the giant pine that lives for a thousand years."

The people of India and of China worshipped the powers of nature—sun, the sky, wind and the rain, the fundamental problems of existence, and the nature of the soul. In both, the fostering of tradition and the sacrifice of the individual to the larger social unit produced conventions in

their arts, and an expression more racial than personal.

In the Brahman faith the Hindu sought fundamental spiritual truths. He believed that every deed in this life plays its part in determining the next life, that individual souls pass at death from one body to another. Good deeds reward the soul by reincarnating it in a higher form of life; evil deeds bring it to a lower. Existence is one continuous succession of rebirth, of which the goal is freedom from existence by absorption into Brahma, the ultimate.

Such expression of this belief is apparent in Indian art in spite of the strong foreign influences that pushed eastward under the impetus of Alexander, and the later invasions of the Persians. From 320 to 647 A.D., considered the golden age of Hindu culture, India was in a rich and prosperous condition. Charitable institutions, hospitals, places of learning, monasteries, and palaces were built and richly decorated, according to a fifth century account. Sculpture, painting and music flourished, and Sanskrit literature reached its greatest height.

The ebb and flow of conquest by barbarous, nomadic tribes reached a climax about 1000 A.D., when the Muhammadans overran the country and established the Mogul Empire which remained the ruling power until the 18th century when the English and French imposed their influence, which led to English rule in 1818.

Indian Art

Of the earliest cities of India, nothing is left except temples carved out of solid rock, which were popular because they gave shelter from heavy rains and intense heat. Walls were decorated with fresco murals, and painted banners hung from the roofs. The earlier examples of architecture were made of wood and could not survive the destructive climate.

Hindu sculpture was chiefly a religious art and served as temple decoration. In early eras Buddha was not represented but was referred to by symbols such as a bird or an elephant. Statues appeared several hundred years later and showed the deity seated with legs crossed, hands folded in lap, eyes downcast—the Indian artist's idea of spiritual simplicity.

The lotus, a favorite flower, was used symbolically. When shown growing upright, it signified the human spirit growing out of material life toward Brahma. The open lotus, with turned down petals used in capitals and the pedestals of statues of Buddha, suggests the vault of heaven.

Temples differed in various areas. In the north, they were shrines and places of assembly, frequently roofed over by a high tower. In the south, the shrine was enclosed in a walled quadrangle which surrounded minor temples and bathing pools. Towering gateways were ornamented with gods and monsters, animals, and floral motifs.

Wealthy Mogul rulers erected magnificent tombs, the finest of which is the Taj Mahal, built between 1632 and 1653 and shown in the accompanying montage. It is a masterpiece of lightness, grace, and delicacy, and has windows of perforated marble, carved in a lace-like design.

Chinese Art

Native conservatism has been Chinese strength. Foreign influences, though powerful, have been absorbed by the Chinese as they adhered to fundamental traditions four thousand years old.

China's greatness was based on the highways to the west, the trade routes for the delivery of silks to the Mediterranean. Over these roads the religion of India crossed with the culture of China, and the result was a great art. Buddhism was the inspiration of the period of the T'ang dynasty, which is recognized as the golden age of all Chinese arts. It lasted from 618 to 907 A.D., when a revolutionary reaction to the religion brought about the destruction of many of the period's noblest examples. The Sung dynasty followed (960–1280), an era similar to the Renaissance in Europe. During this period many of China's greatest statesmen, philosophers, poets, and painters flourished. It was the Sung capital that Marco Polo visited.

The Sung dynasty was overthrown by Mongols led by Kublai Khan (1280–1368), which in turn led to the Ming dynasty (1368–1644), a period of prolific achievement which sought its inspiration in the T'ang era, though it lacked much of the quality of the latter. With the Ming, the great periods of Chinese art ended.

Jade, obtained from the mountains of western

China and from the rivers, was the material of which many statues, bells, bowls, vases, and articles of personal adornment were carved.

The Art of the French Renaissance

Gothic influence was still strong in France when Francis I (1515–1547) engaged in military and political missions in Italy. Charmed by the warmth and splendor of the new art that had swept the southern country, the king not only brought back ideas, but induced some of the outstanding Italian artists to return to France with him.

Up to this time, the Church had dominated the lives of French people. It had inspired a religious art, which, throughout the Middle Ages, had borne the free expression of local craftsmen. In contrast, the classic art of the Renaissance was a formalized set of design principles practiced by artisans trained to cooperate in producing a studied and unified effect. The art glorified the ruling classes in Italy, and Francis saw in it the flattering of a monarch.

For the following three hundred years, the Renaissance in France epitomized the elevation of the king in the suppression of the feudal lords, and the concentration of power that eventually led to the injustices of taxation, persecutions and special privilege. It was the period marked by the reigns of Louis XIV, Louis XV, and Louis XVI, and terminated by the great social outburst of the French Revolution.

Italian ideas appeared first in the architecture of chateaux and civic buildings, in greater regularity of design and a better balance of vertical and horizontal lines than marked Gothic structures. The northern climate imposed certain structural characteristics, such as steep roofs, many windows, chimneys and fireplaces—all of which were executed with French feeling.

Rooms in early Renaissance buildings were large. The ceilings were sometimes vaulted, showing traces of the Gothic builders, and sometimes exposing the structural wooden beams which were richly ornamented. Tapestries that adorned the walls also provided some warmth, and the fireplace that furnished comfort in the colder seasons became the center of the decorative scheme as well as the focal point of hospitality.

Italian influence was predominant in the design of the Hotel des Invalides, which serves now as a war college and the tomb of Napoleon. Renaissance orders with columns and pediment are surmounted by a dome not unlike that of St. Peter's in Rome.

Formality of the Italian Renaissance plan included the gardens, and the landscape architect became an important factor in the development of the magnificent parks which surround the chateaux. During the reign of Louis XIV, Versailles was built. Lagoons were introduced into the design of the gardens to reflect the grandeur of the architecture, and statues of mythical heroes accented the long balustrades and terraces. Even the trees were clipped to a common height to complete the formalized effect.

The Petit Trianon, shown in the center of the accompanying montage, was built for Louis XV. Upon his death, it became the favorite palace of Louis XVI and Marie Antoinette, who laid out its gardens.

Royal sponsorship of the arts caused a centralization of manufacture of all articles of furniture and decoration so that when assembled the result would be harmonious. During the 17th century, Louis XIV placed many commissions with the Gobelin's establishment which extended their activities to include metalwork, furniture and jewelry in addition to their tapestries.

The style of design associated with the monarch is massive, simple, stately and symmetrical. Draperies of silk and velvet were rich in their simplicity and contrasted with the brilliantly painted panels on the walls and ceilings.

With the death of Louis XIV, in 1715, the trend of design turned from the masculine to the grace and more feminine lightness which characterized the style of Louis XV. Angles were avoided in furniture patterns, with the emphasis on slender proportions and a repetition of curves. The use of rockwork or shellwork as units of ornament gave to this style the name Rococo.

The reign of Louis XVI saw a restoration of straight lines, though the proportions of the furniture did not resemble that of Louis XIV. There was a lightness in the style, but much of the manly character of the earlier examples of Renaissance work was restored.

In the 18th century, the potters of France discovered the secret of making true porcelain which equalled some of the 11th and 12th centuries Chinese porcelains that had been famous for their translucency. Royal Sevres porcelains

soon appeared painted with figures and landscapes which harmonized with the elegance of the interiors.

The efforts of French painters during the 14th and 15th centuries were directed toward church work which they executed in the Gothic manner, producing many altarpieces. With the increase of Italian influence, the idea of portraiture found willing patronage among the leading nobles. The lower strata of society, however, gave popular acceptance to a form of genre art, influenced by the Dutch and Flemish schools, in which sober colors predominated.

It was in the landscapes of Claude Lorrain and Nicolas Poussin, both of the 17th century, that France made a notable contribution in painting. Showing definite Italian feeling, Claude composed imaginative studies of classic ruins and verdant groves, all possessing an impressive grandeur.

François Boucher and Antoine Watteau reflected the regal setting of the court of Louis XV, painting nudes in blissful idleness, and lovers loitering in shady glens. Though fanciful, their pictures showed a sense of balance and strength in design.

The outstanding painter of the 18th century was Siméon Chardin, who painted in the spirit of the French middle-class homes, showing figures and still life objects in light and contrasted against dark backgrounds, in a manner not unlike the Dutch masters.

English Art in the 18th Century

As the 18th century dawned, the English interpretation of the classic spirit of the Renaissance was enjoying its most expressive period, but when the century waned the Renaissance faded with it.

This art movement had spanned a period of three hundred years which almost paralleled its life in France. England's southern neighbor had set the pace, and early in the 16th century, King Henry VIII engaged Italian workmen to carve certain memorials. This work led to the absorption of many Italian ideas that were suitable for architectural use.

Because of the conflict between King Henry and the Roman church, which had reached its climax at that time, Italian fashions were not received popularly. Dutch and German influences made effective progress in the fields of architecture, interior decorating, and painting. Hans Holbein contributed heavily to this influence. The result of these opposing influences produced Renaissance details on Gothic castles; Italian facades with symmetrically placed windows, but surmounted by castellated parapets; and a mixture of Roman classic orders and Dutch and German ornament.

With the death of Elizabeth in 1603, and the establishment of the Stuart kings, the Renaissance became full-flowered as a classic style which stamped itself as an urban architecture nationally throughout the 17th century. During this period the architects Inigo Jones and Christopher Wren produced their great works. It was also during this time that the great fire of London (1666) swept away the last vestiges of the Middle Ages in that metropolis.

The 18th century emerged with Wren still alive, and his influence guiding many talented architects who designed scores of churches and other buildings, some over the ashes of the fire. Among these are St. Martin's-in-the-Fields, St. Mary-le-Strand, and St. Clement's Dane, all of which have endured through the two recent world wars, despite some damage.

The Renaissance style became so formalized during the middle years of the century that many amateur designers practiced architecture and left some landmarks of questionable merit. The emphasis, however, was shifted from the exteriors of buildings to the interiors. These were treated lavishly by skilled designers, among whom was William Kent, who introduced strong classic architectural features into rooms of great scale, and who designed equally elaborate furniture and decorations to match. Plaster ornament covered the ceiling areas, and wood carving was skillfully executed. Great freedom was shown in the adaptation of the classic manner to the living comforts of the English gentleman, and many examples were equally as rich in treatment as their counterparts in the palaces of the French kings.

During the closing decades of the 18th century, a strict adherence to the original patterns of Greece and Rome was practiced by the Brothers Adam. Much of the dynamic quality of the Renaissance was lost as the copy-book principles, formal and frigid, pushed the exponents of a freer expression aside. Entire sections of London bore the stamp of the Adams, and on

this shrill high note the Renaissance died.

Against this classic background England produced many of her outstanding authors, artisans, and painters. At the start of the century the playwrights Congreve and Farquhar and the artist Hogarth amused the people with social caricatures. Later, a long train of literary personages included the poet Pope, the lexicographer Samuel Johnson, and the poet-playwrights Goldsmith and Sheridan.

Little sculpture was done and the painting was limited to portraits and landscapes. Probably the most notable of the painters was Sir Joshua Reynolds (1723–1792) who studied for some years in Italy, and showed the influence of the Venetians and of Van Dyck, who had painted the court of Charles I most profusely. Reynolds was a man of lofty imagination and painted with dignity and an elevated spirit. When the Royal Academy was founded in 1768, Sir Joshua served as its first president.

Gainsborough (1727–1788) showed a dislike for conventions and formulas, and his famous Blue Boy was painted in protest against the conventional theory sponsored by Reynolds that a composition should be warm in color and light. Both in portraiture and landscape he was original, showing less foreign influence than any other British painter.

Romney (1734–1802) was as proficient in portraiture as Reynolds and Gainsborough, but he gave less attention to composition. His paintings of women are warm and winsome, and display a fine sense of grace of line and charm of color.

Toward the close of the century a new group of artists appeared who are more definitely identified with the 19th century. There are: Lawrence (1769–1830), Blake (1757–1827), John Constable (1776–1837), famous for his landscapes, and Turner (1775–1851), who is possibly the best known of all British painters. Imaginative, and unschooled in the popular art formulae, Turner painted impressively, even theatrically at times, creating his effects by imposing scale and grandeur.

Tapestry weaving in England can be traced to the efforts of James I, who in 1617 encouraged the establishing of the industry at Mortlake staffed by about fifty weavers obtained from the Netherlands. Designs by Raphael intended for tapestries for the Vatican were acquired upon the advice of Rubens and were woven at Mortlake. The factory was supported by the Crown and continued in operation until early in the 18th century.

Furniture by Thomas Chippendale (1705–1779) remains one of the outstanding contributions to art made during these times. A cabinet-maker whose name will always be associated with furniture, he produced his work in three different styles, showing Gothic feeling, Chinese adaptations, and pieces fashioned in the spirit of Louis Quinze. Mahogany came into use for furniture making about 1725, and the new wood, stronger and more elastic than materials used formerly, permitted more graceful contours, and lighter form. Chippendale took advantage of this flexibility and created a new mode which has persisted to this day.

Early American Art

Following the arrival of the earliest settlers, the transplanting of a European culture amidst primitive conditions took approximately one hundred and fifty years. Lacking proximity to centers of manufacture, the colonists were forced to create the things they needed in a manner governed by the tools they had at hand. They became skilled carpenters, and they refined their earliest forms to imitate the patterns imported from England by the more wealthy merchants.

During the early part of the 18th century a broad demand for more luxurious furnishings provided a market in which the arts and crafts could flourish. The War for Independence interrupted this rapid development and opened the way for a conflict of ideas which represented different influences, effected by the trend of events in Europe. As the frontiers of America moved westward individual treatment prevailed since there was no established school of thought in design matters to govern popular taste.

Architecturally, the earliest homes and churches built reflected the middle-class English Gothic or Tudor in New England, Dutch in New Amsterdam, and Jacobean in the South. As economic conditions improved and contacts with Europe were more frequent, the late-Renaissance or English Georgian style supplied the patterns for timber construction in the Colonies. Classic symmetry, regularity of window openings, and Roman forms suggested Renaissance palaces translated into wood.

Southern mansions featured pedimented porticos and Palladian window details. Many were built of brick against which the white wood trim contrasted pleasingly. The churches, both in the north and south, were modifications of London city churches, with spires reminiscent of Wren's wide variety.

Following the War for Independence, sentiment for British innovations lessened and the classical wave which marked the Napoleonic era was aided in its American acceptance by Thomas Jefferson. This versatile statesman designed the library of the University of Virginia, in addition to his own home at Monticello, and helped to found a style of architecture considered traditionally American.

In New England, the classic influence was expressed in carving, paneling, fireplace mantels and stairways. Samuel McIntire, carver and builder, left many notable examples of his work which may be seen today in Massachusetts towns.

European fashions in furniture also provided models for American designs, Chippendale, Hepplewhite, and Sheraton being most frequently copied. Two outstanding American designers were Duncan Phyfe, of New York, and William Savery, of Philadelphia. Phyfe's designs were rather severe, being patterned chiefly after those of Sheraton. But in spite of the European influences which prevailed, American designers showed a fresh outlook that reflected vigor and shunned the mannerisms of European models.

American Painting

Aside from the portrait of a revered ancestor, little painting was in evidence in the earlier homes of the colonists. The Puritan prejudice against personal vanity discouraged the practice of painting living subjects for a long time. However, the urge to leave some memorial of the family's founder increased, and many examples of portraits by untrained artists and sign painters are extant.

It was not until John S. Copley showed ability to paint strong characterizations, and a technical skill in presenting realism in details, such as satins and laces, that American portraiture became an art. Copley made his permanent home in England and followed the fashion of the day, but he never equalled in candor his earlier Colonial work.

Benjamin West (1738–1820) also left America to seek training abroad, and arrived in London at the time Sir Joshua Reynolds was at the height of his popularity. West followed the current style and became wealthy. At Sir Joshua's death he succeeded him as president of the Royal Academy. He painted historical subjects in the manner of the French Romanticists, and can hardly be associated with American art in spite of his birth.

John Trumbull (1756–1843) recorded on canvas the history of the Revolutionary period, and showed a masterful handling on complex compositions. Some of his pictures are in the rotunda in the Capitol at Washington.

The best of the early portrait painters was Gilbert Stuart (1755–1828) who is remembered chiefly for his likenesses of the great men of his time, especially George Washington. Trained in England, he freed himself from the influences of the British school and created a more vibrant characterization by the sharpness of his modelling. He was one of the first in American art to display skillful accuracy in his brush strokes.

Early American families often counted their wealth in the amount of silver they possessed, which they passed on to successive generations. Silversmiths, therefore, held a high position in the community, and they created articles with distinctive American spirit. The work of the patriot Paul Revere shows a fine relationship between the masses that compose his designs, graceful contours, and restraint in the use of ornament.

The character of early American art was a reflection of the people themselves, blending the influences and prejudices of their European backgrounds, yet with an interpretation that showed they sensed that they were free from the pettiness and artificiality of the fickle modes of European society.

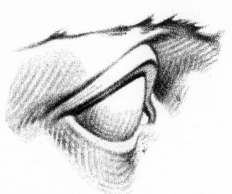

CHAPTER 3

Drawing—The Language of the Artist

Drawing is the basis of the artist's craft. It is the language of the artist in which, through study, he hopes to speak fluently. And he can do this with a minimum amount of instruction. His degree of success will be determined by his powers of observation, a willingness to submit himself to strict discipline, and patient endeavor.

Let us see how an artist's way of looking at the world distinguishes him from most people. In the first place, he usually sees more than they do because, if he is a true student, he has a tremendous amount of curiosity. He is not satisfied with surface appearances. He gives close attention to every detail he can see in whatever he wishes to draw. Characteristics in the object, which the casual observer would not be likely to notice, are important to the artist.

For instance, if he were drawing a horse, he would not be satisfied to have his drawing present an animal resembling in a general way what a horse looks like. His drawing might even show a faultless knowledge of the anatomy of a horse. But some distinctive characteristic which made the horse he was drawing different from others would be recorded by the artist though it might not be noticed by scores of other people. Evidences of keen observation are the marks of a good draftsman. And this is not all.

The artist also analyzes. He tries to find out all that can be known about the thing he is drawing—how it is made, how put together—and he searches for this information whether he is drawing furniture, an airplane, or the human figure.

His curiosity, observation, and analysis of objects combine to give the artist the knowledge he needs. Without this he could hardly hope to present a full statement about the subject he was drawing. With it, his work assumes authority, a quality that gives it lasting value.

When a student desires to express the results of some observation in a drawing, he usually makes his first attempts by suggesting the form of the object with the use of lines. He instinctively identifies the characteristics of the object by its contours and, to further suggest its form, he subdivides the area within the contour by additional lines. The result is purely diagrammatic. The object has no lines; it has area, volume, substance, and its mass appears in varying degrees of light and shade. When the student chose to use line to suggest the object, he succeeded only in defining its form in a sort of stenographic way. He failed to tell the whole story.

The Use of Line

Let us observe the object we wish to draw. Assume it is an orange. At first glance it appears to us approximately in the form of a circle. To express this form we use the most convenient medium, which may be a pencil, a crayon, pen and ink, or a brush with hairs tapered sufficiently to a point to permit us to define the form in line on a piece of paper. But we note that the orange has a rounded surface which our single line fails

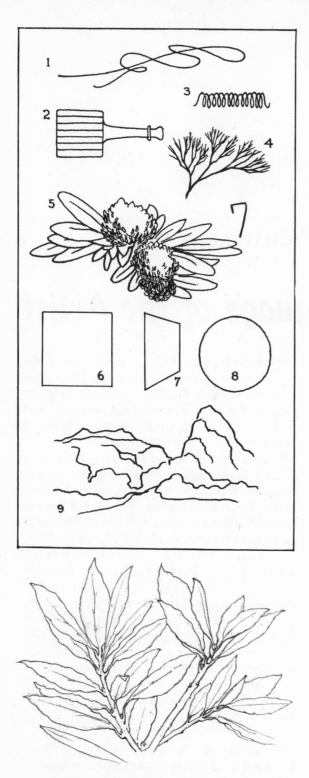

The group of diagrams shown at top illustrate both the limitations and the possibilities of line alone as a means of representing known facts. A line may be conceived as limited to two dimensions, or it may suggest movement in any direction in three-dimensional space. At bottom, line is shown accented, which suggests that the subject has substance.

to express. We see that lines are important in defining the shape of objects but that their value is limited.

How much can we do with line alone?

A single line can represent form by bounding areas and by defining their contours. Lines can be used symbolically; straight lines suggest rigidity, curved lines, movement and grace, while horizontal lines can give the feeling of restfulness. Oblique lines can imply violence, as in a slanting sweep of rain. But, living in a three-dimensional world where objects cannot be defined entirely by their contours, an art student finds that line alone will not tell the complex story of rounded surfaces, textures, and the varying degrees of light and color which make the object visible to us.

What do we mean by three dimensions?

Width, height, and thickness. If you draw the orange as a circle on a piece of paper, using a line of equal width throughout, you will have drawn a shape in two dimensions—width and height. It will suggest no thickness.

Can a line suggest that the object has three dimensions?

Yes. By varying the character of the line. Lines may be considered as a series of points extending contiguously. When these points are alike in character, the lines they form appear uniform and suggest no variation in the contour of the subject. As such, lines are mechanical and serve to bound areas or divide areas into smaller shapes. Lines are not one of Nature's forms. Artists can use lines only to represent the contours of Nature's forms.

However, when the points which form the lines change in character, something new has been added. As the points increase in size and the line appears to broaden, the object the line defines appears to have thickness. The line ceases to function as a diagram and takes on expression.

A line can suggest that an object has three dimensions also in instances where the object resembles a solid having edges which appear to recede from the eye. By defining these edges with lines, the student will experience his first problems in drawing in perspective, the principles of which will be explored a few pages further on.

Lines of uniform thickness may be used to represent a piece of string or wire, spider webs, and a ship's rigging. Thin twigs and branches,

34

seen at a distance, appear as uniform lines. Even in these instances the line is used symbolically because all of these objects have substance.

A line can express Beauty. It depends on the relation that one part of the line bears to another part, such as a variation in the curves, or possibly the contrast in effect obtained by the change of a straight section to one of curves.

While we may draw a line to define a contour, we really think in terms of the boundaries of shapes and, where a variety of shapes are fitted together, we use a line to separate these shapes. The rugged contour of a distant rocky cliff may be marked by a line to define the silhouetted edge where the mass of rock appears in contrast against the sky. A grove of trees may be grouped at the foot of the cliff, and these in turn may be suggested by a line separating them from the cliff. But we soon find that line alone is insufficient to express the true effect we see in Nature. We need the element of dark and light to create the picture, and the addition of color to approximate naturalness.

Illustrating the limitations of line are the panels on these pages. On page 40 is shown (1) a piece of string, or wire; (2) a broiling iron; (3) a coil spring; and (4) twigs near the tip of a branch. These objects are suggested fairly well by line, but with a couple of rhododendron blossoms (5) we begin to suspect that line alone cannot satisfy a person who expects a far different effect—one of white blossoms clustered among dark green leaves.

Other illustrations in the panel show a square, a rectangle, and a circle where line is adequate to bound the areas. Number 9 has been drawn to suggest in line the cliff, trees and sky referred to above.

The Use of Light and Shade

Now examine the panel on this page. See how important the contrast of dark and light can be in establishing the contour of shapes. The objects now appear to have substance and no longer need line to define them.

Let us pause long enough to acquaint ourselves with a few terms referred to in the study of light and shade. Although we do not live in a world of black and white but rather in one of varied color, it will be simpler if, in our study of light and shade, we think in terms of the

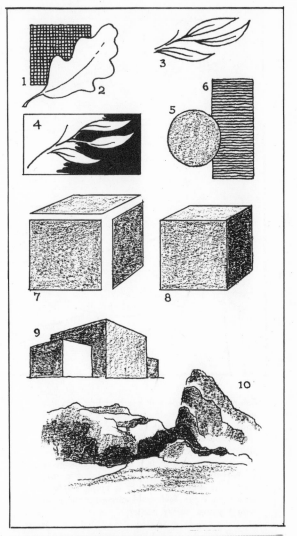

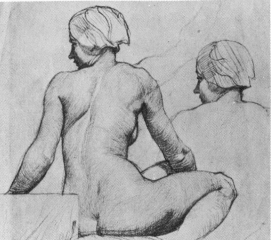

Diagrams at top show the concept of line in relation to tone. Figures 7, 8, and 9 show how tone creates the effect of three dimensions. At bottom, tone supplementing line gives roundness to form.

Emphasis on variation in width of line aids this example to show effect of muscles in action and under tension. Although no tone is used, the line alone has been made to suggest anatomical structure. Below, a concept of space, distance, and infinity is created in a lettering problem by a student. Depth in space is rendered graphically. The illusion that light is projected from below adds the feeling of airiness and great height above earthy matter.

presence or absence of light. The degree of intensity of light which illumines an object will determine the key of the picture. High intensity will force a high key of tone, low intensity will cause a low key of tonal value. Within each key, note how important varying degrees of tone can be in helping to define an object and increase the interest of an observer in it. The word "tone" is used to refer to a single degree of gradation between the extremes of black and white, or light and dark. Since there are many such gradations, each differing slightly as they approach the extremes, the range of gradations is known as a "tonal scale." It represents the variations in intensity of light.

We see objects only because of the light rays that are reflected from them. The more intense the light rays, the more clearly the object appears; likewise, with the absence of light rays we see nothing. More light rays are reflected from an object light in tone, whereas with objects of darker values the rays are absorbed and less of them are reflected. Therefore, objects appear in varying degrees of dark and light because of the nature of their textures which govern the degree of light they reflect.

When objects of contrasting tone are grouped together they create a sharp effect which draws attention. The simpler the effect, the more easily is it understood. We note the contrast between the formal regular shape of the square and the informal, irregular shape of an oak leaf (figures 1 and 2.) Both of these areas are further defined by outlines. The same is true of figure 3, but in figure 4, the sprig of leaves has no outline. The area of the leaves is defined by the contrasting area of the background. This is more nearly the effect we see in nature.

In figures 5 and 6—the circle and the rectangle —we realize that the shape of an area is more important than its outline. If the area is in contrast with the areas which surround it, it needs no outline to define it. In fact, areas that are not in tonal contrast with the areas around them are seldom visible.

In figure 7 we have three areas, one a square and two rectangles having two parallel sides, which when joined along the sides of the square produce the effect of a cube, with the square appearing as the light side. The rectangles, toned differently, create the effect of solidity. Figure 9 carries this idea further to suggest an architectural composition. In figure 10, the cliffs and trees are rendered in a variety of tonal values which suggests their effect to an observer under normal light conditions in nature. We can see that gradations of light and dark are necessary to produce an illusion of solidity. Tones without variety appear flat and suggest flat areas. To give variety to values is known as modelling, a skill necessary to the artist if he desires to give accurate presentations of the shapes he has in mind.

Therefore we see that we do not live in a world of lines but in one of areas, of surfaces, and of solids and in their complex relationships of textures, values and colors. It is a three-dimensional world and the student must give early consideration to the optical differences in objects nearby and at a distance. To create these effects is called drawing in perspective.

The Principles of Perspective

Drawing in perspective is indicating things as they appear to be rather than as we know them to be. As we look down a street we notice that the distance between the curbs at the point we may be standing is much wider than they appear to be further away, although we know that the width of the street is the same at both places.

Three concepts of three-dimensional form, two by students using alphabetical characters, and a painting by Corot, in the Louvre, Paris. The students relied on linear perspective for their suggestion of thickness of the letters; Corot depended on tonal values to create a sense of aerial perspective.

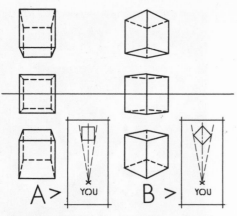

The appearance of things depends on the point of view from which you are looking at them. In Illustration A you are looking directly at the flat side of a cube. The middle illustration shows how the cube appears when its center is at your eye level. The upper illustration shows how it looks when above your eye level. The lower shows how it appears when below your eye level.

The illustrations above the letter B are shown at similar levels but viewed from a corner of the cube instead of one of its flat sides.

We also notice that objects decrease in size apparently as they are moved further from the eye. Furthermore, objects appear in their true proportion only when they are seen with their surface perpendicular to the observer's line of sight. As flat surfaces are turned away from the line of sight, the relationship of width to height changes, a condition called foreshortening.

These three observations govern all the conditions a student will experience as he indicates objects in perspective. There are principles to guide a student in his indication of perspective that have been known from the days of the Italian Renaissance. They are easily learned but a student must master them to be a good draftsman.

Perspective can be suggested either by gradation of tonal values or by convergence of lines. The former method is referred to as "aerial" perspective, the latter as "linear" perspective. Both are helpful toward the success of a drawing. In "aerial" perspective, the effects are created by use of tones, with the sharper, more contrasting values appearing in the foreground, the contrasts less pronounced as objects are suggested at greater distances from the eye. This effect is usual in nature when the light is distributed equally over foreground, middle distance and background alike. Exceptions do occur when the distribution of light is unequal.

It is in "linear" perspective that more formulated rules apply. The student should begin by becoming thoroughly familiar with three terms: the picture plane, the eye level, and the vanishing point.

The Picture Plane

Think of the picture plane as a piece of window glass through which we see a group of objects. If we hold the glass in a fixed position and trace with a crayon the shapes of the objects we see, we would find that the limits of our drawing would be determined by the size of the glass. When we draw this group of objects on a piece of paper, we will find that the size of the paper imposes restrictions as did the glass. We must select the things we wish to draw as though we were moving our piece of glass so that the subject we select will fall within the limits of the glass.

Throughout this experiment we note that the center of our attention is close to the center of the group of objects selected for our picture. This direction of our vision is called the line of sight. We also note that this line of sight is perpendicular to the surface of the window glass. And it may be considered the same when the paper takes the place of the glass. The line of sight is frequently horizontal with the eye or slightly below it. It is a common practice, though by no means necessary, to look downward toward an object to be drawn.

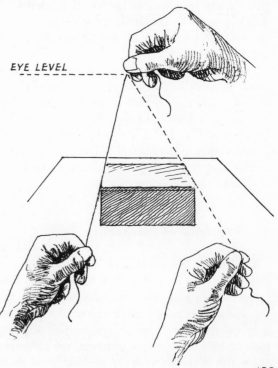

EYE LEVEL

The point in the grouping on which our attention is centered is known as the focal point and, with this point as a center, the material selected for the picture should fall equally on either side and within a 60 degree angle from the eye. If a greater degree of angle is attempted, the student will experience difficulty in avoiding confusion. This is because an eye receives a single impression clearly only if it falls within a 60 degree angle which is approximately the limitation of sight in a fixed stare.

The Eye Level

Think of the eye level as a horizontal line extending across a plane, level and at the height of the observer's eye. It may have an indefinite length along which a student may establish points at which the parallel edges of vertical and horizontal surfaces of objects in the picture seem to converge. It matters little whether the eye level passes through the picture material or not. If the line of sight toward the grouping to be drawn is directed sharply downward, the eye level will most likely be outside and much above the limits of the picture. However, it will still provide the line along which the points of convergence for horizontal edges in the picture can be found.

Let us experiment with a small box having parallel edges. Place the box in front of you so that it is horizontal and slightly below the level of the eye. You will notice that the edges receding from the eye converge upward. Take a piece of string and hold one end in each hand, tautly and between the box and the eye so that the string appears to lie along the receding side of the box. Hold the upper end and swing the lower so that the string lies along the other receding side, and make such adjustment in the position of the upper end that it serves as a common radius for the string as it lies along either of the receding sides of the box.

The Vanishing Point

This point of radius is located along the eye level and serves as the vanishing point for all edges of the box that are parallel to the two receding sides we have used in our experiment. If the box is placed so that all of its horizontal edges recede—some toward the left and some toward the right—the lines of convergence in each case will be located along the eye level.

Let us suppose that the box has a cover hinged

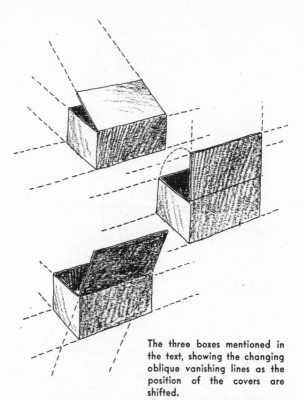

The three boxes mentioned in the text, showing the changing oblique vanishing lines as the position of the covers are shifted.

at one of its longer edges. If we raise the cover so that its shorter edges are no longer parallel with the corresponding edges of the box, we will note that the lines of convergence will no longer meet at a point on the eye level. They will meet above it. An additional point must be established. When we raised the cover of the box we did not change the relationship of the short sides of the cover and the box except in a vertical plane. Therefore we will find the vanishing point governing the edges of the cover directly above the vanishing point governing the corresponding sides of the box.

When the edges of the cover are in a vertical position there will be no convergence. But when

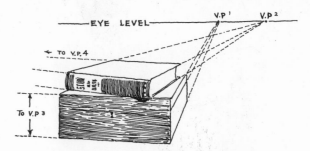

The principle that governs the use of different vanishing points on the same eye level is shown in this sketch of the book on the box. A curving stairway is drawn in a similar manner.

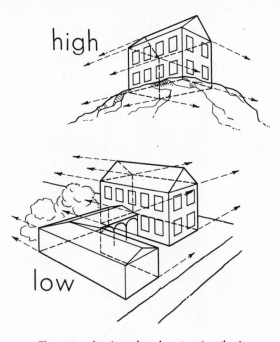

These two drawings show how to give the impression of looking up or looking down. In the "high" position you establish a low horizon and in the "low" position you establish a high horizon. If you wish to find the vanishing points of these two buildings, you need only to project the dotted lines left and right in the direction indicated by the arrow points.

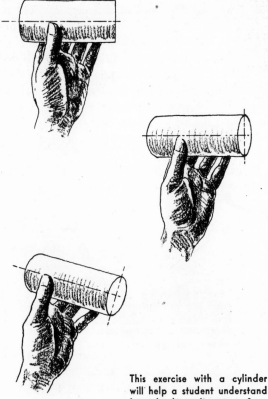

This exercise with a cylinder will help a student understand how the long diameter of an ellipse is determined.

the cover passes the vertical position and reclines backward, the convergence is downward and the point will be found directly below the vanishing point governing the horizontal edges of the box.

These simple principles in convergence of lines used when drawing in perspective will aid the student when he has to construct geometric forms in horizontal and oblique planes, such as roofs of buildings.

How to Draw a Circle in Perspective

Cut a circle about 10 inches in diameter out of cardboard. When you hold the circle in front of you so that the cardboard's surface is perpendicular with your line of sight, the circle appears true, but when you tip the cardboard slightly, the circle appears shorter in one dimension than in another. In this flattened appearance, the circle is called an ellipse. It is symmetrical and its shape follows a changing curve. Students frequently fail to observe that the sharp ends of the long diameter of the ellipse are still curved regardless of how rapid the change of direction may be. Avoid the common error of letting this sharp turn of the curve appear as a point.

Occasionally the student will have a problem where circles of different diameters are grouped so that they have a common center such as an archery target, or a nest of bowls. Using the same center in the cardboard circle, construct other circles of varying diameters. Tilt the cardboard so that the circles appear foreshortened. It will be noted that the distances between the circles along the greater diameter are not changed but that those along the short diameter become narrower. The student will also note that the distances between the circles on the short diameter are graduated, the wider nearer the eye, the narrowest furthest from the eye. This principle will govern many instances where concentric circles appear such as ripples in a pool caused by the tossing of a stone.

Up to this point we have observed the circle when held vertically and horizontally, but a student must be prepared to draw the circle in any position it appears. When you look up at a clock on the face of a building, or at a circular window, the circle is both foreshortened and at an oblique plane from the line of sight. If the correct angle is not determined for the long diam-

40

eter, the construction of the circle will appear faulty. Let us experiment at a closer range.

Take a cylinder, such as a water glass with parallel sides, and hold it so its axis is horizontal and level with the eye, and so that one end appears as a vertical line. Now turn the glass so that the end appears as an ellipse but keep the axis of the glass horizontal. The student will note that the long diameter of the ellipse will be vertical and the short diameter horizontal. Now tip the glass so that the axis is no longer horizontal. The long diameter of the ellipse now takes an oblique direction and it will be noted that this new direction is perpendicular to the axis of the cylinder in its tipped position. With this observation the student is ready to draw cylindrical objects in any position. The principle also governs the construction of the arch in perspective, and it is advisable to draw first the complete circle, removing the unwanted portions later. Just remember that the long diameter is perpendicular to the axis of the cylinder.

Reflections Drawn in Perspective

For the purpose of the following observations and study let us place before the mirror over a bureau, dressing table or a fireplace mantel, some object having sharp edges and parallel sides such as a jewel box or square-edged clock. Set the object so that the rear side is flush against the frame of the mirror. You will note that the edges of the object perpendicular with the mirror are continued in the mirror without any change of direction. The same vanishing point used to determine the edges of the object can be used for the reflection.

Change the position of the object so that the rear side is not parallel with the face of the mirror. The object in reflection now seems to assume an angle with the face of the mirror like the angle of the object itself in relation to the mirror. Therefore, the relative position of an object with a reflecting surface can be established by the reflection indicated. If the object in the mirror appears to tilt upward at the back or slope downward, it is evident the face of the mirror is not vertical.

Let us place a glass on a horizontal mirror surface. The glass appears upside down with the bottom of the reflection supporting the actual object above it. Observe also that while you can

41

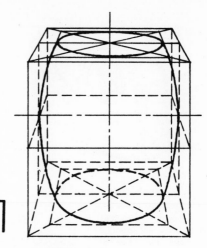

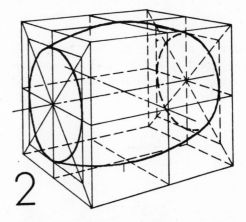

Since curves are much more difficult to draw in perspective than straight lines, your first approach in drawing the barrel (3) should begin with drawing in perspective a box shape which would exactly enclose the barrel. With this box shape as a guide, it will be easy to locate the centers of the top and bottom, as well as the limits of the circumference of the barrel (Figure 1).

With these points established, you will find it less of a problem to draw a barrel regardless of the position it is in.

The edges of the clock are continued in the mirror without change of direction. However, if the clock was placed so that its surfaces were not parallel with the mirror, the edges of the clock would be deflected at the point of contact with the mirror.

the image to be seen across a wide expanse of water. Only when the surface of the water is smooth can images be reflected with a resemblance to the original object.

One of the confusing situations in reflected images is caused by a buoy or stake marking the channel of a stream. The stake is seldom seen perpendicular to the surface of the water. If, for instance, it leans toward the observer its reflection appears longer than the stake itself. If it leans away, the reflection appears shorter. This is caused by the stake being foreshortened above the surface of the water but appearing elongated in the reflection. Hold a pencil upright on the horizontal mirror you used in the experiment with the glass and tilt it toward you and then away from you, noting how the reflection changes.

look into the glass as it rests on the mirror, the inside of the glass in the reflection cannot be seen. It is like drawing a cylindrical object with the mirror passing through the middle of it, but with the same points used for determining the ellipse representing the top of the glass and its counterpart in the reflection at the bottom of the cylinder.

Reflecting surfaces are not always smooth. Think of a body of water, not agitated to the extent of a storm but having a rippled surface. The reflection of an object on such a surface is lengthened causing the image to bear little resemblance to the original. This is because the surface of the water has been broken up into many reflecting surfaces and the movement of the water creates different angles at which the surfaces mirror the image. This causes parts of

The Importance of Proportion

A drawing, to appear accurate, must show the various objects depicted properly related in all of their parts, and in proper relation to one another. This means that the student must measure the parts as to the relation of width to length—the times the width of an object can go into its length or height. For instance, to attain the proper proportion of a human figure, the height of the head from the point of the chin to the top of the head can be measured in relation to the full height of the figure. Using the head as a unit of measure other parts of the body, such as the length of arms and legs, can be determined.

Proper proportion should also be established between the size of the figure and the articles

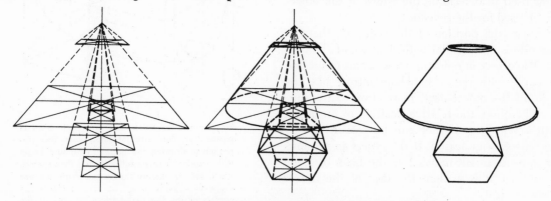

A lampshade and base are constructed over a framework of squares carefully drawn in perspective. The method is similar to that used in the drawing of the barrel on page 47. A center core is indicated on which the various horizontal planes are developed. Each plane serves as a guide in determining an important construction line in the lampshade and its base.

associated with the figure—the height of the door, size of a chair, and other things scaled for use by a human figure.

Many art teachers suggest the use of a square as a unit of measure for determining the proportions of objects other than the human figure. They reason that the eye more quickly detects the commonest of our geometric forms accurately than any other recognizable shape. The four sides of equal length are rapidly apprehended and the shape of objects can be judged as, for instance, "two squares long" or "three squares high."

In order to acquaint oneself with this convenient device for attaining correct proportion, cut a square a couple of inches wide in the center of a piece of paper and, holding the paper at a convenient distance from the eye, look through the opening at an object or a scene. Adjust the opening so that some major division of the object meets the sides of the square. Note the relationship of other features in the object to the square. Draw what you see on a piece of paper. Then adjust the opening to fix other elements of the object. With the aid of this measure it should not be too difficult to construct a drawing with the various objects in proportionate relationship to each other. Practice will train the eye to visualize the square when judging proportions without the aid of the window-like opening in the paper.

A square window cut in a piece of cardboard and held at a distance from the eye so that height and breadth of objects can be compared will prove helpful to the young student and will aid him in drawing the various elements of the subject in proper proportion to one another.

When drawing objects where the base is not horizontal or the sides are not vertical, hold a straight edge before your eyes so that the angle of difference between the prominent contours and the straight edge are easily checked. This simple procedure will aid you in conveying the correct relationships to the paper.

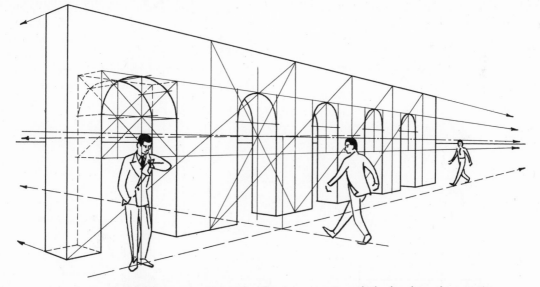

Here we have an illustration of a series of arches in perspective, which also shows the necessity of having the human figure in correct relationship to the various arches at varying distances from the eye. You will notice that in the drawing the eye level has been established at the full height of the figure. Perspective which governs the arches governs the figures as well, and as the arches recede from the eye, the figure is kept in proper scale by being related to the perspective lines determining the arch with which the figure is associated.

How to Draw a Perspective of a House from Plans

This diagram shows the correct way to lay out a perspective of any building from its plans. A plan and two elevations are needed. The elevations should show the two sides of the building required for the drawing and will provide us with information concerning heights of things. Let us proceed in easy steps:

1. You are standing at A.

2. You wish to draw the house B so that its front elevation is seen to a greater degree than its side elevation (for instance, 30 degrees off the front, 60 degrees off the side).

3. Using a T-square, draw a straight line D—E which will serve as the "picture plane" and place the plan C with its near corner touching the line D—E directly in front of your position A. This line X is called the line of sight and is always perpendicular to the picture plane. In placing the plan, be sure that the front elevation and the picture plane form a 30-degree angle. Use a 30—60 degree triangle for this purpose.

4. Draw two lines Y and Z from point A parallel to the two sides of the house on the plan to where they intersect line D—E. Points F and G become the vanishing points on the picture plane.

5. Now, assume a base line J—K for your drawing of the house L. This line will indicate the ground level.

6. Establish another horizontal line above the base line. This line H—I will be the horizon or eye level and can be placed at any distance above the base line you wish dependent upon whether you desire to show the house from a position near the ground or high above ground level.

7. Then drop the two points F—G from the picture plane to their relative positions on the eye level.

8. Next, draw lines from the various features and projections on the plan directly to the eye A. Where these lines intersect the picture plane, drop them vertically to your drawing. This will establish the position of the corners of the house, windows, and door, chimney and porch, in perspective.

9. In order to get the heights, you project these over from the elevation B as shown, to the corner line X and then back to the vanishing points H and J.

10. This will give you an accurate perspective of the house. Note on placing eye level: The normal eye level of about five feet above ground level will give you a normal view of the house.

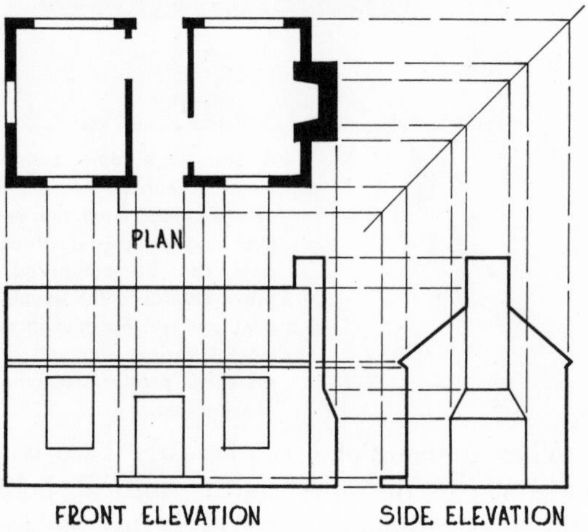

PLAN

FRONT ELEVATION   SIDE ELEVATION

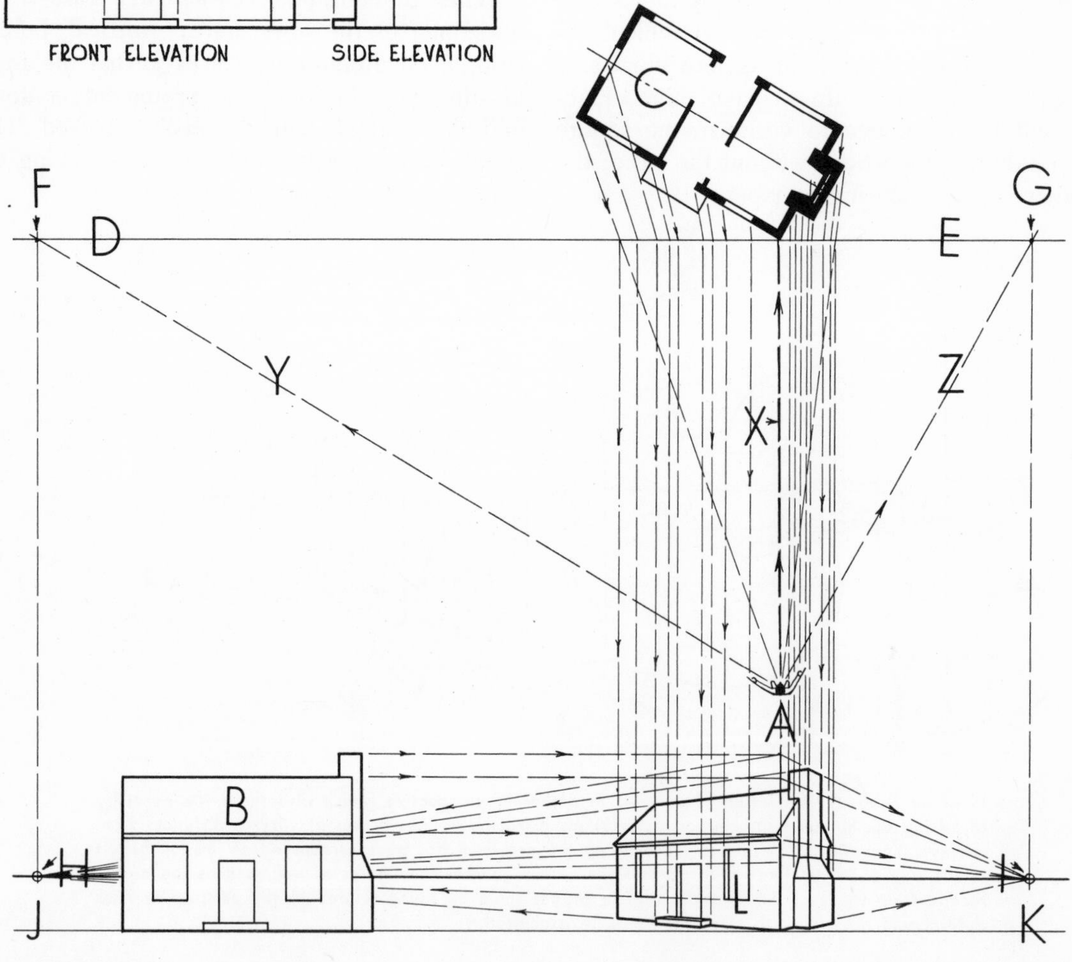

Let's Review What You Have Learned

In Chapter 3 we have discussed the elements of freehand drawing and when a student acquires an understanding of the principles outlined he will have a knowledge of the fundamentals in drawing. He will be acquainted with the "tools of the trade," and his success in this branch of his progress will depend upon constant practice in the application of this knowledge whenever he makes a drawing.

Let us review these principles by practicing with them.

Take a piece of wire which is sufficiently stiff to hold its shape when bent. Bend it in several directions, observing its positions in space. View it from different angles observing the variety of directions in which a line may move in *space*. Draw this piece of bent wire, when held in different positions, as accurately as possible. This exercise will demonstrate the *nature of line,* and will reveal to you that in our three-dimensional world lines exist in space. When you are indicating form, or suggesting the angle at which the

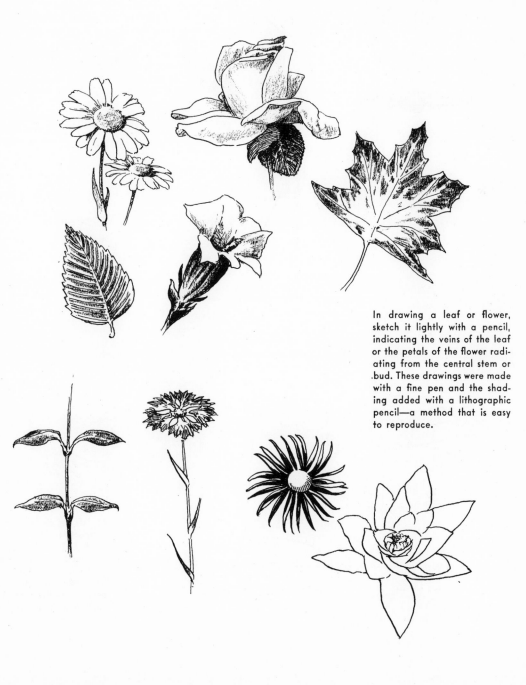

In drawing a leaf or flower, sketch it lightly with a pencil, indicating the veins of the leaf or the petals of the flower radiating from the central stem or bud. These drawings were made with a fine pen and the shading added with a lithographic pencil—a method that is easy to reproduce.

surface of an object may be inclined, it is necessary to draw with line while comprehending fully its three-dimensional existence.

As an exercise, collect a variety of flowers and leaves. Study them for their particular characteristics and draw them in outline as carefully as you can. Practice in drawing natural forms cannot be stressed too much. Knowledge of these forms will be put to use, not only in drawings which include them, but also in planning conventionalized design patterns.

Continuing with exercises in line, construct a perfect cube using cardboard, and draw this cube from different points of view. You will notice that the sides of the cube will cease to be "perfect squares" as soon as any additional sides are seen. Foreshortening takes place, and we are now governed by the principles of perspective.

When you have drawn the cube in so many positions that you feel you can construct it from memory, it will be time to progress to the drawing of a pyramid. Consider the base of the pyra-

Practice Drawing Geometric Solids

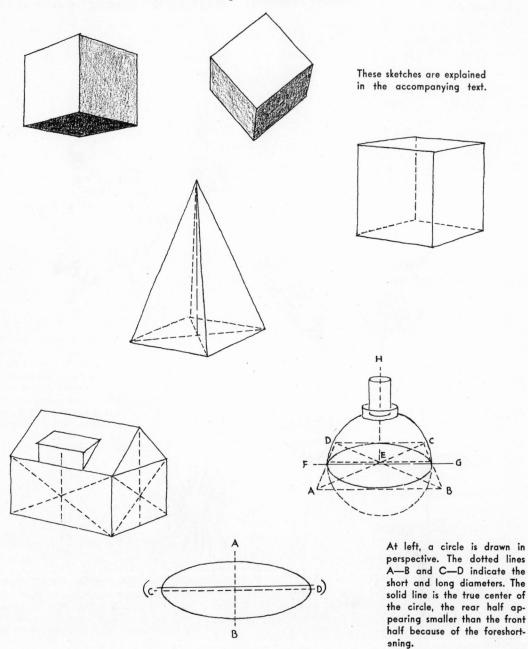

These sketches are explained in the accompanying text.

At left, a circle is drawn in perspective. The dotted lines A—B and C—D indicate the short and long diameters. The solid line is the true center of the circle, the rear half appearing smaller than the front half because of the foreshortening.

mid as square. Draw lines diagonally across it from opposite corners. Where these diagonals intersect, construct a vertical line upward. Along this line will fall the apex of your pyramid. When the height of the pyramid is determined, complete the drawing by constructing the lines from the apex to the "visible" corners of the pyramid.

The principle indicated here in locating the center of a square shown in perspective can be applied in many ways. It is most commonly used in architectural drawing where the roof ridge is to be shown over the center of a gable. The side of the house, in most cases a rectangle, is bisected by lines from the opposite corners, and where the lines intersect, we find the center of the mass. A vertical line passing through this center will furnish the position vertically for the ridge.

The construction of a cylinder on a half-sphere is accomplished by drawing a circle in perspective so that its circumference is tangent to the four sides of a square. Bisecting the corners of the square makes this solution as simple as that of the pyramid. This form is also used in architectural work where the cylinder, serving as the "lantern," surmounts the dome.

Exercises in Light and Shade

Hold a rubber ball where it can be illumined by a single source of light, preferably against a black background which will minimize the rays of reflected light. It will be observed that the light will appear most intense on that portion of the ball's surface directly facing the source of light, and that the light appears less intense as it gradually approaches the place where the surface of the ball recedes away from the light rays. We see things to the degree light rays are reflected from them.

With a stick of artist's charcoal and a piece of drawing paper having a coarse surface, draw a square of evenly toned dark gray, smoothing out the area of tone with the use of a finger or a specially prepared "stump," purchasable at art supply stores. With a kneaded eraser, remove the tone where the highlight on the ball is to be indicated and graduate the tonal values away from this highlight as the gradation appears on the surface of the ball. Drawing with light will prove a fascinating study because you will be creating

An interesting exploitation of three-dimensional form in a painting by Herbert Bayer. Here a cone is represented in direct elevation and also as it would appear if we were to look down on its apex. The shadows cast by the objects add to the pattern interest.

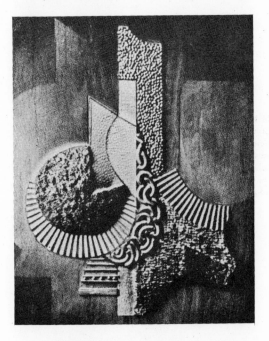

An abstract design in the form of a "collage" by a student at Carnegie Institute of Technology, Pittsburgh. In this example the collage is composed of a variety of contrasting shapes and materials, making an interesting arrangement in light and shade.

This mechanical close-up, seen in terms of abstract design, is the work of a student of Neodesha High School in Kansas. (Courtesy of Scholastic Awards.)

In the drawing of the arch, the principle of the long diameter being perpendicular with the axis of the "cylinder" helps solve the problem. Drawing machinery requires a knowledge of this principle.

the appearance of objects in the same way Nature discloses them to us.

Practice with numerous areas, creating patterns of varying shapes with tonal values. As you advance in skill, make simplified copies of works of famous painters. In this way you will have an opportunity to analyze the patterns of tone which contribute greatly to the quality of the painting.

Another exercise that will help develop your creative ability is the composing of a "collage." This is an area where various materials, selected for their contrast in color and texture, are grouped as a design. Materials selected may be wire fly-screen, corrugated board, burlap and other textiles, oil-cloth, a wood shingle, sandpaper, etc. Your selection should make the most of differences as between rough and smooth, dull or neutral colors and bright, vivid colors, and with contrast still further heightened by giving the various areas strikingly different shapes.

This exercise points up the nature and possibilities of areas in design, and your finished result can be an interesting decorative unit, the likes of which have attained a definite position in the field of modern art.

Exercises in Perspective

The concept of mass involves the concept of perspective, and when you wish to draw an object having three dimensions you are confronted with the problem of foreshortening of those surfaces which recede from the line of sight. A sense of perspective begins with a feeling for lines in space which increases to a feeling for two-dimensional areas and planes in space, and which culminates with a graphic representation of masses or solids.

As the student advances in his studies he will become increasingly aware of the cube and the sphere as comprising the forms most frequently adapted in a drawing. Therefore, it will be simpler to study perspective by the "cube" or "box" approach. In this method, the student sketches lightly and roughly a properly proportioned box which will serve to enclose the object to be drawn. This will help construct many pieces of furniture, buildings, books, and other objects with a base which rests on a horizontal plane.

As an exercise, draw a chair, blocking it out at first with the "box" construction. Remember, that the chair stands on the floor and a floor or base-

This photograph shows how our visual impression of actual form depends on light and shade. Compare the photographic shades and shadows on the column capital with the cast shadows in the wash rendering of a capital of the same type to the right.

Below are two architectural forms—a baluster and an urn, shown first in outline. Though we recognize the forms, they are not realistic. We cannot tell which portions are round and which are square. When shading is added, the forms come to life.

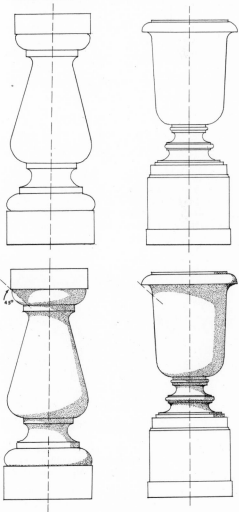

board line should be drawn in agreement with the four points of contact of the legs of the chair with the floor.

To check your freehand drawing, find the eye level and, along this eye level, establish the exact vanishing points for all the horizontal edges and planes that appear in the drawing.

As a further exercise, draw a glass of water. Construct the cylinder within a box which, in this instance will be taller than it is wide. Draw the ellipse representing the top and the bottom of the glass with the circumference tangent to the four sides of the box. Then draw the third ellipse indicating the height of the water in the glass.

Now, let us put together the things we have learned. The drawing which exists in line only tells us what the form is, but a more informative representation requires the addition of tonal values. Indicate these tones in the drawing of the glass of water, introducing a dark tone behind the glass to help establish its light tonal key. Lighter tones of gray will indicate the variations in the glass itself caused by reflections and the deflected rays of light passing through the water. This exercise embraces the study of line, tone and perspective. Continue these exercises with other objects.

49

Using a piece of hard charcoal for his medium, this artist sketched the figure lightly in outline. The little accents developed in varying the strength of the line help create an illusion of roundness without shading.

An excellently expressive pencil drawing of hands by a student of John Hay High School in Cleveland, O. Such work as this represents a very high level of student performance. (Courtesy of Scholastic Awards: Pencil Prize.)

CHAPTER 4

The Human Figure as a Form of Art

From the earliest of times the human figure has been the subject most frequently portrayed in works of art. People are interested most in other people, and every artist who seeks to interest the greatest number of people in his work makes the human figure one of the chief objects for study. As one of Nature's most graceful forms, it lends itself with equal value to illustration and decoration.

In the study of the human figure the student seeks a double objective. He must record the contours of the figure as it passes through countless actions and observe the highly coordinated movement of the various parts. He must likewise study the construction of the parts. The first consideration is necessary to present the figure with naturalness in all its grace of movement. The second is the study of its anatomy. Each objective is important and both studies should proceed simultaneously.

The ability to draw the human figure has been the yardstick by which an artist's progress in his

profession has been measured. From the days of the Italian Renaissance the masters of painting concentrated their greatest effort toward perfection in this phase of their work, and much of their reputation as masters has been established by their expert draftsmanship of the human figure.

For a long time it was the practice in art schools to restrain the students from drawing or painting from life until they had spent a year or more in drawing from plaster casts of antique sculpture. The tempo is faster today, and perhaps it should be. But we should not forget that art students of the past who spent many hours on "antique" drawing became master draftsmen. There is no substitute for good drawing today as there was none in the past.

A few illustrations of exercises which old masters considered essential in the training of students are shown here. They are by Julien, of the famous French art school, and by Van Bree, who was a sincere believer in what could be learned

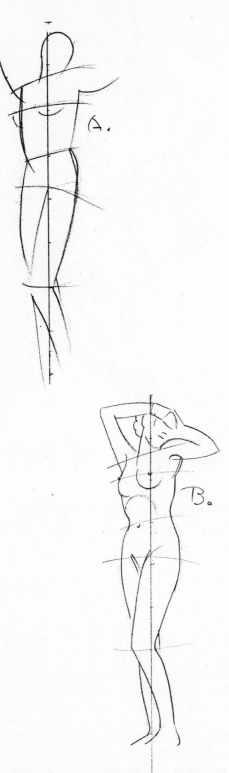

Sketchy lines are used to block in the mass of the figure and to establish the action. Draw like parts in relation to one another at approximately the same time. The line of the slant of the shoulders, the hips, and knees should be indicated before the contour of the figure is attempted.

from drawing the antique with scrupulous care. Students who made drawings of these antique models of hands, heads and other details, were kept at their task until the master of the school was willing to call the result perfect.

Methods for Studying the Figure

It is the practice in most professional art schools to divide the study of the figure into three phases: a study of the skeletal and muscular construction, drawing and painting from the nude figure, and action studies of both the nude and the costumed figure. To accomplish this through the pages of a book is somewhat of a problem. The anatomical phase of the study can be mastered without much difficulty as diagrams of the various members of the body are essential for study whether the student is attending an art school or following the present course of self instruction.

Action studies of the costumed figure are readily available as the student takes his sketch book and makes his drawings rapidly wherever he may be. It is not unusual to see an art student sketching his fellow passengers in a railway car, a bus, or in some other public place. Observing the relationship of the various parts of the figure as it performs certain actions is a most valuable practice. For studies requiring more time, the student may persuade members of the family to "sit" for their picture.

Drawing or painting the nude figure may present a more difficult problem. As the student advances in his study it may help him to inquire in his immediate locality if other students are meeting jointly where a model can be engaged for life drawing. This has been a solution in many parts of the country where professional art schools are not available.

In the posing of the figure, the student should attempt to establish a continuous, undulating line having rhythm and grace. To illustrate this point a series of photographs have been selected as a supplement to this chapter. To sketch from these photographs will provide much helpful practice.

As a further aid in drawing the figure, a manikin, a small model with adjustable joints, may be purchased. At one time this piece of equipment was quite expensive, but, thanks to the modern age of plastics, an admirably designed and proportioned manikin can be obtained at a reasonable cost.

These "lay figures" as they are called, have been used by artists for many years. At one time they were constructed life size and served as the "sitter" for many a famous portrait when the artist was working on the elaborate garments which were draped on the model. Velasquez, the great Spanish painter, had a spirited dummy of a rearing horse, on which he posed many of his famous figures.

Manikins may be obtained for either the male or female figure, and they are made so that they may be placed in any pose the artist desires. They are made small in size, have flexible ball joints, and will prove a valuable investment to the student who will save considerable sums of money in model hire.

Another method of drawing from the figure which is used by many professional artists today is the posed photograph. For this, models are engaged and costumed according to the characters they are to portray in the illustration. They are then posed in the action desired and photographed by the artist. He may photograph many different poses before he dismisses the model, whom he has engaged for a short time. High model fees are saved and, when the films are developed and printed, the artist has a wealth of material from which he can make his illustration.

The Construction of the Figure

As a man stands erect he presents a symmetrical arrangement of parts. The upper half of his body is formed around a central axis which we refer to as the backbone or spinal column. Connected to this axis is a group of bones called ribs which help protect the vital organs of the body. At the upper end of the spinal column sits the skull, and attached at the lower end is the pelvic girdle which comprises the hip bones and the sockets from which the ball-jointed thigh bones are suspended.

The spinal column is made flexible by means of a series of bones separated by cartilage. These bones are called vertebrae. The strength and movement of this vertebral column is dependent on the large muscles which form the back and which lie to either side of the column.

The pelvic girdle is made up of the heavy haunch bones which are attached to the spinal

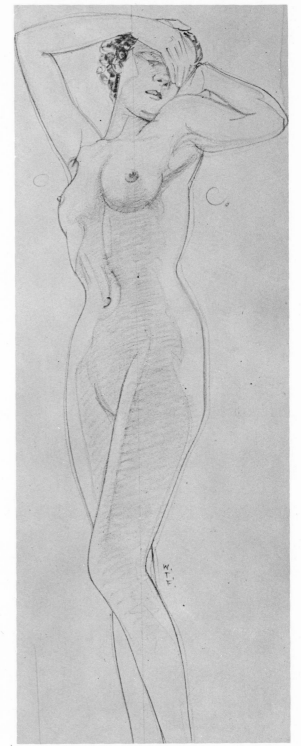

With the outlines of the figure indicated, areas of tone should be studied to give the proper modelling of the rounded forms. These drawings are reproduced through the courtesy of W. T. Foster.

53

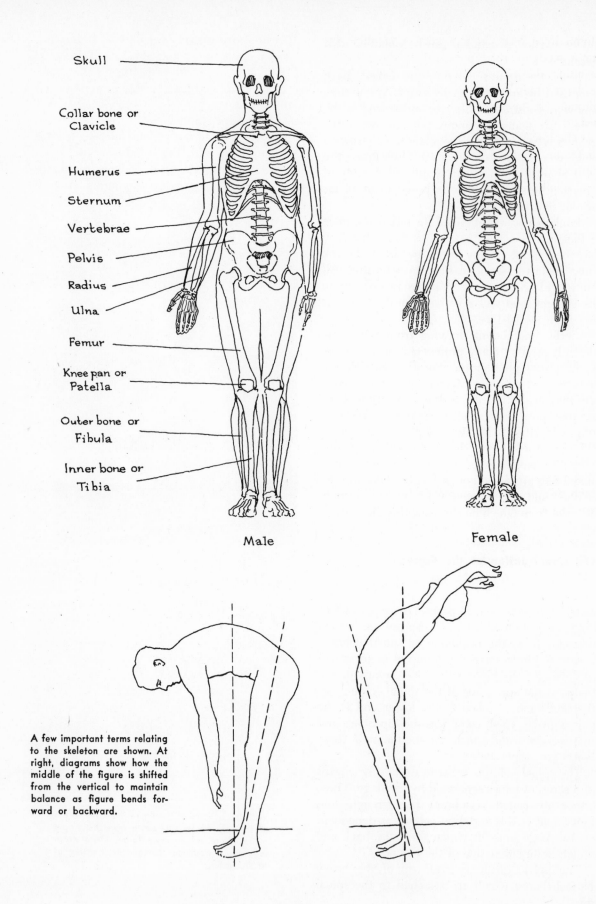

Skull

Collar bone or
Clavicle

Humerus

Sternum

Vertebrae

Pelvis

Radius

Ulna

Femur

Knee pan or
Patella

Outer bone or
Fibula

Inner bone or
Tibia

Male

Female

A few important terms relating
to the skeleton are shown. At
right, diagrams show how the
middle of the figure is shifted
from the vertical to maintain
balance as figure bends forward or backward.

column by a series of five vertebrae which fit into a wedge-shaped bone called the sacrum. On either side of the haunch bone are pivoted the large thigh bones which taper downward obliquely as they approach the position of the knees.

At the lower end of the thigh bone, known as the femur, is a swivel joint to which the two bones of the leg are attached, the joint covered by a small flat bone which we call the knee-cap. The larger of the leg bones is the shin, the smaller is slightly to the rear of the larger, and the two meet at the ankle where the bones of the foot are attached.

Covering the large thigh bone are powerful muscles which are attached to the haunch bone and become narrow as they connect with the bone at the knee. The hip is likewise covered with large muscles which receive great use.

Returning to the upper portion of the body, let us consider the construction of the shoulder. There are two bones on each side which are connected to the central group: the collarbone, which is in front, and the shoulder blade, to the rear. Where these bones meet at the shoulder, there is a socket which receives the upper bone of the arm. This bone is known as the humerus. It connects with two smaller bones at the elbow which give flexibility and movement to the forearm. At the wrist, these bones meet still smaller bones from which are suspended the finger bones, called phalanges.

This brief description of the body's framework is little more than an introduction to anatomy and further study is suggested using the drawings of the male and female skeleton reproduced on the accompanying pages. The names of the bones have been minimized so as not to confuse the student with terms seldom referred to, but to acquaint him with the structure with which he should be familiar when drawing the figure in various actions and under varying light conditions.

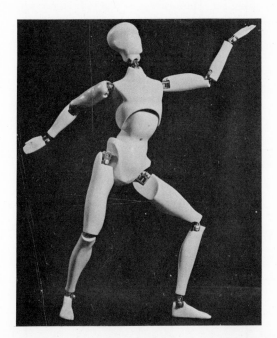

Above and at right: The new plastic manikin which takes the place of the old, cumbersome wooden "lay figures" of earlier times. This versatile figure has been called "the model who never tires."
At right: The manikin is shown draped and undraped. This figurine is skilfully designed to assume an infinite number of poses as either a male or female figure.

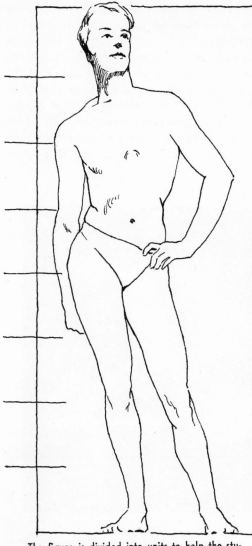

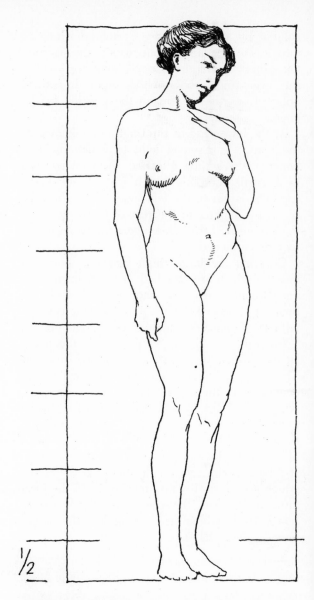

The figure is divided into units to help the student determine correct proportion.

Proportions of the Human Figure

To draw the human figure so that each part will appear in correct proportion to each other part, it is advisable to adopt some unit of measure that can be applied throughout the drawing regardless of the difference in the height of people. From the days of the Greeks and Romans, the head has served this purpose. In Greek sculpture the figure was proportioned eight heads high. Italian Renaissance craftsmen accepted this idea as it gave nobleness to their statues. The female figure is regarded as seven and one half heads in height.

In the width, a man is usually greatest across the shoulders which are slightly less than the height of two heads. With a woman, the width of shoulders usually equals the width at the hips. With arms outstretched horizontally, the distance between the extreme tips of the fingers is approximately equal to the height of the man's figure. The arm from the shoulder to the elbow may be considered as one and one-half heads long; the forearm from elbow to the wrist is about one head in length. The distance from the pelvic girdle to the knee is approximately two heads, and from the knee to the ankle, somewhat in excess of one and one-half heads.

These approximations are given only as a general guide in the student's preliminary studies. They serve as an approach which the student can apply more accurately when drawing from life. In the selection of the model to be used, these generalizations will aid the student immensely.

Drawing the Human Figure

A child is hardly one year old when it acquires a sense of balance. This enables it to stand erect without something to hold on to, and to shift its weight in its earliest steps without falling. This state of balance must be evident in any drawing of the figure in an erect position or in action. If a figure is shown bending, the heavier portions of the pelvic girdle move backward as the upper part of the body leans forward, causing the thighs and legs to take an oblique position. If the legs were drawn perfectly vertical, the figure would appear as losing its balance and falling forward. The counter-balanced weight in the hips must swing backward to preserve the figure's equilibrium.

When drawing a figure in action, sketch a vertical line lightly as a guide over which the figure can be constructed. Then indicate, also lightly, the course of the spinal column by a line passing downward through the knees to the feet or place upon which the figure is pivoted in balance.

At the point of the shoulders sketch a line to indicate the direction of the collar-bone, and another at the level of the hipbones, to show the angle in the tilt of the hips. Both the shoulder line and the hipbone line should be at right angles to the center line passing vertically downward. It will be observed that if the right shoulder is lower than the left, the right hipbone will be higher than the other, and vice versa. The line drawn across the knees will show that the angle of direction of the hipbones will affect similarly the angle of difference in the level of the two knees. The body is so constructed that in its many diversified positions of action, the relationships between the angle of the shoulders and that of the hips and knees will be consistent.

In the seated figure, the place on which the figure is balanced is shifted but balance must be preserved as between the body above the hips and the thighs and legs unless support for the figure is indicated.

The figure is symmetrical and, in sketching the construction, the student should indicate like parts in relation to each other and at approximately the same time. When locating the position of one shoulder draw the other, following a similar procedure in sketching in the eyes, hands, hipbones, knees, breasts and feet. Block out the entire figure before developing any of the smaller details. The student who attempts to

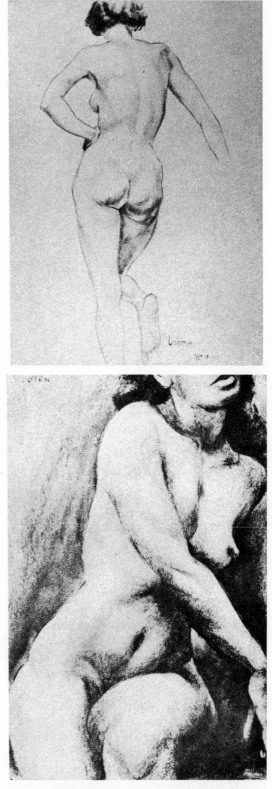

Two studies of nudes by students of the Ringling Art School, Sarasota, Fla. There is no substitute for careful and painstaking drawing of the human figure. Knowledge of anatomy and understanding of human form is essential to every art student.

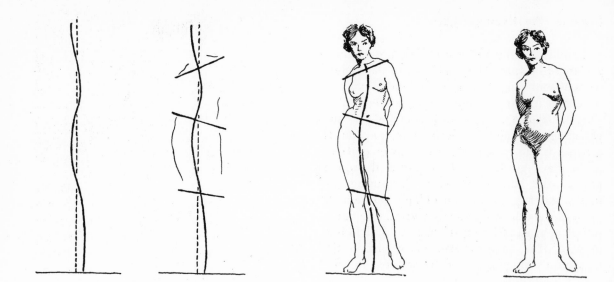

The action of the figure is denoted by the curved line which crosses the vertical. This curved line follows the general direction of the spinal structure to the hips, and of the legs downward. Across this curved line the directional lines of shoulders, hips, and knees are indicated, the contour of the body following this construction. The human figure is a symmetrical form regardless of the position from which it is viewed.

draw one side at a time, or finish one part before the entire figure is roundly constructed will experience difficulty.

The curves of the body are convex. Even when the contour of torso, as it passes outward over the large hipbones appears to create a concave curve, the student will observe upon more careful study that this curve is made up of many arcs, all convex. The "strong line" in figure drawing is the line which denotes the action. It is frequently a long line passing from the upper portion of the body downward to the feet. Often, the action of the arms continues this line to a greater length. In drawing this line study carefully the rhythmic undulations. Where the line indicates that the form passes under and around toward the side facing away from sight, accent the line to give it depth. Consideration of this "strong line" will help the student avoid making his figure appear disjointed and without unified action.

In drawing the figure from life, add tone sparingly. Remember, the flesh color is light and the shadows are not dark unless the figure is illumined by a sharp light which would give the effect of dark shadow by sheer contrast. But this type of lighting does not give the most favorable results. Soft light with secondary side lighting will help preserve the subtle gradation of tonal value that gives to the figure much of its quality in art.

Photographs of models have been furnished among the illustrations of this book so that the student can draw from these life studies in case it proves difficult for him to secure the use of a model for his own study. Much benefit will come from sketching from these photographs and then drawing clothing on them. This practice will aid a student in understanding the form beneath the garment and will make his sketching of people easier and with improved draftsmanship.

It is the practice in art schools specializing in fashion drawing to spend considerable time drawing from the nude figure, and then designing the dress or costume with an accurate statement of form. Points of suspension from which a dress may hang in folds must be correctly placed. Otherwise it would appear as though the dress did not fit the figure.

In this chapter on the drawing of the figure, emphasis on the head and facial features was intentionally omitted. It is better to study the construction of the figure first, leaving smaller details until later. Too frequently a student makes portraiture his earliest objective and, while it may do no harm to enjoy the practice of copying a stage beauty's picture, this indulgence will not lead to an all-around understanding of figure drawing. In order to give this subject proper attention, portraiture has been made a separate study which is given consideration in the following chapter.

Let's Review What We Have Learned

As an initial exercise in the drawing of the human figure, construct a rectangle and divide it vertically into eight equal parts. Using the top division for the size of the head (chin to top of head) locate the other features of the figure following the information furnished in the section of Chapter 3 concerning proportion. Note that the navel is approximately in line with the third division down from the top, the pelvis at the fourth, and the knees at the sixth level.

Follow this exercise with a similar procedure in drawing the female figure. This time, make the rectangle with seven and one-half divisions. Put the one-half section at the bottom. Again, using the top division for the height of the head, construct a female figure. Note that the line of the breasts is about two divisions from the top; the navel is three divisions down, as was the case in the male figure. The position of the hipbones is about halfway between the level of the third and the fourth divisions, and the knees are about

halfway between the fifth and the sixth levels.

Repeat these exercises, using different poses of the figure, until you have mastered the relative proportion of the parts.

Practice drawing the different parts, using the Julien plates distributed through the pages of this chapter. Make a special effort to draw hands in every position you can pose them. If you cannot persuade some member of the family to pose for you, use your free hand as a model.

Take your sketch pad with you when you travel in public. Make quick action studies of people as they do various things. You must work fast for these people are not holding the pose for you very long. Put down the basic lines of the action first, filling in the subordinate parts and details last, providing you have time. A good place to do this is in a railway terminal where people stand around waiting for their train gate to open, or sit reading a newspaper.

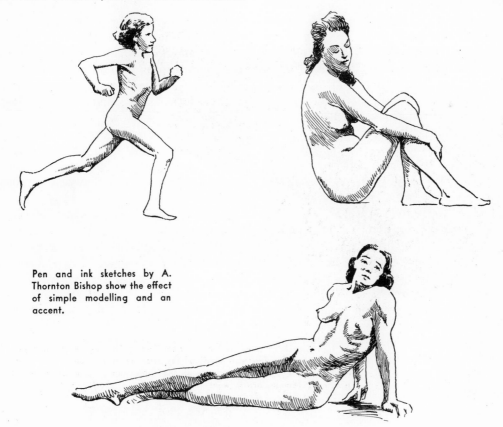

Pen and ink sketches by A. Thornton Bishop show the effect of simple modelling and an accent.

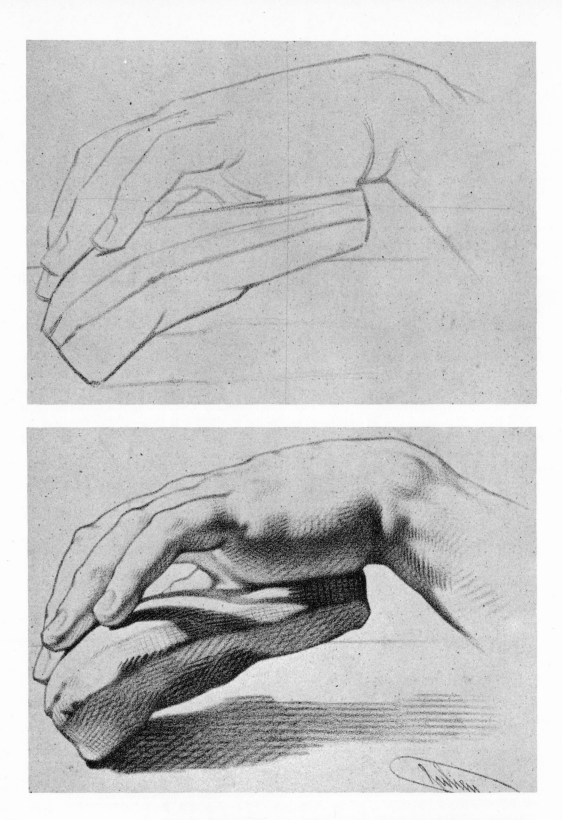

At top: Sketch of mass and proportion. Below: The further development of the same drawing with shading. The drawing is by Julien, the great master of the Parisian academy of the same name, to which many of America's famous artists went for their training.

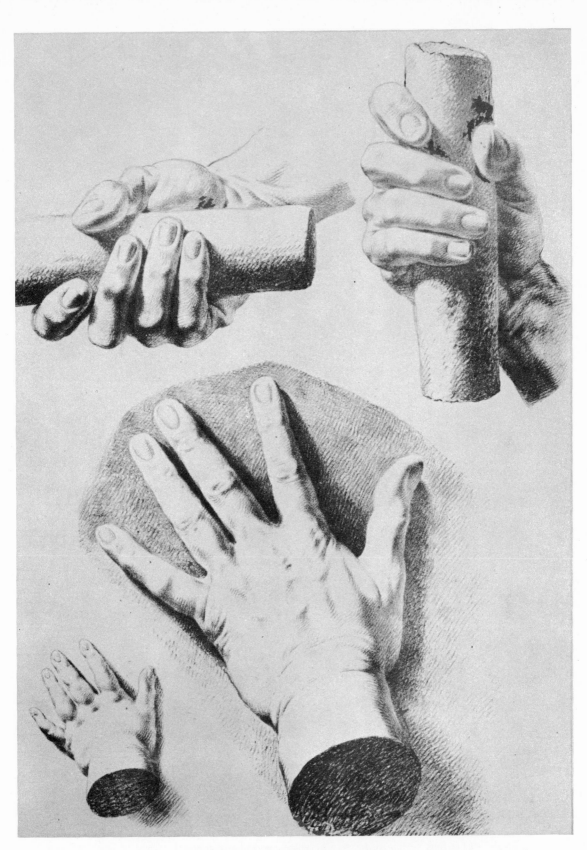

Art schools in earlier days taught students first to draw from casts such as these. The studies above are drawings by Van Bree.

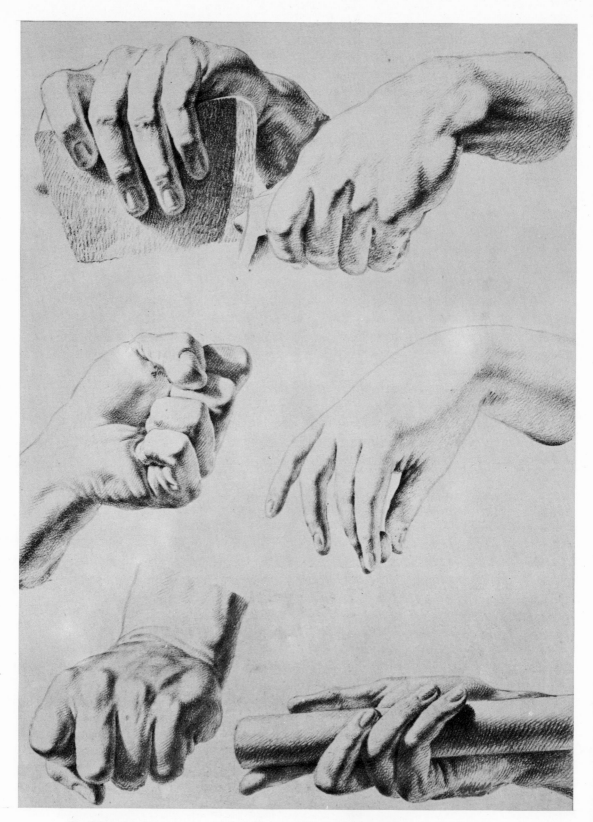

Careful studies from casts were followed by equally careful studies from life. Attention to anatomy and realistic modelling were stressed. Drawings by Van Bree.

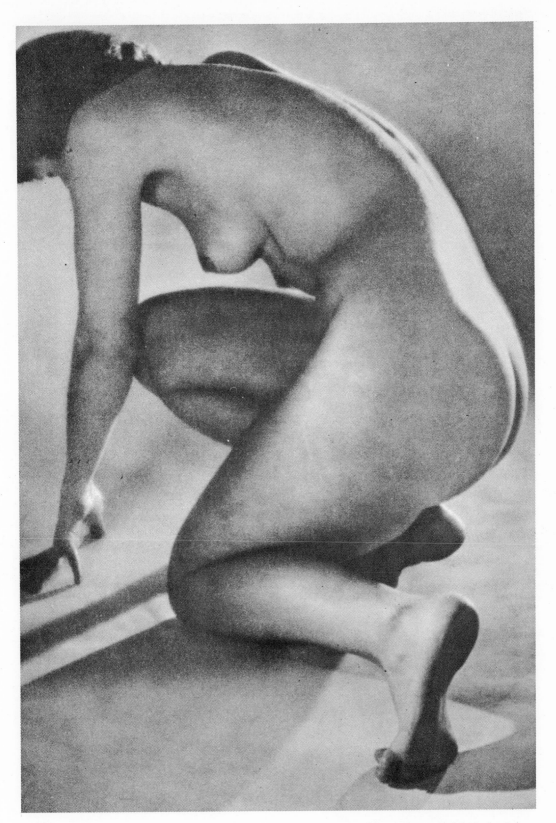

Nude photographic study by Munkacsi.

Nude photographic study by Munkacsi. This
study shows the effect of strong light and
shade effects on the figure.

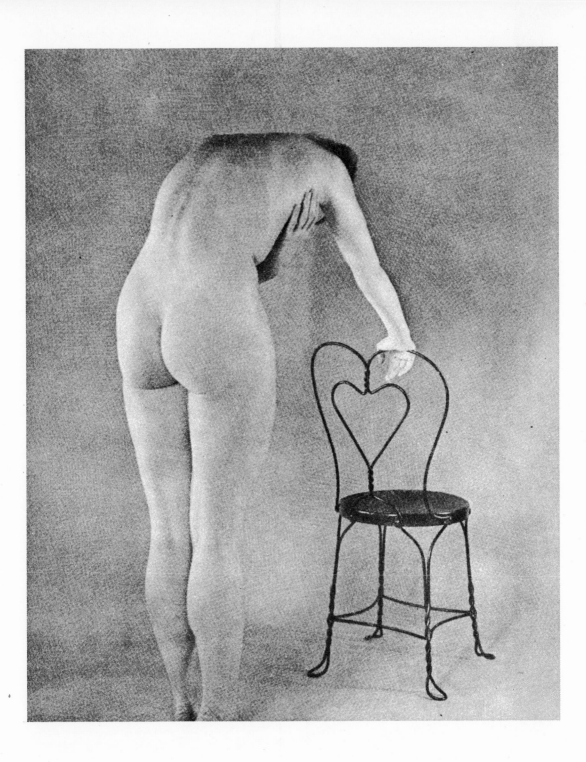

Nude photographic study by Munkacsi.

Sketching from the nude by Zaidenberg.

Two more life sketches by Zaidenberg.

A Julien drawing from the classical head of one of Niobe's daughters, in the famous Niobe group statue. Masterful draftsmanship makes this an outstanding model.

CHAPTER 5

Drawing the Head

Portraiture is a fascinating subject because it offers such infinite variety to an artist to create character. Within the facial features of a person lies the key to personality. The eyes and the mouth tell most of the story but the chin and the shape of the head provide an important contribution. In our study of the head let us start with the skull.

The skull is composed of two parts: the upper portion which houses the brain and the lower portion which serves as the structure of the face. The head is so delicately balanced on the upper end of the spinal column that it needs very little muscular power to maintain it in an erect position. The only movable part of the skull, the lower jaw bone, is hinged from a socket in front of the ear at a position midway between the front line of the face and the back of the head.

Openings for the eyes and nose passages are located in the portion of the frontal bone just above the cheek bones. The level of the eye sockets is about halfway between the lower point of the jaw and the top of the head. This observation will come in handy every time the head is drawn. In direct profile, the lobe of the ear is on a horizontal line level with the base of the nose.

In the earlier experiments start the drawing of the head by constructing a circle. Then draw a line horizontally through the center of this circle. This line will represent the level of the eyes. Draw a line bisecting the circle vertically. At the intersection of these lines, start the drawing of the ear, following a course upward and curving backward and around toward the front of the face, terminating at the vertical line. Construct another horizontal line from the lobe of the ear to the outer circle. This will establish the base of the nose. Now sketch in the other features, indicating the return of the lower jaw to a point in front of the lobe of the ear. Although this exercise produces a result much in need of refinement, it furnishes the simplest procedure to practice the formation of the head and the relationship of the features.

Study of the features should be given next consideration, the plates of Julien furnishing splendid guidance. Learn to preserve the highlights and acquire the knack of placing accents where they will create character. Accents do more to help establish a likeness than any other means used by portrait painters.

Develop the head in light and shadow. Look for contrast in tonal value between the light area of the face and a dark background. Tone on the side of the face can establish in the contour of its area the bony construction of the cheek and jaw. Be careful not to make the

A classical head by Julien, showing the preliminary outlines that are sketched in before the drawing is developed in detail.

shadow on the side of the eye socket too dark; you may want to reserve your darkest accent for the pupil of the eye. Remember that the under side of the chin is not black; it usually is lighter than the shadow on the side of the face because of the reflected light from the clothing beneath, often a white shirt.

All portraits are not painted in a way that extends the paint area to the limits of the canvas. Joseph Cummings Chase, a famous portrait painter, frequently finishes the face in full color then sketchily suggests the shoulders and the outlines of the clothing to about a head's depth below the chin. This is known as vignetting and the effect has spontaneity and freshness. It is most suitable in portrait sketching with pencil or charcoal and concentrates the chief interest in the face.

In drawing the neck, the student should observe that there is a difference in the general character of the male and the female. The male neck is shorter and heavier, rising more vertically from the shoulders; the female neck is longer and more graceful as it extends from the shoulders in a forward direction.

Two powerful muscles support the neck, the sterno-mastoid which passes downward in front of the throat and attaches at the point of the collar-bone, and the trapezius muscle, triangular in shape, which extends across the back to the shoulders and down the spinal column to the middle of the back. When drawing the neck do not emphasize the muscles as the effect will take much grace and beauty from it. A hollow will be observed in the front of the neck between the two sterno-mastoid muscles and under what is called the "Adam's apple" which may be indicated without unpleasant results.

When drawing the hair, block out the areas of dark and light before attempting to introduce any tone. Contrast in tonal values will suggest an interesting light effect and will give lustre to the hair. Shadows cast by hair overhanging the brow are soft. The hair can furnish the dark accent in many drawings of the figure and, in so doing, create the effect of a fair complexion. It is an element in the design of a portrait that the artist can use with much liberality.

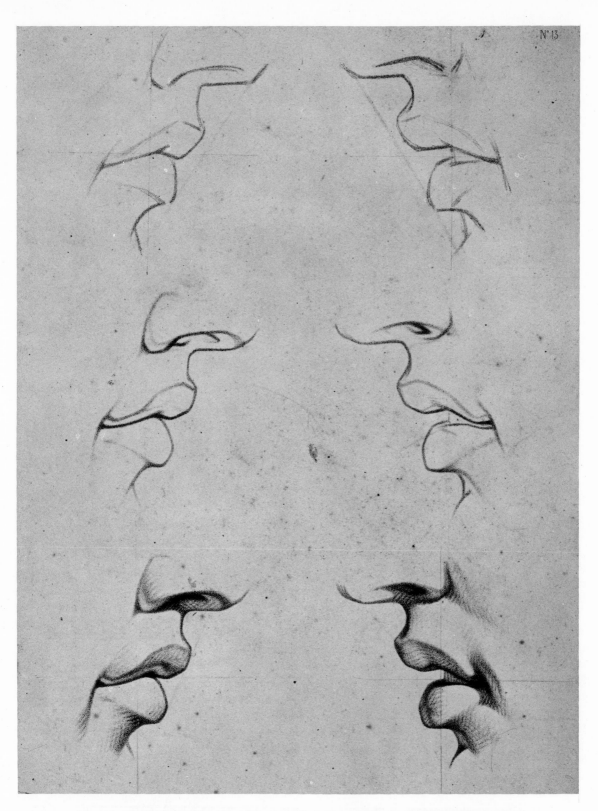

Progressive studies of mouths drawn from casts of classic sculpture by Julien. Note the angle of line from nose to lower lip.

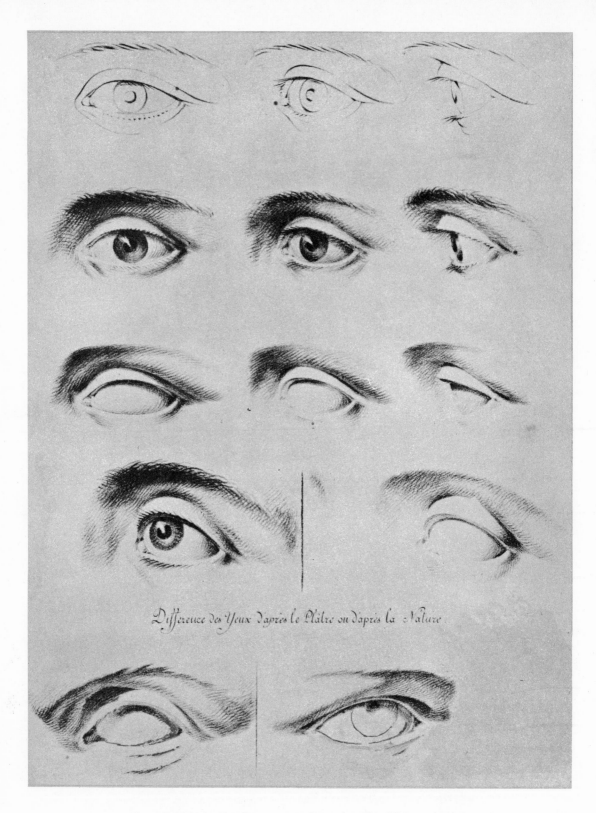

Différence des Yeux d'après le Plâtre ou d'après la Nature.

These drawings by Van Bree were made to show the difference between
the eye in classic sculpture and as drawn from life.

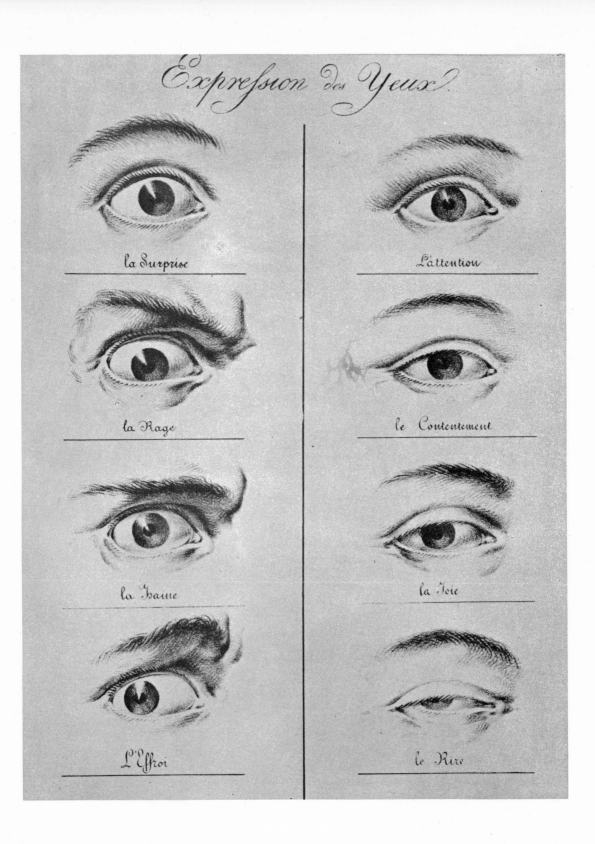

Here Van Bree presents a series of drawings to show differences in expression in the human eye. Left Column (reading down): Surprise, Anger, Hate, Fright. Right Column: Attention, Contentment, Joy, and Laughter.

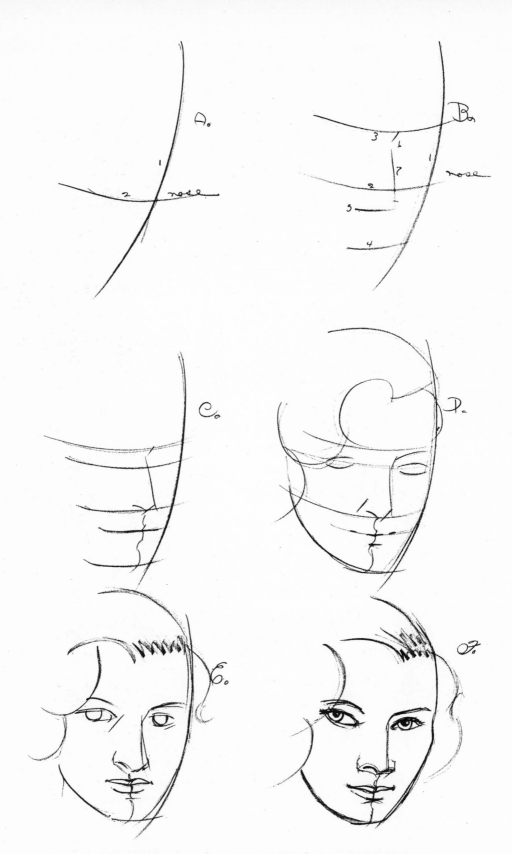

Mr. Foster says in his note on this sequence of sketches: "The first steps in drawing the eye are simple, but it takes much study to put expression or life into them. Do not rush, study them."

The progressive sketches on the facing page are here developed into a more finished crayon drawing by Mr. Foster.

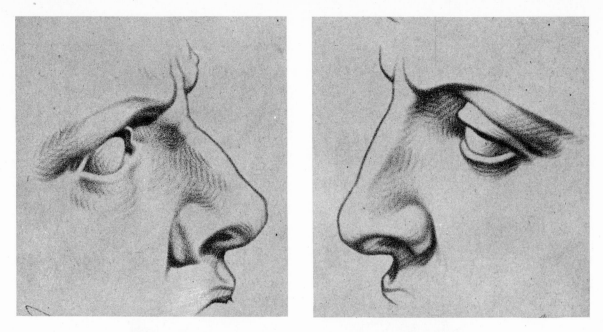

These drawings by Julien of eye and nose were studies from classical sculpture and are admirable examples for a student to copy as an exercise in careful draftsmanship.

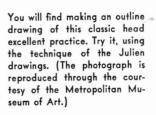

You will find making an outline drawing of this classic head excellent practice. Try it, using the technique of the Julien drawings. (The photograph is reproduced through the courtesy of the Metropolitan Museum of Art.)

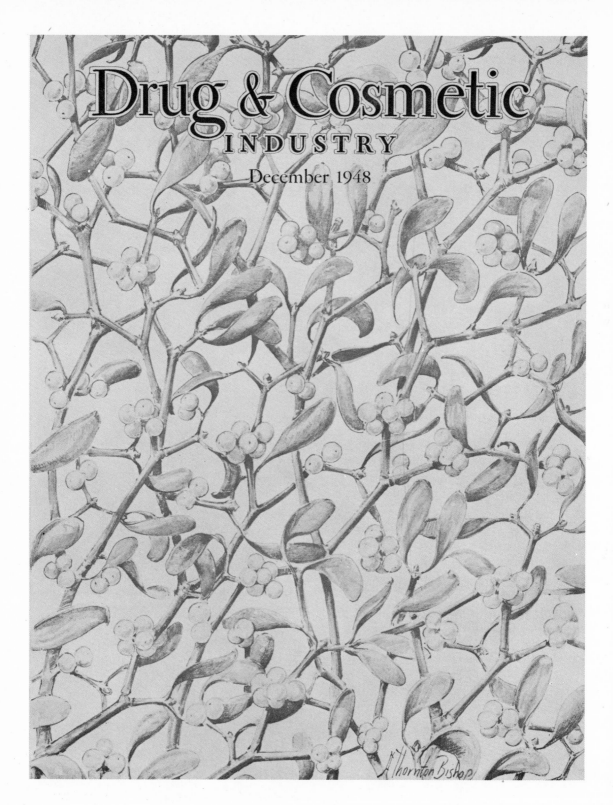

Drug & Cosmetic
INDUSTRY
December 1948

Mistletoe was used as a theme for a Christmas number of a trade magazine. The angular joints of the plant and the waxy leaves provided good
material for an overall pattern. (Reproduced through the courtesy of
Drug and Cosmetic Industry.)

Design for a metal grille. The unfinished portion of the drawing allows us to see how the designer outlined his pattern before filling in the background with ink.

CHAPTER 6

Design – Where Art Begins

In previous chapters we have discussed the language of the artist—the art of drawing, of portraying graphically and accurately subjects selected for presentation. The ability to draw is somewhat like the ability to speak words which describe things. These words, by themselves, may have no art significance until they are grouped into pleasing arrangements that convey not only a meaning but also create an emotional reaction. We have come to the study of applying this ability to draw in a way that will create pleasing arrangements and a unified thought. We also seek through these arrangements an emotional reaction with the observer. This is to design.

Creative impulse stimulates the process. Elements of interest are selected for assembling in a way that creates a pattern or serves a purpose. This procedure involves the function of composing, and it is here the artist's judgment is put to constant use.

With little experience, a student will find that pleasing arrangements result from relationships created between one element in the grouping and other elements. Difference in the size of one to the others brings increased interest. Difference in tonal value, texture and color add happily to the general effect. With these simple

observations, the first steps in the study of design have been taken.

If a student proceeded without other instruction and, allowing for certain basic instincts integrated in the student's mind which have directed him toward the field of art expression, he would evolve in time a set of principles which would appear to apply with marked consistency to every problem of arrangement he tackled. We might summarize his experience in the following manner:

To Design Is to Compose

When we design, we must compose the elements of material we have selected to use in an arrangement that will express most effectively the idea we have in mind. The instincts which guide us in the arrangements we conceive have had much preliminary development of which we are little aware. We have absorbed many impressions, perhaps sub-consciously, in our younger days from the things we have observed, and they have formed a set of preferences which now influence our judgment in the selections we make when we purchase or create things.

These impressions have caused us to respond

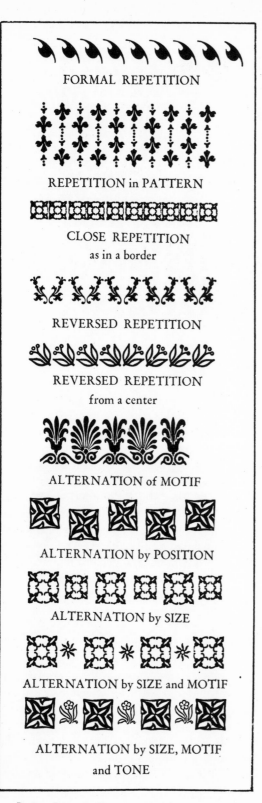

FORMAL REPETITION

REPETITION in PATTERN

CLOSE REPETITION
as in a border

REVERSED REPETITION

REVERSED REPETITION
from a center

ALTERNATION of MOTIF

ALTERNATION by POSITION

ALTERNATION by SIZE

ALTERNATION by SIZE and MOTIF

ALTERNATION by SIZE, MOTIF
and TONE

Design Group I. This group of diagrams show the design principles of Repetition and Alternation. Compare with similar principles in Rhythm by Repetition in Group II. The elements shown, many of which are ornaments used in printing houses, are used chiefly in formal arrangements.

to many natural laws, such as balance, equilibrium and gravity. We learned early in life that these laws are correct and consistent because we live in accordance with them. Naturally, when we now present an idea involving their use, we recognize them.

Let us begin with Balance. Anything that appears out of balance disturbs us. We feel fearful for its stability. But Balance need not be obtained by just two parts, each equal to the other in every particular. Five articles, each weighing one pound, will balance one article weighing five pounds. In art, Balance is obtained through similar reasoning. But now, we must substitute the power to compel attention for the element of "weight." When we think of equalization in weight we can mean equalization in the severity of angles which draw the eye to them, equalization in tonal contrasts, and equalization of color potencies.

Balance need not, therefore, mean symmetrical arrangement, which can lack interest except, possibly, in patterns of unlimited area.

To vary arrangements and to keep them in balance, we need only to recall the play songs of our youth such as *London Bridge* or *In and Out the Windows.* There was balance in the lines but there was no monotony. Some note, usually at the same place in each line, was accented which gave rhythm to the piece. The accented syllables of words not only add variety to words; they give beauty to the language. Rhythm became instinctive with us during our earliest years and we instinctively feel its presence in arrangements of music and poetry that give us pleasure. When we attempt art expression rhythm becomes an important ingredient, and we must remember that it is the *accent* which changes a phrase of seemingly endless, dull repetition into one of interesting rhythm.

The accent plays another and still more important part in a pleasing arrangement. As it stands out from the other elements, it dominates them. Dominance is probably the most necessary ingredient in the arrangement we wish to compose. Once again we find a parallel between the world we live in and the art we practice through which we try to express ourselves.

Dominance is the very essence of Nature's organization in the animal kingdom, plant world, and every other form of natural phenomena. The torso is the dominant element of the human body, the arms and legs subordinate to it. The

Rhythmic effect by repeating pattern and by reversing the principal motif in a parallel arrangement.

trunk of the tree dominates its many limbs and smaller branches, each successive step a transition from an element that dominates it to that which it in turn dominates, as the limb the branch, the branch the twig, and the twig the leaf. Again, applying this principle in the relationships between the elements of interest when we compose, we will see how one element dominating all others will establish a feeling of unity and clarity in the composition. Things alike in character but differing in size make pleasing arrangements. This brings us to a study of that keynote of beauty—harmony.

When we think of harmony we reflect on pleasant experiences, as when we enjoyed an arrangement of flowers, a sunset of varying colors, and a musical composition. There was an absence of harshness, of ill-related things, or disturbing elements. We felt the fitness of each contributing part and the unity of the whole. All of the factors we have discussed—balance, rhythm, and dominance—were present, and with them all, appropriateness.

We think of the mountain having majesty when the trees, the rocks and snow about its peak are presented against a background of clouds and sky. All of these elements belong together. But should we, with a touch of whimsy, introduce an assortment of garden vegetables the note of majesty would fade away; the unity would be broken. This illustration may seem extreme. It is not mentioned facetiously, but to suggest the nature of a disturbing element. Things which we associate because of their use or relationship to each other fit into arrangements harmoniously when the forementioned principles are employed.

Similarity in the shapes of objects, differing in size, frequently produce harmony in proportions. Angles of like degree, and curves that are similar, contribute to make a pleasant impression. Rectangles, related in their proportions

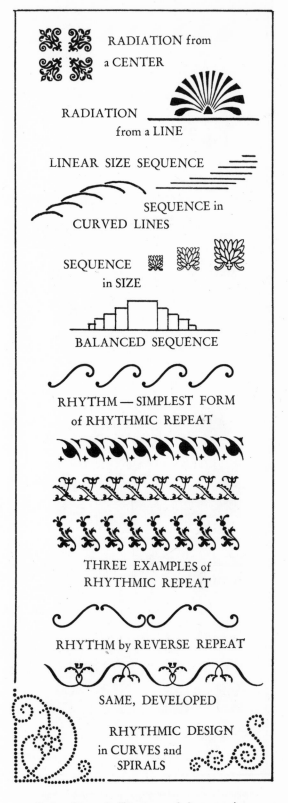

RADIATION from a CENTER

RADIATION from a LINE

LINEAR SIZE SEQUENCE

SEQUENCE in CURVED LINES

SEQUENCE in SIZE

BALANCED SEQUENCE

RHYTHM — SIMPLEST FORM of RHYTHMIC REPEAT

THREE EXAMPLES of RHYTHMIC REPEAT

RHYTHM by REVERSE REPEAT

SAME, DEVELOPED

RHYTHMIC DESIGN in CURVES and SPIRALS

Design Group II. This group of diagrams show the basic principles of Radiation and Rhythm. Many of these principles may be observed in nature, but when used in graphic or design arts they are formalized for rhythmic effect.

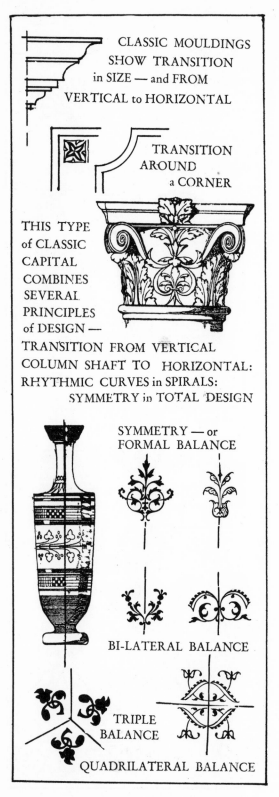

CLASSIC MOULDINGS
SHOW TRANSITION
in SIZE — and FROM
VERTICAL to HORIZONTAL

TRANSITION
AROUND
a CORNER

THIS TYPE
of CLASSIC
CAPITAL
COMBINES
SEVERAL
PRINCIPLES
of DESIGN —

TRANSITION FROM VERTICAL
COLUMN SHAFT TO HORIZONTAL:
RHYTHMIC CURVES in SPIRALS:
SYMMETRY in TOTAL DESIGN

SYMMETRY — or
FORMAL BALANCE

BI-LATERAL BALANCE

TRIPLE
BALANCE

QUADRILATERAL BALANCE

Design Group III. This group of diagrams illustrate the principles of Transition, followed by the principle of Symmetry, or Formal Balance. Other types of balance are also shown. Symmetry creates Balance; asymmetry destroys Balance.

produce a restful harmony. Harmony in the proportionate relationship between two or more elements may result when some basic factor in the dimensions of one finds its counterpart in the other.

Methods used in the arrangement of material include the convergence of lines so as to create sharp angles which attract attention, a modification of this by transitory steps, a repetition of similar forms, and a balance of the material used, either symmetrically or otherwise. Sometimes all of these methods are used in the same composition.

These principles of composition are equally applicable in the use of tones and color as they are in the use of lines.

Importance of Contrast in Tone

Nature does not present, always, a smooth merging of tones. There is the ever-effective presence of contrast and, were it not for this, monotony would prevail. A common defect in the work of the untrained art student is the failure to create contrast, which produces an effect that is flat, dull and uninteresting.

To attain the emphasis in the element of chief interest, unimportant details must be subdued in the contrasts they create. Contrast can be easily controlled, and when the student has mastered this, he should be able to produce effective pictures. Contrast gives to the picture a dramatic quality and its exaggeration at times will prove helpful.

When contrasts are created in color they are attained through relationships in what is known as the "Complementary Scale," a subject that will be discussed fully in the chapter on Color.

Patterns in Design

As we have received much of our judgment in matters concerning design from our exposure to Nature's beauties, we turn to her patterns for an endless variety of ideas and to refresh our inspiration. Patterns created by the wild flowers in the fields, the formation of clouds, the seafoam at the beach, the arrangement of rock formations, and the shadows of clouds cast on distant hills provide infinite possibilities for adaptation in the design of pictures, wallpaper,

82

textiles, rugs and tiles. While many of these subjects are irregular in form, Nature offers many symmetrical patterns, and a few that are geometric.

The value of a student's knowledge of natural forms becomes apparent as he adapts these forms for his designs. The outstanding characteristic of plant-life, for instance, is the symmetrical balance of its parts. Radiation from a center stem is a distinguishing feature. Although leaves spring from the stem of many plants in an alternate manner, first on one side, then on the other, there are other examples of Nature's symmetry where the leaves branch out from the center stem in pairs.

Petals of a flower radiate from a central bud or stalk offering a motif frequently employed in formalized design. The snowflake is geometric, hexagonal in shape, with an infinite variety of patterns creating its structure. Shell forms present rhythmic arrangements suitable for adaptation in design. It is a common practice of designers to take a single flower form and draw it in many different positions to study its many possibilities for use in design. Any time the student spends in study of natural forms will prove to be a most profitable investment.

How to Develop Creative Ability

We have observed in this discussion of the elements of design and the methods used in composing that design is a planned relationship of patterns and forms in two-dimensional arrangement. For the design to be successful it must fulfill the purpose for which it was created. That it functions as it was intended to do is of paramount importance. And it must also produce a feeling of satisfaction and pleasure with those whom it serves. To design successfully the artist must attain both objectives.

While much of this discussion has pointed to a rich source of material for design purposes, there is much more to this study than reproducing facsimiles of nature. Let us give first consideration to the appropriateness of the material selected for the design. Geometric forms, which have a static quality, are successful when employed in designs for linoleums, carpets and rugs. They adapt themselves readily to large areas and flat surfaces. Their use on walls is frequently less successful. The wall introduces

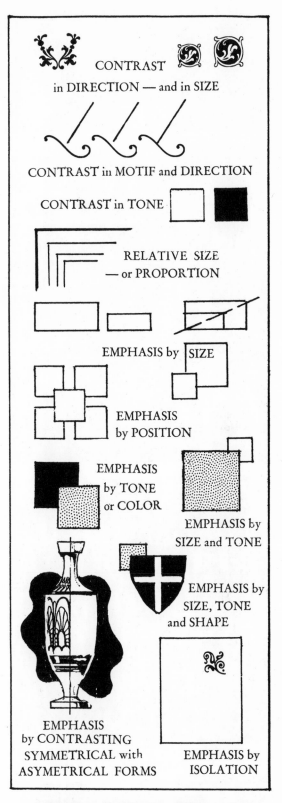

Design Group IV. This group of diagrams illustrate the principles of Contrast and the closely related principle of Proportion (meaning relative size). Several means of achieving emphasis are shown, including the important one of Isolation.

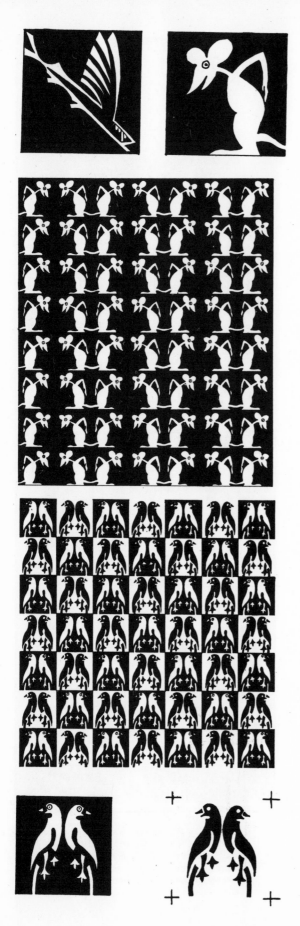

Above: Four unit motifs for pattern design seen in accompanying illustrations of student pattern studies in three different design schemes. At Left: student pattern study based on simple repetition of the design motif. The unsymmetrical figure of the mouse was converted into a symmetrical motif by reversing it in pairs.

the element of height, a factor we think of in vertical measure. Stripes are often selected as decorative motifs on walls and, when natural forms are used, it seems appropriate to suggest those forms as implying growth in an upward direction. Medallions are used for wall decoration but the material comprising them is selected generally so that a static feeling is avoided.

Patterns suitable for use on a finely-woven fabric would not adapt well to a heavy brocade. The use to which the textile is to be put will determine the nature of the design. More detail can be included in the design for silk than on a coarser material. The size of the design will be governed also by the use of the textile; it should bear some relationship to the scale of the material with which it will be used. Since the dimensions of the human figure set the scale by which furniture and other articles devised for its use are measured, there are certain conditions imposed on the designer to make his patterns appropriate to the circumstances.

Originality

The desire to be original seems to attract the average student as an objective having greater importance than other goals in his training. There is virtue in devising something new; it is frequently marketable and occasionally sets a vogue for a short time. But if the article is carefully analyzed, it usually has an ancestor. It is amazing how many things we enjoy today, think-

At Left: Student pattern study of Repetition by Alternation. Reversed values in the same motif create an interesting vibration in the overall effect.

ing them products of our times, had prototypes years ago.

There is plenty of opportunity for the student to show originality in the way he adapts old ideas to new use. The first step is to acquire knowledge of the conditions in which the design in mind can be fitted. Design has always been a thing of growth and movement, being constantly altered in form to serve successive generations of people. Principles in design have remained constant; motifs have changed. The designer's facility for originality has been practiced in adapting forms which served centuries of discriminating purchasers of art to meet the demands of a new outlook. The secret lies not in copying the substance of the old but in recognizing the essence of good and incorporating it into the new. This essence of good consists of pleasing relationships in the various elements of the design, and the appropriateness of the design to the purpose.

Seek Forms Having Beauty

Students of design during a recent period have been encouraged to experiment with rectangles, circles, triangles and wiggly forms, presenting them in formations that produced spotty effects. It can only be assumed that the intention on the part of the instructors was to introduce the simplest of forms for early study. The circle, a monotonous contour without any beauty whatsoever, the square, nearly as monotonous, and the triangle, entirely without grace, offers nothing inspiring to work with, and the student should not hamper his progress or stultify his inspiration by struggling with such sterile material. There are countless other forms offering opportunity for graceful and pleasing designs. Plant life, animal life, bird life, the sea and the denizens of the deep, fire, clouds and rain, are

Student pattern studies, the upper circle showing Repetition by Radiation; the lower, Repetition by Alternation. The alternation is in a reversal of values, with the motif in straight "checkerboard" repeat pattern.

85

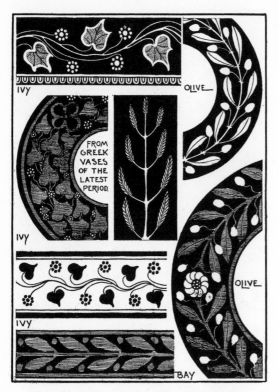

Details of ancient Greek vase paintings in which natural forms have been formalized and worked into border designs. Ivy, olive, and bay leaves supplied the motifs.

rials has been added to natural materials, and an equally amazing complexity of tool and machine processes are now working and fabricating all materials.

Because of our proficiency in producing all kinds of things today, the task of the designer has become increasingly complex. He must be familiar with the mechanics of production, a matter far more involved than confronted the artisans of an early way when hands supplied the skill.

Design of Two Dimensions

There are two kinds of design; that of two dimensions, and that of three dimensions. The first is known as decorative design, the other spatial. The fields for decorative design include

Greek design compositions to conform with circular spaces. Medals, coins, plates, or any other circular space impose conditions to which the design must be accommodated.

at your service and can supply more motifs and ideas than a student can employ in his lifetime.

Uses for abstract forms in design are relatively few. The abstract has no effect emotionally on people. Emotion is evoked through the senses, and the senses respond to concrete things either experienced or imagined. The designer's conception should first be of things known to man. His interpretation of them in design is influenced by his emotion, which the Greeks said is the force that makes us create.

How frequently we interpret the forms of clouds into pictures of animate objects and associations! The clouds present abstract shapes which we view without reaction. It takes the association of reality to incite reaction.

Application of design has followed a steady course from that of primitive people to our present day. An incredible range of synthetic mate-

mural painting, textiles, tiles, book covers and posters, and all surface patterns measured only by two dimensions. Designs for spatial relationships include building, furniture, sculpture, and all problems involved in the three dimensions. Our present study concerns only decorative design.

Designs of two dimensions may be also divided by use in limited areas and in unlimited areas. Limited areas imply an enclosed area surrounded by a border; unlimited areas include wall paper, carpets, linoleums, fabrics for drapery and upholstery, and dress goods. These designs may be composed as single units, groups of units, or patterns of continuous expansion.

Material selected for use in designs is generally simplified from the way it appears in its natural state, and, when we simplify it we reduce the number of details by which we recognize the form to the fewest number by which it retains its chief characteristics. This means of simplification is also known as conventionalizing. However, in conventionalization, the treatment may be formalized or left in an informal arrangement.

Simplicity is the essence of beauty, and the simplest units in designs are often the most effective. Beauty of a pattern depends more on the rhythmic repetition of the units over the surface of the decoration than upon the form of the unit.

Systems of creating rhythm in patterns of unlimited area consist of (1) units placed in vertical rows, (2) units placed in horizontal rows, and (3) units placed in diagonal rows. In many of the designs for dress fabrics on display in shops today, the units are varied, many suggesting pictorial material but in their arrangement, a system of continuity is necessary for production, and this is frequently accomplished with much subtleness.

Nature has provided a valuable idea to the designer which is called radiation. Plant life supplies this motif in two ways, (1) radiation from a line, as the leaves branch out from the stalk and (2) radiation from a point, as the petals spring outward from the bud.

Formal repeat patterns, some based on natural forms, others on abstractions. Nature provides an inexhaustible range of motifs and, through the ages, first the Eastern World then the Western availed themselves of the endless possibilities, their arts being governed by selection and organization.

A pattern design from natural motifs created by a student of Franklin High School, Rochester, N. Y., and winner of a Scholastic Award in its class.

An illustration of the term "applied design," today more correctly recognized as "applied pattern" or "applied decoration." Here is a decorative Oriental dragon motif used on the decoration of a box.

Conventionalizing Design Material

To conventionalize is to omit the less important details of the material and shape it along formalized lines. Strict formality means using the material in a symmetrical arrangement; informal conventionalizing means developing of decorative shapes in arrangements having balance without symmetry. Sometimes the latter introduces the suggestion of perspective; the former never does.

The use of conventionalized forms implies the intention of the designer to create ornament and, for consistency and simplicity, formal and informal patterns should not appear in the same design.

Design in Drawing and Painting

The need for good design, or pleasing arrangement, in pictorial art is just as great as in any fields of decorative art. Here, we frequently think of it as Composition, but the knowledge of a trained designer is needed to divide the spaces within the area of the paper or canvas. Each division of the main area becomes a problem in design. A pattern of well-related shapes does not happen like an accident, it is planned. Each shape made larger or more colorful than its neighbors in a given area will dominate that area. Each part of the drawing or painting is organized so that it plays its desired role in an integrated whole.

In a picture involving more than one figure, the problem of design includes not only the relationship of one figure to the others but the relationship of them all to the background, foreground, or whatever the picture contains.

Probably one of the most remarkable designs involving many figures is Michelangelo's painting for the ceiling of the Sistine Chapel in Rome. As a design the master had not only to plan a total scheme and to relate figure to figure in the vast project, but to relate individual figures in mass to the existing architecture. It is a study gigantic in scale and suggesting infinite space.

No painting or illustration should be undertaken as a finished work until many rough sketches have been made. You need to be certain of what you intend to do. Some illustrators and painters go so far as to make rough paper "scenery" for the "stage-setting" of their compo-

Portrait of Anna Pavlova, by Sorine, is an admirable example of design as applied to portraiture. This painting is in the Luxembourg, Paris.

sition, and in this they have placed little movable models of their figures, in order to convince themselves that a certain placement or relationship of these figures is the most effective. This applies, of course, to planned pictures. When drawings are made of existing conditions, the designer must make his adjustments in favor of a better arrangement of the material.

Design in Landscape Painting

Landscape exists for the artist in an infinity of natural compositions. Yet even here the designer functions, not only in selecting the material to be used but in intensifying the idea that prompted the selection of the material. Nature presents harmonious effects in a wide panorama in which units of interest pass in review, each having potentialities for a strong composition. It takes a discerning eye and a keen designer to assemble the elements he wishes to use. In his selection he typifies the spirit of the landscape, and he compresses its general effect into a picture frame much smaller than the vast scene that stretches before him.

Artists are known to stop on a drive or a walk

in the country to say, "There's a picture I want to paint." Or, in a different situation, they are known to climb to an almost inaccessible spot to secure the arrangement that satisfies them. There can be no rule for this. It depends on your "picture sense," which is really your *sense of design* applied to pictorial arrangements.

"All Saints Day," by E. Friant, is another painting where pattern plays an important part in creating an interesting picture. This also is in the Luxembourg.

The human figure as an art form has been utilized to fit into a myriad of design problems. Above: It fits into a rectangular panel. Below: It is used to achieve symmetry. The old masters were very objective in the use of the figure in their paintings.

Applying the principles of composition, outlined previously, the painter of landscapes will make a more effective picture if he introduces into its design some prominent feature which will dominate all other elements. This feature becomes the focal point, to which the eye of the observer will be drawn. In the planning of the picture, the designer should also permit the attention of the observer to follow a course of interest progressively through the other elements of the composition but returning to the center of interest with satisfaction.

The power to create should be disciplined. The freedom of an artist to improvise can lead to artificial results if he has not observed keenly and practiced conscientiously how to draw and paint the forms he wishes to use in his imaginary compositions. Certain painters of the 18th century romanticized landscape to the degree that the effects were artificial. Trees were deprived of their nobility, the rocks of their ruggedness; the whole effect prettied and stripped of its character.

Students should refrain from creating imaginary landscapes until they have spent considerable time in observation, study, drawing and painting of rocks, trees and other incidents of Nature. Carry a sketch book with you at all times and, in the thousands of lost moments we all have, sketch the things you see that you believe typify the rocks, trees and clouds you would desire to paint. This is the way to build up the background you need to become a creative artist.

The effectiveness of the silhouette was fully appreciated by the master painters, and they used it frequently.

FULCRUM

Symmetrical Balance—Two elements of equal weight and placed equidistant from the center of a limited area.

Unsymmetrical Balance—One element and five elements which total in weight that of the one element and placed so that the average of weight, or balance, falls in the center of a limited area.

One element is balanced by a smaller element when the fulcrum, or point of balance is moved to a position closer to the larger element than to the smaller. The law of equilibrium functions in art as it does in physics.

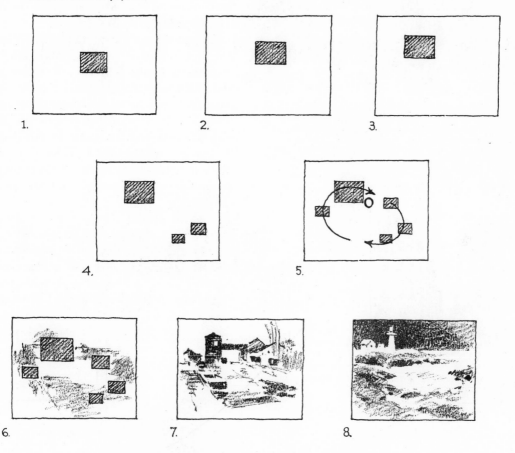

1. 2. 3.

4. 5.

6. 7. 8.

The Evolution of Visual Activity

1. An element of weight is placed within a limited area equidistant from parallel sides. In this position an observer's eye has a tendency to regard the element of weight as falling slightly from its centered location. The area of space below the element seems insufficient to support it.

2. The element of weight is raised above the center but remains equidistant from the two sides. The space below the element seems to support the weight, and the effect of better stability is attained.

3. The element has been moved to the left but the balance does not seem badly disturbed. The large amount of space created in the lower right hand corner of the area has a tendency to assume a weight of its own which helps to offset the visual lack of balance.

4. Two small elements of weight have been introduced in the open space.

5. Other elements are grouped in the area and movement begins. The eye has a habit of reading pictures in a clockwise motion. We now have a series of interests dominated by a chief interest, the group distributed so that the average of interests or balance falls at a point about centered between the two sides and slightly above the center of the area. (Marked by "O")

6. Let us develop these interests. A gray tone is created along the path indicated by the arrow in Figure 5.

7. The chief interest is developed into a tower connected by a bridge. This introduces forces in convergence, a powerful factor in compelling attention.

8. An alternate arrangement where contrasts are created in reverse tonal patterns.

A Single Subject Offers Many Pictures

Here is a typical scene in one of Paris' parks with people grouped near a pool. A grove of trees separates the foreground from the buildings beyond, typical apartments in Parisian architecture with their mansard roofs.

How much should we include in our composition? If we desire to make a vertical picture, we select the vista down the street to the left of the scene; if we want to concentrate the attention on the people around the edge of the pool, we minimize the buildings in the background and center our interest in the lower half of the picture. The rectangles at the bottom of the page show what is possible when the composition comprises a little of both elements—the buildings and the group around the pool.

Composing to fit a definite space is good discipline for the student. He must learn to choose from the things he sees and group them in a pleasing arrangement so that some one element

of his composition will create a chief interest, while the other elements serve in a subordinate way to round out the picture.

It will prove helpful if you cut rectangles of varying proportions out of pieces of cardboard, then hold one after another between your eye and the subject you desire to draw. Move each cardboard "window" back and forth along the object and stop it when you think you have an arrangement which expresses the vista the way you want to draw it. Then sketch it using the edges of the opening in the cardboard for the limits of your picture.

Observe how the base line of the grove of trees forms a strong contrast with the light walk on the opposite side of the pool. This dominant horizontal line draws the eye to it. When a vertical line meets the horizontal at any point, a conflict of opposing forces is joined which is good material to adopt as a center of interest in good composition.

The old masters "designed" their pictures. Their keen vision saw countless pictures in nature, and they made their own adjustment of natural features to create pleasing compositions. (Reproduced through courtesy of Metropolitan Museum of Art.)

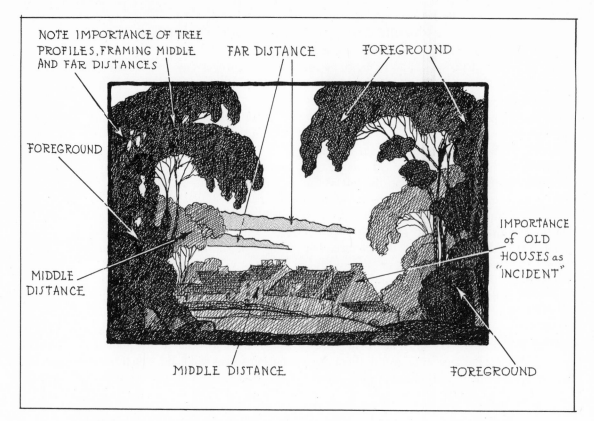

A diagrammatic analysis of one of the landscapes shown below. Observe how the three distances give depth in space, important in a landscape composition.

LESSONS

Begin by selecting a flower, preferably a daisy, cornflower or rose, and draw it in many different positions. With these sketches as a guide, redraw the flowers, simplifying the forms to eliminate the little accidents of growth, and less important details. Keep the drawings confined in treatment to a single outline filled in with a flat tone.

Prepare various geometric shapes such as a square and rectangles of varying proportions. These shapes will serve as limited areas into which you will develop your designs. The square will provide a suitable area for a treatment of the flower or bud of the plant; the rectangles will offer opportunity for arrangements including the stem. Try designs both symmetrical and unsymmetrical in these rectangles.

Repeat these experiments with other material such as fruit and shell fish. The crab is a popular motif for designs of tiles and fabrics. The pineapple and the pine cone have surfaces which offer fine opportunity to a designer.

When you have arranged the design in the area, darken the background in the area, leaving the flower, fruit or shell form silhouetted in white against it. Alternate this experiment, repeating the exercise with various effects.

Then adapt your material to a hexagonal form, then to a pentagon. You will see how it is necessary to rearrange your material so that it composes gracefully in the various areas.

Now let us prepare a design for an unlimited area. Develop one of your flower forms so that it is standardized in shape and size and repeat

The above drawings are offered to suggest subject matter suitable for a student's study and as exercises.

it in vertical, horizontal and oblique formations. Then develop the form as a single unit, like a medallion, and try this in the various formations.

Now, prepare a design using the form in an all-over pattern. Try this with a leaf form. It will give the illusion of solid mass of foliage.

Draw two lines horizontal and parallel to each other with an interval of two or three inches, and develop a vine pattern as a continuous border within the lines. Draw the stem of the vine in a pattern of undulating curves which will furnish the basic structure of the design. Draw the leaves leaving the stem alternately first on one side, then on the other, so that they fill the spaces created by the curving stem.

The purpose of a border is to surround an area with a repeating rhythmic pattern so that the eye will move smoothly along without interruption by an accent that would arrest the attention unwarrantedly.

As a student becomes more proficient in the control of his accents, he will be able to develop patterns of much variation for unlimited areas, such as wall paper designs having naturalistic scenes alternately interspersed throughout the area. Start with simple forms first and learn to use them in a variety of ways. This kind of practice develops creative ability.

Below is an example of a single unit repeated in a diagonal pattern. See how the arms of the windmill carry the diagonal line.

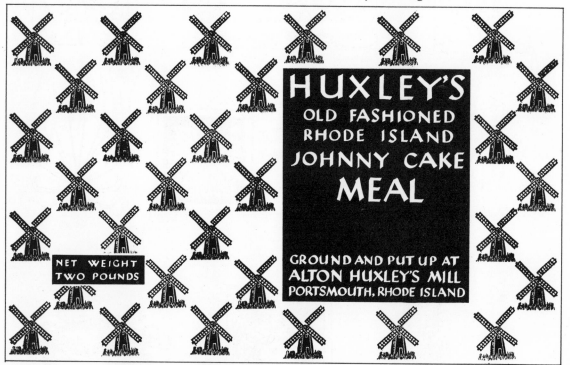

A repeat pattern design for a package, the work of a student. The product —wind-mill ground corn meal—is usually put up in folding paper boxes. This drawing could be printed in two colors, brown on yellow. Pattern, shown here, is adapted to the front, back, and sides of the box. The motif is appropriate.

Lessons in Landscape Composition

The sketches below suggest schemes of arrangement with landscape material. Students should confine their efforts at first to simple subject matter having a center of interest quite prominent in the composition. Difficulty will be experienced if too much material is included in the picture.

This is called a vignette. It is a form of picture making usually associated with sketches. The edges of the vignette should be studied for their pattern interest. Try to get variety into the shapes. A good vignette has spontaneity and defines much of its material by subtle suggestion.

At left: The contour of the foliage and the ground line offers pleasing contrast to the shore line in the distance. When a square is used as a picture frame, it is dangerous to let shapes bordering on rectangles be prominent in the picture. Motifs where curves are dominant will offer a more pleasing result.

Above at Right: The progression of trees and the wagon tracks in the snow seem to meet at the horizon where the center of interest is easily apprehended. Below: A single tree is all that is needed to furnish interest in this bleak landscape.

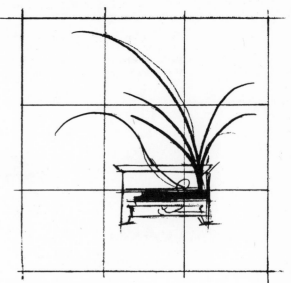

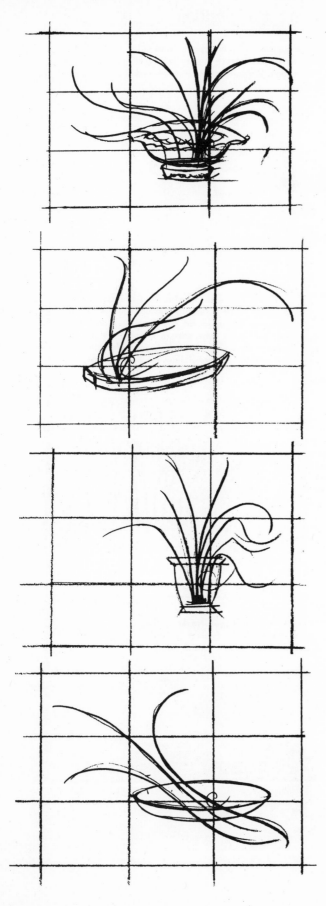

How to Compose a
STILL LIFE STUDY
by W. T. Foster

In the seven rough compositional sketches for a still-life arrangement, Mr. Foster tries out different schemes. Any artist normally makes at least this many sketches, often more. Few, if any, proceed at once to a finished painting from a single preliminary sketch. Into each of the arrangements, Mr. Foster introduces a certain flair. The scheme of arrangement is given first consideration. They may be roses and ferns or magnolia and redbud, he says. There is no limit to the variety of pictures you can do. "With flowers, a vase, and a little ingenuity, you can have a fine time painting," says Mr. Foster.

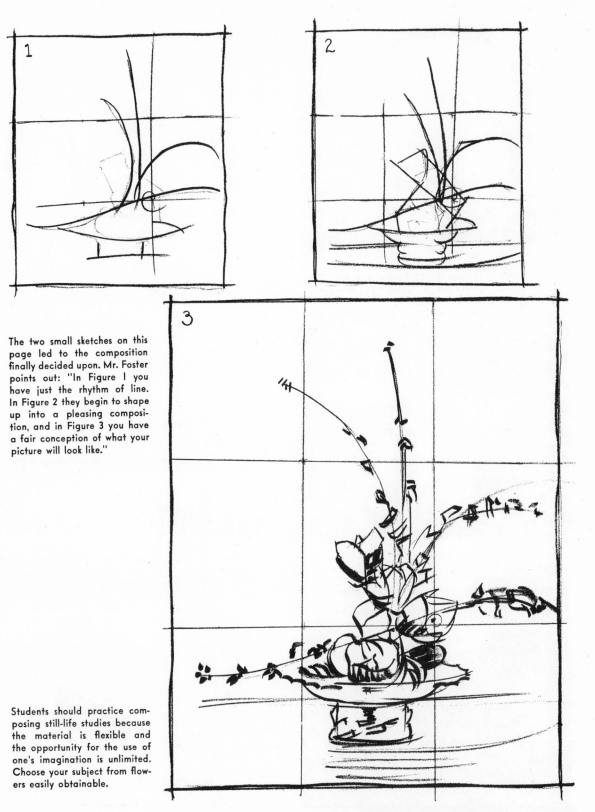

The two small sketches on this page led to the composition finally decided upon. Mr. Foster points out: "In Figure 1 you have just the rhythm of line. In Figure 2 they begin to shape up into a pleasing composition, and in Figure 3 you have a fair conception of what your picture will look like."

Students should practice composing still-life studies because the material is flexible and the opportunity for the use of one's imagination is unlimited. Choose your subject from flowers easily obtainable.

These pages are reproduced through the courtesy of W. T. Foster.

Pictorial design of china and glassware in a still-life arrangement recorded by the camera. Design is just as important in photography as in any of the other media for art.

Lithograph by Louis Lozowick shows that an apple, a pear, a cup of tea, with the shadows they cast, can compose pleasingly. The checkered tablecloth makes an interesting background.

Still-life arrangement designed for use in a merchandise photograph for advertising has much of the art quality of the Lozowick lithograph above.

POWERFUL

Every job spins

Marine law requires ocean-going steamers to carry life boats would be bad business. For the public would have little faith used check paper, and the choice of a great majority of out-for checks. But bankers and business men know that the hax ard correspondingly increased through its use. ▶▶ And it is their are, of course, no laws which require the use of safety paper and rafts of sufficient capacity to accommodate all persons on board. Even though this were not the case — failure to do so in any line which skimped on such vital equipment. ▶▶ There protection which has made "La Monte" America's most widely greater without this precaution — and that public confidence is of loss through fraudulent alteration and counterfeiting is far uncompromising determination to provide the utmost in check standing, banks and business organizations.

Ludlow composit

SPARKLING NEW

COMPOSITION

UNWIT HEYIT
ALL SLUG COMPOSITION

THE MOST

BEAUTIFULS ETERNAL

ch re- and one sponsored the arious incidents of that era One of the most bizarre episod was the presentation of a mu quired, among other things, c fire siren. The author of this strange event, is finally able to culminated in one of the most l Every step was a struggle agai and deep-drifted snow: he had painfully cold, and his muscl T. Williams, the guy who set season on Broadway, doesn't i expected, but the funny part b Besides being pretty and woman" gave Mr. B. what he v intelligent this "other anted most: apprec the fam oblem for v ss as the play rn out t Figures at Mme. Tuss the millions since the tim purting from this tortured nu s testimony to the medieval method sion—and to the unique art at Mme. ous London exhibition, he powerth hear tors: Who's real? Who's wax? I persor

When Will the Spirit Revive

Tinfluential MO

Two examples of typographic abstractions by students. In these instances, the students were encouraged to use type only as design material and show daring and originality in the layouts.

DIAGONALS
vitalize the composition

As mentioned earlier, diagonal lines denote action. They bring to a picture a dynamic quality. They suggest violence at times, such as driving rain. The Flemish and Dutch painters used diagonal motifs, frequently by suggesting a diagonal source of light entering the picture. Even in pictures where the principal figure may be shown in repose, the posing of the figure so that a diagonal composition results adds much to the general interest of the picture. In the typographic arrangement at the bottom of the opposite page, diagonal lines have added force to the page.

Striking design in a scratch-board illustration from an English advertisement. Contrast of major elements creating sharp angles illustrates power of convergence in compositions. (Courtesy of Banister, Walton & Co., Ltd.)

Design plays an important part in this movie still. The pose was arranged to provide both contrast and harmony in the flow of the soft, graceful lines of the skirt to the formal vertical motif furnished by the alignment of the masks on the wall.

Simplicity the Key to Beauty in
JAPANESE INK DRAWINGS

Japanese art expresses a nature-loving people chiefly by means of line and tone. Compositions are harmonic relationships of darks and lights; color is of secondary importance to the Orientals.

In studying the tone relations, the Japanese learned to rely on the beauty in the contour of the forms he created. He ignored modelling within the forms by the use of shadow. Line was his medium—it defined the boundaries of shapes which, in a studied relationship, comprised his design.

The effectiveness of Japanese art lies in its simplicity, its beauty in the harmony between care-fully composed areas of tone. When he works, the Japanese artist studies his picture first in line, tracing over an earlier effort to correct and improve that which he knows will be the structure of his picture. Washes of tone are applied when the line pattern is perfect.

In the reproductions below and on the opposite page, the general effect is of a silhouette. Violent action is suggested in the flight of the crows and in the bat; a languid feeling pervades the horizontal panel at the bottom. There is something sinister about the birds perched on the branch, while Fuji rises quite majestically.

Two crows in a snowstorm—simple enough in subject matter, but brilliantly composed by a modern Japanese artist. How effective and how severe is the bat silhouetted against the moon. The Japanese have never been excelled in the field of pictorial composition. Their understanding of pattern is exemplified in every contour, every area of space left broken by their subject matter.

This famous print of Fujiyama illustrates the masterful division of the main area and the relationship of each division to the others.

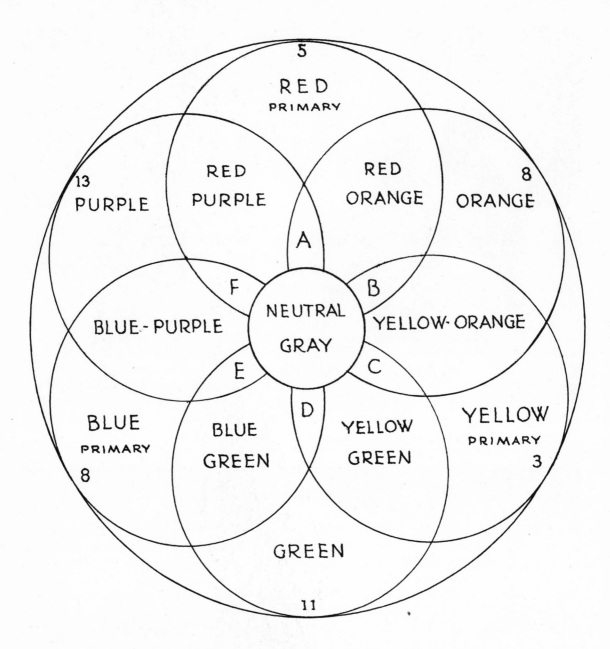

Beginning with the three primaries, three secondary colors are formed. From the three secondaries, six tertiaries are possible when each secondary is mixed with its adjacent primary. The letters A, B, C, D, E, and F represent a further development brought about by the mixing of two tertiaries. These will be Russet, Dark Orange, Citron, Dark Green, Olive, and Dark Purple, respectively. Colors diagonally opposite each other in the chart are complementary. The figures within the circles near the outer perimeter represent the parts of that color needed when mixed with its complementary color to produce a neutral gray.

CHAPTER 7

Color–The Study of Light

Perhaps color is the one subject in an art student's progress where he comes face to face with the study of physics. Color is light, and the more one knows about what it is composed of and how it behaves in this world of ours the better he is equipped to work with it. A sense of color, like a musician's ear for music, may serve as a guide in the appreciation of color, and a preference for certain combinations. The musician may judge harmony in a similar way, but if he is a composer, he must know more about his subject than his aptitude for making a decision solely with the aid of his instinct.

With most children the study of light begins in the lower grades of school when they see how a ray of sunlight, passing through a triangular-shaped glass called a prism, falls on a flat surface in an array of varied colored stripes. The colors take fixed positions beginning with red and follow with red-orange, orange, orange-yellow, yellow, yellow-green, green, green-blue, blue, blue-violet, to violet in that order. It is also observed that these colors are not distributed in equal amounts. There is a large area of red, a smaller one of orange-red, much smaller amounts of orange, orange-yellow, and yellow, and increased amounts of green-yellow, green and blue-green. Almost half the area of the prism's colors are blues and violets. These colors in their varying content comprise a ray of white light.

Objects appear in color as they reflect the various rays in the light which fall upon them. If the object appears red, it is because the red rays in light are the ones making the major contribution to its illumination while the other rays add little. An object which appears black is one which absorbs nearly all of the light rays; it reflects no prominent ray. An article appearing white reflects practically all of the light rays in their original relationship to each other. The material of which an object is made, and its texture on the surface determine which light rays it absorbs and which it reflects.

Interesting experiments have been made with lamps projecting light through colored mediums, used for theatrical effects. When a greenish-blue light was used to illuminate an object which under white light appears red, the object seemed colorless because no ray of red light existed to be reflected from the surface of the object. When a yellow light falls on a bluish surface a similar result occurs, no bluish rays of light are used to illumine the object; therefore none are reflected. The other rays are absorbed by the surface of the object.

These observations will help the student arrive at some definite conclusions concerning color blending as he progresses in his study.

The power of light rays is lessened as it is reflected from an object's surface. Regardless of the material of which an object is made, with the possible exception of a mirror, light rays penetrate the surface to some degree; some of their power is absorbed, the rest reflected. This explains why artists have difficulty in reproducing in color the brilliance and power of light. The designer of stained-glass windows is not so greatly handicapped. The translucency of glass permits light to pass through the color with more brilliant effect than is possible when light is reflected.

Approximating Light with Pigments

There are two chief differences between the study of color in light and that of color in pigments. First, scientists have selected as the primitives of color in light red, yellow-green, and blue-violet. A primary color is one that cannot be made by mixing any other colors, nor can it be separated into any other colors. In pigments, the primaries are red, yellow, and blue. Since there are many kinds of reds, yellows and blues, it will prove helpful at the start to define which color we recognize for our understanding of the primaries.

In an effort to approximate the primaries in light, pigments known as rose madder, lemon yellow, and cobalt blue are generally accepted as primaries in paints. They are the three which cannot be made by mixing other colors.

The second difference between the use of color in light and color in paint is that all colors in light make white light whereas the same colors in paint make gray. But as it was noted that the colors in the spectrum as light passed through the prism were varied in the amount of area each assumed in the scale, so are the amounts of pigment in paint varied to produce a neutral effect.

Let us consider an area of neutral gray as consisting of 16 parts of color. Just as yellow was the smallest in area in the prismatic scale, so it takes less quantity in the pigment scale, or only 3 parts. Red in the spectrum was next smallest in area and it assumes a similar position in the make-up of gray in paint, or 5 parts. The color with the largest volume in light was blue, and in the pigment mixture has 8 parts. If the quantities of color are varied, the result will be other than a neutral gray. When one color is set apart from the others, it takes the sum of the other two colors to restore the effect of gray.

Therefore, the complement of a color is the sum of all other colors when that one color is removed. The sum of yellow and blue is green which is the complement of red. The sum of red and yellow is orange which is the complement of blue. Likewise the complement of yellow is the sum of red and blue, or purple.

Now let us continue with a refinement of these principles through the mixture of colors. The first step in the mixing is mentioned in the previous paragraph. Orange, green and purple are known as the secondary colors. The next step is the blending of the secondary color with its neighboring primary. Through this mixing we increase our combinations to include red-orange, yellow-orange, yellow-green, blue-green, blue-purple, and red-purple. These are known as the tertiaries.

An additional step takes us to the blending of two tertiaries, and for this we should refer to the color wheel to identify the less known colors

by those from which they are made. This fourth stage of mixing brings us a color called russet by blending the secondary color purple with secondary color orange. In this operation red has been used twice, once in the mixing of purple and again in the mixing of orange. Therefore, our proportion of colors used in their primary state would be: blue, 8 parts; yellow, 3 parts; and red, 10 parts, twice the neutralizing equivalent. Any of the colors in this stage of mixing can be obtained by using two primaries in their normal volume and the third primary in double its normal volume.

The Effect of Color on the Optic Nerve

Colors vary in their power to effect a shock on the optic nerve. Light waves produce vibrations on the sensitive membranes of the eye. Red has the greatest effect, and the other colors produce similar reactions in a reduced degree. Blue-greens, blues and violets seem less harsh; they are more restful to the eye. How much less is the strain to look upon verdant foliage than at the glare of a red barn. But when the red barn is situated so that a large mass of green can be seen at the same time, the effect is harmonious. Colors that are complements in a grouping produce a satisfying effect, but much depends on the dominance of one color over the other. In order to produce a harmonious effect they must appear in relative volume or area in which they neutralize each other. The green should dominate in volume the area of red to the proportion of 11 to 5. (The 11 parts are comprised of 8 of blue and 3 of yellow.)

It is an experience common with people who have exposed their eyes to an area of bright color upon shifting their sight to a background of neutral color to see the shape of the area take form in the neutral field having the color's complement. This is known as the after-image and results from the eye endeavoring to balance or neutralize the colors it sees. To attain a harmonious effect there should be elements in a color arrangement which tend to neutralize each other. The eye will do the mixing.

Use of Contrasting and Analogous Harmonies

Any of two complementary colors are contrasting when used in any proportion other than their neutralizing volumes. By volume is meant the space occupied by the color. The greater strength in which the color is used the lesser the space that should be given to it. Potency and volume should be in inverse ratio. The potency of a color may be reduced by blending with it its complement in any proportion less than that necessary to completely neutralize it. This is known as melodizing the color.

When a sequence of colors is used in the same relationship they bear each other in the spectrum, such as red, orange and yellow, or orange, yellow and yellow-green, the arrangement is called an analogous harmony. While not disturbing, it lacks the effect of unity which can be attained by introducing the complement of one of the colors into the arrangement. Effective color schemes result when a small area of potent color is placed against a background of analogous colors, the basic effect of which is complementary to the featured color.

Colors may be regarded as having a tendency to advance toward the eye or retreat from the eye, depending on the relative potencies of the colors and the effect they produce on the optic nerve. Reds, oranges and yellows have "advancing qualities" while the greens, blues and violets have "retreating qualities." A student will find this information of value when he endeavors to put colors in arrangements that will suggest increasing distance in his pictures. The particles of dust that float through the atmosphere reflect the warm light of the sun's rays and create a shimmer of golden light. As the eye's vision views the blue sky near the horizon, the blue appears to be melodized. This is caused by the complementary effect of the golden shimmer serving as a screen in front of the blue sky. When one looks directly upward, the direction of the vision is through the golden haze at its shortest depth, effecting less melodizing of the blue.

Distance has the effect of reducing the potencies of colors. Blue loses its strength first while yellows and oranges retain their intensity for the greatest distance. Bright red will appear first darker, then turn to brown as distance increases. Greens become neutralized as they recede from the eye. Foliage at a distance appears to resemble an olive color.

All colors will change relatively as the quality of light changes and a student should think in terms of the light he is portraying when determining the appearance of objects affected by that light. Shadows out-of-doors are areas denied the direct source of light and they will reflect any secondary source available. This is why shadows on snow appear blue; they reflect the blue rays of the sky.

When painting an object in shadow mix the color of the object with its complement. This is the only way to preserve the true color of the object when the surface in shadow no longer reflects the rays of light by which you distinguish the color of the object. The object in shadow does not assume another color; it merely loses the color it has.

Frequently a student will try to suggest the shaded side of a green tree by painting it a greenish-blue. The effect is unnatural unless one can assume a strong sky reflection, but even in this case the result appears artificial. Avoid the use of black in shadows. To paint the shadow side of a red apple, mix a bright green into the red color; to use black would produce a coffee-bean brown. When painting the shadow side of a yellow vase, mix purple into the yellow; to use black would result in a dirty green. Use the complement of a color to gray the color.

Any student of color will find each new fact he learns a fascinating experience. It is in this study the art student most nearly approaches the domain of the scientist.

This sketch of still-life may offer a suggestion toward a helpful exercise.

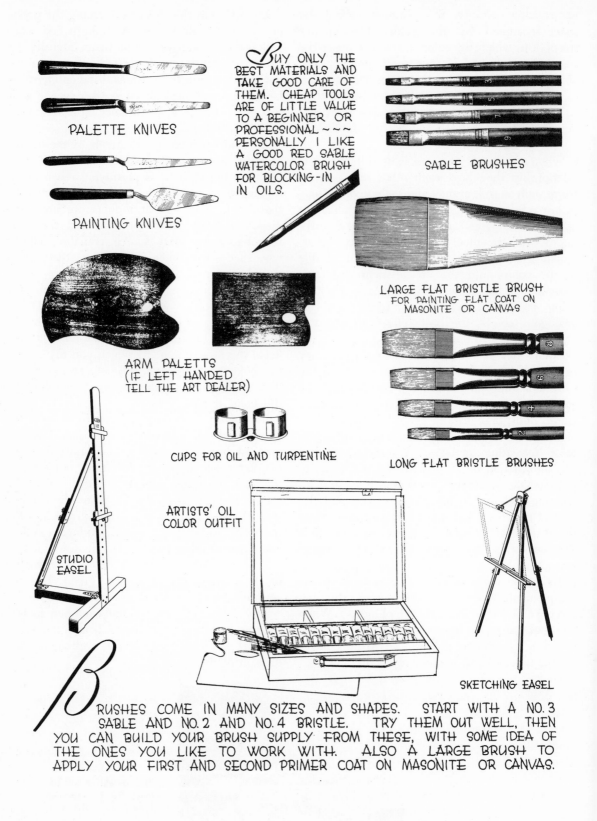

PALETTE KNIVES

PAINTING KNIVES

$\mathcal{B}$UY ONLY THE BEST MATERIALS AND TAKE GOOD CARE OF THEM. CHEAP TOOLS ARE OF LITTLE VALUE TO A BEGINNER OR PROFESSIONAL ~ ~ ~ PERSONALLY I LIKE A GOOD RED SABLE WATERCOLOR BRUSH FOR BLOCKING-IN IN OILS.

SABLE BRUSHES

LARGE FLAT BRISTLE BRUSH
FOR PAINTING FLAT COAT ON MASONITE OR CANVAS

ARM PALETTS
(IF LEFT HANDED TELL THE ART DEALER)

CUPS FOR OIL AND TURPENTINE

LONG FLAT BRISTLE BRUSHES

STUDIO EASEL

ARTISTS' OIL COLOR OUTFIT

SKETCHING EASEL

$\mathcal{B}$RUSHES COME IN MANY SIZES AND SHAPES.   START WITH A NO. 3 SABLE AND NO. 2 AND NO. 4 BRISTLE.   TRY THEM OUT WELL, THEN YOU CAN BUILD YOUR BRUSH SUPPLY FROM THESE, WITH SOME IDEA OF THE ONES YOU LIKE TO WORK WITH.   ALSO A LARGE BRUSH TO APPLY YOUR FIRST AND SECOND PRIMER COAT ON MASONITE OR CANVAS.

LESSONS

In Color Harmony

To begin the study of color, the student should start with water-colors as the medium is more translucent than oils, and can be handled with only the use of water and some white paper or inexpensive illustration board. Sable brushes are recommended, and the student should have four or five of various sizes so that he can work rapidly. Spontaneity is the keynote of water-color. Effects are obtained by direct washes of the color selected to state the fact; the student should not depend on building up to the color desired. Opaqueness destroys the translucent quality that water-color can offer.

In selecting a palette suitable for most purposes, the following is suggested as it has been found satisfactory by many prominent water-color artists. There should be at least three yellows, two reds, two blues, a green, and a warm ground color. Let us list the colors you will find practicable:

Lemon yellow, Aureolin, Cadmium yellow deep, Yellow ochre light, Cadmium orange, Burnt Sienna, Vandyke brown, Rose madder, Vermilion, Cerulean blue, Cobalt blue, Ultramarine blue, Viridian green, Emerald green, and Hooker's green No. 2.

Practice in Small Areas

First experiments in color should be confined to small areas where the student will experience less difficulty in controlling the medium. Begin with the problems proposed in the previous chapter concerning limited areas. Start with simple color schemes based on complementary colors. Practice the problems of design with a viewpoint to the potency of a color and the area in which it is used in relation to its complement.

As you progress, design patterns of three colors, two analogous and one the complement of one of the analogous colors. This complement should serve as an accent and should produce an effective result.

The step from the simple problem in three colors to the larger painting which you may admire on some museum wall is one of development only. The successful painting is not admired because of its complexity, but rather because of its simplicity. It is frequently the development of a three-color scheme.

When creating contrast with complementary color, do not forget the lessons learned in contrasts in black and white. The full potencies of complementary colors can prove troublesome and it is suggested that when complementaries are used, one is kept lighter than its spectrum intensity and the other darker. Tonal contrasts are still to be observed when painting with color.

When painting a large area where a flat wash of color is desired, dampen the board or paper with a sponge, and apply the washes in broad, direct strokes. A wash will float more evenly and dry more slowly on the dampened surface.

Flowers Offer Interesting Problems

A still-life group composed of flowers will give a student a wide variety of color problems. In arranging the grouping, a background cloth of contrasting color to the most prominent color in the flowers will offer opportunity for an effective result. Other articles grouped with the flowers may be analogous to either the background cloth or the flowers. If a set of secondary complementary colors are introduced into the scheme, their contrasts should be kept subordinate to the main scheme, otherwise confusion will result.

When a student has spent some time experimenting with water-color, he will find less dificulty when he starts his studies with oil color.

The soft and atmospheric qualities of this drawing of a scene in an old
European town were obtained with soft pencil or Conté crayon by an artist
who specializes in architectural subjects.

The possibilities of fine line work and delicate detail in scratchboard are well illustrated by this example. It is the work of a student who consistently displays fine craftsmanship.

CHAPTER 8

Media and Methods of Working

Media, the plural of "medium," refers to the tools and materials used by an artist in the making of a drawing. Pencil, pen and ink, pastels, water-colors, and oils—all are media.

Each medium gives certain particular characteristics to a piece of work because of the nature of the medium and its handling. The first media we should consider are pencil, crayon, Conté, chalk or charcoal which produce a certain kind of drawing with a certain quality of line. Any of these media used with an illustration board having a rough surface or coarse texture will create a certain character in the work regardless of the artist making the drawing.

Thus we have the terms "a pencil technique," "a charcoal technique," or a "crayon technique," and, to all art-trained people these terms mean definite types of drawings because they know that certain kinds of media produce certain effects.

Technique and Stylization

Technique refers to the personal way the artist uses his media. It is a characteristic of a piece of work in addition to the nature of the media. With this difference varying among artists, there can be great latitude in the developing of a pencil technique or a charcoal technique—plenty of opportunity for individual expression.

In a similar way the medium of pen and ink produces many techniques. There are also artists who vary the pens they use so that some techniques show a loose quality, others a sketchy quality, and still others a precision quality. Of all media, pen and ink is the outstanding method for drawing in line. With few exceptions there are no instances where artists have endeavored to use the medium to create a "tonal" picture. The most successful examples in pen and ink are those where the major portion of the illustration is outlined with simple detail and dark accents are reserved for defining the center of interest. Too many accents will produce a spotty effect.

It is the same with painting, whether with opaque poster colors, transparent water colors or oils. Every medium, in addition to its own peculiar characteristics, challenges the artist to explore its possibilities for original use.

Developing Your Own Technique

Many beginners strive too early to attain the effects of a personal technique. Even before they have learned to draw they worry about their "individualistic expression." Patient and diligent practice to attain good draftsmanship and a sound foundation in design will prove the better course in the long run. It may take two or three years to develop a truly personal way of doing

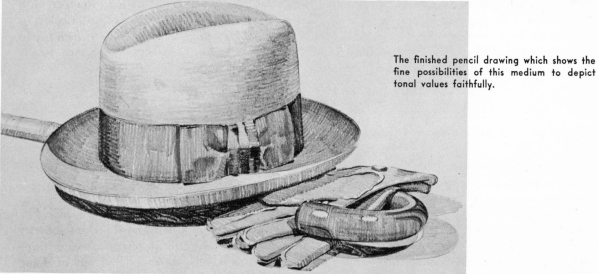

Five special drawings in five different te[chniques?] using pencil, pen and ink, and wa[ter]color wash with a pen and ink outline, h[ave] been made from the same photograph

Hat, gloves and cane are arranged to suggest articles suitable for the man of fashion. The crease in the hat is soft—right off the shelf, so to speak.

A pencil sketch is the first step toward developing a drawing regardless of the technique to be used.

The finished pencil drawing which shows the fine possibilities of this medium to depict tonal values faithfully.

ree Media

ent a comparison. In each drawing
oness is essential as this quality is reed in art work executed for merchandis-
in advertising mediums.

In pen stipple the general effect is one of
softness. The reduction here, as in all of
these examples, is from an original drawing
nine inches wide.

A pen technique which would be effective if
emphasis on texture were desired, or a novel
effect were important.

The technique which can be developed to
resemble a photograph most closely is water
color wash. A pen line outlines the forms
and preserves crisp edges in the reproduction.

These pencil sketches have crispness in some places, softness in others—charm throughout.

A finished pencil drawing showing delicacy of modelling obtainable by skillful handling of a soft lead pencil.

things and, should it take longer, the student need have no fear of his progress. It will stand a better chance of being a personal characteristic if it develops without haste. Too frequently a technique acquired quickly is a borrowed property having no lasting value to the student.

Any student has a natural tendency to admire the work of some professional artist. He may even try to imitate this man's work which will not be harmful if it is only for practice. But he cannot seriously intend to develop his own work into an imitation of that of someone else. It is a better practice to study the effects obtained by different artists whom a student may admire, and to draw from each some quality he would like to emulate in his own work. But as he develops slowly in his own particular manner, the student will find that he has picked up certain ways of doing things that cannot be accredited to any source. This will be real progress.

Popular Techniques

Certain techniques have greater popularity and use than others because of their practical factors. They are more easily adapted to merchandising problems or reproduce more clearly in size much smaller than the original. One of these popular methods is the combination of a pen and ink line with black water-color wash. This "technique" is used generally in newspaper advertising because it combines the definiteness of a pen line with the three-dimensional aspects of light and shade. Even in this method of working, variety exists. Personal characteristics appear from the kind of line the artist uses and manner in which the wash is applied.

Pen Drawing

Probably the chief reason for the popularity of pen drawing is the economy with which it can be reproduced and its adaptability to use on the printed page where it harmonizes with the type matter. The economy results from the method of engraving used to reproduce pen drawings. Pen drawing also offers the artist a wide opportunity to develop a personal technique. It can become as individualistic as one's handwriting.

Early practice should include the various kinds of line that can be made with a pen. The student should learn to draw long sweeping

114

A student in the Technical High School, Erie, Pa., made this masterful drawing with lithographic crayon. This medium produces textures rich and strong. (Courtesy of Scholastic Awards.)

strokes, short vigorous strokes, crisp dashes, delicate lines, and curved lines, either singly or in combination. The pen artist must also develop expertness in creating tones by drawing many single lines evenly spaced so that the tone appears of one value throughout. He must also acquire the skill to "cross-hatch" his lines, and to perfect other techniques for the representation of light and shade, shadows, and textures.

Ernest W. Watson, editor of *American Artist* magazine, says, "An artist reveals his strength or his weakness in a pen drawing. There is a merciless finality about a black line or spot which cannot hide under camouflage of color or diversion of tonal charm. The test of an ink drawing lies

The drawing below was made by a student of Central High School, Syracuse, N. Y. It was made with a soft pencil. (Courtesy of Scholastic Awards.)

Lithographic crayon used on a pebbled drawing surface called Ross Board has the effect of an actual lithograph. Ink, applied with a brush, accounts for the solid areas of black.

Portrait study in pencil by a student in Lincoln High School, Cleveland, O. Pencil is one of the basic techniques in art and should be a part of every artist's equipment. (Courtesy of Scholastic Awards.)

in what is left out, fully as much as in what is put in. A good ink drawing is a display of imagination, strong sense of design and technical resourcefulness."

Although there are many kinds of pens, the kind recommended for the student is a medium one, such as the Gillott 303 and 404, or, for bold drawings, fine-pointed writing pens. Draw on smooth, white paper or plate finish Bristol board, using a waterproof black ink. A drawing board, some thumbtacks, penholder, penwiper, pencils and erasers will complete the necessary equipment.

Before applying ink, sketch your subject lightly in pencil and determine the areas where the tones and accents will be placed. Keep your drawing confined to essentials; simplify your tonal scheme. Keep your drawing clean; particles of dirt or pieces of your eraser will be picked up by the pen point, and a defective line will result. Use the pen about as you would for writing but be ready to change from a "finger" stroke to one made by the wrist, as the occasion arises.

The charm of a pen drawing lies in the contrast between the bright areas of light and the sharp accents of shadow, as well as in the skill with which textures have been created with the pen.

A "spot" drawing in free pen technique by Miriam Bartlett, for use as a chapter heading. Size of original: seven inches wide. From "So You're Going to be an Artist," Watson-Guptill Publications.

Pure line in pencil should be practiced extensively. This is an excellent study by a student in Cass Technical High School, Detroit, Mich. (Courtesy of Scholastic Awards.)

A pencil drawing of period furniture. This is the work of a professional artist and represents the combination of subject and technique which developed into a specialty.

Shaded Effects by Stipple

A highly controllable pen technique is stipple work, in which the most elaborate and delicate range of tonal values may be rendered. The technique is simple and consists of making countless little pen dots, spaced with such regularity that they can produce an even value, or graded values. By controlling these gradations of dots, a modelled effect can be obtained.

In addition to producing any value desired, pen stipple work also gives a drawing an effect of soft texture, sometimes resembling that of a print from a drawing on lithographic stone. The effect is often used to suggest distant hills and mountains, and rough surfaces as stone or stucco walls. The more dots used, the darker the tone will be.

Shaded Effects by Spatter-work

This technique, largely described by its name, is used to add textured effects to a drawing. It can also be applied to painting, using color instead of ink. Although simple, the student will

need a little practice in order to gain the degree of control he will need for the technique's successful use.

For this work a toothbrush and a saucer, into which some ink is poured, will be necessary. If the entire area of the drawing is to receive a spatter treatment, dip the toothbrush into the ink so that the bristles are wet for an eighth-inch or so. Then, holding the brush horizontally with the bristles up; stroke the bristles toward yourself with a toothpick or matchstick, causing them to be released so that they cast tiny drops of ink on the drawing. The effect will be grainy, the drops differing in size, and the irregularity will be its chief characteristic.

Another method is to rub the toothbrush, held with the bristles downward, over a piece of wire screen a couple of inches above the drawing.

If only portions of the drawing are to be treated with spatter-work, the other portions will have to be protected by a mask. This protection may be provided in many ways. If the areas to be spattered are simple in shape, paper strips can be cut to fit along the edge of the area to be treated. Some artists "paint" the protected area with rubber cement, which dries and

The technique in this illustration, in its directness and freedom, is one of the most desirable in pen drawing. The original drawing has a width of seven inches.

To show the quality and character of the pen line, a portion of the drawing above is reproduced here the actual size of the original.

forms a film to be removed after the technique has been applied. Drawings may be covered by a frisket paper, which is like a thin onion skin having one side treated with an adhesive. This paper is spread over the drawing and, with a sharp knife point, the portions covering the area to be treated are cut away and stripped off. When the spraying is finished the frisket can be removed.

Line and Wash Drawings

One of the popular techniques used for merchandise drawings is the pen line supplemented by simple black and gray water-color washes. The line is drawn for defining contours only, with no pen shading.

The drawing is then given a few transparent washes. Three tones usually suffice—a light tone, a dark tone, and one about half way between in tonal intensity. Use charcoal gray water-color instead of ivory black or lamp black, and dilute with water to create the varied tones.

Because of the use of water color, the Bristol board chosen for this work should have what is called a "kid" finish. It is not too rough for pen work but will absorb the dampness of the water color more evenly than a board with a smooth surface.

Do not cover all surfaces with tone. Remember that the area left white will serve as one stage in your tonal scheme and will give brightness to the drawing. The student should also be aware of the tendency of photo-engraving to reduce the tonal contrasts in the original drawing and, to offset this, the areas of tone should be definitely marked. Don't paint with too dark a range of tones; the engraving will print a little darker than you expect.

A large majority of furniture illustrations and fashion work are executed in this technique. Professionals frequently refer to it as the "bread and butter" method because of its general acceptance as practical merchandising art work.

Scratch-board Work

This highly specialized technique reminds one of the old-fashioned woodcut. The method is the reverse of the usual way of making drawings: whites are cut from a black surface instead of blacks being built up on a white surface. A

Pen drawing by a famous marine painter reproduced actual size. This sketch, drawn without
any pencil outline, was a composition the artist
developed into a large oil painting.

specially prepared board, coated with chalk, is
available for this kind of work.

The area of the board, where the drawing is to
be made, is coated with black India ink, applied
with either a brush or a spray. The process is
then to scrape off the ink with a fine, sharp-
pointed tool that will create a white line. The
ink comes off with the chalk.

Tools may be as fine as a needle, mounted in
a holder, or may be broad as a pen-knife. En-
gravers' tools are suitable. Once the chalk has
been removed from the board, the board cannot
be re-inked for a second attempt. The directness
of the medium is part of its fascination.

Scratch-board lines may be bold or delicate,
as shown in the accompanying illustrations and,
when reproduced, are difficult to distinguish
from lines cut in wood in the old technique of
the woodcut and the wood engraving. The similarity of the tools and the method of working
gives this technique much of the character of the
fine book illustrations created by our wood en-
gravers almost a century ago.

Free pen sketch of an imaginary garden in
Florida designed in the Italian manner. The
values are handled interestingly and the
vignette shape of the whole drawing is well
conceived.

119

There are many techniques suitable for pen drawings of architectural perspectives. This example is definitely exact in its rendering of details. A few artists have specialized successfully in this type of work.

Dry-brush Work

Another technique used, sometimes alone and sometimes in combination with transparent or opaque paint techniques, is the dry-brush. It is not an easy technique to control and therefore

Bold pen technique in black and white, with no intermediate tones and no cross-hatching. Made with a broad stub pen. Drawn by W. P. Spratling for "Old Plantation Houses in Louisiana," William Helburn, publisher.

requires considerable practice. The method consists of a brush moistened with black paint or ink, then dabbed on a piece of blotting paper or a rag to remove surplus moisture, leaving the hairs spread in a semi-dry condition but containing sufficient black paint or ink to produce a streaked line on the drawing paper. The rough texture of the line is the characteristic of the technique. The effects produced are sketchy and suggest spontaneity.

The rougher the paper used the more effective the dry-brush is, and the easier it is to do. In studying this medium, give attention to the work of Chinese and Japanese artists, who have been masters of brush and ink work for centuries.

Air-brush Work

Although there may be little practical value in a discussion of this method of working unless you should happen to possess an air-brush and a compressor, some knowledge of the subject may be helpful. The air-brush is used chiefly in art departments of advertising agencies and art studios, and the student who should happen to work for such organizations will find someone on hand to show him how to use it.

By means of the air-brush it is possible for the artist operating it to produce absolutely even tones, perfectly smooth gradations from one tone

Drawing with Pen and Ink

Pen drawing by a European in bold and dramatic technique. In addition to its strong composition, this drawing gives a fine rendering of a dark, rainy and windy day.

to another, or a soft gradation from the general tone of a painting to white paper without any visible edge appearing where the color or tone stops.

The air-brush provides the technique for making the soft "vignetted" edge of a photograph. A vignette is a picture in which the outer edges imperceptibly fade away. The treatment helps focus the attention of the observer on the portion of the photograph the artist intends to feature.

There are special "re-touch" colors, prepared in a range of photographic values. The difference between these colors and other grays mixed from black water-color and white paint is that a certain amount of yellow ochre has been added to give the tones more photographic quality. Yellows photograph gray in a darker value than

they appear in their full color intensity.

The air-brush works much like a perfume atomizer or an automobile carburetor. It has a nozzle with a delicate adjustment through which a mixture of paint flows from a small cup at the side of the nozzle. A tube leads from the air-brush to a tank of compressed air. The air pressure is controlled by a trigger valve on the top of the nozzle and, as the airbrush is held in the hand much like a pencil or pen, the forefinger can operate the trigger valve emitting a fine spray of color on the drawing or photograph.

The nozzles vary in degree of fineness so as to be suitable for different kinds of work, and the delicate adjustment of the trigger valve, which controls the air pressure, enables an experienced operator to achieve accurate and subtle results.

While the air-brush is essentially a mechanical device, in the hands of an artist it can produce work which merits regard as art. Many art-minded young men, whose aptitudes tend toward mechanical sensitivity, have become successful specialists in airbrush work.

Stylization Explained

Stylization is individual interpretation of a subject. It differs from technique much as the eye differs from the hand. Stylization is the way an artist sees his subject, how he conceives to render it; technique is his method for rendering it.

Any modification of the realistic appearance of a subject can be considered as an interpretation, differing with each artist. It becomes an artist's way of approaching the problem, and he acquires a habit of conceiving his interpretations in a similar way. He regards them in severe contrast of elements, or perhaps in the reverse. He sees the subject in a fanciful way and renders it in a higher tonal or chromatic key. There is no cleverness attempted in the development of style; cleverness is reserved for technique. Style must be developed out of the deepest integrity and seriousness of the artist, even if this style should be his way of presenting humor. In the field of caricature, which is a form of stylization, the drawings of Gluyas Williams, Peter Arno, and Charles Addams are notable.

Both stylization and technique are later products of a student's growth in art, and are not to be hurried or expected of a student in his early stages of training. To stay "on the beam" concentrate your first efforts on draftsmanship and design.

Specialization

In commercial work, artists are inclined to specialize, partly from a particular interest in one field of work over another, and partly because of an aptitude that they have developed for which they have gained some reputation. It is pretty difficult to be perfect, or considered so, in very many fields of art. Constant practice in one field will naturally lead to an accumulation of information about a subject that an artist cannot get in any other way. He can be said to

Pen line technique suitable to withstand great reduction. A portion of the drawing at original size is shown with reproduction above.

In pen and ink drawing for reproduction it is vital for the artist to know how the drawing will stand reduction without becoming weak and "brittle."

This pen drawing is shown the actual size of the original. It was made by the artist for reduction to one inch in height, as reproduced at the left.

"major" in his subject. His interest will carry him into ramifications and research in the subject that will give his work outstanding value.

Some artists have been called on for advertising drawings of furniture because of the authenticity of their work. They know furniture—how it is made, the history of its development and the difference in the graining of woods.

Fashion is a definite specialty for artists who have, or are able to develop, a keen sense of styling in men's and women's clothes. The power of line, of silhouette, to enhance the grace of the female figure, for instance, is a study in itself. Specialists in animal drawing or architecture attain their proficiency from the intense concentration of their effort on all phases of their respective subjects. Let your interest guide you as you approach specialization. Refrain from selecting your field of work on any basis other than a desire so strong that it will drive you to explore every avenue available wherein you suspect some information on the subject may be found.

Use of Reference Material

Some mention was made of the value of a "scrap file" in Chapter I, and it may be worthwhile to elaborate on the theme at this time. Whenever you are confronted with a job that requires any kind of visual knowledge you lack, do not try to bluff it through. Originality does not mean that you must supply details of a drawing by guess-work, especially when those details are strictly factual things. Objects like nautical gear, ships, a log cabin, a scene in Algiers, a spinning wheel, a blacksmith's anvil, or historic

Decorative fine line pen technique is suitable for "spot" illustrations or for children's books. This example by an art student combines technique with stylization.

Pen illustrations by Miriam Bartlett for a text-book on furniture styles. These drawings combine the boldness necessary for reduction in size and for printing on rough paper with the necessary accuracy of historic detail.

Drawing shown at top of page was made nine and a half inches wide for reproduction. Quality of pen line used is seen in this actual size portion. These drawings were made for use in newspapers.

costume should be drawn accurately and from the best reference material you can find.

Nobody expects an artist, even an experienced one, to have a mind full of images of all kinds of material. There are libraries for this. Almost everything may be found in books, if you look for it. Even the dictionary gives you accurate illustrations of things you need to know about, and the encyclopedia gives you more. If you need to draw something you know exists, look it up. Don't take it for granted that every observer of your drawing will be as uninformed.

There is probably no artist today who is better known or more widely admired by his fellow artists as well as the public than Norman Rockwell. One of the chief characteristics of his work is his fidelity in the accurate portrayal of simple details. His paintings are filled with objects everybody recognizes as authentic. The public appreciates the rightness of every detail he puts into his pictures.

Aside from the material you may collect in books, the best source for reference is in the actual things about you, if you will look for them and sketch them. Sketches of details are invaluable because you get to know things better when you draw them. It is like analyzing them and memorizing them, all in the same operation.

The difference between the use of reference material and copying the work of another artist should be understood. It rests in the design and composition of a picture. The distinction should be obvious. What is creative in another piece of art should be avoided by any student who refers to that example for information. This also applies to the copying of figures where the pose and general appearance have a distinctive

A precision pen drawing by Harry G. Kitson. All the modelling of figure and drapery was done without the use of cross-hatched lines—a peculiarity of Mr. Kitson's remarkable technique.

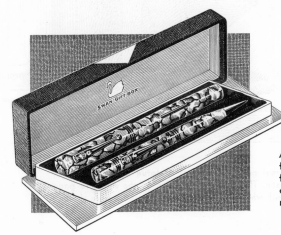

A "technical" pen drawing of a pencil and fountain pen in a gift box. This technique, for merchandising purposes, is developed only by specialists like Mr. Kitson, who also made this drawing.

An exceptionally fine formal pen rendering of a statue by Michelangelo, the work of Harry G. Kitson. The smaller illustration on the opposite page shows the care and skill with which the outline was prepared before shading was added.

From a photograph of Mr. Kitson's outline drawing of the Michelangelo figure shown on facing page. It has all the quality of an old steel engraving. Despite the variety of tone achieved in the finished work, the lines are sufficiently separated to avoid the ink filling in between and destroying the effect.

NIL DESPERANDUM

Example of formal pen technique by O. W. Jaquish. This drawing of an heraldic lion was made five and a quarter inches wide and was kept open to allow a great reduction. Small reproduction at left shows to what degree the work was successfully executed.

quality in the work of another. Do not depend on the successful arrangement of a grouping in some other picture as a basis for the solution of your problem. It is more than a matter of personal ethics. It is poor judgment and bad business. Too frequently the lazy-minded artist will suffer loss of a promising future because he copied something he did not think the public would recognize as the work of another.

A sound method of work will help to prevent this situation. Think out your own arrangement. Make small sketches or studies for the essential elements in a rough way. After you decide the design of your drawing or painting, then seek the information you will need to develop your design. It is in your conception—your design— that you will express your originality.

Design and pen drawing of an old Colonial sign board by a student of lettering. Much imagination and skill are evidenced by the antique effect achieved entirely by pen technique. The original drawing is 10 inches wide, the open line treatment reproducing without loss of clarity.

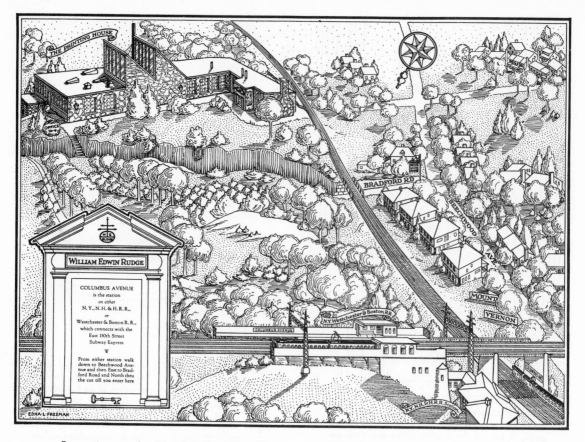

Decorative pen drawing of a perspective "location map" for the former W. E. Rudge printing plant. The artist, Edna L. Freeman, is also a career typographer.

Decorative pen drawing by Will Bradley. This kind of technique is eminently suitable for book illustration.

A decorative pen drawing based on the fantasy of a fairy tale. This type of work frequently departs from realism.

.FIREPLACE SIDE OF INN SITTING ROOM.

- Full Size of Inn -

Two brush drawings in India ink and wash for movie sets. They are rough ideas sketched by W. Cameron Menzies, Hollywood, for later development.

Drawing with Brush and Ink

Six examples of effects to be obtained by the dry-brush technique. The success of this technique lies in the degree of dryness of the brush when being used. The separated hairs take on a character of their own, and the variety of the pattern they produce adds interest to the effect. To the right, an unfinished sketch by a student which shows the technique in a heavy treatment.

Brush drawing in India ink. This technique is suited to modern book illustration and to decorative "spot" drawings for magazines.

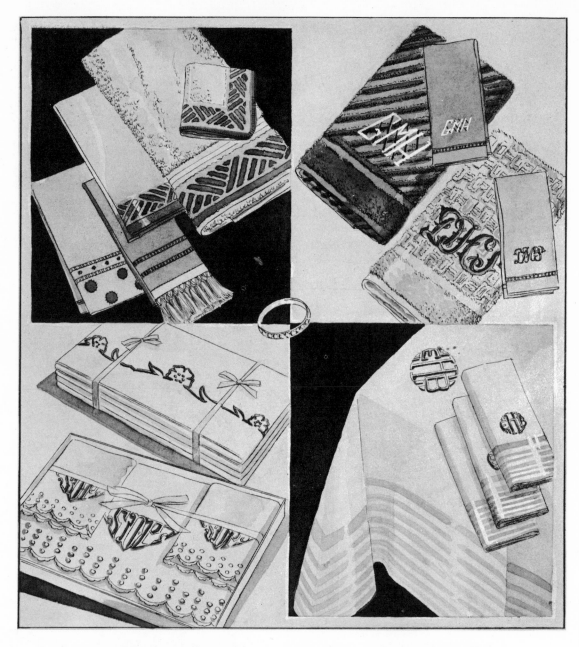

Line and wash merchandise drawing for newspaper reproduction. In this type of work, fidelity in illustrating the merchandise is of extreme importance as well as the reproductive qualities of the art work. The technique has proved successful because it shows the customer all he or she needs to know about an article being advertised.

Drawing with
Pen and Ink and Wash

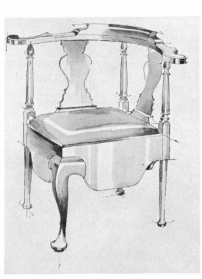

Furniture illustration in pen and ink and water color wash by Miriam Bartlett. An unusual feature of this professional's work is her frequent combination of ruled lines with those drawn freehand. This drawing was made for newspaper use.

Below, three drawings in line and wash by students. The one to the right, a little too dark for newspaper use, would do nicely for magazine illustration. The center sketch would appear to better advantage in newsprint. The chair to the left has been drawn in a highly professional manner.

FROM THE BOOKS OF
ELSIE KRAUSE

*Stipple Drawing
with Pen and Ink*

*combines delicacy with
wide range of tonal values*

Book-plate designed by a student. The design combines the line, solid, and tones produced by the stipple to achieve a very interesting effect. This technique is one of the easier methods of working because a student can proceed carefully toward the effect desired. Other techniques requiring dash and spontaneity for their quality demand much more practice.

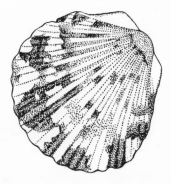

A professional illustration of pen stipple that demonstrates the extreme delicacy obtainable. Suitability to subject is also apparent in the use of this technique to portray shell forms.

THE CHRISTMAS
BOOK BVYER
1898

CHARLES SCRIBNER'S SONS
NEW YORK

An early cover design by Maxfield Parrish, showing extreme finesse of technique obtainable by means of the pen stipple. The tiny dots are controlled to create gradations of tone.

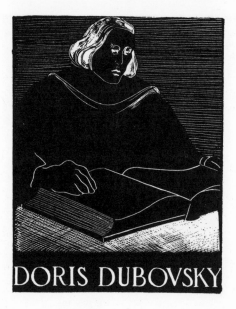

DORIS DUBOVSKY

Scratchboard Drawings

Scratchboard drawings are made by creating white areas in black backgrounds. A specially prepared drawing board is used on which there has been placed a coating of chalk. When ink is brushed over the board to make a solid background, a sharp instrument, like a knife blade, can remove the ink and chalk, leaving a white line. At left, a bookplate has been executed by a student in scratchboard. White accents in large black areas are characteristics in this manner of working.

To right, an actual size reproduction of a portion of the scratchboard drawing shown on opposite page. Note particularly the effective treatment of the trees.

1. Black is brushed on the board.

2. The whites are scratched with the X-ACTO knife.

3. Strokes can be varied in width by changing the knife position.

An excellent illustration of the strong decorative qualities of scratchboard technique. The radiation of light rays in the background create a dramatic effect. At left, three examples of the technique are explained.

The air brush, once regarded as a technical and mechanical aid, has been utilized by artists who have skilled themselves in its use and so broadened their range for effects. This is by Ben J. Harris.

Air Brush Work and Spatter Effects

This drawing was made by the spatter technique, the face and hands protected by a frisket paper during the time the background was made. Reproduced through the courtesy of X-acto—"12 Technics."

In spatter work, or with the air brush, the portions of the drawing which are not to be treated must be protected. This is done with frisket paper, a thin, translucent sheet having a coating of rubber cement on one side and a moisture repellent on the other. The paper can be laid over the drawing with rubber cement face down and the portion covering the parts of the drawing to be treated cut away with the aid of a very sharp, razor-edged blade. The rubber cement will hold the covering in position as long as desired, then removed leaving the protected parts free of the air brush or spatter treatment.

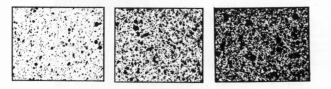

Three specimens of spatter work from Higgins "Techniques." Review the text on page 117 for a full explanation of this method of working.

This Japanese print of a great wave is as fine
an example of stylization as could be found anywhere. Method of depicting foam is individualistic, and the power of the wave is highly dramatized.

Stylization

Stylization in masterful line
technique of remarkable delicacy and subtleness, by Robert
Leonard. There is swank in this
drawing. The pose of the hands
shows gentility, the jewelry,
richness. Shading was kept to
a minimum.

137

This set of six "spot" drawings, made by a senior art school student, capture the characteristics of the various musicians.

Stylization is doing the usual thing unusually different. It sacrifices nothing needed to tell the story but introduces the personality of the artist in even the smallest of drawings and regardless of their intended use.

A highly stylized drawing which makes the most of a decorative line against areas of solid black.

Costume figure by an art school student achieved by formal pen line with light transparent washes.

A bold and decorative example of stylization by an art school student. In stylizing, an artist frequently departs from a realistic attempt, yet he may retain all the essentials of the subject in form and action.

Two "spot" drawings of classic motif made by a senior art school student are shown at left. They illustrate how the conception of a drawing can be styled as well as the manner of working. The palm tree, above, is also by an art school student. The original, painted in green and black, could be adaptable for use in fabric or wall paper design.

THE ILLUSTRATION above is a reproduction of a drawing made at Coral Gables by the famous artist Vernon Howe Bailey. It was made with Wolff pencil, a medium which gives a crayon effect having deep values of dark or, when drawn with lightly on a rough Bristol board or paper, gives a soft and delicate line. The rough texture of the lines results from the roughness of the paper. This quality cannot be obtained on a smooth surfaced paper.

When you make a drawing like this, whether from nature or from a photograph, it is best to emphasize the important features and put in only as much detail as is needed. Consider, for instance, the Spanish tile roof in this drawing. Mr. Bailey knew he did not have to draw every tile in order to make his drawing say that the building had a tile roof.

The character of the palm trees was realized to be of particular importance to give the tropical atmosphere, so the palm trees were given effective attention.

On the opposite page is a photograph of one of the gateways in Coral Gables. Using a mat finish Bristol board and either a Wolff pencil or a very soft drawing pencil, make a study from the photograph in the same technique as the drawing just discussed. You might also try a similar drawing using the smaller subject. In this you have a picturesque series of Spanish tile roofs with dark planting at the base of the wall and characteristic palm trees. An artist would, of course, omit the hurricane braces on the trees, since these are not at all attractive. This chance to eliminate detrimental details is an advantage the artist has over the photographer.

140

Two exercises for which a Wolff pencil or crayon is recommended.

For further exercises thumb through travel magazines such as Holiday or National Geographic. You will find plenty of subjects to intrigue you.

The farm buildings shown in a photograph with light and shade clearly defined.

The first step. Block the subject out roughly in line, checking proportions and the angles at which the lines intersect one another.

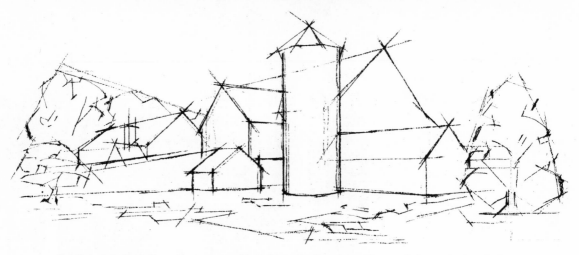

Flat water color washes are applied. Note which is the darkest, and those tones which are relatively lighter.

In this drawing, the outlines of the buildings were drawn in a single pen and ink line before the washes were added.

This drawing was made completely in pen and ink. Note the change of direction of certain lines in shadow areas.

ON THESE two pages are four drawings made from a photograph of a group of farm buildings which happens to present an interesting composition of masses, of angles, and of light and shade.

The first drawing, on the facing page, shows you how you should sketch in the main essentials, with particular attention to proportions, heights, and directions of angles. The second drawing, below the first, is carried out entirely in washes, with no attempt to show details. This is a value study, made only to isolate and thus emphasize the main masses. This value study gives quite a good impression of what the group looks like.

However, if you were making an actual drawing of this subject, you might do it in either one of the two techniques illustrated above on this page. The first of these is in line and wash, the wash giving the values and the line indicating the detail. You will note that not much detail is needed. The second drawing is entirely in pen and ink, the handling taking care of both values and detail. Compare both of these drawings closely with the photograph and note how the all-over tonal effect of the photograph has been simplified to give contrast and clarity.

As a lesson, select a photograph of a building. Draw it carefully; then experiment in values and in line and wash, and in pen renderings. When you are beginning, always choose a photograph in which the detail is clear.

143

slowly drawn

quickly drawn

varied pressure

irregular lines

Practice the above eight specimens of pen lines.

These pen line specimens are
reproduced from "Techniques,"
published by the Higgins Ink
Company. They are the basic
strokes of every proficient pen
draftsman.

A photograph of an old cabin in West Virginia.
It offers fine possibilities for rendering in pen
and ink. Sketch it lightly in pencil first, then
simplify its tone areas. Reserve the accent for
some one place. Be careful you do not scatter
accents too profusely.

An Exercise in Pen Rendering

Although pen and ink is essentially a line medium, tones can
be created so that the area
seems of indefinite breadth.
Some pen draftsmen have accomplished the tonal qualities
of a painting.

Above is a suggested treatment for the pen rendering. Observe that the accents were confined to the area near the door. Note the effect of soft shade on the side of the building, and the introduction of a couple of figures to lend additional interest. To the left is a very effective pen drawing made by a young artist who has since become prominent. Notice the contrasting values in the dark trees and sun-lit building beyond, also the transparent quality of the shadow as it falls across the path. The palm leaves have been handled with excellent boldness and simplicity.

Using the photograph of the gate, pictured above, try to render it in the manner of the sketch on page 144.

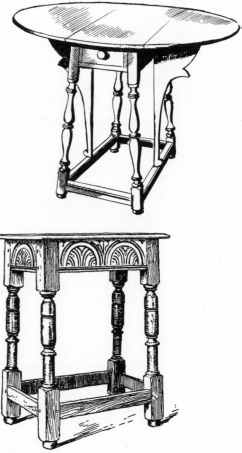

At the top of this page is a fine English pen drawing of an old doorway. Beside it is a photograph of a similar door. As a lesson, make a pen drawing from the photograph, in the same technique as the example. Above: a manufacturer's photograph of a replica of an old English (Jacobean) stool. To the right are drawings of a similar stool, in a fine line technique, and a butterfly table in a bolder technique. The shadows under the leaves were done in dry-brush technique. As a lesson, make two drawings from the photograph—one in fine line and the other in the bolder manner. Give attention to the perspective and the turnings of the legs.

Here is a photograph of a replica of an old Colonial interior, by a Philadelphia architect.

Sydney R. Jones '14

A more ambitious exercise. This drawing is by the great English pen artist, Sydney R. Jones. Note particularly how every detail and object in the old interior stands out, yet how harmonious is the drawing as a whole.

As a lesson, make a careful drawing from the photograph a little more than twice the size of the reproduction, and draw it in the style of the Sydney Jones rendering.

An artist making a pen drawing of such an interior as this would use every device of pen technique to give it an antique atmosphere. He would experiment until he worked out a pen technique that would suggest the roughness of the hand-hewn beams. His drawing would not look any more like a photograph than does the masterful pen drawing by Mr. Jones.

At the top are a pencil drawing and a pen and wash rendering of a Windsor chair, both by a capable student. Observe that the pencil line must be accurate before the inking begins. The line and wash drawing was made on matt finish bristol board, the washes with charcoal gray water color. As a lesson, make a drawing of the Windsor armchair shown in the photograph, then render it twice—once in the line and wash technique and once in the simple pen style shown immediately above. (Illustrations by courtesy of Scholastic Awards.)

A Lesson in Techniques

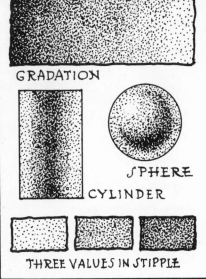

GRADATION

CYLINDER

SPHERE

THREE VALUES IN STIPPLE

Above is a landscape drawn in outline with a fine pen. If you were planning to render it with water color washes, you would use a matt finish bristol board. In the upper right, the same landscape in outline has been rendered with water color tints for values. Below these are two renderings of the landscape, the one on the left drawn with a broad pointed stub pen, the other, a combination of a bold brush drawing with the lighter values made by spatter work. These four illustrations are selected from ten different renderings of the same subject reproduced by courtesy of Higgins Ink Company from "Techniques." At right, are a few specimens of stipple, which is the most easily controllable of all pen techniques. Reproductions are actual size of original stipple work. By increasing the density of the dots you can create any value you wish.

The Legend of Ste.
Genevieve
by
Puvis de Chavannes
(center panel)

Legend of Ste. Genevieve
At right: the panels comprise
a painting 52¾ by 32⅛ inches.
Puvis de Chavannes (1824-
1898) is particularly famous
for the carefully planned pattern of his paintings, many of
which are murals. His outstanding masterpiece is The Sacred
Grove in the Sorbonne, Paris.
He was a master of composition. Above: the center panel.
(Courtesy of The Art Institute
of Chicago.)

An outstanding portrait study by a sculpture student in the School of Industrial Art, New York. (Courtesy of Scholastic Awards.)

CHAPTER 9

The Fine Arts for Self-Expression

Stepping away for a while from the practical or commercial aspects of an art career, let us search for the artist within us which, after all, is the inspiration for our progress, and by whose stature our success will be determined. Although this book is intended to discuss the art of painting and its allied forms—drawing, designing, print-making—we will have to delve deeper into our background, both the individual and the race, to find the element of creative impulse that is the soul of the artist.

In our infancy we did not draw forms with crayons on paper; we played with solid objects. We did not interpret three-dimensional objects into two-dimensional presentations. This came much later. We piled block on block. We built and, when a substance was placed within our reach pliable enough to respond to our impression, we moulded.

It is interesting that, to a great degree, the development of a human individual mirrors the history of the development of the whole human race. The earliest evidences of human creative endeavor are expressed in solid form, and were extended to surface modelling at a later date. Writers of cultural history, and art critics in general agree that there were three distinct culture-zones—a Northern, a Southwestern, and an Eastern—which have been indicated by nature and established by archaeological discoveries. These culture-zones met at the Mediterranean and

created a mixed culture. The North produced an abstract, geometrical style of art, the South developed naturalism. The East furnished an intellectualism which blended the mythological, religious and philosophical ideas into man's development. As we respond to the urge to create, we should not be surprised to find this mixture of early cultures influencing our conception of form.

Some knowledge of and experience in the spatial arts are essential to the development of every artist. To understand and to create substance in the round is, naturally, a step in advance of its representation in the flat. Let us consider the value of architecture and sculpture for the self-trained artist.

Architectural Form

The study of architecture today is becoming more and more dominated by the science of engineering. Much of its cultural inheritance has been ignored. New forms, inspired by utilitarian considerations, have been accepted as industrial design. Economics seems to have dislodged Beauty as the modern architect's muse. The quantitative standard appears triumphant over the qualitative. As Ruskin puts it: Bedevilled by machinery, the smoke of many chimneys clouds not only our physical, but our metaphysical sky.

Illustrating the characteristic incised carving of ancient Egypt. Note outline is cut straight and the image is rounded.

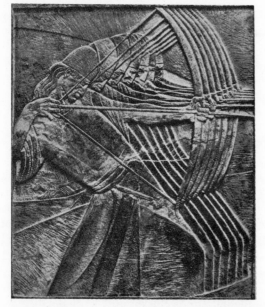

"Archers," a striking example of bas-relief carving in wood, by the famous sculptor Mestrovic.

Familiarity with the great architectural forms of the past can be a liberal education for an artist regardless of the field in which he intends to practice. Its rich material lies in a study of the purpose for which its outstanding monuments were designed. Cultural springs refreshed the imagination and gave vitality to the decorative forms of the art. Ornament, like a dead language, speaks to us of a race of men who, struggling as we struggle to express ideas, took the fundamental concepts of their time and left for us a record of their fears, their hopes, and their aspirations.

Architectural form has been an expression of man's sense of organization and his desire for orderliness. According to the Roman architect Vitruvius, "Architecture depends on order, and . . . order gives due measure to the members of a work considered separately, and symmetrical agreement to the proportions of the whole." Most formal design has an architectural basis. Architectural design, regardless of period, has expressed the sound structural principles that make the building the essence of a timeless idea.

From the days of the palaeolithic nomads, there have been three ideas which have had a profound influence on the development of architecture. First an early conception of the soul of the departed presupposed a continuance of the spirit in a subterranean home. This idea led to tomb-building. Next, the dwelling place for the living spirit was developed with practical considerations. The third idea was a temple, or a dwelling place for the Great Spirit. These three fields of architecture are now called religious, social, and personal. Their respective histories are a chronicle of human achievement. Their forms are a language as extensive as the world is wide, as old as civilization.

Though you have no intention of studying for the practice of architecture, you should become familiar with architectural forms and ornament so as to express correctly the motifs you adapt from this rich source of material.

Sculptured Form

Like architecture, the study of sculptured form offers the student the fullest scope for creative effort but, where architecture formalizes an abstract idea, sculpture personalizes it. The design of a building may express the purpose for which

152

it is built, in fact, it should; the sculptured form can express thought. An artist can convey through modelling ideas, specific reflections, and emotion in a more direct manner than through structural forms.

Sculpture is a profession which can be practiced best through apprenticeship with an outstanding sculptor. Only a few art schools are fortunate enough to have the complete equipment, space and instructors available for students. However, the problems of modelling can be attempted in small scale, and the student can profit by his own experiments. The creation of small sculpture is good design study of three-dimensional forms, and for the understanding of form itself.

Models for book-ends, lamp-bases, ash-trays, paper-weights, and ink-well frames might be offered to concerns which are in the business of manufacturing pottery, bronze, or other similar products. Skilled modellers are in demand for the making of dioramas, the three-dimensional models now popular for advertisements and for exhibit displays. Aside from the practical uses where modelling might be applied for profit with a minimum of training and experience, the greatest value spent in its study will be the knowledge acquired of planes and the light they reflect, and

A bas-relief plaque, in the style of the Italian Renaissance, as a decorative incident. Much early work of this kind was gilded and poly-chromed.

the depth and solidity of mass.

The relationship between modelling and the two-dimensional phases of art, such as illustration and portraiture may be readily recognized. Were a portrait painter to study the planes of his model's face and head in a life-size model, he would gain much knowledge of his subject, far more than he might through quick observation.

An interesting incident illustrates this fact. A blind war veteran was modelling a portrait head of his child in clay, substituting touch for sight. It challenges the imagination to think of this blind sculptor obtaining a "visualization" of a human likeness through his sensitive fingers and reproducing this likeness in clay.

Similarly, modelling can help determine the best composition for an illustration. The setting might be roughly constructed of cardboard, at a scale of one inch equalling one foot, and roughly modelled figures could be made and posed in the set in varied groupings until the most satisfactory arrangement was achieved.

Materials Available for Modelling

For the beginner, a suitable material is plasticine which retains its pliable state for considerable time, allowing the student ample opportunity to experiment before the material hardens. Many industrial designers use this

Stylized study of a cat, by a student of Columbia University's School of Art. Modern sculpture tends to simplify form, even to the degree of ignoring literal form.

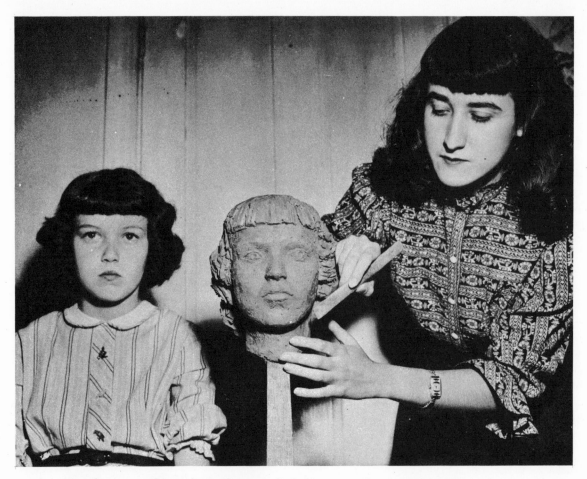

Less than a year after graduation from art school, this young sculptress is seen working on a portrait of a junior neighbor. (Courtesy of the Evening Bulletin, Providence, R. I.)

modelling substance for early studies of new products. This material is soft and needs a framework to support any members of a design requiring a degree of rigidity. A heavy wire, bent to shape the form on which the object is to be built, is fastened to a board. This form is called an "armature" and serves as a skeleton around which you model your plasticine or clay. If the statute is to be a human figure, the armature should consist of a center "spine" with other heavy members fastened to the spine to serve as reinforcement for arms and legs. The armature should be bent into a pose as near as possible to the finished action you have in mind for the figure.

Reaching far back into the past, a fascinating material for small sculpture is now available for professional or amateur, thanks to modern methods of promotion and distribution.

This material, geologically known as Steatite and now popularly known as Sculpstone, appears as a carving medium in ancient Sanskrit and holy Hindu texts. "In parts of India it is called image stone," according to a report, "which indicates its early use for carvings for worship. Centuries ago the clever Chinese were the first to discover its beauty and workability. . . . Egyptian excavations have revealed beautiful carvings in the form of jewelry, scarabs and other precious objects. Travelling through the homelands of ancient civilizations—Egypt, China, India, Mycenae, Babylon, Chaldea, Greece and Rome—the archaeologist meets Steatite in the shape of idols, temple ornaments, household equipment and ceremonial tools and vessels. Though it is easily carved it is not attacked by acids or injuriously affected by normal heat."

No special tools are needed, and the material may be filed, drilled, planed, sand-papered, smoothed and polished with fine steel wool; it can be turned on a lathe to form vases and jars, and is also easily carved with power tools. Polishing with oil or wax brings out the interesting

154

quality of the stone itself. Such treatment also aids the presentation of sculptured pieces generally.

For purposes of identification the distributors have assigned to different varieties names highly appropriate to the exotic character and natural colorings of the material itself. These are: Jade, a translucent green; Luxor, a transparent light jade green; Yukon, an ebony black stone; Helena, partly translucent deep green and black; Madras, various shades of green; Himalaya, cream-colored with various tones; Hindustan, light buff with varying blue-green colors; Shangri-la, off-white with fern patterns (used for jewelry); Grey Congo, a slate-gray stone; and Claire-Monte, green translucent with ornamental textures.

Interesting instructional folders illustrate many things not shown among the illustrations on these pages, as, for instance, a set of chess men, a variety of turned vases, ash trays, paper weights, and other unique bits of sculpture.

Incised Carving

This term refers to carving no part of which rises above the surface of the stone. It is the technique used for cutting letters into the faces of monuments. It is also practiced in linoleum which may be carved for decorative panels, lacquered in colors.

The design, inscription or whatever is cut, is first drawn or painted on the stone, then cut in outline. The ancient Egyptians were skilled at this kind of carving, and gave it added character by rounding the contours of the figures, leaving the outer edge of the incision cut straight down, which cast effective shadows.

This treatment is the basis for relief carving (called bas-relief) in which the design appears slightly raised above the surface of the stone, as a result of cutting away the normal surface. As in the case of any carved work, the effect of finished low relief carving in stone can be studied in plasticine, a method used by professional sculptors.

On an accompanying page this method is illustrated by a photograph of four relief models in plasticine made by lettering students who had been working on drawn studies of Mediaeval letter forms. The Mediaeval letter, even more than some other letter forms, has a definite struc-

Expressive sculpture: "Sea Rider," an imaginative study of forms in action, modelled by W. D. Paddock.

A finished model for a wall fountain figure, also by W. D. Paddock.

155

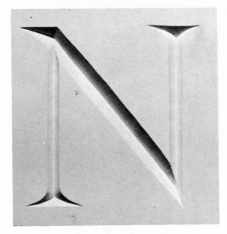

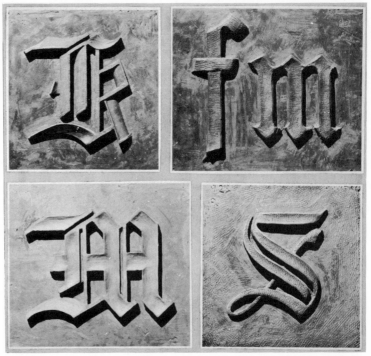

Above: an incised Roman letter, modelled by a student. Sculpture is a good way of studying form. At right: plasticene studies of Mediaeval letters, modelled six inches high, designed for carving in wood, made by lettering students in an art school.

ture, which a student only partly realizes when he draws it. Modelling aided the students to acquire a knowledge beyond anything their drawings had given them.

Wood Sculpture

This kind of work may be practiced by anyone who has manual skill in the old Yankee craft of whittling, aided by woodcarving tools. The Swiss have always been expert at this, making thousands of little wooden figures and toys for the export trade. The French Canadian in the province of Quebec carves and paints wooden figures, using native characters for models.

The easiest wood to carve is balsa wood which may be obtained in fairly large-sized blocks. If this is not obtainable, clear white pine makes a

Wood sculpture, long associated with native and peasant art all over the world, is becoming a widespread hobby with many interested amateurs. These little wooden figures, painted in natural colors, are by "habitant" carvers in Quebec province.

good substitute. Skilled carvers produce beautiful pieces of wood sculpture from hard woods like mahogany, oak and maple. Hardwood figures should be finished with wax and stain, not painted, because the grain of the wood adds much to the beauty of the work.

Wood Carving

Wood carving, either incised or in relief, is an art not too difficult for a student to acquire. It was used in earlier times to carve house names on signs, or to inscribe a motto or crest on a panel. Perhaps the outstanding exponent of the art was Grinling Gibbons who, with a large school of students, carved many overmantels, organ cases, and the reredos and altar rail for many a church in London during the latter part of the 17th century and the early part of the 18th century.

Incised letters in wood, carved with a simple set of wood-carving tools, are effective when color is rubbed into the letters, or if treated with gold-leaf.

Polychrome

Polychrome, meaning "many colors," is used to designate wood carvings, picture frames, and other objects painted in various colors, often with the addition of gilding. It was practiced by many of the artists and craftsmen of the Italian Renaissance in the making of religious figures, altar pieces, panels and furniture.

In the field of sculpture, polychrome was practiced by the Egyptians·and the Greeks, particularly in architectural carving. During the Italian Renaissance, portrait busts were treated with color, a practice which a few modern sculptors have revived.

Soap Carving

This diversion has become an interesting hobby with those whose skill has not progressed to the stage where they can handle the problems presented by wood which can split if one is not careful. As an exercise in three-dimensional thinking, a classic horse head is suggested by Lester Gaba, who is the author of a stimulating book on soap carving.

An effective piece of wood sculpture, excellent in both form and treatment, by a student of Berlin, N. H. High School. (Courtesy of Scholastic Awards.)

A carved panel in white oak, stained with colored ink to accentuate the design. Such panels might be made for a chest or cabinet, or for an ornamented door. (Courtesy of Higgins Ink Company: "Arts and Crafts Projects."

157

Four stages in the execution of a carved bas-relief plaque in sculpstone. The ease with which this material may be carved has made it very popular with amateurs and beginners.

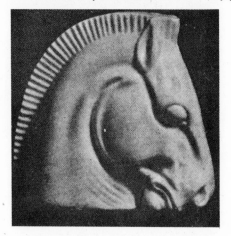

Pattern of a Classic Horse Head

FRONT   BACK

SIDE

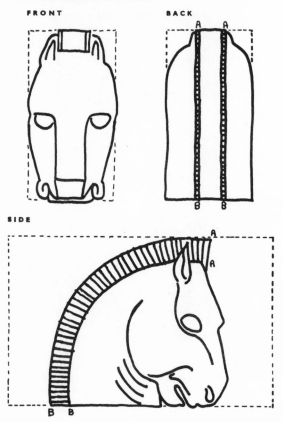

The horse's head is chosen for its decorative possibilities. Three outline drawings are shown here, a back view in addition to the front and side, to help the student in the modelling of the horse's mane.

The side view is drawn on the flat side of the block of soap and the profile is determined in preliminary cuts. Block out the head first. Do not try to make the deepest penetration until the piece is molded in the rough.

A horse's head also lends itself to a decorative bas-relief medallion, or square plaque, with the ivory color of the soap contrasting against a black or a dark blue background.

Sculpture relief carving by Joseph Loevenick, suggesting the decorative units which may be created in this newly popularized, though ancient, material.

Practice for the beginner in sculpture should start with soap carving. Lester Gaba, regarded generally as the foremost artist in this medium, furnishes working drawings for the modelling of a classic horse head. With these drawings to guide you, try your hand at this exercise. (Courtesy of Studio Publications.)

Modelling in plasticene is an aid to architectural study. An unusual house site has presented a problem which the model at the left projects in a manner more completely than any set of drawings could do. The scale model, colored to simulate the actual materials, is shown from two points of view.

Mention of the various kinds of sculpture and carving has been kept brief with the intention of suggesting its study solely to aid the student toward a better understanding of the problems of light and mass and contour that he will endeavor to portray in two-dimensional media. Should interest in sculpture and carving exceed this point, the student should seek further information on the subject in the many helpful books available.

Above: "Deep Sea," a sculpstone carving by Joseph Loevenick, which would look well in a modern interior. At right: two bas-relief carvings, also in sculpstone by Mr. Loevenick.

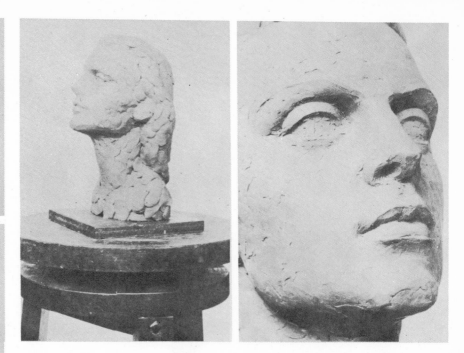

Note the ridge modeled around the outline of the lips; and how deeply the eyes are set into the sockets. The outside points of the eyes are farther back and slightly higher than the points nearest the nose. The hair has been treated as form.

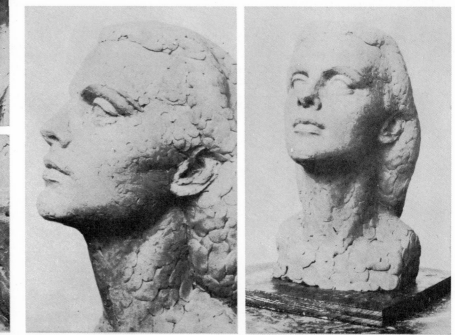

The step by step detail photographs shown on these pages clearly illustrate the modelling phase of sculpture, and the logical progression from basic form to full representation. (Courtesy of W. T. Foster: Sculpture for Beginners, by Henry Lion.)

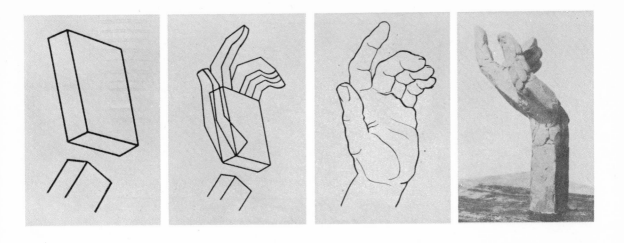

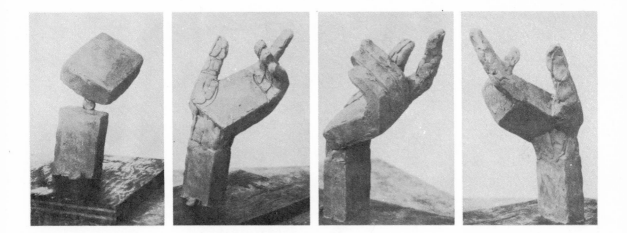

The hand, like the torso, is constructed of basic forms. The palm of the hand is a flat oblong box with the thumb fitting onto one corner and the fingers attached directly onto the end plane. In modeling a hand, it would be a good idea for beginners to follow all of the different stages illustrated on this page.

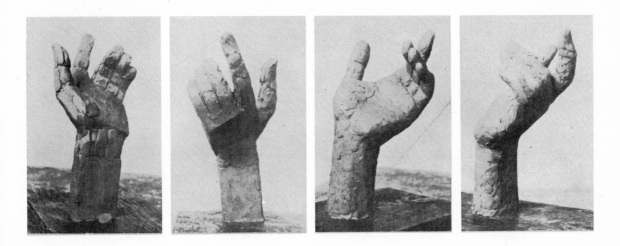

"From One Root," a sculpstone carving by Betty Lewis Isaacs, which reflects the trend of modern sculpture.

The *whisky* of old London

Old London Tap Room

HAIG & HAIG

Whoosh! the customers have me nearly tuckered out serving them—
haig & haig.

A student project for a window or counter display, combining painted balsa wood sculpture with carved and painted lettering and other elements. If reproduced by color photography, the display could be used as a full-page color advertisement.

"Flute player," an excellent interpretation of primitive "tribal" art, carved in sculpstone by Olive O'Connor Barrett.

A graceful silhouette in sculpstone carved by Jacques Heliczer. The character of the material is apparent in the photograph.

Painting

As we approach the study of painting we must review what we have learned so far and organize it for use. We will need all of it—object drawing, proportion, design, and the schemes of arrangement called composition, and color. Thought must be given to the selection of subject matter —what to paint. And in our training we should observe a procedure that will help us apply the things we learn to the more advanced problems. For this reason, art schools begin this series of experiences with what is called still life.

Still Life

Still life consists of objects, usually associated with domestic or personal use, arranged in such a way as to make an interesting grouping. Objects are selected for still-life groups because of their color, texture, and decorative qualities. The objects should have some common association with each other, such as kitchen utensils have with vegetables, or a vase of flowers with a book. Articles suggesting antiquity, such as an old violin and a piece of porcelain or an old clock, compose well together.

Backgrounds are chosen for their color, pattern, texture, and the way they help to unify the objects. Frequently backgrounds are selected for their low color key against which the brighter objects in the grouping create an effective contrast. Such arrangements are regarded as particularly suitable for student training.

Whether the student renders the grouping with charcoal or paints it with water-color or in oils, the problems of careful observation, proportions, light and shade, and interesting pattern are always before him. The advantages of studying still life include the intimate scrutiny one can engage in under conditions that offer unhurried observation. The source of light can be controlled so that the effect is not changed during the course of the study. Objects may be assembled with a broad range of variety.

Frequently beginners become impatient when they are required to draw or paint still life. They prefer to begin immediately with the human

The two still life paintings, above and to the right, are reproduced by the courtesy of the Metropolitan Museum of New York. Still life furnishes an endlessly varied opportunity for skilled technique. The floral still life, at the right, is by a student in the Central High School of Jackson, Miss. (Courtesy of Scholastic Awards.)

Subject matter may be close at hand—your own town, even your own neighborhood. It is the individual interpretation that makes it art. The picture to the left, by a student of the Erie (Penna.) Technical High School, is in oil. The one to the right, by a student of Cass Technical High School, Detroit, Mich., is in black ink.

Nautical subjects have always been favored by artists, as is proved by the popularity of seashore places for vacation sketching and painting. This study in oil is by a student of Montclair High School, New Jersey.

An unusually fine rendering of trees in oil by a student of Hope High School, Providence, R. I. The picture is nicely composed and the artist has made the most of the shadows cast by the trees on the snow. (All illustrations on this page are by courtesy of Scholastic Awards.)

model. These students fail to appreciate that the problems in painting the human figure will seem simpler if preliminary study is devoted to still life. Premature attempts at art problems can prove discouraging. Progress made slowly is more secure. The length of posing time for the human model is short, whereas the still life can be drawn or painted and re-painted until the student reaches the limit of his abilities.

Copper and brass are favorite objects for still-life painting. The surface reflects much of the color of other articles in the grouping which gives rich variety to the picture. The highlight provides a dramatic touch, and here one would do well to examine closely the reproductions of many of Rembrandt's portraits.

The market for still life painting is broader and offers more opportunities for sales than other kinds of painting. A canvas of flowers well painted is by far the most popular subject sold by art stores and department stores dealing with this kind of merchandise. The modern professional painter finds still life a good field for the display of his particular style of technique, and he often shows something novel and surprising in his choice of things selected as subjects. A student should never consider himself too advanced to engage in studies of still-life painting even long after he has learned the lessons it can teach him.

Landscape Painting

Drawing or painting landscapes brings into play a sense of large-scale perspective and of distances relative to the place from which you

The student of North Phoenix High School, in Arizona, who chose this industrial subject matter had a good eye for the dramatic quality in compositions.

Dramatic incident has been painted in an every-day setting by this student of Cass Technical High School, Detroit, Mich.

Again, the artist's immediate environment frequently furnishes the best and the most authentic subject matter. By a student of Chattanooga High School, in Tennessee.

What may be seen from your window may provide excellent material for an illustration or a painting, as is indicated by this drawing by a student of the Worcester High School of Commerce, in Massachusetts.

(All illustrations on this page are by courtesy of Scholastic Awards.)

With pencil and sketch book, landscape painters have long made the practice of recording notes they will use later in their paintings. This is from a sketch book containings hundreds of sketches.

view the vista. The artist is concerned chiefly with three principal distances: foreground, middle distance, and far distance. There are many intermediate distances in addition to these but the beginner will be wise to practice with the three most important ones until he has mastered the delicate gradations of tone and color, and the relative varieties of form as they appear at varying distances from the eye.

If you will check the relationship of these three major considerations of distance with your own visual experience, you will observe that the only stage where a great deal of detail is distinguishable is in the foreground; that less can be seen in the middle distance, and that no detail at all can be seen in the far distance. In the far distance only the profiles of hills and mountains can be seen, perhaps the silhouette of a large building. Individual trees and houses cannot be seen at all. They are discernible in the middle distance only to a slight degree.

Nature invites the painter of landscapes to a countless variety of subjects and effects. Landscape painting is not akin to coloring a photograph. The scene you wish to paint should stir an emotional reaction within you, causing you to create a picture of which the vista before you is only the inspiration. The valley appears fertile,

sunny, and vibrant with life, or perhaps, the hill seems bleak, bald, and tragic. The sea is calm and clouds float listlessly by, or maybe the surf is turbulent. The idea you paint is freshness in the first instance, desolation in the second, solemnity in the third, and conflict in the fourth.

Art typifies life; it should not imitate it. The accuracy of the reproduction of a scene on canvas is not so much in the pictorial detail as in the *spirit* of the place by which everyone familiar with the scene will recognize it. The need for design is also a requirement in landscape painting. The picture should satisfy the observer by the pattern quality of its composition. In order to compose a landscape into a pleasing arrangement, liberties are taken with the material which in no way changes the spirit of the picture. Rather, these changes may add immeasurably to the effect desired.

Planning a Landscape

Much can be learned from the study of the work of master painters of landscape such as George Inness, John Constable, Claude Lorrain, and from a later group consisting of Jonas Lie, Gardner Symons, John Carlson, and Gari

An old apple tree —
rugged and forceful, poster treatment
just solid black and a poster gray

1st
Paint in
blacks with water
proof ink

2nd
poster gray
or mix chinese white
and black — use it solid — no tints

Together with much other valuable advice and example, the hand book
from which this illustration is borrowed urges the student to make many
sketches of trees from nature. In this way he can study tree anatomy in the
best possible manner. (Courtesy of W. T. Foster: How to Draw Trees, by
Frederick I. Garner.)

Melchers. But nothing will be as helpful as taking your sketch pad, your water-colors, or your oils and studying nature at first hand. A combination of these two approaches is, of course, most desirable.

Form a habit of studying the formations of clouds, the interesting shadows they cast on rolling hills, the color of these shadows in relation to the sunlit areas, and the way that the contours of distant hills weave across the horizon, obscuring one another at times. Sketch these effects. Keep your first studies simple. Don't try to put in everything you see. Draw in the essentials and organize them in an arrangement that will have a center of interest, a group of lesser interests, and a feeling of balance established between the two. As you learn to control compositions of two elements of interest, one primary and one secondary, it will become easier to add gradually more and more of the details you wish to include in your picture without detracting from its total effect.

From all appearances there has been a relaxation from the practice of outdoor sketching on the part of modern students. At least, the current trend suggests this deficiency in their training. The feeling for distance, the relationship of colors affected by distance, and the concept of space seem lacking in many modern efforts. Closer association with nature through the habit of sketching would make a world of difference.

There was a time when an artist would take his sketchbook everywhere he went, and in the course of a year his studio would be filled with sketches of first-hand impressions and observations of people and places—all vital material for future canvases.

At the risk of laboring the point, consider the champion golf or tennis player who has developed his skill and style over a great length of time in trial matches and practice games, not in play-offs. The practice strokes are what you put in your sketchbook that add up to professional performance later.

Sketching Foliage

Trees and shrubbery are an essential part of landscape sketching and can be given whatever shape is required to create the mass of dark foliage needed to help the composition. Foliage adds a touch of "livability" to a picture of a house. It also relieves the stern and angular roof lines of any building. Trees can be used to frame the picture. Vistas seen through wooded groves or between the branches of trees are frequently pleasing. Foliage, placed so its dark mass aids in drawing attention to some point of interest, can serve as the chief accent in the picture.

Trees have personality. Huge oaks, maples and chestnuts give a feeling of protection to a home standing in their shadow. Low fruit trees seem associated with the rural scene; they cast little shadow but suggest the productivity of the farm. The tall cedars, cypresses and hemlocks contrast pleasingly with monumental architecture and seem to project the eternal idea associated with this character of building.

Trees have *anatomy,* and it is well to study their structure carefully before drawing them. Without balance they would fall over. Therefore, the masses of foliage must be distributed on either side of the trunk in a way to convince an observer of the tree's stability. There are exceptions where scrub pine and oak are to be found emerging from the crevices of rocks, but in these instances the roots are firmly anchored and, although the tree seems to overhang its base, its balance is not endangered.

A good time to study the anatomy of trees is in the winter when the limbs are not concealed by their foliage. It will be seen that the limbs grow out of the main trunk, the smaller branches grow out of the larger limbs, the twigs grow out of the branches and the leaf stems spread outward from the twigs. It should also be observed that the limbs do not leave the trunk at the same height from the ground nor do the branches spring from the limbs in pairs. It is a characteristic of Nature to follow a system of growth by which new life springs from a stalk. The point on the stem from which a leaf emerges is known as a node. The space between nodes on a stalk is called an internode. These internodes vary in length dependent on the kind of tree and the exposure of the foliage to the light.

The length of the internodes becomes less as the size of the stalk becomes smaller. This system of tree formation should be made apparent whenever trees are drawn so that the limb and branch structure is visible. When the foliage is so thick that no branches are seen, the artist is confronted with the problem of creating interesting masses of light and shade, and he is concerned essentially with the mass profile of the tree rather than with its detail. Foliage is often a

168

An Oxfordshire Cottage
A Thornton Bishop

Sketched with a Wolff pencil on a dull coated
printing paper which produced a soft effect.

study of pattern and here the artist must depend
upon his sense of good design.

In drawing a tree, start with the trunk and
develop it *upward* in the way it grows, branch-
ing out first on one side then the other in order
to keep a feeling of balance in the main structure. If the tree is planned in balance it will
probably end up that way. Then determine the
masses of foliage, giving consideration to the
general silhouette of the tree you are drawing.
The elm resembles a triangle balanced on its
apex; the pine keeps its columnar appearance;
the oak and chestnut have straighter sides; the
maple more of a half-dome; and the evergreens
are symmetrical. One characteristic of the spruce

is that the divisions of light and shade are
definitely horizontal.

When drawing evergreen shrubs, such as the
rhododendron, lay out the blossoms first, then
draw a uniform leaf treatment around them.
Place the accents between the leaves and tone
down the leaves slightly but do not make them
too dark. Mountain laurel and rhododendron have
a waxy appearance and reflect light.

Groups of birch appear light, partly because
of the white trunk and branches and partly because of their light green, shiny leaves. They are
effective when shown against a dark background. The foliage appears crisp if dark accents
are introduced around the small areas of foliage.

169

It is only from filling many sketch books full of studies from life, such as these, that observation is developed and knowledge acquired. Much is described when accents vary weight of the line.

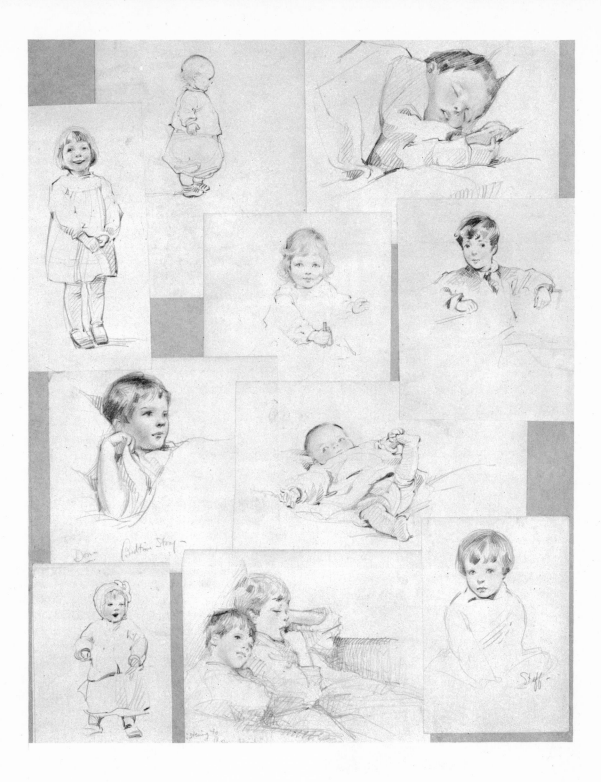

The drawings on this page are developed toward finished illustrations. They are by the same artist, a specialist in the drawing of children, who made the pencil sketches on the page opposite.

A well handled water color of a local situation by a student of the Miami (Florida) Senior High School. The strong diagonal helps accentuate the violence of the storm.

A water color, handled with admirable freedom, by a student of the Peabody Demonstrational School, Nashville, Tenn.

A waterfront scene inspired this water color by a student of the Midwood High School, Brooklyn, N. Y. (All illustrations on this page are reproduced through the courtesy of Scholastic Awards.)

An atmospheric water color by a student of the Miami (Florida) Senior High School. The piles furnish a rhythmic pattern that supplies the major interest.

Painting—an Art and a Craft

There is more to painting than choosing the colors you want to put on canvas. There are different kinds of colors in which the chemical ingredients vary, making certain colors unsuitable in combination with other colors. Preparing the canvas so that a special effect can be attained is a kind of knowledge quite apart from a general art training.

The master painters of the Italian Renaissance did not consider themselves as artists, but as craftsmen. They had to prepare their own colors and make other materials with which to treat wood or canvas so that their work would be permanent. Art students in that day learned their craft through apprenticeship, and much can be said in praise of this "ancient" practice. Today, many of the technical problems of the old master painters have been assumed by the laboratories of the modern paint manufacturers.

There are three principal kinds of color paints: opaque paint used for posters, water color, and oil paint. A few elementary facts about each will give a student sufficient working knowledge to start his own experiments. Let us discuss the opaque paint first because it is the least difficult to use, if you use it properly.

Poster Paint

Poster paint is soluble in water and should be used in a consistency as thick as heavy cream. Remove a small quantity of the paint from the jar in which it comes and put it in a small saucer or mixing pan. Using a brush, add just enough

172

water to bring it to the right consistency. If you use too much water, poster paint will dry out streaky and uneven. It should be *uniformly smooth* and *absolutely opaque,* capable of covering a line as black as ink.

Your first exercises should teach you to (1) paint flat, uniform areas, and (2) paint with clean edges. Do not paint up to the edge of another area which is not yet dry. The colors will run together.

Your second exercise should be to paint a "scale" of grays, in values ranging from black to white. Graduate this scale by mixing white and black paints yourself. Practice in determining values in the mixing of color is important.

Your third exercise should be to mix two or more poster paint colors to create colors different from the selections which come prepared in jars. Consulting the color wheel shown in Chapter 7, mix the colors necessary to duplicate this wheel.

The fourth exercise should be the addition of a sufficient amount of poster white to create delicate "pastel" shades of several full-strength colors, such as orchid from purple; coral from red; light, sky-blue from dark blue, and white-green jade from bright green.

These exercises should prepare you to mix the ready-made colors to any tint or shade you may wish, and to control your paints so that you can produce flat areas with clean, sharp edges.

Poster paints do not blend easily into one another, but a certain amount of blending may be achieved after you have become more expert in handling the medium through experimenting. A "blended" opaque painting in reproduction closely resembles an oil painting. Actually, the medium is not intended for use where blended effects are desired or expected. Poster paint simplifies a subject and, to a degree, stylizes it. The medium is not suitable for realistic representation. Therefore, the student is cautioned to confine his practice to the simple poster treatment of his designs.

The process of simplification leads to the importance of shadows in effecting striking contrasts. Two degrees of shadow will prove sufficient for most practical purposes—a deep shadow to signify cast shadow, and a lighter shadow to approximate the effect of reflected light in shadow. This is illustrated by a poster paint rendering of a photograph in which the many values of the shadows, as seen by the camera, are actually reduced to two.

One of the greatest of poster designers was Ludwig Hohlwein of Munich. The simplicity of the silhouette makes this one effective.

Since shadow creates the most important design pattern in a poster, many artists successful in handling the medium paint in the shadows first, adding the lighted areas afterward. The edges between shadows and the lighter areas may be softened by brush work to avoid the appearance of being cut out of paper. Further softening effects can be added by spatter work.

Ludwig Hohlwein, one of the greatest of poster artists, provides us with examples of what can be accomplished in this medium, four being reproduced here. Poster paint can produce work particularly suitable for a process known as silk screen reproduction, the principle of which depends largely upon simplification of the areas of color.

Water Color

Like poster paint, water color is soluble in water but here the similarity between the two ceases. Where poster paint is flat and opaque, water color produces transparent effects, and it is this quality that gives to the medium its popularity. Freshness, sunlight, spontaneity, and life are sought for through water color, and artists

Water color of the Lincoln Memorial in Washington, by Mr. Bishop, pictures the famous shrine in a setting of fall coloring. (Courtesy of Vernon Lincoln Faulkner Collection.)

like Sargent, Homer, and Starkweather have produced some of their most famous work in this medium.

One thing to remember about water color is the importance of directness in applying color. You cannot go back over an area and patch it up. It has to be right the first time. The wash may be graded, delicately from light to dark or in reverse, but the operation must take place while the wash is still moist.

Sable brushes of varying sizes are recommended. Do not try to work with only a few; you will need large brushes for broad areas and smaller brushes for details. Illustration board or rough surfaced drawing paper will offer good texture for water color paintings. Regarding a paint box, it is advisable to get one where spaces are provided for the mixing of washes with ridges to prevent the wash in one space from mixing with that in another. A list of colors suitable for water color painting is suggested in the Supplement to Chapter 7. With this equipment you are ready for your first experiments.

You'll need two pans of water, one for lightening a wash, and the other in which to wash out your brush as you change quickly from one color to another. Moisten a small patch of

the drawing paper with clear water, and drop into it some red, blue and yellow, working them together, and noting the results. Next, cover a second space of the paper with a very watery wash of yellow, and drop red and blue into it. Compare this result with the first experiment. Try the experiment again, starting with a red wash into which you work a drop of yellow and blue. This kind of practice will reveal the difference in effects obtained with the same colors but under varying circumstances.

Water Color Techniques

Because of the transparency of water color, the necessary sketch layout of the picture should be made with pencil lightly. Confine the layout to outlines only; all values, shades, and shadows are to be painted directly.

Technique in handling the medium varies. Some artists paint very "wet" and broadly, with little detail. This is most difficult to do and requires a great deal of experience. Some combine breadth with a certain amount of detail, allowing the broad tonal areas to dry before applying paint in the smaller details. Then, an artist who works more in detail applies his color pretty much as he would with opaque paints. Over-painting is possible in small detail when the color is applied almost dry and with a fine brush. This method is necessary to indicate delicate detail such as ship's rigging, the branches and twigs of a tree, or the divisions of window panes.

The most fascinating results in water color are obtained by the broad treatment of rich color applied directly and with a minimum of over-painting. With this as an objective, the student should apply himself to endless experiments and not feel discouraged by his early efforts. He is after a technical proficiency that only experience can give to him. A few suggestions follow which may make his path less stony.

How to Lay a Flat Wash

Mix a quantity of color in a receptacle large enough to hold more than might be accommodated in one of the compartments of the paint box. Dampen the board with a small sponge using clear water, and tilt the board at an angle of about 30 degrees. With a large brush filled with the color, draw it across the top of the board with a smooth, even stroke. Refill the

A portrait study in oil by a student of Lincoln High School, Cleveland, Ohio. (Illustrations on this page by courtesy of Scholastic Awards.)

Definite delineation characterizes this portrait study by a student of the Arsenal Technical High School, in Indianapolis, Ind.

A portrait in oil, painted by a student of the High School of Music and Art, in New York City, displays an artist with keen sensitivity.

Photographs, sketches, and paintings of the same person by different artists in different media.

These two pages are presented to show the varied approaches, in both perception and medium, employed by different artists in the portraiture of the same person.

The portrait above, as well as the one to the right, were by the same artist, and it is interesting to note that the painting at the right and the photograph at the left on page facing, were made independently.

The informal pencil portrait above was made by the same artist who painted the oil portrait at the right. His vision of the subject, evidently, differed from that of other artists' interpretations assembled here.

brush and allow the second stroke to overlay the first so that the color runs in an even manner. Continue down the board with successive strokes and watch the color gather at the bottom. Wipe your brush quickly and "pick up" the color as it reaches the bottom of the area you wish to cover. Work fast at this point in the operation, drying your brush on a blotter or cloth you should have at hand.

How to Lay a Graduated Wash

Mix a quantity of color of medium strength. Dampen the board and lay the first brushful of color as before. Then, quickly, without cleaning the brush, fill it with water. Add this to the mixture of color and make the second stroke. Continue the process until the area is covered. The weakening of the original solution with water after each successive stroke will produce a graded effect in one color.

When the gradation is to include two colors, such as a sky where a deep blue is to graduate downward to a rose-gray, one color must be allowed to dry before the other color is applied. Suppose we consider the horizon first and, turning the board around, flow a tint of the rose-gray from the horizon toward the "top" of the drawing, following the procedure suggested above for one color. When this wash is dry, turn the board back again and, starting from the top, float on the dark blue, weakening it with each stroke as you approach the horizon.

The more direct method of working with two pools of color, starting with one and changing to the other, is difficult and will probably result in a streaky effect. Clouds can be cut into a sky by cleaning the brush, drying it, and wiping out cloud formations in the flat wash. Where crispness is desired, the board must be dry when color is applied.

As in opaque painting, consider the dark areas first. They create the stronger element in the pattern. Then establish the focal center of your picture, introducing the contrasting color. This is the crucial part of the painting; if it is successful you have made a great start but if it fails, you might as well start over, because regardless of what you do in the less important areas, the painting will lack its sparkle where it needs it most. Learn by doing, and strive for the richness and depth of color this great medium can give you.

Casein Painting

There has been introduced recently among art materials a new medium called casein which can be used either as a water color medium or to produce the effect of tempera painting and oil painting. This versatile medium provides the student with a range of technical possibilities.

All techniques employ water as the only agent for thinning the colors. The range of techniques is determined by the amount of water added to the colors. When used very thin, casein is suitable also for airbrush work.

According to instructions issued by M. Grumbacher, Inc., manufacturers of casein and other art materials, painting with casein should never be done with unmoistened colors squeezed directly from the tubes. Casein also requires water to dry properly. The colors are permanent, full strength, pure and brilliant, and easy to manipulate.

Casein is adaptable to any surface that will absorb water. Paper, canvas that has not been sized to receive oil, wet or dry plaster and similar surfaces are suitable. Canvas must be sized with a ground that will not repel water.

Casein can be pre-mixed and kept in tightly capped jars until used. This is especially convenient when large surfaces are being worked on and an area cannot be completed at one time, such as in mural painting. The colors will remain uniform and, if any evaporation has occurred, they can be diluted with water to the consistency desired.

Should a semi-gloss be preferred rather than the natural velvet-matt finish the colors produce, a special casein medium, prepared by M. Grumbacher, Inc., is available for adding to the water when thinning the colors.

Henry Gasser, director of the Newark School of Fine and Industrial Art, has been particularly successful in the handling of this medium. A report of his experiences appeared in the *American Artist* magazine, published by Watson-Guptill Publications.

In this article he states that the water color technique with casein is achieved by simply thinning the colors and applying them to the paper as washes. Oil painting effects are attained by moistening the brush with water and applying the color much in the same manner as one would do with oil paint. The tempera or opaque techniques are obtained by adding Grumbacher Casein Titan White to the colors used. Care

178

"Colorado Landscape" by Xavier Barile. Painted with Casein and handled as oil color on illustration board.

"Vesper II," by Grace T. Steinmetz. Here Casein was used for tempera effect on illustration board.

should be taken, however, to avoid several applications of pigment, as the thick coats of paints applied directly are liable to chip off. Water must be used frequently; the brush should be kept wet.

When an oil painting effect is desired, varnish should be applied as soon as the painting is dry to the touch. Use Grumbacher Casein Varnish with either a brush or an atomizer.

When varnishing with a brush, place the painting on a flat surface and apply a light coat of varnish with overlapping, parallel strokes, using a moisture-free brush. If an atomizer is used, stand the painting upright so that the spray will hit it at a 90-degree angle. Clean varnishing tools with alcohol. Clean brushes and palettes with soap and water. Brushes that have been used for casein colors may be used in any other medium if they are properly washed and allowed to dry.

John J. Newman, artist, lecturer, and color consultant to M. Grumbacher, Inc., describes casein colors as pigments mixed in an adhesive emulsion prepared from curd of milk and lime. He declares that the medium is fast drying and that it has a waterproof feature which "permits the making of corrections with an ease and simplicity that is astonishing."

Clarence A. Brodeur, painter, lecturer, and instructor at Pratt Institute, gives as another recommendation for the medium the fact that it has an "advantage over the chameleon-like habits of opaque watercolor or poster paint tempera. Casein retains its full richness without turning chalky in the darks."

179

Oil Painting

Like water color painting, the successful use of oils will come from experimentation and practice. Much good can come from reading the biographies of great masters of the art which disclose many points of view and methods peculiar to these personalities. But this kind of reading is background, and what the beginner needs most is the "know-how" with which to make the first steps intelligently.

Oil paint, ably handled, has many advantages. While still wet, it can be wiped off for correction or repainting. While still wet, any color can be graded off into subtle tones and values, tints and shades, or blended with other colors. When dry, the painting can serve as a base for overpainting, adding details, or making corrections in the original effort. Some painters develop their canvases by building up stage by stage, creating effects they feel they cannot obtain in any other way.

Lastly, there is a permanence in oil painting which has long made this medium the most favored for work intended to survive long periods of time. It has been the medium of the old masters and has recorded likenesses throughout centuries.

Most of the works to be seen in museums and private collections are oil paintings, and many of them are as fresh and bright today as they

All illustrations involving use of Casein paint reproduced through the courtesy of Grumbacher Collection.

were when they were painted. The permanence of oil paint has been the chief object of study by the old masters who ground their own colors and who experimented ceaselessly to discover the secrets that assured permanent quality in color. Many modern painters have mixed their own oils, but the problem of permanence has been assumed by our paint manufacturers with outstanding results. However, there are a few facts the young painter should know at the beginning of his experiments.

Since a painter uses a greater amount of white than any other color, let us begin with a study of this element. There are three kinds of white, known as White Lead, or Flake White; Zinc White, or Permanent White; and Titanium, called "Titanox." White lead has a tendency to powder, brush off, and turn yellow, but it covers well, and that is the reason it is used commercially by house painters.

Zinc White is whiter, stays whiter, and dries harder than White Lead. It is preferred by picture painters because it is more imperishable when exposed to salt atmosphere.

Titanium is a newer product and is favored by many painters. But for the student, Zinc White is suggested.

The Yellows

Of the yellows, Lemon Yellow is the lightest in the yellow family, and the best yellow for graying purple, its complement. It is nearest the "spectrum" yellow although it has a slightly greenish cast. Because of its quality most nearly approaching the yellow rays of white light, it offers the student the best element in his effort to approximate light.

Ochres and Siennas are earth colors, made of a combination of clay and iron rust. They offer a range of warm hues from a cream to a reddish brown.

Cadmium Yellows, pale and deep, range from a light lemon, through yellow-orange to a deep red-orange. Cadmiums are permanent when used with Zinc White; they are not permanent used with lead.

Chrome Yellows are a lead product, with fair permanence. They are less expensive than Cadmium Yellows, which range of color they approximate.

The Reds

Chemically, there are two kinds of reds, one made from earth colors and the other from coal-tar dyes. These two different elements do not mix well together. Venetian Red and Indian Red, both permanent colors, are made from iron rust, an earth ingredient. Light Red also is a clay-iron product.

The Madders, Rose Madder and Alizarin Crimson, come from the coal-tar base. They have a transparent quality and are the reds recommended for mixing with blue and in graying their complement, green. Rose Madder is the red most nearly like the "spectrum" red, and therefore helps to assimilate this color in painting.

"Metropolitan Harbor Scene," by George Schwacha, who used Casein to obtain a mixed transparent and opaque technique on mounted Superba cold-ressed water color paper.

"George Washington Bridge at Twilight," by Mary Black Diller. An impressionistic water color technique on bristol board.

The Blues

Blue pigments, artificially made, are fairly permanent. It is in the mixture with other colors and white that their difference is important. Ultramarine has more red in it than Cobalt and Cerulean Blues. Mixed with white, the result is a purplish tint. When Cobalt and Cerulean are mixed with white the result is a greenish-blue tint more nearly approximating sky color, especially in the eastern part of the United States.

If Ultramarine is used for mixing green, the yellow should be a Cadmium, not a Chrome. Chrome will have a tendency to gray and darken the green; Cadmium will keep it bright. Ultramarine and Rose Madder make a good deep purple.

Tints of blue for sky color are best produced by use of Cobalt and Cerulean, which is also a cobalt product in a lighter degree. The complements of the blue family are found in the warm earthy colors which will gray the blues when mixed with them.

The Greens

Viridian Green and Emeraude Green are favorites with landscape painters. They are permanent, dark, and lack brilliance. To enliven them, use Cadmium Lemon Yellow. Take care not to be confused with the similarity of spelling of Emeraude and Emerald Green, which is bright but becomes chalky when mixed with white. Emerald is not permanent; it darkens and, if used, should be protected with a coat of varnish.

The Purples

When mixing purple, depend on Rose Madder and the blues—Ultramarine, Cobalt and Cerulean. Cobalt Violet, more a purple than a violet, is the only permanent pigment of this family made. Results will be more successful if reached by the mixture of other pigments.

Be Careful of Black

Black can muddy more color on a student's palette than any combination of colors. When needed for a depth unattainable in any other way, a small amount of brilliant red or a bit of Prussian Blue should be added. Black should not

be used to darken color; that color's complement should be used. Black simply blackens color. In many instances, black creates a different color. Mixed with vermilion it will produce a coffee brown; with yellow, a dirty green.

When used on a palette, Lamp Black is preferred to Ivory Black. Lamp Black is mostly carbon, the result of burning wood tar and pitch. Ivory Black, made from charred ivory chips, is blacker than Lamp Black and dries more quickly. Black was a prominent pigment with the old masters, and they developed a skill in using it which has baffled many of our modern painters.

A Safe Beginning

When you start painting in oil, choose still-life subjects for your early experiments. Refrain from the urge to paint portraits and landscapes until you feel thoroughly acquainted with the medium. With still life you can control the lighting and you can spend any amount of time needed to achieve a worthwhile result.

In case you have wondered why artists' studios are planned with a north light, the reason is: north light remains nearly the same for a long period of time each day, and this permits a painter to work under similar light conditions throughout the daylight hours.

As you select the material for your still life, remember the scale of complementary colors, and place objects in contrast near one another to create the chief interest. Distribute objects of harmonizing color in an arrangement that will establish them as a secondary interest to the chief interest. Build your composition before attempting any painting. A painting is good only if its design is good. No technical tricks can save a painting if it is poorly designed. In still life, you can control all of the factors which go into the design before you paint it. When you progress to the stage where you paint landscapes and the elements in your view are not distributed as you would like them, you will have to make these adjustments mentally—a task made easier by early problems of arrangement in still-life studies.

The Viewpoint of a Painter

Within the pattern of a good design, the painter seeks to express an idea. Something has

The vast storehouse of historic design will help you to solve formal design problems if you devote a little study to the great styles of architecture and furniture. It is a field served by many excellent books.

moved him and he wants to pass it on to others. There is an emotional process going on. Henri Matisse is quoted: "If one feels no emotion, one should not paint."

Mood is the keynote of the picture. Mood can be created by color key, by tone, and by prominent lines appearing in the picture. Horizontal lines are suggestive of restfulness and peace; vertical lines give a feeling of dignity and strength; diagonal lines imply violent action; the circle suggests unity and the "S" formation, gracefulness. Symmetrical arrangements have a static but decorative quality.

If the color of a picture is bright, the mood is similar; if gray, the mood is more pensive; if dark, the mood can be sorrowful, even tragic. Tones can affect the mood in a similar way. The painter expresses how he feels through the key of his color and tone, and the basic construction of his pattern.

A famous painter, member of the National Academy and known for his illustrations of rugged Americanism, was painting a picture of his native environs—the Dakotas. The horizon predominant, with a whitish sky above, seemed to attract the observer's eye and hold the attention without much competition from other interests arranged in the foreground. The scene depicted a rural burial on the crest of a mound in the foreground. Greater attention could have been drawn to the burial action if one of the figures had been permitted to intersect the strong horizontal line at the "earth's edge."

The painter, a master of composition, was asked why he had neglected to create such an obvious focal point. His answer was: "In the Dakotas, the horizon is always dominant. Nothing intersects it." The element of bleakness and the finality of the burial seemed best portrayed with the unbroken horizon.

Portrait Painting

When you paint a portrait, you are engaged in the most difficult task a painter faces. You have the problem of obtaining a likeness with subtle gradations of color so as to reproduce correctly the complexion of a person. Color adds to this problem of capturing a likeness.

Some people have a talent for drawing a likeness; they are fortunate. The secret, as revealed by a prominent portrait painter, is to note the

An excellent student performance in a pen drawing which simulates the technique of a copperplate engraving. Valuable experience was gained in style appreciation, precision drawing, and technique in this effort.

most characteristic feature of an individual and start the drawing with that.

Portrait painting, even portrait sketching, has a never-ending market for the artist who can catch a likeness. A good training for this field is constant sketching. Sketch your friends. Make a close study of the different kinds of eyes, noses and mouths. Do not depend on drawing a "typical" feature to serve any portrait. Ears differ, and personality can be suggested by them. As likenesses differ, every feature becomes an object of

A formal pen rendering of the British coat-of-arms. Ability to do this kind of work qualifies a student to undertake important professional assignments. Such a drawing is exacting.

scrutiny. Draftsmanship is the most important tool for this job. Sketchers who are successful at capturing a likeness usually do so in a matter of a few minutes. They either get it in a quick impression, or they don't get it at all. Laboring over the sketch seldom helps. It is better to start over again.

Painting the portrait in oil is a different matter. There are few artists who can finish a likeness in one sitting. The normal approach is to make a number of studies of the model, in order to become visually acquainted. Sometimes when the model or subject is not available, the painter has to work from photographs. This is considered an unsatisfactory method of working and imposes additional problems on the painter.

A portrait painter interprets character as he experiences it, which accounts for entirely different presentations of the same individual by different artists. To illustrate this point, there are shown on the accompanying pages a number of photographs, sketches and paintings of the same person. The sketches were made at different times. Perhaps the most interesting comparison lies between an oil portrait and a photograph which was taken after the portrait was painted by a photographer who had not seen the portrait. Both, evidently, caught a characteristic pose.

Other Considerations

The natural training for a portrait painter is the charcoal drawing where the values of flesh in light and shadow can be studied before the added problems of color are experienced. It is here that a keen observation will help a student acquire much knowledge. He will observe the difference in the highlights on the forehead, the cheek bones, the bridge of the nose, and on the chin. He will see that the shadow on a white collar is darker in tone than the highlight on a blue serge suit. He will learn the secret of obtaining the feeling of depth in the background.

A trip to a museum will yield a vast reservoir of ideas, especially if that institution happens to have some Rembrandts, Copleys, Reynolds, and Lawrences. Study the difference in light when the subject is shown out-of-doors instead of indoors.

In the above exercise, students were asked not only to familiarize themselves with historic forms of eighteenth century French, but also to practice the technique, in pen and ink, of copperplate engraving. The ornaments drawn are typical of that period's style of decoration.

First Steps in Color

Some artists sketch the "layout" for the finished painting in pencil, some in chalk, and some in paint. The composition is determined by the placing of the head within the rectangle of the canvas. Slightly less space should be allowed between the back of the head and the side of the rectangle than on the opposite side of the portrait. More space should appear at the side the features are facing. Care in placing the head will make a world of difference.

The usual method in painting is to develop the large masses first, defining the angular planes of the face in broad areas. Establish the background next to create the contours of the head, then return the attention to the head, refining the rough masses into features. Concentrate on the exact features of the model after the head takes on the appearance of solidity.

Flesh color, in most cases, may be made of Zinc White, Yellow Ochre, and a touch of Vermilion. When the side of the face turns into shadow, study carefully the color of the flesh you are using in the light, and mix its complement with it to preserve its color in shadow.

In portrait painting, more than in other fields of art, the teaching of an experienced painter is worth more than any words on a printed page. But there are many successful painters today who learned nearly all they know through ex-

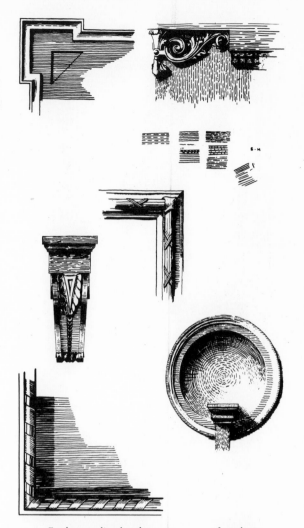

Further studies by the same group of students. Through these exercises they acquired style knowledge and technical skill in formal pen rendering of decorative forms.

perience. They hold out the greatest hope for the beginner when they say that even portrait painting may be self-taught. They qualify this statement somewhat when they add that a natural talent for capturing a likeness will help tremendously, and the habit of making countless sketches will be a necessary adjunct.

However, there is more to portrait painting than capturing a likeness. The painter endeavors to record on canvas the personality of his subject. Of course, this is an interpretation of the personality through the painter's mind. The first step toward attaining this is permitting the subject to

An excellent piece of precision drafting in a black and gold menu cover design in the style of Louis XVI, by a sophomore student in art school.

In the two menu covers above, designed by sophomore art school students, the period called Baroque, characterized by an elaboration of ornament, has been well understood and gracefully executed.

assume a position and attitude of naturalness. Anything forced—causing the pose to appear affected—will destroy a representation of the personality.

Another factor important to successful portrait painting is the omission of unnecessary details and extraneous articles from the picture that are not definitely associated with the subject. A person known for literary pursuits may be shown with a book in his hands, and a military man would not seem unnatural if he were shown with maps in the background or a geographical globe on a table nearby. Relationship of such material to the subject may help to establish the character and personality.

In these days of advanced photographic skill, when a representation of one's features can be recorded accurately on film, the value of the portrait painter rests chiefly in noting the hidden qualities of the subject's personality the camera may miss.

Joseph Cummings Chase, one of the foremost portraitists of the past 40 years, encourages his sitters to converse with him while he is at work on the painting. Strange as this may seem, the change of pose resulting from this practice is more

Student design for a menu cover in two colors. The layout follows a modern trend, but the details are in conformity with the Georgian Colonial style.

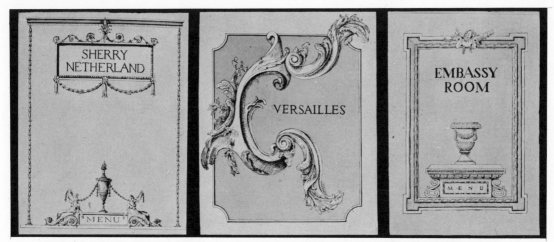

Three designs for menu covers developed in historic period styles by sophomore students in art school. At left: the style of the Brothers Adam (eighteenth century English) was the inspiration; center: the Rococo (Louis XV); and, at right: the period of Louis XVI was the style source.

than compensated for by the display of mannerisms and individual characteristics he could not obtain if the sitter assumed a fixed pose and a "frozen" countenance.

Designing with "Period" Feeling

On this and accompanying pages are examples of students work wherein the objective was to design menu covers using ornament of historic periods for motifs. In these the students were highly successful, capturing the outstanding characteristics of the various styles. Much of the ornament designed years ago was intended for use on architectural forms, or in interior decoration. The material used adapted itself readily to borders, panels, and other geometric shapes, and therefore are as easily used in flat rectangular spaces like those common to the graphic arts.

Careful study of this ornament will show a student the precise differences between styles that appear similar. These differences are the important motifs to select when embellishing an area with a particular style.

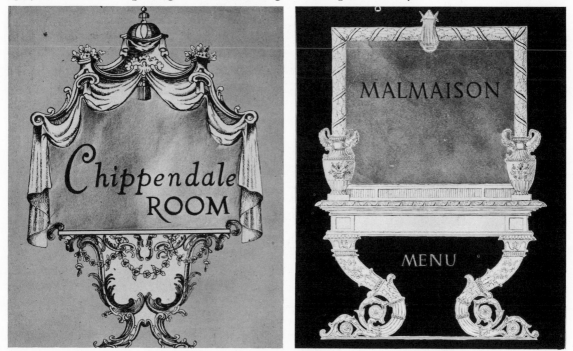

Sophomore art students designed these two "period" menu covers; the first, at left, suggesting the late English Renaissance, and the one to the right, the French Napoleonic Empire style. In this period much of the pure Roman tradition was revived.

Finished art work for the frontispiece of Ernie Pyle's "Brave Men." Various studies and other illustrations for the same project appear on following pages. In these illustrations, the artist sought to convey the impressions of the man at the front rather than depict a single incident.

A magazine illustration in crayon. The illustrator has concentrated his lighting on the figures, surrounded by dark, which gives the scene its dramatic effect.

CHAPTER 10

The Field of Illustration

Illustration for American books and magazines has undergone a change as have other fields of art. The field has always challenged the best of American artists. A review of copies of Scribner's, Harper's and Century magazines over the past fifty years will acquaint the student with the best examples of characterization and the most carefully planned compositions he can find anywhere. The traditions of American illustration as exemplified in the works of Howard Pyle, A. B. Frost, Frederic Remington, E. W. Kemble, N. C. Wyeth, Harvey Dunn, and Dean Cornwall set standards as high as any might hope to attain in the Fine Arts.

Although fashions have changed in the type of illustration used in current periodicals, the objectives are much the same as they ever were. The purpose of an illustration is to interest a person casually thumbing the pages of a magazine, and cause him to buy the magazine to read the story. In book illustration, the objective is similar and the appeal, if pictorial, is focused on the book jacket. Illustrations within the book are usually planned to give it visual enhancement as a whole, rather than to "sell" people on reading it.

To see what fashion in illustration decrees today, take any magazine which features fiction —*The Saturday Evening Post, Collier's, Cosmopolitan,* or the *American*—and observe the eye-appeal which goes into the layout of the pages. Strong, splashy illustrations dominate a two-page spread. The emphasis is placed more on the factors which compel attention than on any incident in the story. It seems that everything is directed toward getting the story read. Terse writing today handles action dramatically. It was not always so. Storywriting has changed, and modern illustration has adopted a new approach to keep in step.

As you examine a contemporary magazine, decide which illustration, or set of illustrations, make you want to read the story illustrated before any others. Then, read the story and critically check the merit of the illustration against the particular incident in the story it is supposed to illustrate.

One of the three conclusions which follow should have come to mind:

1. That the illustration "over-played" the incident, so that on reading the story you were disappointed.

Clippings used as reference in developing the illustrations for Ernie Pyle's "Brave Men." Unless an illustrator is able to be on the scene and get his information first hand, he must depend upon good photographic material.

2. That the illustration either missed the point of the incident, or failed to "play it up."
3. That the illustration visualized the characters, action and the setting so well that it was not out of agreement with the way you imagined these things to be.

Not every illustrator selects the most important action in a story for his picture. As mentioned earlier, the concise, terse and provocative style of writing found in today's periodicals presents an incident so graphically that an illustration of it is hardly necessary. Therefore, many illustrators try to give an overall picture of the characters, setting, and *mood* of the story. Each story has to be analyzed with thought given to the type of readership of that particular magazine.

An illustrator today has a great opportunity to study a story in moving form. The motion picture can furnish hundreds of ideas for illustrations if the artist is keen enough to recognize the dramatic incidents as they are pictured on the screen. Each "shot" has been studied for its composition, its story-telling qualities, and its emotional appeal. Motion picture directors work closely with trained artists who visualize each sequence of the picture before it is planned in full scale.

Let us break down a motion picture into the four main elements which every illustrator should study when he plans his picture. These are:

(1) Characters, (2) Action, (3) Costume, (4) Settings.

First, each illustrator is a casting director who, like the casting director in a motion picture studio, must choose characters for the type of part they are to play. A great surgeon must look like a great surgeon, and all who see him should not have cause to think otherwise. A country lawyer is a different type. Regardless of how well-dressed a lawyer in a small town may be today, the picture of a country lawyer which comes to mind is that of a man, neither shabby nor well dressed, friendly and trying to serve his townsfolk on the few small fees he can earn. There is nothing urbane and stylish about him. Inherently honest, he just "gets by." Put him in your picture, and your audience will believe he is a country lawyer.

A similar approach should determine the "casting" of a big executive, a refugee nobleman, or a clergyman. This leads, sometimes, to selections closely bordering on caricature, yet the movie producer frequently runs this risk rather than cast an actor for a doctor when he better suggests a questionable character.

Next, let us consider the action.

Every picture script has been worked over with the viewpoint of translating as much of the story as possible into *action,* and to reduce *narration,* which is not visual, to a minimum. The artist, reading a story he is to illustrate, should do the same thing. He should select incidents in the story which are pure action. These will be the most effective because they will be the most generally understandable. These will also be the incidents most likely to cause people to read the story. A picture of two people sitting on chairs and conversing is not very exciting, al-

190

Organizational thumbnail sketches aid the illustrator in developing legible pattern and significant shapes.

Here the original rough ideas begin to assume design and organization as they develop into the finished composition for the
frontispiece for Ernie Pyle's "Brave Men."

though their conversation, according to the story, may be.

Correct costume is important whether the picture be that of a trainman, a soldier, a modern businessman, or a knight in armor for an historical story. Here again, the movie producer pays enormous sums to experts on small details because the picture must pass the scrutiny of the sharpest critics, including the producer's competitors.

The situation is no different with the illustrator whose picture will appear before the eyes of thousands with plenty of time on their hands to compare the details with some authentic source if a discrepancy is suspected. Professional illustrators devote many hours in research for the correct details they paint into their pictures.

It was the motion picture that brought into prominence the difference between the "long shot" and the "close-up." The long shot is a scene in which a considerable portion of the picture consists of setting—a vista, or the entire end of a room. The movie close-up is a fleeting thing which momentarily concentrates the attention on a single detail. Illustrators of the past did not use the close-up as we know it today. They did not devote an entire illustration to just a facial expression. The close-up is now available for the use of the illustrator because of the change in the manner in which illustrations are planned for today's magazines.

Planning the Illustration

After the manuscript of a story is read and various incidents in it are selected for possible illustrations, the illustrator makes a number of small, rough sketches, either in soft pencil or charcoal, to help him visualize the best picture possibilities in the material. From these preliminary sketches he chooses the best three or four which he develops in a larger size, giving attention to the compositional factors of the picture. Frequently, he submits these sketches, which are called "comprehensives," to the editor for discussion and criticism. The sketches which survive this test are the ones to be developed as the finished illustrations.

Developing the Picture

Many illustrators today solve the problem of model hire by taking photographs of models and working from these instead of paying for long hours of posing. In their search for models who fit the types described in the story, they refer to albums supplied by model agencies. Over a long period of time an illustrator will accumulate a file of such photographs of models, classified as to character, together with information by which means the model may be contacted for hire. Costumes and incidental articles appearing in the picture are secured, and the models are grouped as they appear in the sketch and photographed.

This method makes possible the catching of the desired expression on the faces of the models in the photograph, or the taking of many photographs until the expression and action are just right. The cost of extra photographs is relatively inexpensive compared with the hourly fee for posing. These photographs supply what the illustrator needs for his picture.

Although this method is the practical way of overcoming the model problem, it is not the best way. Nothing can take the place of drawing or painting from life. To have the three-dimensional subject before you will furnish you with ideas that no photograph can provide.

The next stage is the working up of the drawing. This is frequently done on tracing paper, over which another piece of paper will be laid for further study and corrections. When the arrangement has been determined in outline, an additional piece of paper is laid over it on which the drawing is studied in tone, either with charcoal or water color wash. It is after all experiments have been made, and the artist knows the exact effect he is after in each detail that the drawing is transferred to the illustration board for the final effort.

The finished drawing is usually made about one and one-half times the size it is intended to be when it appears in the magazine or book. Too great a reduction in reproductive processes will prove disappointing. Some reduction is helpful as it softens many irregularities in the technique of the artist, but a student should not depend upon reduction to obliterate the evidences of poor workmanship. Perhaps the results of a student's first drawings reproduced will tell more to shape his technique than any other form of criticism. What the engraver's camera sees is what the public will see.

Illustrations for Ernie Pyle's book *Brave Men* should prove a most helpful aid to any student of illustration. This work, done as a graduation project by a senior student in the Rhode Island School of Design, comprises not only illustra-

"He had been at the FRONT for over a year"

SICILY
— JUNE - SEPTEMBER 1943

1. INVASION PRELUDE

The illustrator, functioning as book designer, tries out full-page roughs and spot illustrations in relation to type to study the effect of the finished book page.

The caption for this illustration in Ernie Pyle's "Brave Men" is "He had been at the front for over a year." The horror of the experience is dramatically portrayed. Such illustrations may be created by talented students with imagination.

tions, but shows the relationship of the illustrations to the printed page. The sequence, presented here, demonstrates the various steps taken by the illustrator.

First, there is the assembling of a mass of reference material, of which a few typical examples are shown.

Next, very rough preliminaries are made; these are the illustrator's graphic means of "feeling" for ideas. Then the preliminary organization of these ideas is sketched into rough compositional form.

The next illustration shows further progress in developing the general composition. The detailed treatment of the illustration is also shown in its finished form.

Shown in miniature are eight page layouts, made to visualize the appearance of the large illustrations as well as the "spot" illustrations in their relationship to the type. Several of these spot illustrations, including the artwork and lettering for the dedication page are shown with another full page illustration, concluding the sequence of work on the Ernie Pyle book.

The sequence dealing with the Nativity incident at the inn, done for Ginn and Company by the same illustrator, following his graduation, gives us a complete review of the illustrator's method of working.

First we see his memorandum sheet in which he lists all the requirements, both literary and technical.

Next, six small rough sketches in which he is "feeling" for his basic pictorial composition.

Sketches as rough as these may mean little to the untrained eye, but they mean everything to the illustrator who makes them. From such sketches grow final finished illustrations.

The second "rough," developed from the preliminary thumbnail sketches, is comprehensible to anyone.

With the composition crystallized, the illustrator gives us a vivid photographic demonstration of how he gets into his illustration himself, how he actually feels himself a part of it by acting the pose of the inn-keeper.

Photographs 1 to 5, in the first group, readily explain themselves. The photographs 1 to 3 in the second group are "close-ups" for the difficult back view of the turned head and for the pose of the hands.

These two groups, together with the following group of photographs for the Jonah illustration,

Finished art work and hand lettering for the dedication page for "Brave Men." It is a good example of dry brush ink work.

give you a very clear idea of how effectively the camera may aid the illustrator.

When the illustrator poses himself he can put into a figure, a head, or a face the exact mood in which he wishes to interpret the character and the action he is illustrating.

Not all illustrators, perhaps, are such good actors as the young man who acted these poses, particularly as in the dramatic scowling close-up (1) for the head of Jonah. In this Jonah sequence (numbered 1 to 4) drapery studies were taken, as well as the poses for the figures in the background group.

The rough sketches for this illustration are unfortunately not available, but they were carried out in the same way as the Nativity sequence here reproduced.

Illustrations for Advertisements

Drawing or painting pictures to be used in advertisements differs little from magazine and book illustration. A story is to be told and it's the picture's job to do it. Artists are usually selected for certain advertising drawings because of the reputation they have made in the particular field of art chosen by the advertiser or its agency for the presentation of their product. Specialization is common in the advertising field, and the artist

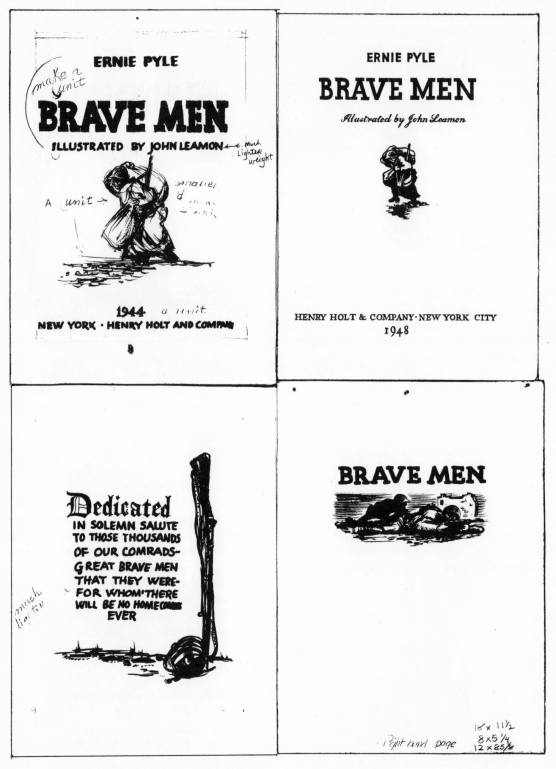

Here the illustrator, again functioning as book designer, plans spot illustrations for their relationship to title-page, dedication, and half-title pages. Some of the finished art work appears on the facing page. A combination of pen work, dry brush, and solid blacks painted with a brush produced these effective illustrations.

Chapter Heading for Chapter One

Half-Title Spot

Tail-Piece Spot

Title-Page Spot

The likeness of the author, Ernie Pyle, at so small a scale, is a noteworthy achievement.

3 Illustrations for GINN.

Due: Finishes – MAY 15
Sketches – APRIL 10

Medium : Black and white wash   contrasty
Black and white + 1 color   modeling in blacks & whites

Audience : 6th grade reader
Realistic drawing
Pictures must follow details in text

Working Drawings : vignettes –
Color indicated in soft pencil on acetate drawn overlay.
Work 1½ times up
OK to omit folios on one of 2 pages

Sketches ; Working drawing size – 1½ up
DUE APRIL 10
Color (any color)
Careful and detailed sketches needed

Reproduction : Relief

Above: the illustrator's notes on his assignment covering technical details as well as literary objective, together with six rough preliminary sketches for the general composition of the Nativity illustration.

At right: the rough sketch, as developed by the illustrator, now embodies most of his final version. His photographic poses, shown on the facing page, helped him to visualize studies for the inn-keeper. This shows how intelligently and effectively an illustrator may use the camera as an aid.

who specializes will be sought for instead of the one who may do a creditable job in many fields.

A student should not confine his earliest efforts to one kind of work. He should obtain as much training as possible in a variety of subjects. Undoubtedly, some subjects will interest him more than others and he will acquire more knowledge about them than he does about others. He will become a specialist at some later time in his career. That is one reason why so many advertisements bear the name of a well known artist. It is the illustrator with years of experience in his specialty who is sought to make the drawings for a national advertiser. The space bought for the advertisement is costly, and so are plates for full color reproduction. The advertiser is not likely to save money on the art work. He entrusts it to the most reliable artist he can find.

Decorative Illustration

Illustrations made for decorative purposes need not be realistic. Often the more fanciful and imaginative they are, the better they fit their purpose. They are used most frequently in children's books, where characters and settings are likely to be fantastic.

The natural aptitude of a student will direct him into this kind of work or will point to a different path of endeavor. Without a strong liking for fanciful illustration, no student should attempt it. It calls for an imaginative and inventive mind capable of whimsy and humor, and a technique suited to delicate suggestion.

Pen and ink has been the favored medium for decorative illustrators, one of the best of whom

is Willy Pogany. The effect of realism is less evident in pen and ink drawings than it is in illustrations where tone helps to naturalize the picture. The delicate lines seem to weave a spidery web of mystery and fantasy about the drawing which other mediums fail to capture. Areas of solid black are introduced for compositional purposes. One way to obtain a striking effect with decorative quality is to make a simple line drawing on white bristol board and then have a negative photostat made of it. The black lines will appear white on a black field. Trim the field of black down to a desired size and mount it on a white board.

Cartoon and Comic Illustration

This field of art is another specialty requiring training and experience that would be difficult to cover in a book of this kind. Comic drawings appearing in current periodicals are executed by well trained artists whose talents can match the abilities of artists engaged in any particular field.

If you will study the careful draftsmanship shown by Harold Foster in his picture story of Prince Valiant you will realize the thorough training he has had. Another carefully drawn comic strip is "Terry and the Pirates," as originally drawn by Milton Caniff.

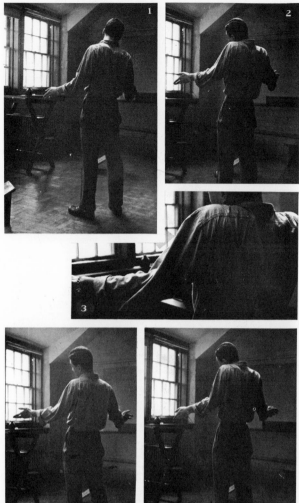

The illustrator himself posed for the action which he wished to put into the figure of the innkeeper in the Nativity illustration.

As in other types of illustration, the success of the comic is based on its composition and its story-telling quality. Various arrangements of the characters to be shown in a single panel are made before the one selected is inked in. All factors in the panel require study, including the size of the balloon carrying the inscription and the sequence in which the story is to be read to be coherent to the reader.

Some details are recorded in these close-up poses which will give the illustration authenticity and aid in draftsmanship.

Accurate tracing of final composition is transferred to illustration board for finished art work.

The final finished art work for the illustration of the inn scene in the Nativity story.

Comic strip artists require a sense of the dramatic in order to present a story in an abridged form. Like other special fields, cartoons and comics are recommended only to those who have a particular liking for them and who realize the need for thorough training in illustration to be successful.

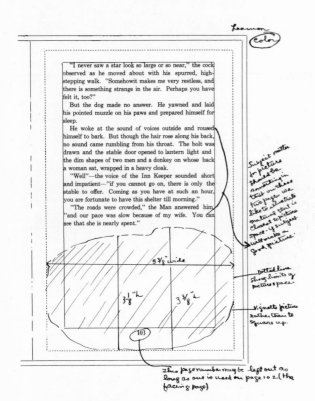

Above: a blank dummy page is furnished by the publisher to give the illustrator the exact size for the finished illustration, as well as its relationship to the type.

The complete page with finished illustration as published. (Courtesy of Ginn & Company.) It is both interesting and important to note the consistency of the illustrator's vision through rough sketches and action poses to the finished illustration.

stable to offer. Coming as you have at such an hour, you are fortunate to have this shelter till morning."

"The roads were crowded," the man answered him, "and our pace was slow because of my wife. You can see that she is nearly spent."

"Yes, yes." The innkeeper was already shutting the door. "I am sorry for your plight, but I tell you there is no room left."

The dog was on his feet. He could hear the other animals rising about him, yet not one of them uttered a sound. Their throats were as silent as his own.

In the flickering lantern light he watched the man lift the woman from the donkey's back and set her upon her feet. She was so weary she would have fallen, but for the man's arms.

"Joseph," she said, "you must not be troubled for me." She rested her head on the man's shoulder and sighed so softly it might have been one of the doves in the rafters.

Inventions"; "How Culture Grows—by Invention, Accumulation, and Borrowing." You may want to retell the story of the alphabet.

Do you like to draw? Make a map showing where our everyday objects came from. One possibility is a list of the foods we got from the American Indians. Some suggestions can be found in an encyclopedia, but here are a few—corn, potatoes, turkeys.

Make a poster showing how picture writing may have turned into an alphabet. One way to do this is to put the different stages in writing, as described in this chapter, on different lines, one below the other. Start off with picture writing, then show the picture-outlines only, and finally show the letters representing the alphabet.

Do you like to read? In connection with Mr. Jackson's last comment, page 36, read the book of Jonah. If you are a fast reader you can finish this four-chapter story in five minutes. But you will want to scan it carefully to get the point of the story that appears in the fourth chapter.

"Jonah, in the Bible story, had his own set idea about what God ought to do to the wicked people of Nineveh. He found it very hard to grasp the bigger idea of love and forgiveness."

Four photographic poses enacted by the illustrator himself. 1 is an excellent study for the scowling face of Jonah in the foreground of the illustration. 2 is an equally dramatic study of the arms and hands for one of the background figures. Others in the background group were studied and enacted as poses 3 and 4. This group of photographs provides a clear demonstration of the way in which illustrators use the camera profitably.

Below at right: actual size reproduction of the Jonah illustration as published. The illustrator, J. T. Leamon, decided upon a technique of excellent clarity and simplicity. Above: complete page, showing the illustration in relation to the type. (Courtesy of Ginn & Company.)

Learning
from
Movie Stills

At left: movie still of a street scene in a mediaeval town. Because of the care given to technical details by motion picture directors, any illustrator can learn a great deal from movie stills.

Merchandise Illustration

In merchandising drawings you work either from a photograph or from the merchandise itself. It is the field in which most art students acquire valuable training, as this kind of work is largely done by art services where a student frequently gets his first opportunity in the professional art field. Art departments in department stores also execute drawings for their own newspaper advertisements, and a student who can work in such a department will profit greatly because of the diversity of objects he will be required to draw. Household appliances, furniture, cosmetic articles, luggage and toys are but a few of the things to be drawn. Learning to emphasize the features in each article is an education in itself. Pen and ink is the preferred medium for this kind of work, with black and white wash added occasionally. With this background the student will advance rapidly.

Another field of merchandising illustration is Fashion Drawing which is highly specialized. This subject will be treated more thoroughly in Part II.

Two more stills of a mediaeval setting. It can be observed that the same bracketted balcony appears in each picture, indicating the broad possibilities of varied vistas in a single setting. The irregular pattern of streets in some of these old cities produced interesting arrangements of architectural features.

On page facing are a group of stills indicating how expertly the movie casting director picks his types, like the old chemist, for instance, and how the art director plans sets and accessories. If, as an illustrator, you were asked to make a painting of a rural church scene, or a wedding in the 1880's, could you do it as convincingly as the movie stills shown here?

203

Practice Drawing Hands

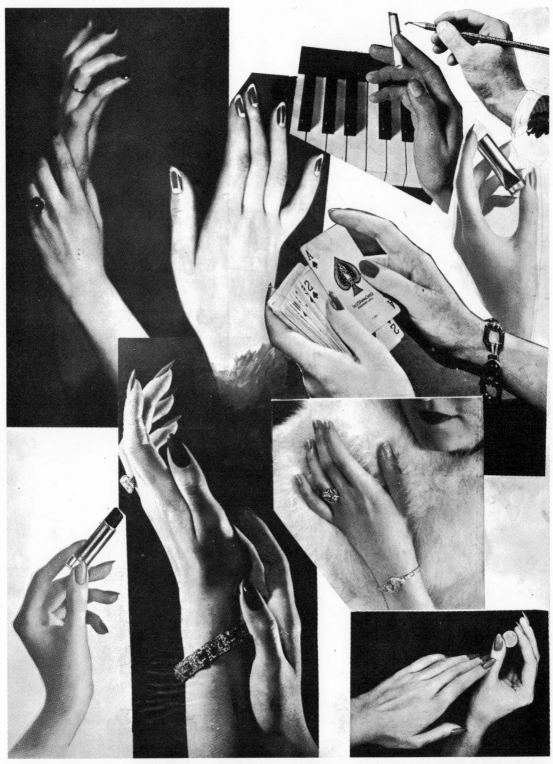

An illustrator's file of hands is only one of the subjects he keeps classified for ready reference. Hands are perhaps the measure of an artist's skill in drawing. They are used in almost every picture where a figure is included. Draw them as often as possible so that the drawing of them will not mar the quality of your illustration.

Suggested Exercises

To Test Aptitude and Progress in Drawing
And Composition at this Stage of Training

In the chapters of the first half of this book, we have discussed the essential points of drawing, design, composition, and color, together with their application in illustrative art. It is now time to find out how much we have learned and, to this purpose, certain problems are presented which will call into play information treated in the foregoing text.

Supply yourself with drawing paper of a quality that will be suitable for pencil drawing, pen and ink work, water color wash, and poster color. No attempt will be made at this time to offer problems involving the use of oil paint.

Exercise No. 1

Two photographs are shown, one of a porch of a large Colonial home having a classic door-way with a Palladian window over it, and the other of a simple entry to a more modest dwelling. The problem is to compose a picture with two or more figures introduced, using the photographs as the setting for each composition.

An important thing to remember is the scale the figures should be in each of the pictures. In the porch scene a chair is shown which should help establish the height of the figure. Also, the door, usually a seven-foot high opening, can serve as a yardstick in determining the size the figures should be. In the smaller entry, the doorway is probably a bit lower, and the figures will appear in this picture a bit larger in proportion to the door than they will in the other entrance.

Another point worth considering is the style and costuming of the figures to be appropriate in

This setting is suggested as the basis for an illustration, figures and action to be supplied.

Another setting suggested in the text above as a basis for an illustration with figures included.

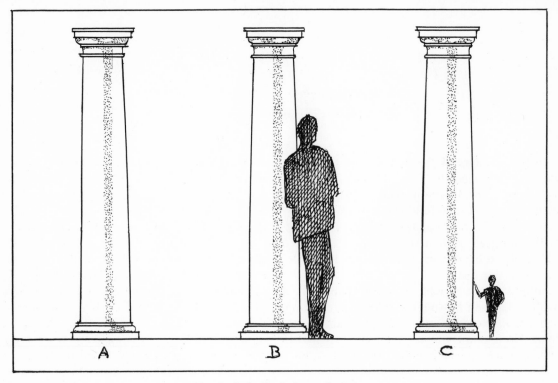

Exercise 2. Studies in Proper Scale

each setting. Then, think of something for them to do that will suggest an incident in some story.

Exercise No. 2

Photographs of three figures are shown on the opposite page. In three sketches create imaginary illustrations with settings appropriate for each figure. In this problem, care should be taken to establish a fitting balance between the figure and the background. All three figures seem dressed for a stroll down a city street, so some consideration should be given to the nature of the setting.

These two tests have been presented to emphasize the importance of the relationship between figures and settings. We have learned that the height of a normal human male figure is about five feet and ten inches; women are a few inches shorter, as an average. The height and width of doors, the distance above the floor line for the height of a window sill, the size of rooms and furniture—all are determined by man's height.

Note the three columns diagrammed above. First, cover up B and C. Looking at Column A, you have no immediate idea of its size. Now, uncover Column B. Immediately you perceive that the column is small. You do not think that

a man 15 feet tall is leaning against a column 25 feet high. You know that a man is not 15 feet tall, and you scale down the column in your mind to a proportionate relationship with the man.

Now, uncover Column C. Immediately the column seems to shoot up to a considerable height. You do not think that the column is, perhaps, 10 feet high, with a dwarf leaning against it.

In a similar way, the diagram of the letter H, below, seems to give the impression that the letter H is big. These simple illustrations are given to stress the importance of establishing the scale of the things you draw in pictures to the size of the human figure, as you represent them in your drawing. The realism in an illustration is seriously affected if any element in it is obviously out of proportion.

Exercise No. 3

As an exercise in observation and accurate delineation, draw a "double hung" window from the outside. A "double hung" window consists of an upper and a lower sash, each counterbalanced by sash weights, and operated in separate channels so that they may be opened or closed separately.

206

Study the construction of one of these windows, and draw it as carefully as you are able. Compare your drawing with the sketch of one of these windows shown on this page.

Exercise No. 4

In the city of Rouen, France, is a famous clock located over an arch which bridges one of the narrow streets. In the accompanying drawing of this arch, the clock has been left out but the limits of its circular rim have been indicated by straight lines, drawn lightly. Draw in the clock,

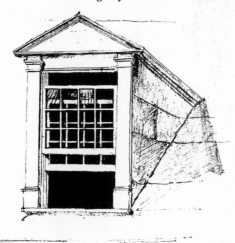

Above, at right: a pencil drawing of the rear of an old New York house introduces the studies of windows shown immediately above and at right. Double-hung sashes were drawn as an exercise in observation.

A lesson in still life. At left: articles to be drawn are arranged so that they seem too spread out. Also, the box looks flat. Below, at left: the arrangement is also faulty as pitcher covers the glass and its own silhouette presents an uninteresting effect. Below: a much better grouping.

After arriving at a satisfactory grouping, it should be sketched freehand, to see if your eye is sufficiently trained to record forms, angles, and relationships accurately. The grouping could also be developed as an accurate composition in perspective, as shown below, with the extension of the lines in the directions shown by the arrow points to furnish the exact vanishing points.

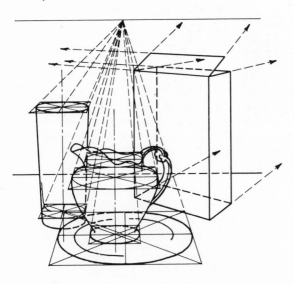

referring to the photograph of it, remembering that you are looking at it from below. The clock will appear as an ellipse, the long diameter of which will be your problem to determine.

Exercise No. 5

Plan a still-life grouping, using vegetables, fruit, porcelain or metal objects. Include at least five objects in the arrangement. Give thought to tonal and color contrasts. First, draw the grouping in outline. Then, place a piece of tracing paper over the outline and, with a soft pencil or crayon, render the grouping in tone. On another piece of tracing paper, laid over the outline drawing, paint in the colors giving thought to the lights and shadows. This study will serve as a preliminary sketch.

Take a piece of illustration board, trace the outline of the grouping on it lightly, and proceed with a finished water color drawing.

Exercise No. 6

Draw a person seated and reading a book. Have the light above and slightly to the rear of the person, as it would be to give proper illumination on the pages of the book. Make the drawing from a point in front of, or somewhat to the side of, the person.

For this test, you will require the cooperation of some member of the family or a friend. The pose suggested will be simple for the model to hold, far more so than an action pose would be.

The value of this test lies not only in the drawing of a person seated, requiring the introduction of a chair and possibly a table, but in the casting of the shadows which will fall on the surfaces facing your point of sight. Make

A suggestion of how the shadow tone is simplified when face is subjected to side lighting.

the drawing in a medium tone, that is, with a soft pencil, crayon or charcoal. As a suggestion, a small sketch appears on the page of a subject drawn under similar light conditions.

Exercise No. 7

Conventionalize a butterfly for use in various designs. The butterfly need not be shown with both wings extended. Think of how it appears when it alights on some flower with the wings together, or nearly so.

Use your motif for a wall paper design, that is, for use in unlimited area. Do not overlook the possibility of showing it in rows, vertically, horizontally, or diagonally, or within a weaving pattern of a vine or tall grass. Put your imagination to work in the application of the "butterfly" motif.

Work your pattern out in tones of black and gray before interpreting it in color. If color is used, confine it to three colors, and treat the areas in flat color.

Exercise No. 8

Make a poster for a high-school play. The play is Shakespeare's *The Tempest*. If you are not acquainted with the play, read it. Plan the idea for the poster after you catch the spirit of the play. As no instruction has been offered in the previous chapters of the book concerning lettering, compose a panel in the poster area to accommodate information about the performance to be set in type. The panel may be treated with a border in keeping with the idea selected for the design. Render the poster in four colors, and keep the color areas flat.

Exercise No. 9

Sketch a landscape consisting of trees and a building or two, placing special attention on the composition. It is suggested that for this test you use a cardboard with a rectangle cut from it so as to create a "window" through which you can study various arrangements of interesting subjects. Choose one which pleases you and draw what you see through the opening when the cardboard is held at arm's length distance.

Aside from this being a test of your ability to select a pleasing arrangement, the practice should be carried on until you are capable of visualizing groups of objects suitable for compo-

sitions without the cardboard window.

Exercise No. 10

Compose an illustration for Longfellow's poem, "Paul Revere's Ride." This tale is full of action beginning with the watching for the signal light, the crossing of the river under the bow of the British frigate, incidents along the way, to the awakening of the minutemen who leave their homes, many still dressing, in the cool April morning.

Make the drawing in soft pencil, crayon or charcoal. Get the tenseness into it, the gray dawn or the moonlight. Do not struggle with too much detail. Think of the composition. Suggest conflict, danger, and action.

These ten problems should disclose to you the amount of interest you have in the study of art, your willingness to study and work, and your aptitude for a successful career. If you are still enthusiastic, let's continue.

Drawn with a lithographic pencil on kid finish bristol board.

Part II

Professional Arts

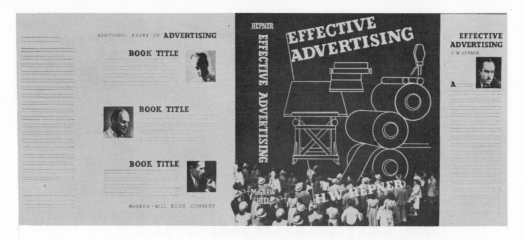

Book jacket design by a third-year student. The complete design of a jacket includes front, "spine," "flaps," and back. This one was designed in dark green and black, with effective use of white.

Contents of Part II

CHAPTER 1

The Application of Design

In Part I, we discussed the fundamental considerations in the study of art. In Part II, we will take up the application of these fundamentals in various fields of art endeavor. As we pursue our study we will become keenly aware of the most essential of these fundamentals, the essence of art itself—design.

There is a great difference between design and other aspects of our study, such as drawing and color. To become a successful draftsman, you must seek information and acquire the skill to use it. To become an accomplished colorist, you should be extremely observant, analytical, and skillful in the use of color. Designing requires a peculiar kind of ability which involves, on one hand, a practical approach to the problem and, on the other hand, imagination and good taste.

You might take stock of your ability as a designer by submitting yourself to an aptitude test embracing the following questions:

1. When presented a problem, can you analyze the chief objectives involved and plan a practical solution to attain them?
2. Have you the ability to visualize, the imagination to picture in the mind the object you think will serve the purpose?
3. Are you sensitive to relationships existing between areas of various size and shape, textures, colors, and arrangements?
4. When you see a design, can you analyze it and determine how it was made?

It will be understood that these aptitudes are inherent and do not result from book learning. Quite apart from any training a designer may get in any field of art, he will be far more successful if he has an analytical and creative mind. The above aptitudes may be developed through practice. They can also deteriorate through neglect and misuse.

You will probably begin, as most students do, by following in the footsteps of certain prominent designers, and give evidence of their influence as you learn the reasoning behind their designs. To know why they do a thing is just as important as to know how they do it.

During our studies in Part II, you will also observe that the principles of design, as outlined in Chapter 6 of Part I, are applicable in every field of art. It matters little whether you are designing the title page of a book, an advertisement, some pattern for a fabric, or an area of wall decoration, the principles of good arrangement, balance of interests, harmony of colors, and the suitability of the design to the purpose will govern the success of the effort.

You may be interested chiefly in a certain type of work and, concentrating your attention on acquiring the training needed to permit you to seek an opening in some professional studio specializing in this work, you may ignore the benefits of a broader training acquired through practice in a variety of art fields. It is not unusual for a designer successful in one line of work to attain a high ranking in other fields, regardless of the specialization in each field.

It is not necessary for us to go back to the days of Michelangelo to find the many-sided artist. Contemporary artists are just as versatile, if not as famous. Claude Bragdon, an architect of the past generation, gave up his practice in that profession to design theatrical productions for Walter

Hampden. He also created a school of design patterned after geometric form and devoted many hours to experiments with color lights. Norman Bel Geddes began his career as a commercial artist in Detroit and likewise extended his activities to the theater, designing the Max Reinhardt production of *The Miracle* produced in New York in 1924. His sense of the dramatic led him to the designing of dioramas used in the New York World's Fair in 1939. He has also entered the field of industrial design, an activity which is still offering broad opportunities to the new generation of art students.

There are some outlets for the designer that border more on the fine arts than on commercialism. One of these is Print Making. It is in the interest of that student who seeks to prepare himself for a professional career in art that the subjects that follow were selected. Some could be practiced either as a hobby or professionally; others could be practiced only in the professional field.

The Designer Approaches a Problem

The designer's first problem is to determine the purpose for which the article he is asked to design will be used. The intention of the client must be carried out. The means through which this is done depends on the designer's ingenuity. He does not arrive at his solution accidentally. He must consider all possibilities and make a selection. His planning and thinking are affected by various conditions. Let us consider some of them.

Aside from the purpose and function of the article to be designed, he must consider the space it will require and the material of which it will be made.

Then, if it is to be an article of which there will be many reproductions, will these be made by hand or by machine? If it must be made to sell in a certain market for a certain price, what will it cost to produce, and how much time will it take?

An example: The design of an all-over pattern might be affected by its purpose which, in turn, would affect its motif and its scale. If it were for a Christmas wrapping paper, the motif would be selected for its appropriateness. Also, as wrapping paper, its scale would be smaller than if it were being designed for a wallpaper.

Shape and size will affect the design. A circular shape, like a coin, medal or a plate, will require different treatment of the space than a square or rectangular area. Although the shape of the coin and the plate is similar, the difference in size would affect the design, as well as the process by which each would be reproduced.

There are various kinds of design; as many in number as there are purposes for things to be designed. For practical purposes we may confine ourselves to the consideration of seven.

1. Abstract design.
2. Applied ornament.
3. Design related to use.
4. Two-dimensional design.
5. Three-dimensional design.
6. Structural design.
7. Functional design.

Abstract Design

This kind of design, sometimes referred to as "pure" design, is unrelated to purpose, function, or any particular use. It is, or can be, visually pleasing, consisting of interesting relationships of lines, areas, forms, colors, or textures, or of relationships that combine two or more of these elements. The design is not required to mean anything, or to accomplish anything other than to provide a visual experience. It serves its chief purpose as exercise for art students because the beginner can concentrate on the essential nature of line, area, form, color and texture without, at the same time, being concerned with the advanced problem of application to purpose and use.

Applied Ornament

This is design as applied to anything which might otherwise exist and function without having design applied to it. It might be more appropriately termed "decoration." Designers claim that ornament should never be added to a thing already designed, that is, added as an afterthought. The inference is: If there is need for decoration in the design, it should be part of the original intention of the designer. This in no way belittles the use of ornament. It simply emphasizes the proper function of ornament—an integrated part of the whole design.

A china bowl will serve just as well as a bowl if it is plain, but there are many people who feel that the bowl, in addition to being useful, may be

A group of art school students working on a large window display for World Affairs Week in Providence, R. I. The theme was "the danger of boundaries." (Photograph courtesy of the Providence Journal-Bulletin.)

made more beautiful by the application of some ornament. Primitive craftsmen, with no art training as we know it, seemed to feel this need for ornament, and their instinct for appropriate decoration was highly developed.

Today, use and beauty are still considered important, and their union is desirable.

Design Related to Use

This is design chosen or created because of its particular relationship to its use through association of ideas. Orange blossoms are an appropriate motif for a wedding ring; wings for an aviator's insignia pin; or nursery rhyme figures for the decoration of a child's room.

To think of good ideas for designs related to use, the designer should have a large storehouse of visual knowledge. All kinds of symbols, their meanings and appropriate uses can be found in books, and a designer with a broad, general education will find constant use for it in this phase of his work.

Two-dimensional Design

This kind of design, explained in Chapter 6, Part I, is subject only to the condition of area. Within this limitation are wide possibilities for relationships of line, shapes, colors, and of textures.

It is considered good practice in two-dimensional design not to "counterfeit" three dimensions. It is an attempt to exceed the conditions imposed by the problem. Wall papers and textiles, two prominent uses of two-dimensional design, are used to define through suitable decoration, the limitation of space. Two-dimensional patterns cause the observer's eye to travel in a flat plane perpendicular to the line of sight. When three dimensions are suggested, as in wall paintings, or wall paper with landscapes, we are seeking to violate the limitations of space by creating the effect of greater space. There is plenty of precedent for this; the walls of many buildings are adorned with paintings and decorations where three dimensions are suggested. But this

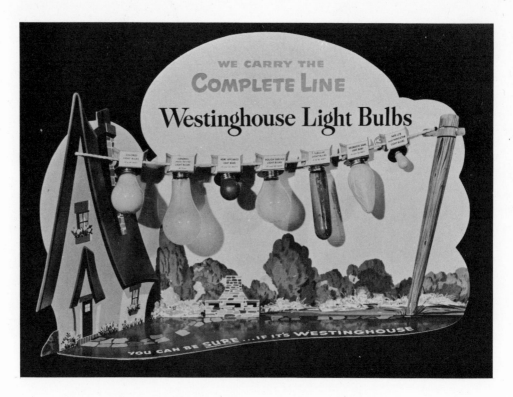

Window display design, lithographed in full color, with actual light bulbs on the "line." (Courtesy of Einson-Freeman Co.)

introduces a different problem with a different purpose, and is not related to that kind of design which is defined as two-dimensional, which is particularly related to designs in the graphic arts.

Three-dimensional Design

This is design which actually exists in space. Here line is of less importance compared to form. Color and textures affect the visual appearance of three-dimensional designs but they, too, are secondary to the more important factor—form. Show a designer a red ball. The fact that it is a sphere is more important to him than the fact it is red. Think of a chair. The form of its design will influence your acceptance or rejection of it rather than the color or the detail of its upholstery. True, color and texture are factors, but the beauty or ugliness of the furniture will depend upon its form.

A pleasing contour and good relationship between the parts determine the merit of all articles designed in three dimensions. This kind of design is of paramount importance in the fields of architecture and sculpture.

As an interesting experiment, the student should visit a store where unpainted furniture is on display. Test your judgment in appraising the worth of the pieces from a design point of view. There will be no color or texture to influence you.

Structural Design

This is a kind of design in three dimensions in which the structure constitutes the most important elements. A bridge, especially one of steel, is a good example of this kind of design. The purpose of every truss is apparent, and its importance in the design seems to be in relation to its structural value.

Furniture serves to illustrate the same point. If a chair looks so poorly constructed that it might not support a weight, it is the elements in the design which are related to their structured pur-

218

Three-dimensional window display in full color, including the vista of the lawn and garden seen through the lithographed wood-grain foreground, with actual products. (Courtesy of Einson-Freeman Co.)

pose that send out this message to the observer. The structural designer, once he is satisfied that his design is structurally sound, turns his attention to the appearance of strength the design must also have to be convincing.

Functional Design

This kind of design is similar to structural design. The difference lies in the qualities of the design which effect the article's efficiency although these qualities may not suggest its structural factors. How well a thing works in relation to the purpose for which it is designed is the primary consideration of the designer.

As an example, let us consider two electric toasters. The purpose of both is to toast bread. One of the toasters might burn the bread too easily, or its release mechanism might be so poorly designed that it would be difficult to get the toast out easily. This toaster would not function well; it is not well designed from the standpoint of function. It would matter little how attractive it appeared to be.

The other toaster might toast the bread exactly as you wished, and might deliver it quickly and easily. It would be a good example of functional design well carried out.

We live in an age of things designed to function well, from fountain pens and cigarette lighters to refrigerators, automobiles, locomotives and airplanes. The designer's problem is to create articles that are functional, sound in structure, as well as attractive and desirable.

During the past two decades art has joined with industry to improve the operation of the products of manufacture and, at the same time, to widen their appeal to a public with money to spend.

An unusually attractive window display, designed to fold flat for shipping. A miniature of the Dobbs hat box is seen in the foreground. (Courtesy of Einson-Freeman Co.)

Student layout in crayon—the eighteenth century French figure in the background is in red, contrasting effectively with the bolder rendering of the modern figure.

CHAPTER 2

Design for Advertising

For the young artist the lure of the advertising field lies chiefly in its availability as a broad schooling in art while offering some compensation. Wide circulation of art work carried on advertising pieces, and in magazines and newspapers, offers the artist the foundation of publicity and the opportunity of establishing himself.

High prices paid for advertising art also have their attraction for the young artist. These prices are not determined solely on the artist's ability as a technician; they are earned because of his ability as a good merchandising man who is familiar with the processes of reproduction, printing, typography, and dramatic presentation. He must also have the ability to think quickly, and to work for and with business executives. He should know something about the operations of an advertising agency, how advertising is planned, produced and distributed.

A Map Analysis of the Total Field of Advertising Design appears on adjacent pages and shows the many special kinds of advertising on which the artist may be expected to work. These

various fields will be referred to constantly throughout this chapter. It will be readily understood that this field of art endeavor cannot be practiced as a hobby. It can be approached only in a professional way.

Practicing the Profession

When the young artist begins in the advertising field he finds three courses open to him:

1. In an advertising agency art department, or in the art department of a store, or of any other organization which maintains an art department.
2. In an art service which is a business organization operating a supervised art studio for the production of a variety of art work for a diversified clientele.

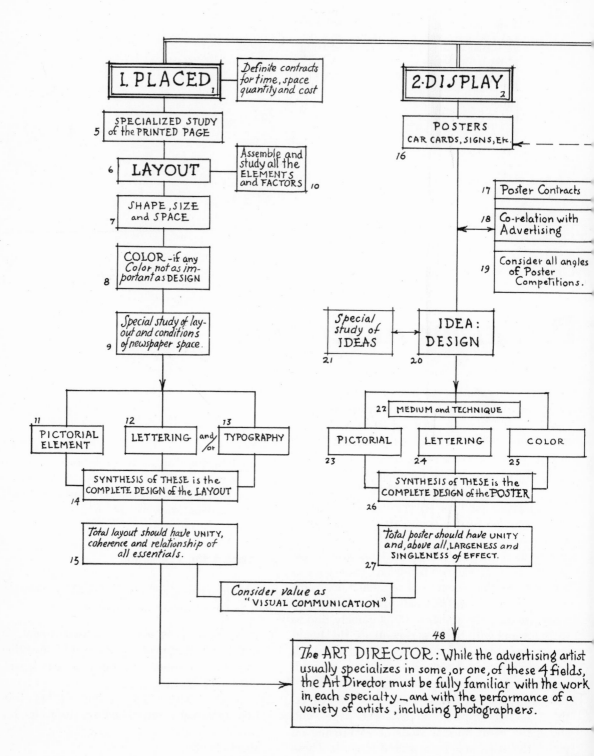

1. PLACED [1]

Definite contracts for time, space quantity and cost

5 SPECIALIZED STUDY of the PRINTED PAGE

6 LAYOUT

10 Assemble and study all the ELEMENTS and FACTORS

7 SHAPE, SIZE and SPACE

8 COLOR – if any Color not as important as DESIGN

9 Special study of layout and conditions of newspaper space.

11 PICTORIAL ELEMENT

12 LETTERING and/or

13 TYPOGRAPHY

14 SYNTHESIS of THESE is the COMPLETE DESIGN of the LAYOUT

15 Total layout should have UNITY, coherence and relationship of all essentials.

Consider value as "VISUAL COMMUNICATION"

2. DISPLAY [2]

16 POSTERS CAR CARDS, SIGNS, Etc.

17 Poster Contracts

18 Co-relation with Advertising

19 Consider all angles of Poster Competitions.

21 Special study of IDEAS

20 IDEA: DESIGN

22 MEDIUM and TECHNIQUE

23 PICTORIAL

24 LETTERING

25 COLOR

26 SYNTHESIS of THESE is the COMPLETE DESIGN of the POSTER

27 Total poster should have UNITY and, above all, LARGENESS and SINGLENESS of EFFECT.

48 The ART DIRECTOR: While the advertising artist usually specializes in some, or one, of these 4 fields, the Art Director must be fully familiar with the work in each specialty – and with the performance of a variety of artists, including photographers.

IELD of ADVERTISING DESIGN

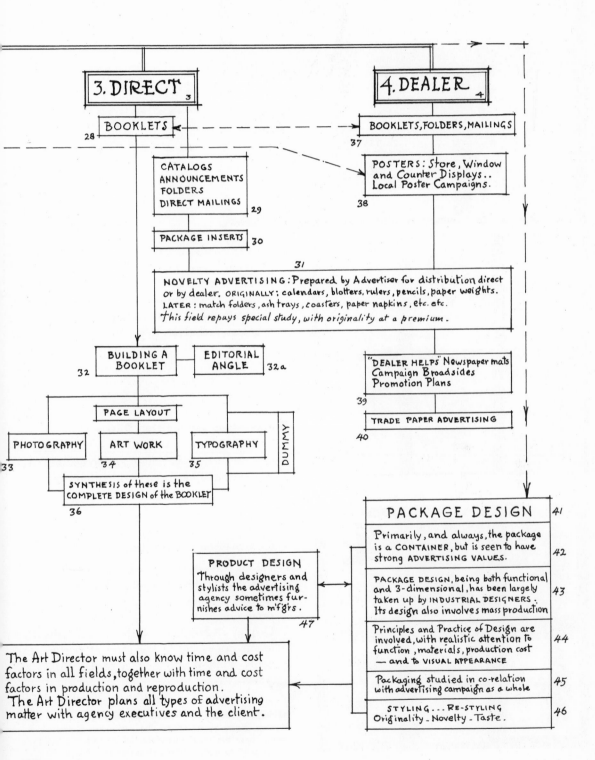

3. DIRECT ³

BOOKLETS ← 28

CATALOGS
ANNOUNCEMENTS
FOLDERS
DIRECT MAILINGS 29

PACKAGE INSERTS 30

31
NOVELTY ADVERTISING: Prepared by Advertiser for distribution direct or by dealer. ORIGINALLY: calendars, blotters, rulers, pencils, paper weights. LATER: match folders, ash trays, coasters, paper napkins, etc. etc. This field repays special study, with originality at a premium.

BUILDING A BOOKLET 32 — EDITORIAL ANGLE 32a

PAGE LAYOUT

PHOTOGRAPHY 33   ART WORK 34   TYPOGRAPHY 35   DUMMY

SYNTHESIS of these is the COMPLETE DESIGN of the BOOKLET 36

PRODUCT DESIGN
Through designers and stylists the advertising agency sometimes furnishes advice to m'f'g'rs. 47

The Art Director must also know time and cost factors in all fields, together with time and cost factors in production and reproduction.
The Art Director plans all types of advertising matter with agency executives and the client.

4. DEALER ⁴

BOOKLETS, FOLDERS, MAILINGS 37

POSTERS: Store, Window and Counter Displays.. Local Poster Campaigns. 38

"DEALER HELPS" Newspaper mats Campaign Broadsides Promotion Plans 39

TRADE PAPER ADVERTISING 40

PACKAGE DESIGN	41
Primarily, and always, the package is a CONTAINER, but is seen to have strong ADVERTISING VALUES.	42
PACKAGE DESIGN, being both functional and 3-dimensional, has been largely taken up by INDUSTRIAL DESIGNERS. Its design also involves mass production	43
Principles and Practice of Design are involved, with realistic attention to function, materials, production cost — and to VISUAL APPEARANCE	44
Packaging studied in co-relation with advertising campaign as a whole	45
STYLING... RE-STYLING Originality - Novelty - Taste.	46

Miniature rough layouts (about 1¾" x 2½") assigned to help the student to develop a visual "feeling" for the page as a whole.

3. As a free-lance artist, making his own contacts with customers, and carrying on the sales and service personally. This method can involve a great deal of unproductive time, insofar as solicitation cuts heavily into the daylight hours when an artist tries to produce his work. Once contacts are established, and the "selling and service time" is reduced to a minimum, free-lance operations may prove to be profitable.

The Field of Advertising Design

Let us survey the chart on preceding page. The entire field has been divided into four main divisions:

1. Placed 2. Display 3. Direct 4. Dealer

They may be described as follows:

1. Placed Advertising includes all advertisements "placed" on definite contracts, and at definite space rates, in newspapers, magazines, and programs.
2. Display Advertising includes all advertisements appearing in the form of posters, car-cards, window and counter cards "displayed."

Miniature "roughs" or "visuals" for full-page layouts, made by an advertising design student. These are required before the student is assigned to making abstract paste-ups,

3. Direct Advertising includes all advertising matter which is sent "directly" to you, by mail or by other means. It includes announcements, folders, booklets, and certain forms of novelty advertising, which may also reach you through a dealer.

4. Dealer Advertising is advertising sent by the manufacturer to the dealer, as well as advertising material prepared by the manufacturer for the dealer's use. The latter, the dealer distributes to the customer, or places in his window or on his counter, or uses in his local newspapers.

The Importance of the Layout

Layout is the planning of the design. Referring to the chart and reading down the extreme left axis, we see the conditions (7, 8, and 9) which affect the layout, together with the three principal things which have to be organized by the designer. They are: the pictorial element, if any, the lettering, and the typography. The "synthesis" (14), because the bringing together of the three major elements which comprise the advertisement.

If the advertisement calls for color, this phase of the study should wait until the layout is determined in black and white. It must have its appeal on the basis of its arrangement of masses. Color will not make it a better layout. For this reason, it is suggested that all preliminary study of the layout be done without color.

As in all design, it is advisable to approach the layout by making a number of small sketches. These sketches should determine the approximate relation of the illustration, if any, to the other elements on the page, and show its shape and its placement. Headlines and type areas should also be indicated. A number of such preliminary studies are illustrated on opposite page. They may be considered the designs for advertising pages.

A student layout in crayon for a two-column newspaper layout. A "finish" for this layout might require little more than an accurate drawing of the razor and a better rendering of the informal lettering.

Four small-space newspaper layouts for a series. These layouts, by a student, present a comprehensive visualization of the appearance of the finished advertisement. At the left, one is shown at larger scale.

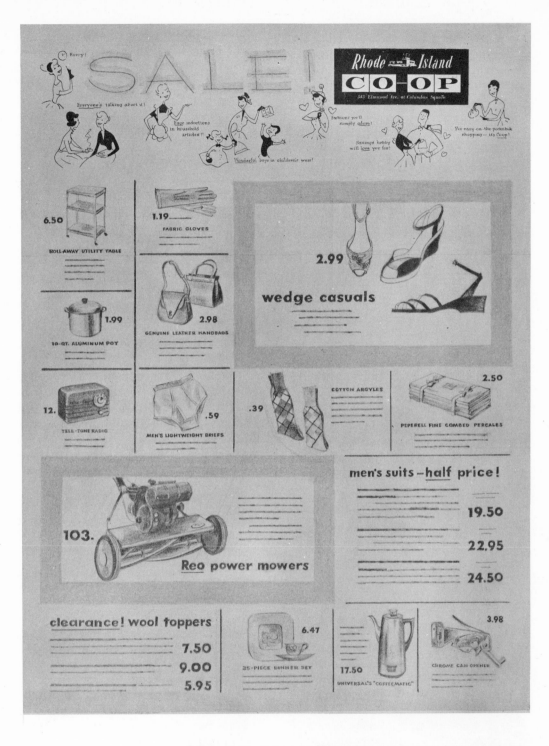

Soft-pencil layout for a newspaper full page featuring a variety of merchandise. This is the work of an advertising design student, and no exercise could be more valuable as preparation for a staff position in an art service or the art department of a retail store.

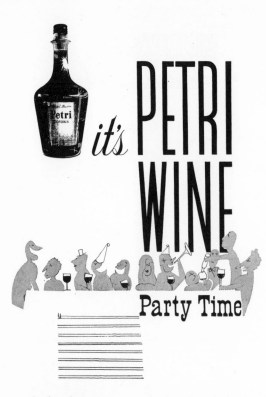

Student layout in pen and ink and applied shading medium, with hand-lettering and the illustration of the bottle in scratch-board technique.

Paste-up layout by a typography student Material for this layout is clipped and pasted to represent a complete page.

Concentrate on the Design

It is recommended that while a student is learning to design advertisements, he refrain from struggling with a rendering of the proposed illustration. Even a good illustration will not compensate for a poorly designed layout. Concentrate on the layout. Seek interesting arrangements with areas of type matter. Give importance to white space, for without this basic element in your design, confusion will probably be the result.

Where illustrations are to be used, work with photographic material which can be clipped from magazines. It will simplify this part of the problem and permit you to direct your full attention to the design.

The Early Decisions

The first decision concerning the layout that a designer must make is whether it is to be formal or informal. As we have observed in our studies of composition, formality is attained by orderly arrangements, frequently involving symmetry. A balance of like parts, a simplification of the units, or a static appearance in the arrangement will produce this effect.

The informal design has movement and, while not appearing to effect orderliness, nevertheless can be made to produce balance with the elements used.

The Picture Element

When a picture is specified for an advertisement, three considerations will govern its use:

1. Size. Is the picture to occupy approximately half the total area? More than half? Less than half? If more than one picture is specified, are they to be shown the same size, or is one to dominate?
2. Shape or Treatment. Shape makes a tremendous difference in the appearance of a picture, and this difference affects the layout. The contour of a photograph will frequently suggest an object related to the theme of the advertisement, and this shape will create a strong appeal in the design, apart from the appeal of the photograph. In addition to the

228

shape of the picture, special effects are gained also by special treatments, a few of which were mentioned in Chapter 8 of Part I, Media and Methods of Working.

3. Placement. The appearance of a layout is affected by the placement of the picture or pictures. Where several are involved, the arrangement of these is essentially a matter of design.

The Reading Matter

Most advertisements break "the message" into three parts—the heading, the body of the text, and the signature, which consists of the advertiser's name, address, and branch offices, if any. This "copy" is an integral part of the design, and all three elements should be studied at the same time consideration is being given to the illustration.

Headings may be hand-lettered (see Chapter 3) or may be set in type (see Chapter 4). In either case, the heading should make the reader stop, look, and read further. Examples may be seen in the numerous illustrations for this chapter and in current periodicals. No text book on this subject can be as up-to-date as the magazines on display at the newsstands.

The body of the text is chiefly a matter of typography. Sufficient space should be reserved in the layout so that the type can be of a size readily legible.

Signatures may be hand-lettered or typographic. When a signature utilizes a specially designed style, or kind of letter, such as a trademark, it is called a logotype. Specially designed signatures frequently carry "Registered U. S. Patent Office."

Space Considerations

The space which presents the simplest problems in layout is the full page, whether for magazine or newspaper. The smaller the space and the greater the difference between the width and depth of the space, the more difficult the designer's problem will be.

One of the more difficult problems of layout is the catalog page on which a large number of articles are to be displayed. Sometimes the articles vary greatly in size which makes the group-

Two paste-up layouts by typography students —the first an "all type" page, the second a formal relationship of type and picture.

Two paste-up layouts by typography students. These layouts are assembled from existing material but presented in strictly original relationships.

When articles can be grouped, it is the problem of the designer to arrange them so that the important parts of each article will be seen. Other parts may be obscured from view by another article in front of it.

Space in catalogs is considered at a premium by the advertiser. The artist is supposed to economize on this space by arranging the articles to their best advantage in the smallest space possible. Provision must also be given for copy descriptive of the articles. Study the folders that are mailed to you advertising clothing, silverware, luggage, and furniture. Refer to them as you make your early experiments in this field.

Dramatize the product you are trying to sell. If it is not very exciting in itself, make it so in the layout. Be willing to experiment with different shapes, both of type and of illustration. There are no rules to confine you other than the sound principles of good design—pleasing arrangement of elements, balance of parts, harmony in the size and shapes of masses, and clarity in setting forth your message.

A Few Thoughts About the Layout

Frequently poor photographs are submitted for use, and the designer finds it necessary to obscure the faults and favor the virtues of this material. A good picture is a good start. That is why it is helpful for the designer to supervise the making of the photograph. He may not possess the technical information of a professional photographer, but his sense of the dramatic and his understanding of pictorial composition will aid greatly in obtaining satisfactory results.

Dominance and contrast are the outstanding principles of design that control dramatic presentation. When everything on the page is the same size, the effect may make a good pattern though it will not be dramatic. Our sense of design tells us that to dramatize one thing, all other elements in the composition must be made subordinate to it. To make it large in contrast with smaller things will make it appear larger than it actually is.

Contrasts can be created in ways other than those of size. Formal arrangements contrast with informal ones; straight contours with curved contours; rectangular pictures with silhouetted pictures; and the contrast of direction obtained by oblique placement of material on the page

ing of them impractical. A thimble can hardly be shown in the same grouping with a sewing machine; the scale of one is ill-related to the other. When articles differ in size too greatly to be grouped together, they are set apart so that the problem of scale is avoided.

230

against the rectangular shape of the page itself.

It is a good idea to compose small pictures vertically rather than horizontally, and to group them together rather than scatter them and so lose a structural formation.

Formal, symmetrical pages are harder to dramatize than unsymmetrical ones. The symmetrical page usually depends for its effect on dignity and elegance. Restraint in the use of contrast tends to reduce the dramatic effect.

The Design of Posters
(16 on the map)

The value of a poster is its power to attract attention and convey an idea at a glance. The secret of its power is its simplicity, both in the treatment of the message and the presentation of the illustration, if any.

While a poster may be pictorial, and many are, it should not be an illustration. It should carry but one idea, not many. It should be a visual message—an idea presented clearly and dramatically to the mind through the eye. It should never be so elaborate as to require close study for any length of time. It should act as an "interrupting idea," interrupting whatever the observer may be thinking about at that time.

This important fact is frequently overlooked, particularly by beginners. When they are designing a poster and it is absorbing their entire attention, they may assume that it will merit public attention in the same degree. It will be interesting to make this experiment: The next time you see what appears to be a good poster in a store window, stand by for a few minutes and count the people who, going by, pause to look at it.

Four Qualities a Poster Must Have

Regardless of the purpose for which a poster is designed, it should have four important qualities:

1. Attention Value
2. Comprehension Value
3. Impulsion Value
4. Memory Value.

Let us define these briefly:

1. Attention Value speaks for itself. The poster must provide a shock for the optic nerve. This shock can be produced by strong contrasts

Soft-pencil layout for a newspaper advertisement, done by a senior art student. The ability to draw and render store merchandise of all kinds is a never-failing asset to any artist who is concerned with earning a living.

in dark and light, and in color. Simple, powerful masses with striking contours create the desired effect.

2. Comprehension Value means that the idea in the poster should be so clearly stated that it can be comprehended by anyone at the

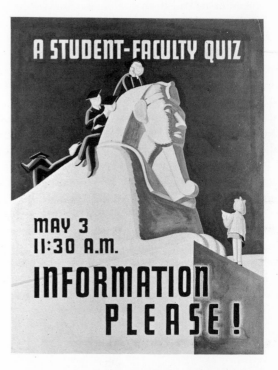

Poster design for a car-card; the color scheme, black and orange; the cigarette, a creative idea of the student-designer.

Two posters by students in training as art teachers. The first is interestingly stylized, the second with the gigantic red, white, and buff steamship funnel has "largeness and singleness of effect."

In this full-color poster for a school "assembly" program, a third-year art school program produced an excellent example of the extent to which a well-planned poster can tell its entire story pictorially, in this case, with both strong technique and composition, and with whimsical humor.

This now famous Harrison Fisher poster of World War I days dramatizes its message so clearly and forcefully that no worded text is necessary. Few posters accomplish this.

A typical poster by Ludwig Hohlwein, famous pre-World War I German artist. The leopard is in natural colors on a buff background; the eyes of the black feline behind it are vivid emerald green.

In this collection of lettering chosen in connection with poster design, Examples 1 to 9 would be good choices while Examples 10 to 18 are "don'ts." The 1 to 9 group, obviously not only are easily readable but also have character and distinction. The reason for illustrating the "don'ts" (10 to 18) is that a great many amateur poster designers make the mistake either of forgetting the importance of clear, easy readability or of thinking that a poster calls for some sort of freakish, eccentric letter style. Examples 10, 11, 17, and 18 would not be good anywhere; the others are definitely for use on the printed page.

first glance. Interesting details will not compel attention or arrest the interest of a passerby. It takes a forceful and dramatic treatment to do this. The simpler the idea presented in a picture, the fewer the words needed to explain it.

One of the most striking posters, and one which tells its story without a word of text, is the Red Cross poster made by Harrison Fisher at the time of the first World War. It carries out the words of the Chinese wise man who said, "One picture is worth a thousand words."

3. Impulsion Value means that your poster should impel people to act. This will happen only if the message is direct and forceful.

It isn't easy to think of impelling ideas. The best way is to simplify the idea, to present the essence of the idea in a single picture.

4. Memory Value suggests its own meaning. Anything forceful and unusual will be remembered. A poster fails in its purpose if it is forgotten as soon as it has been seen. Here again, the quality of appeal is needed to reach the inner consciousness of an observer and to make him think about the idea expressed long after he has seen the poster.

Medium and Technique
(22 on the map)

In painting the poster, the selection of the medium is not as important as the treatment or technique. Oil and water color are acceptable media; heavy black crayon has been used with good effect, but brilliant poster colors are recommended for the student's use. The important factor is the simplicity with which the work is done. Areas should be broad and free from distracting details. Some very effective posters have been made with the camera, especially where the subject matter was suitable for use as a silhouette. In November 1949, a camera study was used for a poster on Polio, and it won a $1,000 prize in competition with art work. Ideas are more important than the medium used. (See illustration on page 306.)

Lettering
(24 on the map)

Poster lettering must be easily readable, even by people with less than normal eyesight. Block

In the concept of a poster, neither medium nor color is so important as idea, particularly when the idea is presented as dramatically as Victor Keppler has created, with the camera, this World War II poster, in black and white, with red background to the lettering.

The poster designer here turned to the camera for technique, making a striking composition of mannequin and ornate frame to dramatize the silk, which is the subject.

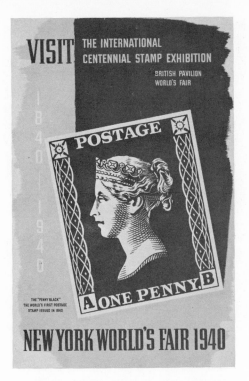

In the hands of a skillful designer, a thing as small as a postage stamp may be given dramatic importance and even an illusion of largeness, as in this poster by Bob Smith.

The modern poster designer sometimes utilizes symbols, treated, as in this poster, in the manner of abstract design. This example is by E. McKnight Kauffer, one of the most outstanding of contemporary poster artists.

letters are preferred. These are letters without serifs—those little spurs that spread outward from the prominent stroke of the letter. However, block letters can be illegible if the strokes are drawn too closely together, closing up the spaces. Space between the letters and within the parts of a letter are necessary so that it can be easily read. Letters that are very thin are difficult to read at long range because they seem to resemble one another.

Letters resembling script are attractive but are not easy to read unless they are simply and clearly drawn. Fine-line script or "autographic" script letters should not be used on posters.

Examples of good poster lettering appear in the illustrations on accompanying pages. Those most easily read are the bold letters surrounded by sufficient space to set each character apart.

When designing a poster, study the lettering on a piece of tracing paper and set it where you can view it twenty feet away. Draw the illustration on another piece of tracing paper and study the two elements of the poster in juxtaposition so that neither will be weakened by the other. Tracing paper studies will save much time when the finished drawing is being made.

Color

Color gives a poster more "attention and attraction value" than the design would have if rendered only in black and white. In the use of color, remember the suggestions offered in the chapter on Color in Part 1. As previously mentioned, select a complementary scheme, but reserve the bright, vivid color for only one strong accent. Too many bright colors will cause confusion; they will defeat one another.

Black is frequently used in posters because almost any other color will seem bright in contrast with it. Yellows and reds are favorites with poster designers because of the strong "eye appeal" they have. If a vermilion is used, a small amount of it will seem to vibrate against a subdued shade of bluish-green. Lemon yellow makes a striking accent against a background of deep purple. But be careful when you use a medium depth of blue; its complement is orange, and each color has the power of balancing the other. The "tonal" values of each are similar, and when they are used together the effect produces a color shock but lacks a tonal contrast. It will be better if a light orange is used against a much darker blue.

Three typical examples of the 24-sheet outdoor poster. These were selected as illustrative of the kind of idea-work, as well as the high level of art-work observable, in this advertising medium today.

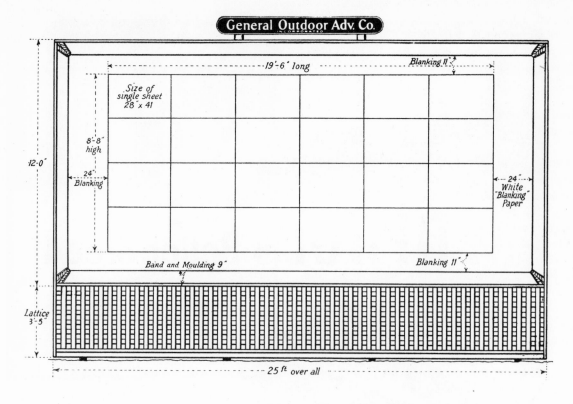

The standard dimensions of the outdoor roadside poster, generally called a "24-sheet." The poster area is here shown in a "poster panel," with white "blanking" at right and left.

Letters in pale, light colors lack sharp visibility unless projected against a dark background. Against a light or neutral background, letters in light colors seem smaller than the same letters would be rendered in black or a dark color. White or light-colored letters on a dark background appear to "close up," especially if thin lines are used. Avoid using thin strokes in making poster lettering. Letters must have sufficient thickness to be legible at a distance, but they should not be too heavy or clumsy.

Sizes of Posters

Size, of course, can make a poster more conspicuous, but size is relative. It depends on where the poster is to be used, and from what distance it is to be seen.

For the purpose of reference, a reproduction of a technical drawing of a "poster panel" is shown on an accompanying page. This drawing, furnished by the General Outdoor Advertising Company, shows a typical panel built to display the big roadside posters. These posters are referred to as "24-sheet posters" because they are

printed in 24 separate sheets and matched together to make the full poster.

Each sheet is 28 by 41 inches, and when the 24 sheets are matched together, they make a panel 8 feet and 8 inches high and 19 feet and 6 inches long. This is a standard size. Artists who design and paint posters to be reproduced in this manner make their finished drawing 40 inches long. It is enlarged mechanically by the lithographer. When making sketches for posters of this kind, follow the proportions of the dimensions given above in a reduced ratio. Remember the long dimension as the horizontal dimension.

Two other standard sizes for outdoor posters frequently seen are the two-sheet and the three-sheet units. The sheets which comprise them are cut the same size as for use in the 24-sheet display, but they are matched to produce a vertical poster. Each is 41 inches wide and the two-sheet poster when matched is 56 inches high; the three-sheet, 84 inches high.

Standard size for car-cards is 11 by 21 inches. Card advertising in buses has introduced various sizes, some standard, some special. It is most likely that the artist commissioned to design one of these will be instructed as to the dimensions required. Dimensions of a piece of work make a most important part of the instructions. Make certain you know how your design is to be used before spending time on the study.

Direct Advertising
(3 on the map)

Designers of direct-by-mail advertising plan announcements, folders, catalogs, novelty items, and booklets (28 on the map), the latter being one of the most important mailing pieces in this class of work.

Planning a booklet requires a certain amount of knowledge of the printing industry—engraving processes, type, standard paper sizes, and printing production. Each page is a separate layout, and all are to be co-related so that the flow of interest throughout the booklet will be maintained. The continuity of the booklet's message should not be broken.

Cost is an important factor in the planning and designing of a booklet. In order to get an engraver's and a printer's estimates, a "structural model" called a "dummy" simulating the finished booklet in size and number of pages should be made.

Making a Dummy
(25 on the map)

Every booklet design naturally depends on the purpose and general character of the material which is to go into it as well as the amount of material. The booklet may be a "quality" presentation, produced at considerable expense for distribution to a limited clientele, or it may be mass-produced at the lowest possible cost. Cost may be high or low on any or all of the following items which make up the total cost, and each of which must be carefully considered by the designer.

Booklet costs which govern design: The designer's fee, costs of artwork and/or photography,

Four typical booklet covers: The Kodak booklet, appropriately, photographic; "Syrie," a topical pattern in stylized art-work; the "Finger Paint" booklet exactly reproducing the medium; "Florence," a poster-like painting in full color.

Three booklet covers designed and styled in character with the subject matter. The "antique" clock book is brown on a buff cover; the recipe booklet is black on a red-and-white check background; the Dobbs booklet is quaintly stylized and in bright colors.

A group of advertising books and booklets designed and supervised by the author.

Typical advertising booklets here chosen to suggest the great variety in size, format, and styling.

plate-making, type composition, kind of paper to be used for inside pages and for cover, general style of binding (called "format" by printers) style and format of mailing container, if any.

Designers who specialize in booklet work never begin directly with a finished dummy. The general procedure is to make a careful study of the material required to go into the booklet, then to arrange this in sequence, page by page. Following this, several very rough dummies may have to be made until the required material is so exactly "edited" that it exactly fills the planned number of pages. At this point the designer would be ready to proceed with a carefully finished dummy for presentation to the client for O.K.

In presenting a booklet dummy for approval and O.K. it is very important to present, at the same time, a printer's estimate based on the dummy. Such estimates are usually figured on the first five or ten thousand copies, with a lower per thousand figure quoted for "additional thousands."

Obtain sample sheets of paper from a printing house and fold these blank sheets to the page size you desire. Sketch the material to go on each page and decide on the positions for the illustrations and type. Many revisions may be necessary. When the position of all the material to go into the booklet is determined, you are ready to ask the engraver and the printer for estimates of cost. They require the information the dummy shows them to give an intelligent estimate. They may also make suggestions as to how the cost may be reduced and, if these suggestions do not interfere with the basic planning of the booklet, much money may be saved. The more careful and precise the dummy is, the closer co-operation may be expected from the various craftsmen in the printing trades.

Before listing the steps in booklet design, it may be well to remind the student that a booklet is never planned to be one of 13, 14, 17 or 18 pages. It can be made in multiples of 4 pages, but is usually planned for 8, 16 or 32 pages.

A booklet is printed on both sides of a sheet which is folded later, bound, and trimmed by machinery. A 32-page booklet is printed with 16 pages on one side of the sheet, and 16 pages

This illustration shows the dummy and finished booklet, with an uncut sheet or "form" of 8 pages. Backed up with the other 8, this made a 16-page booklet.

on the other. These pages are located in the printing form so that when printed back to back, folded, bound and trimmed, the pages will appear in perfect order.

If you take a sheet of paper and fold it once, you will have a four-page folder. Fold it again and it becomes an eight-page booklet. Fold it once more and it becomes a 16-page booklet, do so again and you have 32 pages. These are the economical numbers of pages to plan for use in booklet design.

If your material seems to run to ten pages, a little condensing of your layouts could get it into eight pages. If the material seems to run to 13 or 14 pages, it would seem wiser to spread it enough to fill 16 pages.

When you have received the estimates from the engraver covering the illustrations, and from the printer covering the cost of paper, type-setting, printing, folding, and shipping, submit the dummy and prices for the client's approval.

In many instances a client will supply the text and the illustrations, requiring only a design for the booklet and art work that may be suggested by the design.

Designing the Cover

When a booklet requires a cover of heavier paper stock than that used for the printed pages, different standards of size have to be consulted. The booklet with the 4½" x 6" and 6" x 9" page size will require a sheet of cover stock 20" x 26". The 8½" x 11" page size will require a sheet of cover stock 23" x 33". These two cover stock sizes are standard and the most frequently used.

When a booklet is designed so that the first page serves as a cover, it is called a "self-covered" booklet.

Frequently a cover is designed where portions of the illustration extend to the trimmed edge of the page. This is called a "bleed." When

Four designs for booklet covers in full color, the work of second-year art school students.

Two cover designs and an inside photographic layout for travel booklets, designed by second-year art school students.

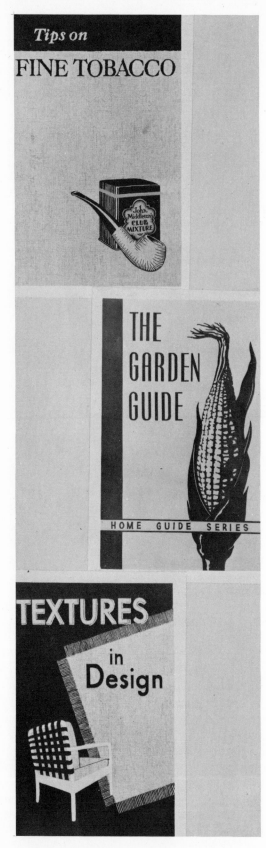

Tips on
FINE TOBACCO

THE GARDEN GUIDE

HOME GUIDE SERIES

TEXTURES in Design

Three designs on cover stock for booklets designed by third-year art school students.

the drawing is made to attain this effect, an additional ¼ inch of the design should be allowed at the places where the design "bleeds" off the sheet. This will assure the effect when the cover is trimmed to its finished size.

Supervising the Production

The designer can serve a client effectively by checking the various stages of the work as it progresses. He can help prepare the artwork and the photography for the engraver. Attention should be given to the accuracy of the proportions of each piece of artwork so that when the engraving is made the image will fit into the space allowed for it. The simplest method of establishing reductions in size is the diagonal, diagrammed on page 323.

Type should be estimated for the space it will take when specifications are given for its setting. Nothing can upset the fitting of the finished material to the dummy more thoroughly than type which either falls short of its space or extends beyond the space allotted to it.

There are many systems of type "casting" used currently in the printing industry but a student can do the job for himself with nothing more than the application of common sense. All that is needed is a sample of the style and size of type proposed for use. Counting the characters of type in a line of given length, and counting the number of lines to a given depth, the total number of characters can be determined. Using this factor as a measurement, and counting the characters in the copy furnished by the client, the length of the copy when set in type is easily estimated.

When type proofs and engraving proofs are received, the designer can check the correctness of everything at this stage by making a "paste-up" dummy, placing the proofs where they are intended for printing. This gives a client a graphic visualization of the completed job, and his approval should be obtained on this dummy before the printer proceeds with the work.

Changes and corrections in the typesetting should be made on the side of the galleys, not on the trimmed proof pasted in the dummy. The dummy establishes the position of the material, the corrected galleys are followed by the typesetter.

Four designs on wood grain cover stock for booklets by third-year art school students. At the right, a working drawing for the carpentry booklet, in black and white for reproduction.

This series of steps represents the kind of design and production responsibility assumed by an art director. The designer, planner and supervisor of booklet production may not do the artwork himself, but he must have experience in all stages of the work.

Novelty Advertising
(36 on the map)

People gifted with an inventive turn of mind are capable of designing pieces of advertising material with unusual folds and die-stamped cut-outs which attract the public's attention more by the uniqueness of the article than by the message it may carry.

The first advertisements that appeared on calendars, blotters, rulers, pencils, match folders, paper-weights and ash trays were novel. They attracted attention and soon became used generally. Novel ideas are needed constantly to interest the public.

Some firms make a specialty of producing novelties for the advertising field. These novelties are used both in direct and dealer advertising.

In this field individual thinking is imperative. Look over the various items of novelty advertising currently in use, and study an extension of the idea to a further use. This offers a good beginning in studying the approach to the problem. The ideas from which new articles are evolved are seldom a radical departure from the

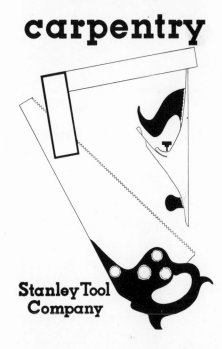

stream of thought governing the present trends. They are different chiefly in their application to a new use.

Thinking up ideas for novelty advertising is an excellent training in creative work. You may be able to think of a good, attractive, and practical novelty that you have never seen. It may be a salable idea. It surely is worth working into a model. If it involves action, it may be suitable for a window display. It might not involve printing; rather it may be something you would have to model in clay, or carve in wood.

Sometimes ideas for novelty advertising come from the nature of a business. You may ask yourself what would be a smart novelty advertisement for a real estate company, or for a local savings bank.

243

A second-year art school student created this quaint booklet cover, carried out in Delft blue and white Dutch tile motif.

Textured and rich-colored cover stocks inspired these two booklet cover designs by third-year art school students.

Let us explore an idea for the first of these. A strip of cardboard, perhaps two inches wide and eight or nine inches long, might be made to slip through a sleeve, also of cardboard and having a window opening in the front wall. On the back inside wall of the sleeve, foliage could be painted. Along the strip a series of small cut-outs could be made, each a home in a different architectural style, and silhouetted. These might be spaced on the strip so that, when moved through the sleeve, only one design would appear in the opening. This idea might help an observer to visualize the home he desires placed in a verdant setting. While it is not the intention to suggest that such an idea has commercial merit, it suggests a way of thinking the student might turn to some advantage.

New ways to encourage thrift are always interesting ideas for bankers.

Sometimes ideas come from things an advertiser would be likely to use. An automobile tire company distributed ash trays with miniature tires fitted around the circumference of the tray. It made a practical article and used a model of the advertiser's product as its feature.

Often, these novelty ideas may be presented directly to the advertiser. It is usually wiser to present them through the advertising agency which handles the account.

244

Dealer Advertising
(4 on the map)

This kind of work is generally designed by advertising agencies or art departments of manufacturers. A student is not likely to encounter the problems of dealer advertising unless he works for some such agency or department. Store and counter displays, store posters and dealer helps are furnished to dealers by the manufacturer.

Show card writing, used by local stores, can be practiced by anyone who is proficient at lettering, especially with a brush.

Package Design
(41–46 on the map)

The Map Analysis in this chapter shows a group of notes on Package Design, but does not show it as a form of advertising. Any package is a *container*, which is its chief function. Only recently the advertising possibilities of the package have been realized and developed by both advertisers and designers.

The main points of package design will be discussed in a subsequent chapter, but the subject's connection with the Map Analysis gives reason for some mention at this time of the basic principles involved. Manufacturers, persuaded by their advertising advisers, came to realize that the appearance of a packaged product might be of great importance in the whole advertising and promotion plan.

It was pointed out that a package should be so distinctive in its design that the buying public would recognize it easily. This would give it memory value. A distinctive color scheme, design, and unusual lettering would give the package trade-mark value, definitely associated with a particular product and manufacturer.

More recently the functional possibilities of package designs became recognized and advertising agencies have engaged industrial designers to study the use of new materials adaptable to this purpose.

Product Design

About 1927 advertising agencies began to advise their clients to redesign their products with a view to eye appeal. This opened a new field for designers as it required them to become fa-

In the category of "point-of-sale" advertising, window and counter displays represent a wide and diversified field for the imaginative designer. (Courtesy of Einson-Freeman Co.).

It has been found that one of the most effective of selling aids is the display unit that puts the product on the dealer's counter. (Courtesy of Einson-Freeman Co.).

Three units for either window or counter display, designed to feature the actual article advertised.

The window display was built around a realistic full-color lithograph of "Miss Rheingold" and was keyed to the Christmas season. Displays of this kind tie in with poster, magazine, newspaper advertising and a total large-scale promotion. Courtesy of the Einson-Freeman Company.

Organized design in a European window display. The arrangement of windows, as well as display material involved, should attract the best efforts of any advertising designer.

miliar with the operations of intricate machinery. It was not long before those aspects of a designer's mind which direct him in his creative thinking won the respect of the industrial world. Industrial designing became a new profession which has been responsible for the progress of modern design in a wide variety of manufactured products.

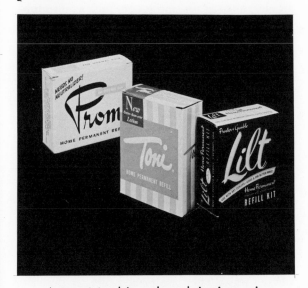

A present trend in package design is seen in these three examples, in which the major element, in addition to striking color schemes, is large scale informal script lettering.

The Art Director
(48 on the map)

The last notation on the Map Analysis gives a brief outline of the duties of the Art Director, an executive the student is likely to meet with sooner or later. Certain artists who have acquired a breadth of information in the printing and advertising fields, and who have practiced art, become expert in layout, and developed their critical powers, become art directors themselves.

The qualifications and aptitudes are not common nor are they easy to meet. Professionally, the art director must be a person of taste and sound judgment in all matters pertaining to art, and he must be adroit in working effectively with all types of artists, designers, and photographers. He must be somewhat of a diplomat, an executive, and a good businessman.

Nowhere is training for such a position obtainable unless it be on the job itself. The men and women who are art directors have, in addition to natural aptitudes, the ability to grasp the mere wisp of an idea and develop it, with all its ramifications, into a message with a strong appeal.

Suggested Exercises

Design for Advertising

Exercise 1

As preliminary practice in layout, make approximately 10 miniature sketch layouts for magazine pages, similar to the sketches illustrated on page 224. These small sketches need not be any larger than 2 inches wide and 2⅝ inches deep, approximately the proportion of a typical magazine page. These small sketches are frequently called "visuals." They are the first rough ideas composed for a layout.

It may be wiser to make these first attempts at layout "abstract"—that is, show the picture only as a dark-toned shape, and the type, headline, and signature by a rough indication, as in the student examples illustrated.

Exercise 2

Following this preliminary exercise, you should be ready to make "paste-ups," as seen in the student examples illustrated on pages 236 and 238. As a basis for these layouts you might select two of your miniature "roughs." Select a picture in any magazine and give it the shape indicated in the sketch. Then find lines of display type and a signature, and a block of body type to serve as the main portion of the copy.

Trim this material neatly, lightly marking guide lines to aid in keeping the lines of type level when pasting them on the layout. With a piece of white show-card board on which a rectangle has been drawn having the actual size of a typical magazine page, paste the various elements of the layout in positions relative to their location in the small rough. Use rubber cement for the pasting; it's cleaner than glue and does not wrinkle the cut-outs. If this is done carefully and neatly the finished work will look like a printed page. Make many of these; the practice will teach you much about making layouts.

Exercise 3

Your next exercise should be the completely drawn layout. For this, use a pad of tracing paper, especially suitable for layout work and sold in art supply stores, and a soft pencil, preferably a 2B or 3B grade. Hard pencils fail to give a result approximating the blacks of a printed page.

In technique, your pencil layouts may range in effect from a rough visualization to a smartly executed sketch which is called a "comprehensive" in advertising circles. This effect is close in appearance to the "finished" page.

Exercise 4

Make the layout for a 6-page folder that, when folded with two parallel folds, will fit into a 6¾″ envelope. This envelope is a standard mailing size. The size of the folder, flat, should be 9¾″ x 6¼″ and, when folded, 3¼″ x 6¼″. The subject to be advertised is a household electric appliance. Space should be reserved for the imprinting of a dealer's name. Consult the popular magazines, select an article, and plan the use of the illustration, copy, and other factors you think will help to sell the product. Hold the printing to two colors.

Exercise 5

Let's design a 16-page booklet. Its subject can be governed by the illustrations you are able to find. However, it should advertise a line of articles, alike in use and scope, such as furniture, garden tools, household equipment, etc. Again, consult the pages of some current magazines where many small illustrations of such merchandise may be found.

MAKE A DUMMY

Determine your page size. For this kind of practice work it may be convenient to determine the size of the booklet by the size of the illustrations available for use in it.

Plan the pages to get as much merchandise included as you can without the effect of crowding. Allow space for the descriptive captions. Descriptive captions are usually handled in one of two ways. They are placed directly under or beside the articles shown, or they are concentrated in one large caption in one part of the page and "keyed" to the illustration by a numeral or letter which appears with the illustration.

Incidental artwork may be used to contrast with photographs, and further variety may be introduced by silhouetting some photographs while leaving others rectangular.

Study the booklet page layouts as pairs of facing pages. These would be pages 2 and 3, 4 and 5, etc. Page 1, being a single page should be designed with, perhaps, a paragraph of introductory text and some kind of decoration.

For the cover find some kind of tinted or colored stock heavier than the inside pages, and on this, letter the title of the booklet in a style appropriate to its contents and add some incidental artwork.

Staple the booklet along the binding edge using an automatic stapler, or take staples from a printed booklet and use them on the dummy in the same manner they were used in the other.

This is the sort of dummy for a booklet which in actual practice would be used to obtain a printer's estimate and the client's approval. In order to put it into production there would need be, of course, actual photographs of the items to be pictured and actual copy with descriptions, prices, etc.

Exercise 6

Make sketches for a 24-sheet poster advertising some brand of gasoline. Prepare black-and-white studies at first, then make color sketches. Remember to keep the idea dominant, the treatment simple and effective. Hold the length of copy used to 12 words, including the name of the product.

Supplement to Chapter 2

Vocational Notes on Advertising, from the American Association of Advertising Agencies publications, "The Structure of the Advertising Agency Business" and "The AAAA Examination Plan," by permission of the AAAA.

The following quotations will be found helpful by anyone who is looking ahead to a career in advertising.

"Advertising is a broad field—broader perhaps than most people realize. Many who are unfamiliar with the business may think of advertising men as primarily writers or artists. But the fact is, advertising provides a field for a wide range of special talents.

"Within advertising agencies there are specialists in merchandising, research, radio, publication space buying and radio time buying, as well as art and copy writing. Many agencies also have a publicity or public relations department. In larger agencies, such departments are staffed by specialists in their fields. In smaller agencies the same person may combine two or more functions.

"But advertising is by no means limited to advertising agencies. The advertising agency business employs a total of less than 25,000 people, and many of these people can be classed as clerical workers rather than advertising specialists. Beyond the agency field there are thousands of advertising men and women employed by department stores, large manufacturers, publications, radio stations and large printing concerns. In some cases people move from advertising agencies into some of the other fields named.

"One reason why advertising is a fascinating business is that it touches all fields of business. An advertising agency man needs to know not simply advertising. He needs to understand the problems of a client's business including, in many cases, distribution, selling, and even manufacturing. He needs also to know how a client's products will be used.

"So in the course of a day's work, an advertising man may need to be equally at home in the test kitchen of a client who develops recipes for using a food product, with engineers who develop such products as radios, tractors, diesel engines or automobiles, and with the sales forces and dealers who sell these products.

"And above all, he needs to know his fellow Americans, how they live and think, their wants, their hopes, their whims, their likes, and dislikes, their ambitions.

"The vast majority of advertising men and women are sincere, hard working people, for they know that upon their skill and judgment depend the success of their clients' advertising and, in no inconsiderable part, the growth of the business upon which a large measure of our nation's economic security depends.

"It is for such reasons that the advertising agency business seeks to attract to its ranks the finest new talent for the years ahead."

You have been reading the Foreword of the Monograph: "The Structure of the Advertising Agency Business" written by Mr. Frederic R. Gamble, President of the American Association of Advertising Agencies. This monograph proceeds with a detailed account of the functions of the advertising agency, and again a quotation:

"Advertising in newspapers, by radio, in magazines, on outdoor boards, in car cards, and in motion pictures, is the counterpart in distribution of the machine in production.

"By use of machines, our production of goods and services has been multiplied. Advertising multiplies selling messages and appeals. Hence, advertising has the greatest opportunity and responsibility for moving goods fast enough and in large enough quantities to keep the machines in our factories running."

Under the heading: "Additional Agency Services," the following is an important paragraph:

"In addition to advertising service there is a willingness among many agencies today to assist the client with his other dynamic activities of distribution. They do special work for the manufacturer in such fields as package design, sales research, sales training, preparation of sales and service literature, designing of merchandising displays, public relations and publicity. But always the agency must justify such work by doing it more satisfactorily than can either the manufacturer himself or a competing expert."

Turning to a second informative publication of the "Four A's", "The AAAA Examination Plan", which discusses Jobs in Advertising and Facts about the Plan, we immediately encounter a significant piece of text which has direct bearing on *aptitudes*. This is so important to any young person who may be thinking of an advertising career that, again with the kind permission of the AAAA, it is here quoted for you:

"What Sort of Person Succeeds in Advertising?

"The advertising industry employs people of many kinds of mind and temperament. There is, of course, the well-known work of specialists such as writers, artists and merchandising experts. And there is need for the diversified talents of research workers, media analysts, administrators, people who know the graphic arts, radio and television production, and others. But, varied as all these jobs are, the people of the advertising industry share certain attitudes of mind with surprising consistency. If you are considering advertising as a career, it may be helpful at the outset to compare your own outlook and abilities with those of the majority of advertising men and women who are already successful.

"Excluding the purely administrative and clerical work, which is about the same in any industry, we usually find that advertising people have three major characteristics in common. They are constructive. They are adaptable. And they are eternally curious. People in other industries often exhibit these traits, too, but the advertising business, by its very nature, requires these qualities in an unusual degree.

"Constructive optimism comes high on the list, because advertising people are called upon to originate ideas, to initiate action—to visualize something in full operation that has not yet even been begun. Logically, this would require a positive and affirmative temperament.

"Adaptability is a second necessity trait because of the infinitely varied problems that the advertising specialist meets. If he is in an agency, he is likely to work with many different persons in a number of client organizations. He must also co-operate with specialists in his own agency and in other organizations that help to build advertising campaigns for his clients. If he works for an advertiser, he has many problems similar to those of agency people, and at the same time must co-ordinate his activities with the over-all business of his company. With today's advertisements produced by many minds and running in many media on close schedules, it takes people of flexible and co-operative temperament to see that advertising is produced as planned and on time.

"Another sort of adaptability is needed to meet the rapidly changing demands made on the advertising worker. As pointed out in the AAAA booklet, 'The Structure of the Advertising Agency Business,' an advertising man may work in the course of a single day with chefs testing food products, with engineers in a plant manufacturing diesel engines, and with the sales forces who sell these products. In addition, he may be asked to speak at meetings, contribute to the design of a package or counter display or do any of countless other things to aid in the sale of the product. If you have the flexibility to meet such demands, you may find advertising an unusually satisfying kind of work.

"Unceasing interest in people and things and the workings of business is a third vital characteristic. The advertising man's first goal is to communicate with the public in an interesting and convincing manner. Ideally, he should be a salesman with a broad background in history, literature, psychology and many other fields. At the same time he should sense the day-to-day thinking of the people.

"As more efficient distribution has become an increasingly important problem in this country, the advertising man has been called on increasingly to aid in planning broad sales and merchandising policies. To do this job effectively, he must be thoroughly versed in the economics of each industry he serves. Meanwhile, he must find time to keep abreast of developments in advertising itself as new techniques are worked out and gains in knowledge are reported. No matter what position he holds, the effective advertising man is a keen and interested student in many fields—and remains one throughout his entire career.

"In advertising, as in the motion picture industry, a relatively small number of people produce work that is seen by millions. Hence both industries are unusually well-known in proportion to their size, and tend to attract far more people than can be employed.

"We estimate that there are only some 12,500 advertising specialists working in this country's 2,000 advertising agencies. Probably 25,000 more are employed in the advertising and sales departments of retailers, manufacturers, newspapers, magazines, broadcasting stations and so on. If we count an equal number of people doing clerical and administrative work, there are jobs for a total of some 75,000 people in the entire advertising industry. By contrast, there are 180,000 lawyers, 165,000 doctors, and 140,000 clergymen in this country.

"The advertising agency business itself needs approximately 1,600 new people a year with perhaps half of the jobs going to experienced persons from other industries and half to younger men and women with relatively little experience."

Needless to say, only a few of these positions are in the art field, but since this book is concerned with various art activities, we shall not quote the detailed particulars and desirable aptitudes applying to many advertising specialties, or to the data on the account executive, the copy writer, the researcher, the radio or television specialist or the space buyer. Of direct interest to you, however, are the qualifications for *art and layout* and, quite possibly, *mechanical production,* covered in the AAAA outline as follows:

"*Art and layout* men, working with the advertising manager, account executive, or copy writer, establish the layout or advertising copy and see that proper art work is prepared. There are roughly 2,000 people in agencies doing lettering, layouts and visualizations, as well as aiding in the planning and purchase of illustrations from outside sources. Many more work in other branches of the industry.

"*Mechanical Production* people have the task of translating art work and copy into the mechanical materials used in reproducing the finished advertisement. A wide knowledge of engraving, lithography, typography, electrotyping and many other technical processes is needed to see that the most effective work is done as economically as possible. Responsible for co-ordinating the flow of advertising materials to publications, mechanical production people often oversee the flow of work ('traffic') through their agencies as well."

Under the heading "Locating Opportunities," this paragraph alone is quoted, though followed by much excellent and realistic advice to anyone seeking a position in advertising:

"In general, there are four ways that you can approach the problem of locating opportunities—through reading the want ads, through personal inquiry and solicitation, through employment agencies, and through the AAAA Examinations for Advertising. All of these methods have their advantages, and if a job opening does not readily develop, it may be well to carry on a campaign on all four fronts at once."

Turning to another highly informative document of the American Association of Advertising Agencies, you are presented with the complete 12 provisions of the AAAA "Standards of Practice in Handling Art Work" (revised statement adopted January 20, 1948)—a document too little known to artists, though written primarily in their interests. It is preceded by the following introductory paragraph:

"These standards are predicated upon the belief that adherence to a code of fair practice, agreed upon in advance, will contribute to the welfare of the Advertiser, the Creative Craftsman and the Agency and will reduce the opportunities for misunderstanding and inefficiency in handling Art Work."

Following are the 12 provisions, which every artist should read carefully, not only as governing his work with advertising agencies, but as highly desirable in governing his conduct of any situation in which art meets business:

1. An artist or photographer should not be asked to speculate with or for an advertising agency, or asked to do work on any basis which entails the possibility of loss to him through factors beyond his control.

2. An artist or photographer should not be expected to suffer any loss that is due to poor judgment on the part of the advertising agency.

3. Dealings with an artist or photographer should be conducted only through an Art Director or art buyer who is the authorized representative of the advertising agency.

4. Orders to an artist or photographer should be in writing and should include all details for which the supplier will be held responsible. The price, whenever possible, and delivery date should be set at this time and included in the written order.

5. Changes or alterations in drawings or photographs that are demonstrably made necessary by mistakes on the part of the artist or photographer should not be paid for by the advertising agency, but the supplier should be compensated for major revisions resulting from a change in agency plans or instructions.

6. If the purchase price of a drawing or photograph is based upon limited use, and later this material is used more extensively than originally planned, the artist or photographer should receive additional remuneration.

7. If comprehensive layouts or other preliminary art work or photographs are published as finished work, the price should be adjusted to include additional compensation.

8. If preliminary drawings, photographs or comprehensives are bought from an artist or photographer with the intention or possibility that someone else will be assigned to do the finished work, this should be made clear at the time of placing the order for preliminary work.

9. Work stopped by the advertising agency for reasons beyond the control of the artist or photographer after it has been started should be paid for on the basis of the time and effort expended.

10. Should an artist or photographer fail to keep his contract with the advertising agency through unreasonable delay in delivery, or non-conformance with agreed specifications, it should be considered a breach of contract by the artist or photographer and should release the advertising agency from responsibility.

11. There should be no concealed charges in art work as billed by the advertising agency.

12. No personal commission or rebate should be asked or accepted by the art buyer from an artist or art service.

The field of lettering, from ancient Rome to the present day, presents to the student as well as to the professional letterer, an inexhaustible range of styles. To know these styles and to sense their appropriateness for a given situation, the student needs sound style training.

Reproduction of a selection of "samples" as shown by a professional letterer. In such a showing he gives evidence of his skill as well as his style range.

CHAPTER 3

Lettering

Every student should learn to do good lettering as it is a most essential requirement for employment on the staff of an art department or an art service. Also it is likely to be the first assignment offered a beginner soliciting free-lance work.

Lettering is used for so many different purposes that it represents one of the readiest markets for anyone who can do it well. Quality in lettering has a way of being recognized as quality more easily than other forms of art, and by people with little or no appreciation for art.

The chief attributes of a good letterer are patience, neatness, perseverance, and a sense of appropriateness and style. If you possess these traits, you have natural aptitudes that should aid you toward success in this field.

As a letterer you should not only master the technique of drawing, spacing and finishing letters; you should also know the style history of letters so that you will be able to choose the right style for every piece of work you do.

The Basic Styles

Practically all lettering may be traced to three sources: the Roman letter with the italic and script variation, the black letter or ecclesiastical text letter, and the block letter. The block letter, in its lighter forms, is called "sans-serif"—that is, a letter without serifs.

255

1. The Classic Roman capital letter.
2. The Mediaeval "blackletter," (called "Old English" by printers.)
3. The "Uncial" form of the Mediaeval letter.
4. The Roman small letter, or "minuscule," generally called "lower case."
5. The Italic, or slanting letter, originated in Venice by Aldus Manutius.
6. Calligraphic Script, a freely written pen letter.
7. The square serif letter, a 19th Century style.
8. The square serif, "lower case."
9. The square serif letter, open and shaded.
10. An "extra-bold," or very heavy 19th Century style.
11. A delicate formal Italic script.
12. A heavier formal Italic script.
13. The sans-serif letter (capitals).
14. The sans-serif letter (lower case).
15. A formal 19th Century open shaded letter.
16. The 19th Century style called "French Antique."
17. A condensed, or narrow letter, essentially typographic in character.

This selection of letter forms has been made to show at a glance the sequence of styles with which every well-trained letterer is familiar. Essential notes, by number, are at the right.

Our alphabet is taken from the Romans who derived many of their characters from the Greeks. Greek, Etruscan, and old Roman alphabets had much in common. The early Roman or Latin alphabet differed very little from the Greek. The later additions were G, H, K, Q, X, Y, and Z.

The Greek gamma or G became the Latin C, and the Greek upsilon became the Latin Y. There was no letter J in either the Greek or the ancient Roman alphabet. The sound was designated by one I being placed over the other. Eventually the lower I developed into a tail and became J.

The black letter was developed by the manuscript writers who worked with a broad-pointed pen. At first they adopted the square capital letter but later evolved a rounder form which is called the "uncial" because it was made one inch high. This type of letter was a transition between the Roman form and the manuscript characters which became narrower when practiced by the European peoples to the north.

With the fall of Rome, all Roman influence waned and this included the Roman character of the alphabet. It is interesting to note in a study of the history of these times how markedly the prevailing social and religious trends stamped themselves on the art of lettering. Following the architectural development in Europe, the black letter took on the vertical character of the Gothic style.

The block letter, while Roman in form, lacks the interest of the Roman letter because of the single width of stroke used throughout the letter. The style can be traced back more than 300 years ago when it was used in embroidery work probably because of its simple execution. That factor commends it to many uses today, especially by engineers, and other individuals, who have not acquired the facility to draw more graceful characters freehand. The block letter can be made with T-square, triangle and ruling pens. It is the basis for the sans serif styles of type which we will study in the following chapter.

Various Uses of Lettering

Kinds of lettering vary with their uses, and it may be well to survey the methods and materials which cause styles and techniques of lettering to differ.

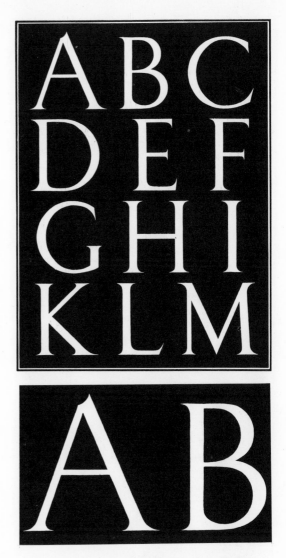

A reproduction of part of a fine Classic Roman alphabet designed by Leonardo da Vinci. The artists, architects, and painters of Renaissance Italy were such well-trained and scholarly designers and craftsmen that most of them were master letterers as well. This reproduction was rendered for The Printing Art magazine by Fances R. Booth.

Lettering is used for (1) advertising displays such as show cards, posters, book jackets, and carton and package designs; (2) silk screen work; (3) the printed page—title page designs, book plates, magazine headings; and (4) general service purposes.

When the style of a letter is determined, based on the purpose for which it is being made, the artist must select the medium that will produce the desired result. For most purposes the choice

is narrowed to either a pen or a brush. The selection is made according to which the artist believes he can control more precisely and with the greater ease. There are times when the very nature of the lettering will dictate the method to be used.

Lettering for Advertising Displays

Lettering in this field usually requires a broad stroke that is accomplished best with a brush. Show-card lettering is executed quickly, and this results from much practice. Since show-card lettering is not made for reproduction, but only for cards to be displayed temporarily in stores, the absolute correctness of each letter is not as important as the general effect of the layout. When done by a person who has complete confidence in this method and in his ability to use it, the result has verve, spontaneity, and sureness.

Show cards can be lettered with a ball-pointed pen, or a flat-edged pen. One of the pens made for this purpose is called "speedball." These pens give a uniform width to the letter, the widths differing with the size of the pens as shown on page 274.

When brushes are used, Havighorst, a show-card expert, recommends starting with a No. 10 red sable show-card brush, to which may be added as need arises, the smaller sizes, 8, 6, 4 and 2, and the two larger sizes, 12 and 14.

There are colors specially prepared for show-card work, or poster colors may be used. Where black or colored backgrounds are desired, colored poster boards may be obtained from any art supply store.

Examples of brush lettering, suitable for show-card work, may be found on the accompanying pages. In studying these examples, the beginner should start with the simpler letter styles and acquire the skill to do them well before attempting the more elaborate forms.

Lettering for Silk Screen

The silk screen method of reproduction is used chiefly for small quantities of posters because of the saving in cost compared with lithography or offset lithography. In preparing the printing surface for silk screen work, the design is cut in stencil form—a different stencil for each color. The printing is done by forcing color through the fabric where the design of that particular color is to appear. The beginner will find that at first it is unwise to attempt to cut fine-line letters in the stencils. Best results are obtained when the letters are simple in form and of medium weight.

Silk screen posters can be made with apparatus and materials which may be obtained from art supply stores together with a manual which will show step-by-step illustrations and directions.

Lettering for the Printed Page

This is lettering which is to be reproduced and, frequently, to appear with type. Such lettering may be part of an advertising layout, a title page of a book, the title of a story or an article in a magazine, an announcement, menu card, or a letterhead design.

The artist's knowledge of styles again is brought into play. Furthermore, he must show professional skill in neatness and craftsmanship in execution. He may work with a small brush with the hairs tapering to a fine point, a fine-pointed pen, flat-edged pens, or a ruling pen and pen-compass. The treatment will be determined according to the kind of letter desired. Each problem should be studied, and the lettering drawn carefully on tracing paper, and transferred to the final drawing when accurately formed. The lines of the transferred letter may be followed with precision, using a brush, a pen, freehand, or with a ruling pen and straight-edge. Mechanically true edges are expected in this type of work.

Many artists with long experience in lettering prefer to execute the sharp edges of a letter with a brush rather than a pen. Of course, a big, clumsy brush would not be used, but there is a certain flexibility in the brush that a pen can not offer. The slight tremors of a hand are not conveyed to the letter when a brush is used;

Reproduction (reduced) from a page in F. W. Goudy's great book The Alphabet. The letter forms shown for comparison indicate the scholarly approach of the trained letterer.

A study in the Mediaeval blackletter by a third-year art school student.

259

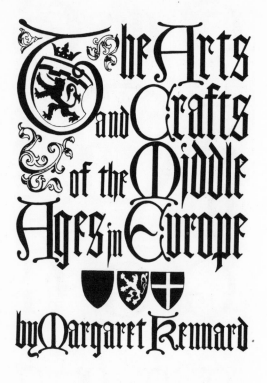

Two design compositions in Mediaeval black-letter by students training as art teachers. These were done in black and vermilion on a tonal antique stock.

there is a "give" in the brush which takes up much of any minor shakiness the hand might have. The penpoint is not as flexible, and will show more readily any wavering of the hand when following a "precision" line.

When lettering with a brush, use India ink, but do not work with a brush too full of ink. Have a piece of blotting paper handy, and with every brushful point up your brush lightly on the blotter and remove the surplus ink in so doing. Use sable brushes and clean them well after using; the ink has a tendency to destroy the brush if left to harden and dry.

Anyone who has borrowed another's fountain pen will know how individual a pen can be. The one best suited for your use is the one with which you feel most confident in doing what you wish to do with it. There are many varieties of pens, from the finest crow-quill pens to the bold stub writing pens, the latter being excellent for heavy, single-stroke lettering.

It usually takes some time to find the one pen which you prefer. Every professional artist has tried scores of them before he found the one for him. The selection depends much on the way you use a pen. Some artists draw toward themselves using the forefinger for the action; others draw sideways, creating the line by wrist motion or by pivoting on the fleshy part of the forearm. The student will develop his own technique as he seeks a way to acquire a sensitive control of his hand.

Many students draw well-formed letters in a layout and then ruin the job when inking it in. They say: "When I come to ink it in, my hand shakes." That is what psychologists would call "a mental hazard." The student's mind allows his hand to shake. Let us see if we can dispel this bugaboo.

The pencil-drawn letter is frequently good, its outline firm and smooth. The point of the pencil is not more than three-quarters of an inch from the tip of your forefinger, and the pencil and finger, as a unit, is rigid. The pen point is not rigid. The pencil gives the student a feeling of sureness and control; the pen doesn't.

Pens as rigid and controllable as a pencil are available. They can be purchased in any commercial stationery store in sizes suitable for fine, small-scale lettering. They are recommended for the student who has difficulties when inking in lettering.

This very fine "study plate," involving considerable research in source material, was done by an evening school student who later became a professional letterer.

Smart
mantle
uniform
weight
shield
California

both definitions
fabled **ʒ** knowledge
earn
anchor **g**
sale **ʒ**

Variety Variety Variety Variety Variety Variety Variety iety

Ask Risqué
day
Beauty
Musaphonic
The

Two study plates made by students to explore
the varieties existing in this particular letter
form.

Lettering for title pages, bookplates, and special announcements requires considerable knowledge of historic styles. It is necessary to design
with lettering so that the spirit of the particular
period with ,which the subject matter may be
associated can be felt in the character and style
of the lettering.

For the designer of lettering, a study of the
decorative arts—ornament, jewelry, textiles, and
manuscripts—is essential. Lettering used in the
inscriptions on monuments and in all craft work
of the historic style periods constitutes source
material.

Lettering for General Service Purposes

The value of simple lettering for general use
is its professional character. Lettering uniform
in style, properly spaced, and of even height
creates a good impression. It may be done quickly, like that used on plans for titling by architectural draftsmen, or on drawings by advertising artists. Even packages neatly addressed and
having "that professional look" carry the thought
to the recipient that the sender is a person of
discrimination and good taste.

A student study plate made for exploration and
practice in the Italic script letter form.

262

Lettering as Discipline

Lettering has often been taught so that it is regarded by students as a tedious chore. This has been the result of stressing the copying of alphabets instead of studying the characteristics of letters. Too frequently an art student, confronted with a problem which includes both an illustration and lettering, will consider the illustration the important factor and neglect the lettering, much to the detriment of the whole design. The lettering is just as important as the other elements and should be given as much study and care in execution.

Students who do good lettering are likely to do other things equally well. This may stem from the fact that lettering is definitely a form of discipline, as compared with some other forms of art. Certain people benefit from discipline, others resent it, failing to realize that discipline is valuable during a person's training period.

It is interesting to note that girls have shown greater ability as lettering students than boys, which may be the result of two outstanding

A few examples of studies in Italic script by art school students in lettering classes.

A student design for a poster which combines an informal Italic script with a thick-and-thin sans serif Roman form.

natural aptitudes or traits more likely to be found in girls than in boys. These are patience and a pride in neatness for its own sake, both of great importance to anyone endeavoring to develop professional skill in lettering. Boys are too often inclined to be impatient, too anxious to see the job finished and to start something else. Impatience is fatal to quality in lettering.

On advice of the instructor, the students who designed and drew these six book-plates adhered (with one exception) to a conventional Roman letter, well drawn and carefully executed.

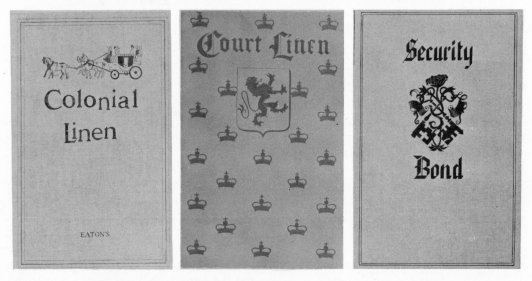

Good lettering is essential to the professional appearance of such work as these three student designs for covers for tablets of writing paper.

A letterer's reference clipping file of monogram designs. Every practicing letterer constantly adds to his collection of reference examples.

This chapter was intentionally written at greater length than some of the other chapters because of the over-all importance of lettering as a skilled accomplishment for the beginner—especially if he is seeking a salaried position in an art service or is starting out as a free-lance artist.

Before bringing the chapter to a close, a few paragraphs should be added on "modern" lettering and on numerals.

"Modern" Lettering

"Modern" is a word devoid of meaning without relation to the period to which it refers. Egyptian hieroglyphs were once modern, Roman letters a smart, new departure, and the Mediaeval blackletter as modern as the times in which it flourished.

If we are to call what we think of as "modern" letters "20th Century" letters, we would more nearly be saying what we mean—but even so, are we so certain of exactly what we *do* mean? Lettering today has a curiously deceptive quality, to understand the nature of which we need to study

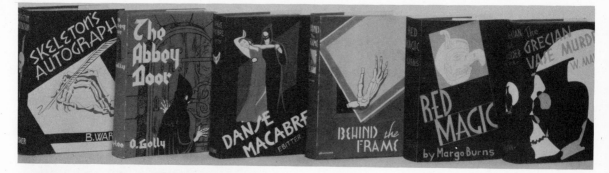

The student designs for book jackets here illustrated were restricted to two printings. Four are shown at larger scale.

it along two lines—individual letter form, and usage, or placement of letters in connection with other and related elements.

Still considering form, it can be said that the only really significant contemporary change in traditional letter forms is seen in the "sans-serif" letter—(Fr. *sans* = "*without*"). The removal of serifs is entirely in accordance with the philosophy of 20th Century design which abolishes forms which have become obsolete, as being meaningless and therefore to be abandoned. This philosophy the individual accepts, rejects or examines with an open mind. The present book is not a controversial treatise on contemporary art.

Returning to the sans-serif letter, seen in the form of its generally accepted "classic" purity in FUTURA type, we see this form at its best. But even so, the sans-serif letter is not so new as many young artists of ten years or so background think it is. It was a common type style throughout the 19th Century.

Nor is there anything essentially contemporary about our "modern" script lettering, which, in its nature is as old as the art of calligraphy. It is only that much of our script is more free, more informal—even in certain contemporary type forms. Its freedom and informality, indeed, would have utterly shocked the calligrapher of the 17th, 18th or even the early 19th Century, whose idea of script lettering was extremely formal and elegant —in character, similar to the formal "Spencerian" script in which professional "penners" of the 19th Century excelled.

If we wish to be truly "modern," our best course is to be continually observant of the styles of let-

The assignment specified only that the story was an imaginary mystery title.

tering seen today in display advertising, book jackets and such contemporary packages as are illustrated on page 247. When a number of packages appear featuring a bold, informal script, as in these examples, it is safe to regard such lettering as indicating a "trend."

What, then, creates the illusion of modernity in so much "modern" lettering? A careful comparative examination of today's printed page, the posters, package designs, covers, book jackets and other evidences of contemporary design, will result in the important discovery that it is the *use* of the letter and not its intrinsic *form* that makes it seem that the letter itself is something new.

It would be a vain gesture to attempt to formulate any rules for the practice of 20th Century lettering. Much of it is not even of this century, and the textbook for its styles and uses, as with any contemporary expression, lies all about us every day. The letterer can only be counselled to be guided by his best taste, to observe and compare examples until he is able to sense trends, and to appraise every piece of lettering or typography he sees on its own merit. But he cannot exercise this necessary discrimination without a sound background knowledge of the origins and evolution of the great traditional letter forms through the centuries down which they have come to us today.

Numerals

No one training as a letterer should overlook the importance of studying Arabic numerals, since

This output of designs for book jackets was the work of a class in lettering.

The book jacket illustrated at right a combination of lettering, art-work, and photography in montage—was accepted and used by a publisher from a well-presented drawing by a third-year art school student, now a practicing designer.

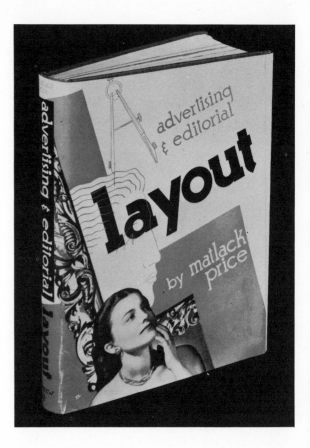

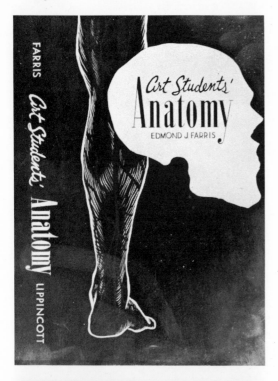

Strong design and good lettering give these two book-jacket studies by third-year advertising design students a distinctly professional appearance.

these so often form a part of lettering projects. Numerals, moreover, are symbols, exactly as letters are and their correct drawing is of equal importance. Well-drawn typographic numerals appear at fairly large scale on calendars and if you are forming your vitally important file of lettering references, include as many different sets of calendar numerals as you can find.

It is interesting to detour for a moment to learn something of the origin of Arabic numerals.

The Arabs, even before the Middle Ages, led all Europe as mathematicians and produced the first textbooks in a field which the common folk of the time regarded as bordering on the Black Arts, if not indeed one of them. Arabian accomplishments in arithmetic, algebra and trigonometry, seen against the prevailing ignorance of the times, gave rise to the widespread conviction that these dark, strange people were magicians. Certainly the Moors in Spain had this reputation, as well as Arabian scholars wherever they appeared on the Mediaeval scene. It is not far from *algebra* to *abracadabra,* and out of the earlier mystery of what could be done with circles, angles and unintelligible magic symbols, *zero* and *cipher,* both

268

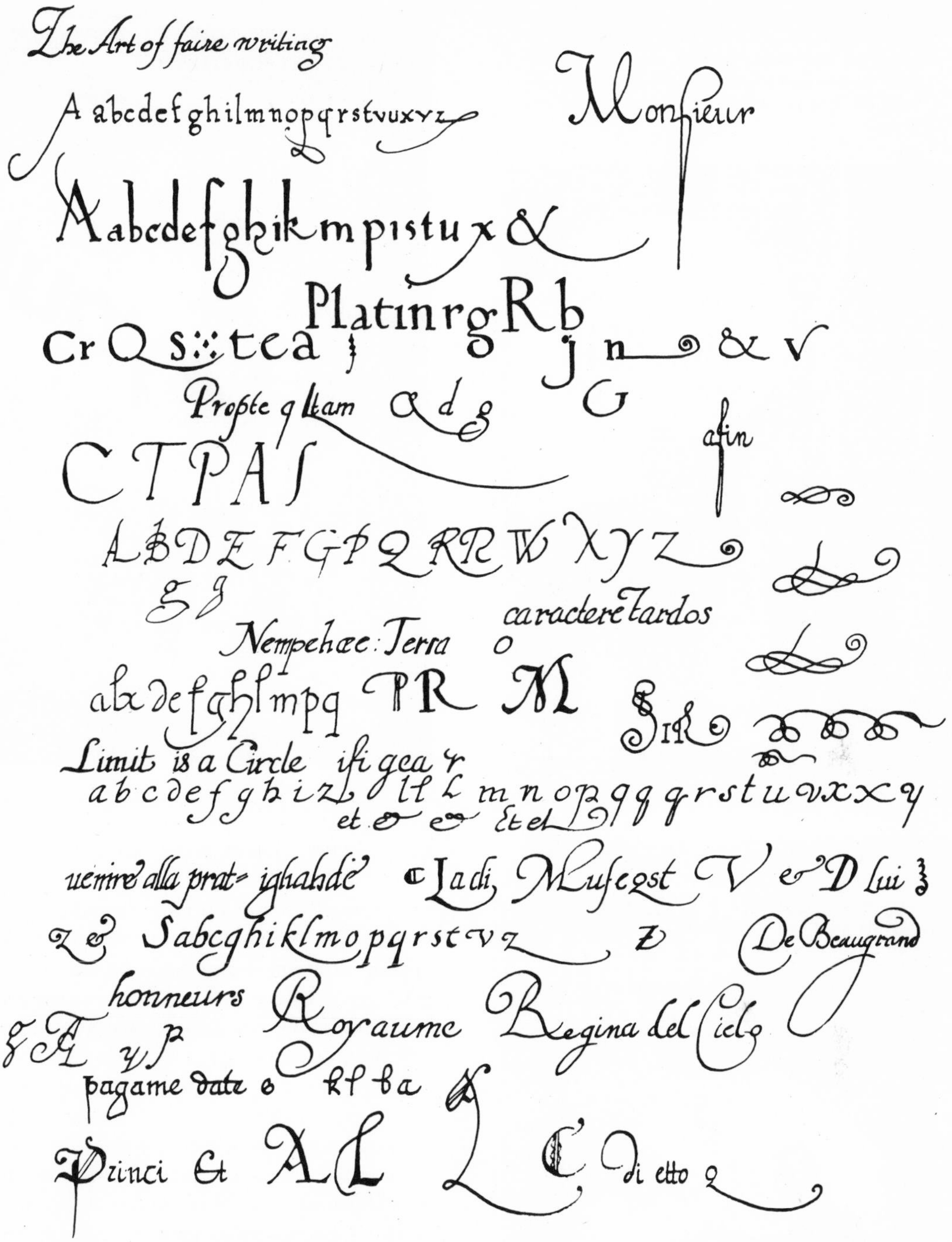

The Art of faire writing

A abcdef ghilmnopqrstvuxyz   *Monſieur*

Aabcdefghik mpistu x &

Platinrg Rb

Cr Q S∴tea   *o*   *j n*   *& v*

Propte q ltam   *d g*   *G*   *afin*

CTPAS

ABDEFGPQRRWXYZ
g g

caractere tardos
Nempehæ Terra   *o*

alx defghlmpq   *PR M*   *Sir*

Limit is a Circle   *ifi gea r*
abcdefghiz ll L mnopqqgrstuvxxy
et et Etel

uenire alla prat ighahde   *Ladi Mufeost V & D Lui z*
z Sabcghiklmopqrstvz   *Z*   *De Beaugrand*

honneurs Royaume Regina del Cielo
A y P
pagame date o kl ba

Princi & AL L di etto

ALPHABETS
BY
IMRE AND HEDWIG
REINER

Above, a page from the note-book of a student of calligraphy. Professional skill in this kind of lettering comes only with long and constant practice.

Left, a fine example of free pen writing, or calligraphy. This was once done (and should be done today) with reed or quill pens.

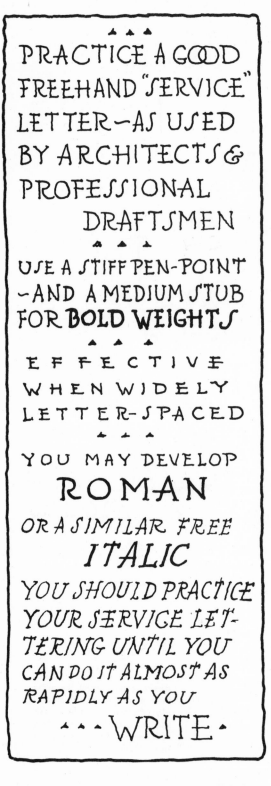

PRACTICE A GOOD FREEHAND "SERVICE" LETTER – AS USED BY ARCHITECTS & PROFESSIONAL DRAFTSMEN

USE A STIFF PEN-POINT – AND A MEDIUM STUB FOR **BOLD WEIGHTS**

EFFECTIVE WHEN WIDELY LETTER-SPACED

YOU MAY DEVELOP ROMAN OR A SIMILAR FREE *ITALIC*

YOU SHOULD PRACTICE YOUR SERVICE LETTERING UNTIL YOU CAN DO IT ALMOST AS RAPIDLY AS YOU WRITE

Every graphic artist and designer should develop a neat, quickly executed letter for use on drawings, addressing, and other "service" lettering.

The student, as well as the practicing letterer, should start and constantly add to a clipping reference file of lettering, classified by style. The most practical and efficient means of keeping these and having them always ready for use is to mount them in ordinary commercial manila folders. The above illustration shows a file of Italic scripts.

Arabic words, have come to us, along with the nine figures and zero with which all the science, the engineering and the whole business of the civilized world is done.

Compared with the alphabet, however, the Arabic numerals are young. The Arabs had studied the mathematical systems of the Egyptians and Babylonians, the Greeks and the Hindus, from the last of which sources they produced their arithmetic book in 825 A.D., the first known. This work was by an Arab, Al-Khowarizimi, which name, in Latin, became *algorisimus* and, by a series of gradual changes and elisions, *arithmetic*.

It was not until the 12th Century that Arabic numerals began to appear in Mediaeval European manuscripts, prior to which time Roman numerals were used—a natural accompaniment to the prevalent use of Latin as the written language of scholars. Until comparatively recently, old custom placed Roman numerals on clock and watch dials, and architects still use them in connection with monumental inscriptions on buildings. Here the obvious harmony in form with Roman capital letters affords some compensation for the difficulty of easily reading dates so lettered.

For the letterer, the drawing and execution of Roman numerals remains wholly in the field of his experience with Roman capital letters.

In the drawing of Arabic numerals there is the constant represented by sensitive freehand draftsmanship, due to the cursive quality of most of the figures. Beyond this, there should be awareness of the two broad divisions into which the design of Arabic numerals fall: the "lining" figures, which are wholly contained within the guidelines, and the figures in which the tails sweep above and below the guidelines. The latter offer the better decorative possibilities, and beyond this the question is one of the taste and judgment needed to design numerals in the right style and scale to conform with the letter forms which they accompany.

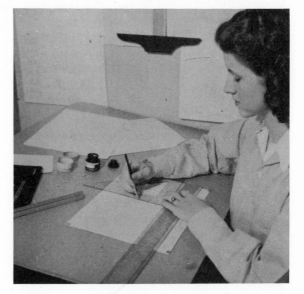

This is an illustration of the proper way to handle T-square, triangle, and ruling pen, as practiced by all professional draftsmen.

Aids to Precision in Lettering

The average art student probably considers a set of drawing instruments as equipment only for mechanical engineers or architectural draftsmen. Anyone who works on layouts, lettering or typography will find that sooner or later he will need instruments to help him attain precise drawings. These are the principal instruments he will need:

Dividers—These are for marking off exact distances without the use of a ruler.

Compass—This is for drawing perfect circles of any radius within the limits of the compass. It is usually equipped with an interchangeable pen and pencil attachment.

Ruling Pen—This important instrument is designed to permit you to rule straight lines of uniform width.

Spring-bow Instruments—In a complete set of drawing instruments will be found a small pair of dividers, a small pencil compass and a small pen compass, all adjustable with a set-screw and useful for fine precision drafting. The compasses are used for drawing circles of small radii, the dividers for assuring uniformity in small measurements.

Rulers

Many beginners believe that using a ruler, with its orderly markings of inches and fractions of inches, will guarantee accuracy in their drawings. Accuracy depends upon the person using the ruler. A slight difference in a single dimension becomes a large error when the dimension is multiplied. Aside from rulers used as straight edges along which to rule a line, there are three kinds which help in measuring things accurately. They are:

The Steel Rule, or the Printer's "Pica" Rule.

The Transparent Plastic (Lumarith) Rule.

The Architect's or Engineer's Rule.

The Steel Rule, stamped with its sub-divisions by machine, can generally be relied on for accurate indications. There is an aluminum rule, made specially for printers, which has its divisions both in inches and in picas and points, units used in typographic work. A student will find this rule has many uses other than as a straight edge. The common school-room or office ruler, with the bevelled edge and a thin strip of brass set into the wood, should not be considered a "precision" instrument if you are concerned with measurements of less than $\frac{1}{8}$ of an inch. The

Transparent rulers with markings in red to facilitate closer registration over black lines and drawings.

TRIANGULAR SCALE RULE

Shown here are two kinds of rulers suitable to use for precision drafting. The only point in measuring anything is to measure it accurately.

For pointing pencils, charcoal, etc. Has 12 sheets of sand paper padded and mounted on wood handle.

45 x 45°   30 x 60°

This illustration shows the always important sandpaper block, the 45° and 30-60° triangles, the T-square, and the ruling pen (shown opened up). (Both above illustrations courtesy of Arthur Brown & Bros.)

markings are so heavy that a single mark may be $\frac{1}{32}$ of an inch thick. Furthermore, the graduations are not at the point of contact with the paper; the width of the brass edge separates the two, so that a critical measurement cannot be accurately transcribed.

The Plastic (Lumarith) Rule is an excellent type of ruler for all-purpose use. The ruler is thin and transparent. The graduations are clearly printed in fine lines directly on the edge of the ruler, assuring pin-point accuracy.

Plastic rules come in many styles and sizes: 6-inch ones for the pocket, a foot length either one or two inches wide, and the largest size 18 inches long and two inches wide.

The architect's or engineer's rule is made of fine-grained hardwood (usually pearwood) and is triangular in section. Some are faced with white plastic so that the finely printed graduations are easy to read. These rulers are not used as straight edges. Draftsmen use the T-square and triangle for ruling lines.

The triangular section is a good example of functional design, as the three faces of the rule present six edges for various graduated scales. One edge indicates the foot divided into inches and fractions; the others are divided into units representing feet in various scales.

At this point, it may be helpful to familiarize yourself with the draftsman's notations for feet and inches, and the use of scales. A foot is indicated as ('); an inch as ("); thus six feet and four inches is written (6′–4″).

Scale means the relation of a given drawing to the full size of the object it represents. Plans for small houses, for instance, are usually drawn one-quarter inch to the foot; apartment houses, where the floor area is vast, one-eighth inch to the foot; and larger structures, one-sixteenth inch to the foot. Details are frequently made three-quarters of an inch to the foot. The inch, on the usual ruler, is divided into sixteenths, twelve of which measure three-quarters of an inch. This scale permits each sixteenth to be considered an inch, a convenient unit of measure.

The graduations on the engineer's rule are metric; on the architect's rule, they are graduated in scales from ⅛″ equals 1′ to 3″ equals 1′. The graduations are so fine that, on the ¼″ scale, the miniature "feet" (actually ¼″) are marked off into twelve miniature "inches." These precision rules are made for professional use and the graduations are absolutely accurate.

Use a Sharp Pencil

Precision draftsmen use sharp pencils, usually of a hard degree of lead. These pencils are not recommended for art effects but for placing lines and points with utmost precision. They learned early in their careers how to sharpen a pencil with a method no mechanical sharpener can equal. Whittle the pencil so about ½″ of wood appears on a long, shallow cut with about ⅜″ of lead exposed. Then sandpaper the lead to a fine point. Sandpaper blocks can be obtained at art supply stores and should be always at hand.

Letter Spacing

Space between the various characters of lettering is not governed by any standard of linear measurement but rather by the equalization of space which separates the letters as judged by the eye. Thin, vertical strokes like that of the "I" and the upright stroke of the "L" need more space to separate the base of the letters than is necessary to effect good spacing between the "I" and the letter "O." Here, the letters may be spaced more closely because of the areas above and below the center of the "O" where it approaches tangency with the "I."

The objective sought in the proper spacing of letters is the effect of "equal" spacing. To achieve this, the attention must be given to the area that separates the letters, not to the linear distance beween them.

Variety in form of letters makes for interest and legibility. Letters which look alike will be difficult to read. This is why the hand-lettered, black letter, with the thick, vertical stroke predominating, needs deciphering when seen in a large area, like that of a full page.

Demonstrating the use of the spring-bow compass in inking a precision drawing.

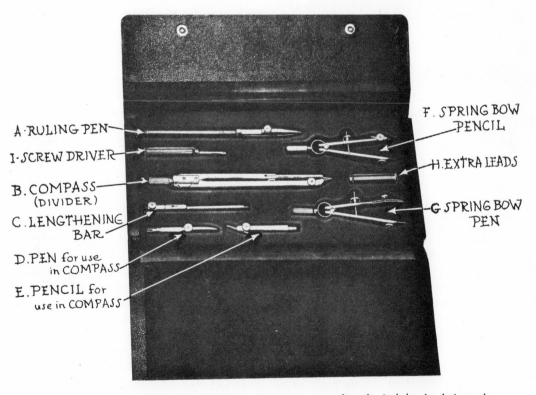

A RULING PEN

I SCREW DRIVER

B COMPASS (DIVIDER)

C LENGTHENING BAR

D PEN for use in COMPASS

E PENCIL for use in COMPASS

F SPRING BOW PENCIL

H EXTRA LEADS

G SPRING BOW PEN

A self-explanatory illustration showing a typical inexpensive set of mechanical drawing instruments. Sets like this may cost approximately $12 (professional sets, more), and sooner or later every designer should acquire a set. (Courtesy of Arthur Brown & Bros.)

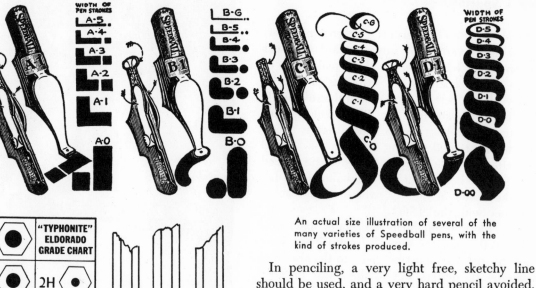

WIDTH OF PEN STROKES
A·5
A·4
A·3
A·2
A·1
A·0

B·G
B·5
B·4
B·3
B·2
B·1
B·0

C·6
C·5
C·4
C·3
C·2
C·1
C·0

WIDTH OF PEN STROKES
D·5
D·4
D·3
D·2
D·1
D·0
D·00

An actual size illustration of several of the many varieties of Speedball pens, with the kind of strokes produced.

6B ⬡	"TYPHONITE" ELDORADO GRADE CHART
5B ⬡	2H ⬡
4B ⬡	3H ⬡
3B ⬡	4H ⬡
2B ⬡	5H ⬡
B ⬡	6H ⬡
HB ⬡	7H ⬡
F ⬡	8H ⬡
H ⬡	9H ⬡

A

B

1/2"

C

3/8"

This illustration shows the range of grades in drawing pencil from the softest, 6B to the hardest, 9H. Diagram Drawings A and B show two badly sharpened pencils, while C shows the precision draftsman's way of doing it. It is futile to attempt a precision drawing with a blunt or badly sharpened pencil.

The main thing to remember in letter spacing, regardless of the style of letter, is that letter spacing is essentially a *visual* matter. No piece of lettering should look either scattered or crowded; every letter should appear to be spaced evenly with every other letter. Also, a beginner's error to avoid is that of failing to leave sufficient spaces between words. Legibility is greatly impaired if words seem to run too closely together.

In penciling, a very light free, sketchy line should be used, and a very hard pencil avoided. The beginner's usual mistake is in cutting into the paper with hard wiry lines that cannot be erased and that hinder the control of the pen or brush. A 2H pencil sharpened to a long conical point serves nicely.

Begin your practice with a study of the old Roman letters taken from the incised panels of monuments. This alphabet is probably the very essence of the classic style and can be used whenever the feeling of formality and dignity is to prevail. It is considered the parent of all the styles, however diversified, which are in use today, and curiously enough, instead of being archaic, it is the most useful and practical one for the designer.

It is interesting to note that although the first movable type faces invented were cut to print the German Gothic text letter, the Roman small letters were soon added to the fonts available for printing. Designed by the Italians in the early part of the 15th century, they were cut on movable type faces by Jenson in 1470.

The Italic face was added in the 16th century. This beautiful letter derives its grace from the easy flow of line. The student will do well to practice this style as it offers harmony and contrast when employed with the Roman characters. Be sure that the angle of incline is the same in all vertical strokes. Do not consider the informal aspect of the Italic as offering excuse for inconsistencies. Keep each character of equal thickness in the heavy strokes and in the light strokes, and do not design one letter of the alphabet differently the second time it appears in the composition.

274

Keep Your Drawings Clean

You will always need erasers, if only to clean up a drawing. The best known eraser for this purpose is artgum. For erasing errors, a harder rubber is needed. The red rubber takes out pencil lines satisfactorily if the lines are not cut deeply into the paper. Green rubbers, made of harder substance than the red ones, sometimes leave a dark smudge and, therefore, they should be used sparingly. You will need an ink eraser for ink lines, but take care when it is used. The drawing paper you have selected may not be durable enough to take much rubbing. It is for this reason that most lettering is done on Bristol board.

Another excellent clean-up rubber is the "kneaded" rubber which not only cleans a drawing thoroughly but which will also erase. It is the best eraser to use on soft pencil lines because it seems to pick them up without smudging them.

Other Equipment Needed

T-Square—For most work, a 24″ or 30″ blade will be suitable. It should be used with the head placed against the left-hand edge of your drawing board for drawing horizontal lines. If your drawing is thumb-tacked or taped down, all your horizontal lines will be parallel. Be sure the head of the T-square is always firmly held against the drawing board, or the lines may not be horizontal. This instrument is essential in ruling guide lines for lettering.

Triangle—The 45-degree triangle is most useful. For drawing vertical lines, hold one of the short sides against the blade of the T-square.

The proper position and left-hand control of T-square and triangle is clearly shown in the illustration of the girl draftsman. Other notes on drafting uses of the 45-degree triangle will be found in the chapter on Interior Design, which follows.

Knives—They are needed to cut heavy illustration board and mat board. A set of varied X-acto knives is recommended for all-purpose service. An accompanying illustration suggests some of their uses. The Stanley mat knife is heavy enough to do the toughest cutting jobs.

An illustration of X-acto knife blades and kit chest—useful in many ways to the artist-designer, as is the heavy-duty mat cutting knife. (Courtesy of Arthur Brown & Bros.).

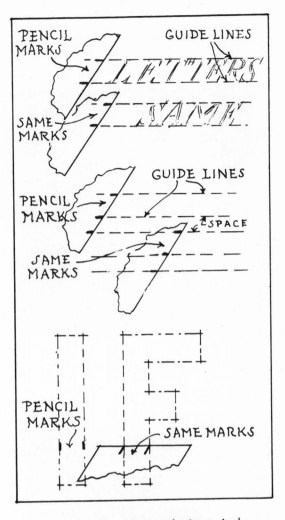

A diagrammatic drawing showing a simple, quick, and accurate way of transcribing measurements which are required to be identical and accurate.

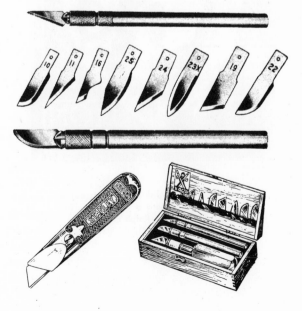

English designers have developed a manner of creating painted signs far more attractive than most similar work seen in this country. (Painted by the Dorian Studio.)

A very handsome English inn sign, its design based on heraldry, with a decorative "lion rampant." (Painted by Ralph Ellis.)

One of the early forms of lettering art, and one which engaged the artist rather than a "sign painter", was the assortment of signs that marked the business places of earlier generations. The commercial shop today fails to recall the quaintness and originality that made these signs a bright spot along the English, French, and American Colonial roads.

Two illustrations of English tavern signs, reproduced on the accompanying page, should offer an inspiration to modern designers. Today we haven't the same kind of taverns, but we do have roadhouses, many of which aim to suggest a quaint, old-time atmosphere. We have our tea-rooms, coffee-shops, gift shops, and antique shops everywhere, in both town and country. The very association of purpose with their earlier prototypes seems to suggest an old-time character to their architecture and their signs.

Classes in lettering have been given the "olde-quainte" sign problem frequently, in which the lettering required is the same style as that found on most old Colonial signs. The letter used then was a version of the conventional Roman capital and lower case letter. The sign-painters of those days who traveled around the countryside on foot, with a knapsack painting kit strapped to their backs, did not know any other style. Their only guide for lettering was a current newspaper or handbill where the type was of one style only. It was the Caslon face brought over from England, and the only type face Colonial printers had.

Colonial Signs by Students

Examples of Colonial signs designed by students appear on accompanying pages. The names were composed by the students, then lettered in a fairly bold weight, suitable for painting. The arrangement was then transferred to wood-grain paper and executed in black poster paint. The problem was extended to include the Colonial frame for the sign, and also the design for the crane, or post and bracket. The problem involved some observation and study of the simple, though necessary, carpenter work, as well as iron-work.

In classes where the sign problem was extended to include pictorial art work suitable for

276

an outdoor sign, the artwork was designed so that it could be used for a menu or booklet, according to the nature of the business, and for a business card. "The Decoy Duck Tea Room," "Red Barn Antiques," and "The White Lamb," are projects done by students.

How to Make a Real Sign

It is not difficult for a student to get this kind of a job to do. He should begin by making a number of sketches from which the client can select one for execution. From that point the following excerpt from an article by Mr. Price may be of help. The article appeared in *The American Artist* magazine, October 1945.

"First, the design: determine the size of the finished sign and lay it out to scale for sketches. The sketch should indicate the enframement, which is a job of carpenter work (perhaps some carving by the artist, for polychrome), and the means of hanging, which, if it be a swinging sign on a crane, is a blacksmith or iron-worker's job.

"Returning to the design: choice should always fall on good classical letters, bold or refined, according to the nature of the sign. The pictorial treatment is best handled in a poster style.

"With the lettered and pictorial scheme for the sign now worked out, the painter would make a full-size working drawing for the enframement, whether this be a simple moulding or a crested affair, perhaps with turned spindles on the sides. Ready-made stock spindles do very well, and can be had at any mill lumber establishment which carries stock mouldings, sashes and doors.

"Next, a full-size working drawing of the iron-work, and here the painter has a rare chance to discover whether or not he is also a practical designer. Whatever other consideration he incorporates in such a design, it must be strong, even stronger than might appear necessary.

"The board on which the sign is to be painted should be thoroughly seasoned so that it will not warp or shrink. It must withstand both rain and sun. Three-quarter inch plywood is a board that Colonial sign-painters would have welcomed, if there had been

An art school student in training for teaching created this well-studied design for an antique Colonial sign. It is a rendered pen drawing, with very well-styled Colonial lettering.

A thorough understanding of the style character of the typical Colonial sign was shown by the student who made this sensitively rendered design.

Old London Tap Room

The Roadside Tavern

The Herring Run

Above: Three studies by students in designing the old Colonial style of painted signboards.

Left: The complete design of the hanging signboard involves, as well, the realistic design of its iron crane.

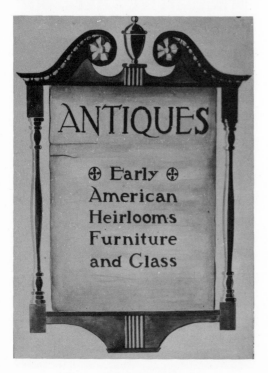

ANTIQUES

⊕ Early ⊕
American
Heirlooms
Furniture
and Glass

any in those days. Or one of the easiest good choices is a drawing board, with flush end-cleats. The wood is seasoned, free from imperfections, smoothly surfaced, and the cleats will prevent it from warping.

"The board should be thoroughly grounded with several coats of paint, beginning with a first coat of outdoor flat white as an undercoat. The lettering and pictorial part should be thoroughly painted, using plenty of paint. In a few signs which I have painted myself, I found that what is called "wagon and implement" or "truck and tractor" paint, being made for severe outdoor use, will stand a lot of punishment in weather, but even this should be given several protective coats of spar varnish."

There is room for a great deal of esthetic improvement in the design and lettering of painted signs, and although commercial sign painting is highly unionized, art-trained people, working in a sign shop, might well exert some influence toward better styling.

Research problem by a student. In designing this kind of sign, make certain that the turned spindles and other "architectural" features are correct.

In designing a sign particular attention should be given to the style of letter used. Since the purpose of any sign is "quick visual information," it is most unwise to use any freakish or unusual style of letter.

Probably the most easily legible letter is a medium or bold weight rendering of the standard capital and lower case Roman alphabet, since "caps" and lower case are more quickly read than all capitals, as may be realized through your own reading-reactions to the accompanying illustrations.

If capitals are used for the whole job, it is well to keep them to a medium weight for the reason that too bold or heavy letters tend to "fill up" visually.

The designer of signs, moreover, should not assume that everybody has normal or better than normal eyesight, and the designer might well make a few simple legibility tests, such as viewing his sign from a much greater distance than the depth of his studio and also viewing it with half-closed eyes, or through dark sun-glasses. If, under such tests, it can be easily read, it should fulfil the necessary practical requirements of a good sign.

The pictorial element in a well-designed sign should meet the same kind of test. The best treatment is one of the utmost simplicity, bearing in mind that shapes and flat areas have longer range visibility than fussy detail. Nothing is gained if persons viewing your sign, perhaps from a passing automobile, cannot make out what it is trying to tell them via visual communication.

This design for a Colonial signboard was done on wood-grain paper to simulate the effect were the sign actually to be painted on knotty pine.

279

This well-studied design for a signboard carried out by a second-year student. The drawings were done in pen and ink and water-color.

The problem as presented called for a motif which could be used on a card and menu cover, featuring the pictorial and name motif of the sign.

THE DECOY DUCK
Tea Room
150 High St.   Bristol, R.I.

Telephone 0-152

THE DECOY DUCK
Tea Room

Here a country antique shop was chosen as the subject for a Colonial sign, with the motif carried over to a leaflet and business card.

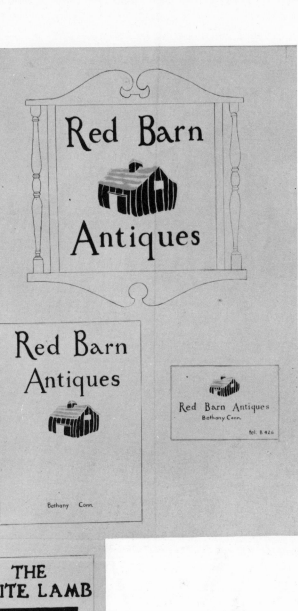

Red Barn Antiques

Red Barn Antiques

Bethany Conn.

Red Barn Antiques
Bethany Conn.
tel. B 426

THE WHITE LAMB

GIFTS ~ YARNS

The WHITE LAMB

15 CHAPEL HILL.
KINGSTREE, ME.

THE WHITE LAMB

GIFTS

This ensemble of signboard, leaflet, and business card shows a student design for an imaginary gift shop.

THE CLASSIC DIGNITY OF THE ROMAN LETTER

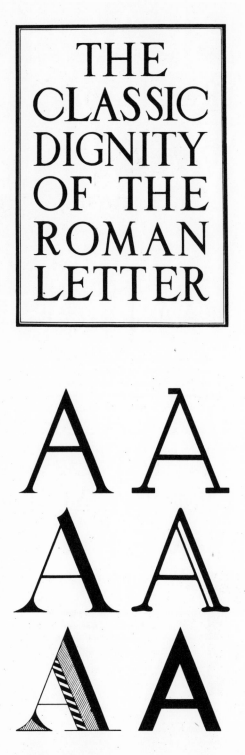

A student lettering exercise in uniformity of weights and spacing in the Classic Roman letter. Further study of the Roman capital letter explores the striking visual differences which the same letter may assume with varied treatments.

Students of lettering have been required to make "study plates," like the two above, not only for practice but in order to realize the striking style differences existing in this lettering category.

Notes on Lettering Lessons

At this point, a few words of remindful advice:

1. Any professional letterer will agree that time spent on the pencilled layout will save more time later, when you come to ink-in.

2. Also, while a piece of lettering is still in the pencilled stage, this is the time to check it carefully to make sure that you haven't left out a letter or even a whole word, or mis-spelled a word. (It can so easily happen.) Pay particular attention to spelling of proper names and check on correct initials, if any.

3. When the pencilled layout is ready to ink in, resolve to do it with a slow, even tempo. It is fatal to become impatient or to feel hurried, putting on a sudden burst of speed which will more than likely ruin the whole job.

4. Uniformity. Few essentials of good lettering are more important than *uniformity*. All weights should be the same, all serifs identical. The best way to achieve this is to put in all the heavy weights at one operation, then all the secondary weights, then all the curvilinear portions of the letters—and lastly, all the serifs (if you are doing a serif letter). If you attempt to finish up each letter completely, as you go along, you are very likely to lose sight of the important maintenance of *uniformity*.

BLACK *and* **WHITE** *for* **SMART CONTRAST**

This exercise was required to be executed without the use of Chinese white—purely an exercise in precision technique.

IMP·CAESARI
TRAIANO·AVG
OMNIS·GALLIÆ
SIME PATER
TECHNIQUE

Studies in the Classic Roman letter done in school by a student who later became a career letterer.

Diagram showing the "half-up" size at which lettering (and much other artwork) is made for reproduction.

YOUR DRAWING 15"

DRAGON

HEIGHT OF DRAWN LETTER

REPRODUCTION SIZE 10"

The & *from*

of L'Aiglen

Majestic

Paris *Super*

There is so much Bad in the Best of us ...
And so much Good in the Worst of us ...
That it hardly behooves any of us ...
To talk about the rest of us ... →

Student pencil layout for a lettered composition in spacing and arrangement. The letter style is that of Trafton Script type.

Below: Two student studies in combining Roman capital letters with script.

Fight

?

Everything!

To Buy!

Compare

O

L'Aiglen

I need

W

shee

BRIGHT

Sliced

&

Sliced

As in the study plate for Roman "lower case" letters, the student is here required to select and draw a number of examples of italic and script lettering, not only for practice but to develop a consciousness of style differences.

Técla Pearls for the FORMAL *Ensemble*

Técla Pearls for the FORMAL *Ensemble*

Standard brün

Lancaster Bond

Christmas S Greetings

S S

I Quā magnifi

Company York

Donnelley

Art S

Deutsch

As with all letter styles, the student should execute "study" plates if he plans to carry out a "design" problem like the one at lower right. These study plates are done in black and vermilion red opaque color.

Note: The student of lettering, if self-training, should make all the plates here illustrated under "Lessons." The examples shown, all by students, were done on Bristol board, size 11" x 15", in India ink and poster paint.

285

Student pencil study for a design problem in the Mediaeval letter. The pencil study should be complete and accurate before being transferred for final execution.

The Arts and Crafts of the Middle Ages in Europe

Nicholas Kochansky

Student design problem in the Mediaeval letter. Executed in black and vermilion on a brown, textured paper.

Whether a student or a practicing typographer, the designer of printed matter has access to a wide range of type styles. Every type has a name, and many of them are cast in several weights and a range of point sizes. The typographer is visually familiar with these aspects of type.

Examples of printed matter designed by typography students. Some pieces are for direct mail advertising, some are typographic "paste-ups" for advertising pages.

CHAPTER 4

Typography

A Word About Printing

As typography is one of the many procedures in printing, it will be well to pause long enough to get an overall view of this vital industry. Many historians have acclaimed Gutenberg's invention of movable type, about 1450, as probably the greatest and most far-reaching of all human inventions. (It is well to remember that Gutenberg is credited with the invention of type, not of the printing press, as many people erroneously believe. Printing presses were in operation long before Gutenberg's time, but they printed mostly wood-cuts of religious pictures, playing cards, and book pages where the text and the illustrations were cut on a wood block.)

Following Gutenberg's invention, books became widely circulated for the first time. No longer were they locked up in monastery libraries.

William Caxton, known as the founder of English printing, was born in Kent in 1422, about 22 years after the birth of Gutenberg. He lived for a long while in Flanders where he acquired knowledge about the new typographic art. When he returned to England, he set up a press in Westminster where he brought out about 100 works, many of which were translations by himself.

From a typographic point of view, the 18th century witnessed the flowering of the art of printing. Great names became identified with type design. William Caslon cut his first font in

1722, and many more before 1734, by which time his types had won general acceptance. When he died in 1766, he left a type design which has been adopted as "standard" by print shops for almost two centuries. The face has both beauty and legibility, and makes a peculiar appeal to the Anglo-Saxon taste.

About the middle of the 18th century, another English type cutter produced a font which still bears his name—John Baskerville, of Birmingham. Shortly afterward, Giambattista Bodoni, in Italy, designed a font having greater contrast between the thick and the thin strokes of the letter. Today, the Bodoni "family" of faces is an important part of every typesetter's equipment.

Educational circulars issued by the American Typefounders aim to encourage an interest in good typography and printing. Excerpts from these circulars follow:

"The varied aspects of school printshop work, such as composition, artwork, proofreading and press-work, provide an outlet for many diverse talents and abilities. Every student discovers in printshop work a subject which he can undertake with interest and profit. The formation of habits of accuracy, thoroughness and perseverance is encouraged by the necessity for these qualities in producing good printing. These habits acquired in the printshop are important contributions to success. . . .

"Itself a fine art, printing naturally fosters an appreciation of its sister arts by developing the student's sense of balance and proportion, his feeling for beauty of line and form, his respect for fine craftsmanship. Good printing requires foresight in planning, and an understanding of the human reactions to the printed page. It is in every sense an expression of the finest qualities of the artist as well as of the artisan."

While typography is considered a subject appropriate for a professional art school, printing is generally considered part of a trade school program. Such a distinction is an arbitrary one. Anyone intending to be a typographer will function far better if he has had some first-hand experience with type and presswork. The cost of printing equipment, as well as the time needed for the practice of printing, has discouraged most art schools from attempting to teach it. Certainly, the trade school, followed by apprenticeship in a printshop, offers effective training whether you intend to become a typographer or a printer, or both.

Qualities a Typographer Needs

Success as a typographer may be predicted providing (1) the student believes in the importance of getting things right, (2) he has acquired good taste, and (3) he has a strong sense of design. Typographic work demands not only good design, but a sense of the delicate differences in type styles and sizes. Knowledge of style comes from a study of the historic background of printing and of the work of modern typographers and type designers.

How a Typographer Functions

A typographer makes two kinds of layouts: a "presentation" layout for the client's approval and a "shop" layout from which the printer will set the type. The layouts are made to accommodate the "copy" furnished by the client.

288

Compositors working with the typographer in arranging type in two large chases. Patience, "follow-through," and a certain amount of manual dexterity are important here. (From the French Magazine Arts et Metiers Graphiques.)

Aptitude Test for Typography

The simplest definition of typography is "designing with type."

Typography is a field which requires special aptitudes and training. Test your aptitudes by answering the following questions:

1. Do you like books?
2. Are you aware of the different styles of type and the effects created by type?
3. Do type styles seem to you to have any *personality*?
4. Are you sensitive to the arrangements of type, and do slight differences seem important to you?
5. Can you become enthusiastic about the art of printing?

Most typographic work is done in the fields of advertising, publishing, and printing, and is usually done by a member of the advertising or printing organization. After becoming experienced in type, you might qualify as a "stylist" or the organization's typographer.

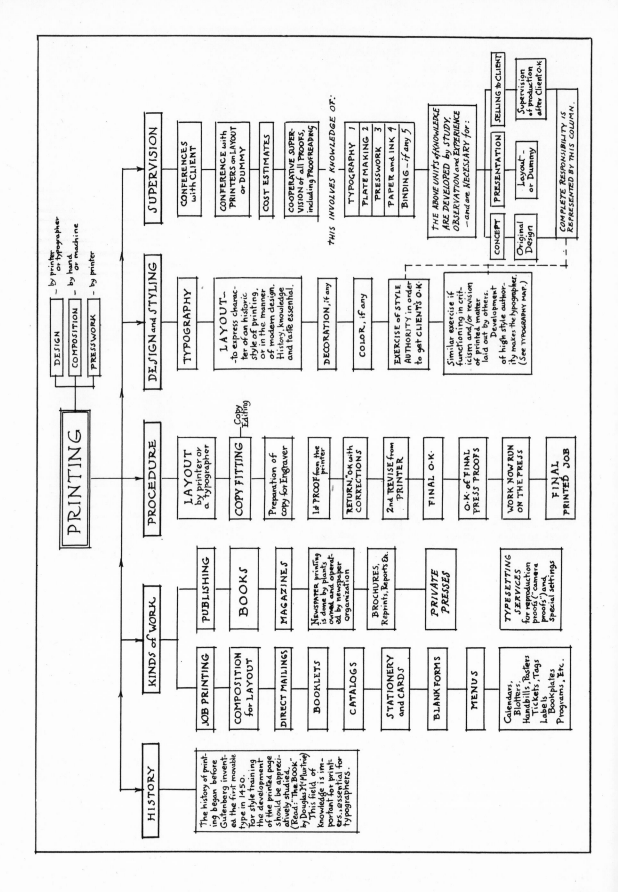

When the type is set, the printer pulls a "proof" which the typographer examines to make sure that it corresponds with the layout. The proof is then submitted to the client for approval or for any changes which may be required. With all changes marked on the proof, it is returned to the printer for correction, after which it is returned to the client for final approval.

An important part of a typographer's work is proofreading. Corrections are costly and, when they are caused by errors in the original copy, or an afterthought by the author, the charges are a legitimate cost to be paid for by the client. It is essential, therefore, that the printer is given "clean copy"—that is, typewritten copy, double-spaced, and carefully checked for any errors before it is sent to be set in type. Complete specifications as to the style and size of type, the depth of leading between the lines, the length of line, and any other instructions peculiar to the problem, should accompany the copy. The typesetter will follow these instructions implicitly but, if no instructions are given and he uses his own judgment, the typographer and the client cannot hold him responsible for setting the copy in a manner they think unsatisfactory.

There are two principal kinds of error: an editorial error, and a mechanical or typographic error. Editorial errors include errors in spelling, punctuation, use of capital letters, poor grammar, as well as erroneous statements. Mechanical errors include wrong letters, words run together, accidental breaks in words, wrong type fonts, words accidentally left out, and misspelled words which are spelled correctly in the copy. For instance:

"Columbus discovered America in 1592." This is correctly set typographically, but there is an editorial error in the date.

"Columbus discovered Americain 1492." This is correct editorially, but running "America" and "in" together without a space is a typographical error.

All reputable printers have proofreaders, but this is no guarantee that every proof they read and submit for approval will be free of errors. It is the typographer's job to check the proofs thoroughly before approving them for printing. The penalty for overlooking a mistake or an inaccuracy in printing is that the mistake is multiplied 10,000, 20,000, or 50,000 times, according to the size of the printed edition. A student may fail

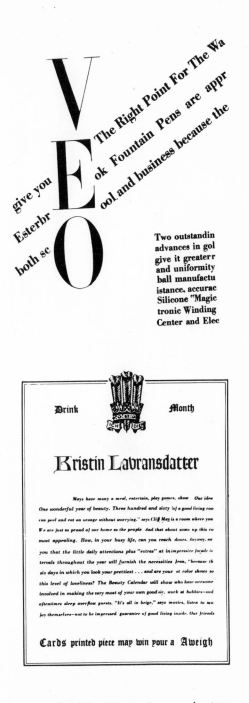

Two designs for "all type" pages by typographic students. These are "abstract," in that they do not convey a message but are made only for preliminary experience in designing with type.

PARIS ... *The World's Preferred Cognac*

David Crystal, Inc., 498 Seventh Avenue, New York 18

Twentieth Century Limited—across the airways and play

interlocking wardrobes designed by this famous creator

of this traveling world. For these are Izod of London to

You'll see them on the Trans-Atlantic Clipper—the plod

You'll find coats, dresses and blouses, too, In one fine st

and good examples of the beautifully correct and all lab

[A MILLIONAIRE CZECH]   [OWENS-C TO CHEER]

MUSIC ON RECORDS

Christened MADEMOISELLE's LIVING because *living* is what it's

permanence of everything you put into the home you make

Watch for it! The new magazine for smart young homemakers.

mortgaging tomorrow. It's full of young workable ideas on

Living, don't skip a single problem from ground-breaking to

Two layouts by students of typography. These are abstract designs in which the type is handled as an accompaniment of the picture. Pictures always dominate any layout, and the type is given secondary place. The dramatization of photographs by means of shaping and art work should be noted by the student of layout, of which typography is a vitally important part.

to realize the enormity of carelessness in typographic work until he is confronted with some such multiplication of the evidence of it.

Training for Typography

There are two kinds of training for the career of a typographer. One is apprenticeship with a printer, which is the best approach for practical training; the other is through training in design. Since the latter is the approach of the artist, it is the phase of the study best treated in a book of this kind.

You should begin your training by learning the different type faces by name and by sight. All modern types have names. If someone wants a layout made with "Lydian" type, the typographer knows exactly what Lydian looks like and in what sizes it is obtainable. The student will find it helpful to study the style manual or type specimen sheets of a local printer, and to write to the American Typefounders, of New York City; the Mergenthaler Linotype Company, of Brooklyn; and the Lanston Monotype Machine Company, of Philadelphia, for booklets and folders describing the type faces made by the various companies.

Another way of becoming familiar with type styles is by cutting different specimens of type from back numbers of magazines and pasting them in layouts as preliminary design problems. Although this method may not aid the student in associating the proper name with the style, it advances him in the use of type in design.

Illustrations on accompanying pages show work by typographic students in the beginning stage. These examples were made by selecting and arranging type from clippings. The problems helped to give students confidence and a certain "type sense."

In making these layouts, the students were concerned only with the *effect* of the arrangements, not with what the words said. The paste-ups were exercises in design by the use of varying styles. You are offered similar exercises in the lessons which follow this chapter.

Facts About Type

Before discussing styles of type, it may be well to introduce a few technical terms used frequently in typography.

✕	Defective letter	⊙	Colon	*no ¶*	No paragraph
⊥	Push down space	;/	Semicolon	*wf.*	Wrong font letter
⑨	Turn over	∨	Apostrophe	*stet.*	Let it stand
ℒ	Take out	∨"	Quotation	*tr.*	Transpose
∧	Insert at this point	-/	Hyphen	*Caps*	Capitals
✓	Space evenly	///	Straighten lines	*S.C.*	Small capitals
⁂	Insert space	⊏	Move over	*l.c.*	Lower-case letter
‿	Less space	☐	Em quad space	*ital.*	Italic
◯	Close up entirely	|—1—|	One-em dash	*Rom.*	Roman letter
⊙	Period	|—2—|	Two-em dash	(?)	Verify
⸝/	Comma	¶	Make paragraph	◯	Spell out

EXAMPLE OF MARKED PROOF

Printing Educates

tr   Even if none of thees boys should ever follow the craft   e/✕

⊥   of the printer in years to come the education that they   ᵍ/

wf   get in this department will prove of real value in prac-

ℒ   tical life, whatever life of occpation or profession they   n/u

⑨   may later choose. The printing trade isa thoroughly prac-   #

tical school of education in itself//It provides practical   °/Cap.

lessons in the principles of language, composition, punc-

tuation, and other every day exercises, in addition to the   ⊃

vast fund of general knowledge which passes under the

l.c.   Worker's observation.   ---An excerpt from an editorial   ⌐→⌐
                        in the Portland Press Herald.   —*ital.*

This illustration shows the marks commonly used by proofreaders and typographers, and shows, also, how they are applied to a paragraph of copy.

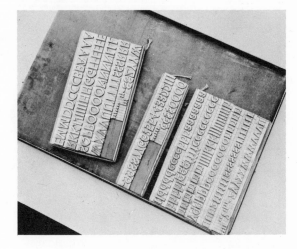

There are three units of measurement for type —the "point," the "pica," and the "em." For the printer's purpose the inch is divided into 72 parts; each part is a "point." Twelve points make a "pica," which is one-sixth of an inch. Type size is measured by points.

The "em" is the square of the body of a style of type. It is a measurement used chiefly in spacing horizontally.

A set of type, as made by a typefounder, is called a "font." A font of type varies in size according to the number of A's and E's it has.

A font of "Lydian" type—caps, lower case, and numerals, each tied up separately and here photographed in a printer's metal galley tray. (Both illustrations on this page courtesy of American Type Founders Sales Corporation.)

MARK well ti 72 point
3A 4a

MARK well the 60 point
3A 5a

MARK well the b 48 point
5A 9a

MARK well the be 42 point
5A 10a

MARK well the bea 36 point
5A 11a

MARK well the beauty 30 point
6A 12a

MARK well the beauty o 24 point
8A 16a

MARK well the beauty of page 18 point
13A 25a

MARK well the beauty of pages pri 14 point
17A 34a

MARK WELL THE BEAUTY OF PA 12 point
21A 40a
Mark well the beauty of pages printed

MARK WELL THE BEAUTY OF PAGE 10 point
25A 49a
Mark well the beauty of pages printed wi

BERNHARD MODERN BOLD

1 For, let a man be as able and original as he may, he cannot afford to discard knowledge of

If this is what you want — you show it thus

12 point Scotch – set solid

2 For, let a man be as able and original as he may, he cannot afford to discard knowledge of

If you want it more open, you show it thus

12 point Scotch : 1 pt leaded

3 For, let a man be as able and original as he may, he cannot afford to discard knowledge of what has gone

If you want lines widely spaced, show thus, on your layout, marked "lead as shown"

4 All those concerned in what are cepted as the fine arts, the learned sciences, and the professions sur-

Normal "1 M" paragraph indention

For, let a man be as now going on in nal as he may, he cannot afford to discard knowledge of what has gone

5 *Style called "hanging indention"*

---

1 Fairy Tales **2 A printed**

3 FOR your

A **4 efghijkl**

5 ADvertising

6 ABCD 7 ABCDE

8 abc SLIM·BLACK 9

10 abcdefghijklmnop

11 AB abc

12 ANCIENT 13 PAPER

14 ROMANCE 15 DECEMBER

16 portfolio 17 Binding

Above: A quick survey of type styles. 1-2, Mediaeval ("Old English"); 3-4, Roman caps and lower case; 5, Italic; 6, 7, 8, 9, 19th Century styles; 10, sans serif lower case; 11, square serif; 12, "French Antique"; 13, an open shade (Thorne); 14, a 19th Century "ornate" ("Floradora") and 15, same, "Phidian"; 16, a formal script (Typo-script) and an informal script ("Brush").

Left: This shows five typical instructions to the printer, as marked on copy by the typographer to show how type is to be set.

Showing the wide variety in style with which the typographer has to work, here are thirteen contemporary types, listed by name to the right.

A type style means its name designation. It is referred to also as a "type face," and the different styles or faces may be found in type specimen books.

Roman letters are those which are upright; italic letters are those which slant. "Upper case" means capitals; "lower case" means small letters; small capitals are capital letters made the size of the lower case letters less their ascenders and descenders, such as the upright stroke of the *b*, *d*, or *h* and the downward stroke of the *p* or *y*.

A type "family" means the complete variations of the fonts within a type style. For instance, the Bodoni face may be specified in Bodoni Book, a light variation; Bodoni regular; Bodoni Bold; Ultra Bodoni, a very heavy variation; and Bodoni Campanile, a tall, elongated variation; together with capital letters, small capitals in certain fonts, and in italics both light and bold.

Sizes of type vary from 4 points high to 72 points in magazine and book printing, although display faces used in newspaper work are much larger. The standard sizes in which most type faces may be obtained are 6-point, 8-point, 10-point, 12-point, 14-point, 18-point, 24-point, 30-point, 36-point, and 48-point. Some fonts are made in 60-point and 72-point sizes, but style specimen sheets should be consulted before specifying these larger sizes. A sample of a specimen sheet showing Bernhard Modern Bold from 10-point to 72-point is shown on an accompanying page.

Many special types exist as italics only, and in one weight only, such as "Park Avenue," or "Trafton Script." Some exist as capital letters, with no lower case, such as "Empire" or "Huxley Vertical."

Listing, by name, of types shown to the left: 1, Kaufman and Kaufman Bold; 2, Lydian and Lydian Bold; 3, Commecial Script; 4, Keynote; 5, Empire; 6, Trafton Script; 7, Cartoon and Cartoon Bold; 8, Cloister Black; 9, Clearcut Initials (also called Ransom); 10, Lombardic Initials; 11, P. T. Barnum; 12, Rondo Bold; 13, Maria Balle Initial.

Type Styles

Types may be classified as belonging to one of four groups: the Roman classic letter; the black letter, associated with monastery manuscripts; the script letter which developed into the italic; and the block letter, the grandparent of the sans serif family.

Gutenberg's first face was the black letter. The earliest printed books, such as the Mainz Bible and Psalters, were printed in this general character which simulated the pen strokes of the scribes in Germany. In Italy, however, the "Gothic" hand did not satisfy the fastidious taste of the scholars of the Renaissance, who had adopted for their own a handwriting inspired by the letter used in classical Rome, of which so many admirable examples have survived in the old monumental inscriptions.

When Germans brought printing into Italy, the first books showed a somewhat heavy Roman letter of strong "Gothic" tendency. This gave way to further refinement and the Roman type used by the early Italian printers is the prototype from which all other Roman fonts are descended. Its development may be traced through such Roman type as was used by Aldus at Venice, by Froben at Basle, by the Estiennes in Paris, by Berthlet and Day in London, Plantin at Antwerp, and by other printers through the 17th and 18th centuries. Today, this "old-face" character is the basis for the purest of Roman faces.

Outstanding faces suitable for designs in which the spirit of classicism is sought are: Caslon, Garamond, Janson, Granjon, and Elzevir. There are others, but the student will observe a unity of feeling in these which give them crispness.

Following the Roman pattern but with a softer

Listing, by name, of the types shown to the right: 1, Commercial Script; 2, Bernhard Cursive; 3, Typical sans serif; 4, Caslon Bold; 5, Lilith; 6, Legend; 7, Grayda; 8, Umbra; 9, Thorne Shaded; 10, Hauser; 11, Onyx; 12, American Text; 13, Neuland; 14, Beton Open; 15, Ultra-Bodoni; 16, Ultra Bodoni (lower case italic); 17, 18 Girder, caps and lower case; 19, Cooper Black; 20, Nubian.

Another group illustration of the varied styles in contemporary type faces. These styles are to the typographer as colors on the palette are to the painter.

The upper panel shows a number of typographic ornaments, together with compositions of some of these in simple designs for book-plates. Such designs are even more effective when printed in two colors.

In the lower panel is shown a "sampling" of the great variety of "foundry material" available to the typographer, including typographic borders made up of small repeat units, decorative initials, brackets, many varieties of symbolic "spots," arrows, pointing hands, stars, and different sizes of dots.

effect are: Centaur, Kennerley, and Bookman. Heavier variations used for commercial purposes are: Cheltenham, Jenson, and Goudy Lanston.

Differing in character but based on Roman form are faces which feature strong contrast between the thin and the heavy strokes of the letter. They include: Bodoni, Corvinus, and Egmont.

There are variations of the block letter, or sans serif group. The outstanding faces available in most commercial shops include: Futura, Tempo, Erbar, and a wide assortment of similar faces. The chief characteristic of this group is the uniformity in the width of the stroke. The 20th Century faces offer a broad selection of various weights and condensed styles.

To help acquaint you with type styles, a few groups have been assembled on accompanying pages.

Decorative Material

Units of ornament cast like type are available in many patterns. This material is sometimes called "foundry material" because most of the designs for borders and special effects have to be composed of single movable pieces of foundry type. Initial letters make up part of this material and, when used, must be inserted in spaces left for them when the body of the type is set on a machine.

Head bands, "boxes" made of ornamental units, tailpieces, and stock designs suitable for use in various holiday seasons are available in foundry, linotype, and monotype cases. Their use in the design of announcements, programs, letter-heads, and other special work adds greatly to a designer's resources.

Setting Type

Type is set by (1) hand, (2) Linotype, (3) Monotype, or (4) by Ludlow or Intertype. In setting by hand, foundry faces are used. Each piece of type is on a single mount and has to be handled separately. The Linotype machine operates like a typewriter, and as each key is pressed down a matrix or mould with an incised pattern of the letter is released from a slot in a metal container, called a magazine, and takes its place in a frame. When a complete line of type has been so accumulated, it becomes a mould for casting a slug in molten type metal. This is the fastest method of

298

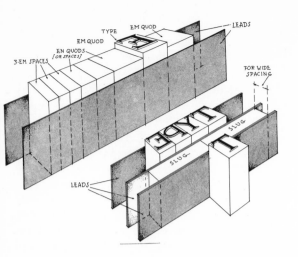

This diagram shows the use of spacing material (quads, leads, slugs) in type composition. These printing accessories are used only in hand-set type.

setting type and is used in all newspaper composing rooms.

Monotype is also set by a keyboard, but instead of assembling matrixes a stencil, like a player-piano roll of music, is made. This becomes the pattern for assembling the type faces. Monotype is movable type and, although set mechanically, can be rearranged by hand.

When the type is placed in a "pan" for handling, spaces between lines are regulated by inserting "leads" which are strips of inferior metal about the thickness of two-ply Bristol board. These strips are not as high as the type face, so do not print when ink rollers pass over the type faces. When type is set "solid" no leads are used between the lines, but good typography requires some spacing.

Horizontal Spacing

This is done with a piece of metal called a "quad." These are cast in all point sizes, and lower than the face of the type. There are "em" quads, which are square, and two- and three-em quads, which take care of the spacing horizontally. There is also an "en" quad, which is half an "em" quad. It is also called an en space. Spaces then diminish, through the 3-em space (which is a third of an em), the 4-em space, and down to the paper-thin spaces which are often called "slivers."

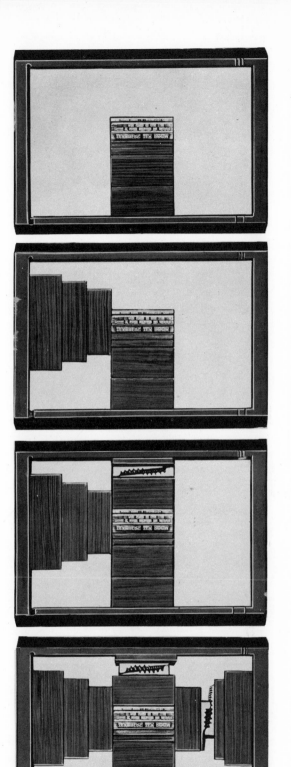

Four stages in "locking-up" a small piece of type composition in the chase of a platen press. This is from a set of instructional plates published for educational purposes by American Type Founders Sales Corporation.

It can be seen that lines of type, or single pieces of type, can be spaced right and left with the utmost accuracy and precision. The normal paragraph indention is a single em quad. If you want a deep indention, you put in two em quads. Refer to the illustration on page 299.

"Furniture"

Lastly, in order to have a type set-up fixed tightly in a frame, which printers call a "chase," the space between the type and the edge of the frame is filled in with wood, called "furniture." Blocks of hard wood are used, varying in size and shape, and these are arranged so that the contents of the chase can be locked up, with pressure exerted by means of specially designed metal wedges which are tightened with a tool made for the purpose.

Everything in the chase must be so tightly locked that, when the chase is picked up to put on the press bed, not a single comma or period can drop out. Type itself, quads, and furniture are all made so mechanically true that the two-way pressure exerted by the wedges will make the whole set-up tight.

Reproduction Proofs

Typographers make extensive use of proofs of type so well printed on a proofing press that they are suitable for reproduction. These are sometimes called "camera proofs." These proofs are made when a display line or a piece of copy set in a certain size and style of type is needed to be pasted on artwork and reproduced at the same time the engraving is being made of the artwork. The proofs are used also as photographic copy for offset reproduction.

There are typographic organizations which specialize in this kind of service and which have on hand a large variety of different type faces not found in the average printing shop.

Printing as a Hobby

With a relatively small investment, typography can be developed as a rewarding, and even a profitable, hobby. If you have a place which you could use as a "shop" and if you can buy a small press and a few fonts of type, you can design and produce a surprising variety of small printed items.

In a small community where you would not have to compete with large and fully equipped printing establishments, it would be possible to build up a sound, even if small, practice, particularly if your main idea in doing it were to engage in a hobby. Owners of hobby presses have even managed to print small books in limited editions, though the press might be so small as to allow the printing of only two pages at a time. This kind of production could not attempt to compete with large-scale printing, but hobby presses have given typographers an opportunity to produce some beautiful little books and to derive much pleasure from the work.

Some Outstanding Typographers

No treatment of this subject would be complete without some reference to Frederic W. Goudy who designed more than 100 faces during his productive life. Many of these types carry his name, and most were cut specially for mono-type casting. With his wife, who worked by his side until her death, Mr. Goudy made most of his faces in his shop at Marlborough, New York. As a student studies the many designs of Mr. Goudy, the impression persists that he was ever seeking the most beautiful adaptation of the old Roman types. Goudy Italian Old Style, Goudy Kennerley, Hadriano, and Forum are but a few of these. Yet, one of the most authentic of the German black-letter types was designed by Mr. Goudy as Goudy Text. This face is complemented with his Lombardic capitals, which are graceful and medieval in spirit.

George W. Jones, an Englishman and a printer who had a sympathetic understanding of the classic traditions of the art of printing, designed the Granjon face. It was based chiefly on a type used in many beautiful French books of the 16th century which can be safely attributed to Claude Garamond. Introduced in England, Granjon soon won recognition in America as a practical face, worthy to rank with Caslon for usefulness and clear enough to use for a dictionary type.

Other type designers whose work is better known than their names are W. A. Dwiggins, whose reputation as an artist and illustrator was enhanced by his design of Electra; Rudolf Koch,

An excellent illustration of a printer locking up a chase containing type and cuts for a tabloid newspaper.

the famous designer of Eve, Neuland, and Kabel faces; and Sol Hess, Associate Art Director of the Lanston Monotype Machine Company, who adapted Janson, 20th Century and other faces for commercial use.

A few additional names should be added to this brief listing. In the 1890's Will Bradley designed an excellent simplified Mediaeval blackletter known as Bradley Blackletter. Bertram Goodhue, later known as a great architect, designed Cheltenham, Bruce Rogers designed the beautiful Centaur to which Frederic Warde added the Arrighi Italic. The Lydian series, one of our most distinguished American types, was designed by Warren Chappell. The chapter headings in this book are set in Lydian Italic.

A few preliminary miniature paste-ups by typography students. These are abstract layouts, composed from clipped material and effective as a means of learning to visualize actual type as it would appear on a page layout.

You may remember the paste-up layout lesson suggested in connection with Chapter 2, Design for Advertising. The same exercise, involving the same techniques, is repeated here.

The illustration on this page shows a group of six miniature page layouts made by an art school student. Where the layouts you made in former lessons concerned both type and illustration, you should, in these exercises, give your best thought and attention to the typography.

Following the same technique outlined in Chapter 2, make two paste-ups for an all-type page layout, similar to those illustrated with the headings "VEO" and "Kristin Lavransdatter."

Since type is the only element you have with which to design a good-looking page, you should try to see the problem as a typographer would see it. The type area for the main text of the advertising copy would be seen by him as an important part of the design, and related to the white space. The type area should be considered as having a certain tone and texture. The breaks between paragraphs and the accents created by the headings, enlarged initials, and the signature, are other elements the typographer would use.

In designing two all-type layouts, you should make one of them formal and one informal.

As a second exercise, refer to the two picture and type layouts illustrated, using "Fine Art Coffee" as the theme, and make two, one formal and one informal.

Remember, in layouts like these it is useless to try to make the type compete with the picture. No matter what kind of a picture it is, it is bound to dominate the page, regardless of what you do with the type. Type should be selected and arranged as an accompaniment to the picture, not in competition with it.

Another instructive paste-up exercise is the creating of a few effective style combinations in type. From a number of clippings of lines of type, taken from back numbers of magazines, combine two on the basis of contrast. The contrast may be in style of type, in weight, in size or in color, or may result from featuring several of these. If you have developed a "type sense" you will be able to judge for yourself whether or not each "style combination" is successful.

The principle governing effective combinations of different types is a simple one, based on contrast by opposition. A formal type may be used with an informal one; large with small; Roman

302

letter with script; black with color; and variety in use of capital letters in headings or sub-headings. The thing to avoid is the use of two types which have too many points of similarity. For instance, it would not be wise to use Kennerley with Caslon. Both are based on the old Roman letter and are alike in form and color. But the Kennerley is florid in character compared with the more dignified Caslon. Unity in feeling should be preserved in type selections. The differences in type used should not destroy the "spirit" of the page.

Next, make a paste-up dummy for a folder to serve as an announcement. Make the page size 4″ x 5″, with the fold on the side having the 4″ dimension. It is a 4-page folder, for which you are planning a typographic treatment for the cover (page 1), and the two inside pages. The cover should be simple, but striking, and designed entirely with type. The two inside pages may be considered as a spread, since they are two facing pages, offering an area 4″ x 10″ for typographic use.

As with any form of art activity, typography should engage your continuous interest. You should take critical notice of all typographic work —title pages of books, letterheads, and announcements. If you are near a large city where exhibitions of the graphic arts are held from time to time, you should attend them in order to keep abreast of the trends in this branch of art.

Start a collection of type specimens, mounted and classified as suggested for examples of lettering and, if you can, build up your own library of books on typography and printing.

Typography as a career is highly attractive, not only because of the nature of the work but also because of the fine opportunities for persons with the proper qualifications. These, to name a few, are knowledge of type and printing, good taste, a strong design sense, patience, accuracy, the ability to follow through, and the ability to supervise work.

In your exercise in creating a typographic design for a direct mail folder or announcement, study such examples as this group and, when you find good examples of this kind of work, file them in your collection of typographic material. The effect of any small printed piece depends mainly on good typography, and may be enhanced by the use of tinted and textured paper stock of good quality.

A character portrait taken without studio lighting with a candid camera. It is apparent here that pictorial composition is more important than elaborate and expensive studio equipment.

A street scene in Newport, Rhode Island—one illustration from a "locale" book by Beth Murray, career photographer.

CHAPTER 5

Photography

Photography is probably the most wide-spread hobby activity in this country. Amateurs, in organized camera clubs which span the continent, often display an ability to create good pictures which rank with the work of well-established professionals. The quality which enhances the work of both the amateur and the professional, and which gives to a picture its excellence, is the design. Aside from the technical aspects of photography, the work of any photographer, amateur or professional, will take on added quality if he has had some training in design.

Many professional photographers began their careers in an art school where they approached their problems in composition as students of illustration. Whatever may have been their aptitudes or their professional aims, they regarded photography as an art—a medium with great dramatic possibilities.

The question whether a good photograph is better than a good painting can be argued indefinitely from either side; there are many things to take into consideration. However, in the hands of

an artist a camera can produce a work of art, and in the hands of a person unskilled in art all the media of drawing and painting will not. In brief, photography is a medium which an artist can use intelligently and effectively because of his art training.

It is interesting that the top award was won by a photographic entry in a poster contest sponsored by the Museum of Modern Art in co-operation with the National Foundation for Infantile Paralysis. The *New York Herald Tribune*, on November 6, 1949, carried the story under the heading: "Camera Wins Over Brush in Contest."

The article mentioned that "among the final entries there were five photographic posters and one montage, ten paintings, six designs, and one sculptured medal. When the jury had evaluated all, they crowned the photographic work of Herbert Matter as the winner of the grand prize of $1,000.

"Mr. Matter's camera triumph over the brush and the designer's tools was a photo-montage showing a young boy and girl running freely

Distinguished amateur photography by an art student who later used several of these shots in a magazine layout.

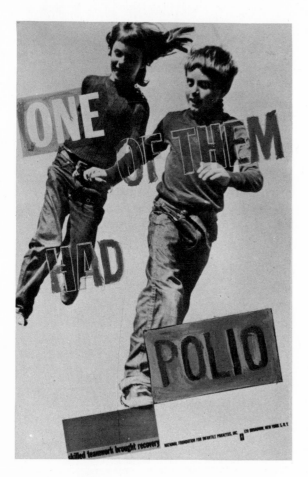

A recent poster for the Infantile Paralysis Foundation—a dramatic creation of the camera, designed by Herbert Matter and winning a $1000 prize.

hand in hand. Across this vigorous expression of youthful activity was inscribed the message, 'One of Them Had Polio.' "

The article contained the further interesting information that Mr. Matter, a native of Switzerland, had originally been a painter and sculptor in Paris, where he also studied typography and layout.

The inclusion of a discussion of photography in this book is for the purpose of directing the student's interest to a medium which he may apply in conjunction with his art work, typographic work, or may use as an aid to illustration and painting. Success in the use of this medium can be attained by a person who has become sensitive to the elements which make good pictures, beginning with good design. Strong compositions, with their factors of balance, harmonious relationships, and contrast are as much the objectives of the photographer as they are of the illustrator or painter.

Technical information about photography may be found in any number of manufacturers' manuals, and in hobby and professional magazines. It is our purpose here to discuss and illustrate the uses which designers of advertising make of photography—not the actual taking of photographs.

Photography as an Artist's Aid

Many illustrators use the camera to save hours of posing time by models. Once the sketches are made with a view to grouping the characters in a composition, the artist searches for the models who fit the types described in the story. These models are located by means of a file furnished by model agencies. When the models are selected, they are coached in the characters they are engaged to depict by the artist who watches their movements from various angles. When he believes that the grouping and action, as well as the expressions, are telling the story, he photographs them. He may make many exposures, taking care to obtain photographically any information he may require in creating his finished illustration. The entire process takes much less time and costs much less money than would be the case if the group of models was engaged to pose throughout the time it would take the illustrator to complete his drawing or painting.

Illustrators often use the camera for "field notes." Suppose, for instance, an illustration called for a scene at an airport, a race-track, a fish-wharf, or any special "locale." The illustrator takes a dozen shots from many different points of view, as well as close-ups of characteristic incidents—pictures which will help him when he is back in his studio to capture the spirit of the scene, the relationship of people and crowds to the setting as a whole.

These are the things an artist would sketch, were time permitting. In practice, where time is an important factor, the camera is the quicker way to get such information.

Although any reputable portrait painter will say that all portraits should be painted directly from life, many painters ask for a variety of photographs of the person to be painted or will take a number of photographs for study and reference to work with between sittings when the subject cannot be available for posing in the studio.

Color transparencies are helpful to the artist for collecting valuable information when the limited time available would hardly permit him to register a scene in color on a small canvas.

Ben Brown, painter-photographer, who so kindly contributed some of the material reproduced in this chapter, finds that the "more he continues to divide his time between painting and photography, the more he becomes fascinated with both media." Many of Mr. Brown's paintings reflect the employment of the camera as a sketch book. But the young artist feels that occasionally he makes a photograph which, by accident or arrangement, is a complete and satisfying accomplishment in itself.

A photograph which could provide a striking design for a poster or booklet cover. Amateurs who are awed by equipment will be interested to know that this was taken by an amateur with an old model Brownie 3 box camera.

The significance of this photograph is that it is not only an amateur shot, but was taken with a dollar camera picked up in a drug store.

"Kids on Charles Street"—a Leica camera shot taken by Ben Brown as a basis for a painting. Mr. Brown has found real esthetic satisfaction in both camera and brush, finding either one a means of expression in its own right.

This is the painting which Mr. Brown made from his Leica camera "impression." Much more about the relationships between camera and painting or illustration may be read in the chapter on Illustration in Part I.

"I find that both of them have much in sympathy with each other," says Mr. Brown, "but they are entirely different media. With oils I can change textures or alter proportions or dimensions. With the camera, it is necessary to work hard for the proper effects, although you have to work with what you have on hand. Both of them have their place."

Photography in Advertising

You have only to turn the pages of any magazine to realize what a vast use exists for photography in this field. The amazing development of direct color photography in recent years has added still greater power to the camera in advertising.

Imaginative layout designers have found additional uses for the photograph which result in a combination of photography and art work. There are many more treatments of a photograph than might be suggested by the usual rectangular shape of the negative and print. The layout-artist, if he is familiar with the various techniques, such as photo-editing, the montage, and the collage, can create many startling effects.

Photography and Art Work

The effectiveness of this combination comes from the essential and visible difference between the photograph and a piece of art work as a means of picturizing anything. It is the contrast that makes this sort of thing effective. Because the keynote is contrast, the photograph must remain obviously a photograph, and the art work must be done obviously as art work. The more closely the photograph and art work resemble each other, the less effective is the result.

From an observer's point of view, a photograph is a statistical document. It proves the reality and existence of a fact. Conversely, a piece of art work is an idea which may or may not have foundation in fact. If a photograph supplies the whole story—conveys the idea completely and evokes the desired reaction in the observer—further use of art work would seem unnecessary. But if the photograph lacks the full story-telling quality needed to convey an idea, art work can be supplemented with good effect.

Care should be exercised to prevent the attention value of one of the elements from destroying the other. If art work adds something, if it strengthens the power of the photograph, then use it.

It has been common to see a photograph of a fashion figure with a background sketched in with pencil or suggested roughly with black-and-white wash. While the background supplied a setting, it in no way detracted from the importance of the photographed figure. Here, the combination of the two was beneficial to the whole effect. In the skillful integration of the art work and photograph, the contrast created should be definitely in favor of the articles advertised.

Photographers who make exhibition or "salon" photography create pictures which should properly be classed with the fine arts.

Compositionally, as well as in the subleties of controlled lighting, the "salon" or exhibition photograph has established its own place in the field of art.

An English movie still, posed with due thought to pictorial composition. Such a photograph is complete in itself and would not be improved by "cropping."

Advertising photography planned and posed to dramatize the merchandise (floor covering) by means of an attractive model and realistic lighting.

Photo-Editing

This technique consists mainly of painting out or cutting out certain parts of a photograph in order to bring into greater prominence certain other parts. In the photograph of the girl looking at the poster advertising "Virginia Rounds," the background has been deleted in order to create a more compelling shape. The same technique may be used to impose one photograph over another, or blend the two.

Photo-Montage

There are two ways of making a photo-montage. One method may be followed by a layout artist who cuts up and combines several photographic prints—a technique that comes from a very old hobby called "decoupage." The other method is a highly specialized kind of photo-laboratory work where the overlapping of images is done with the negatives, instead of the prints.

The value of a photo-montage is in its effective presentation of an idea created by a composite view of many elements. The assembly of illustrations used in the historic review of the arts in Part I is an example of photo-montage.

310

In the first of these fashion publicity photographs the photographer made a daring and effective use of an oblique composition. The two at the right illustrate the present trend toward natural poses and appropriate backgrounds.

An interesting arrangement of shapes, contrasting in contour and tone, is a design objective in photo-montage. As in all good designs, some feature should dominate. The montage should give the impression of a carefully studied "arrangement" of various related illustrations.

There is no limit to the possibilities of photo-montage. All you need is a pair of scissors, rubber cement, and your own imagination, ingenuity and design-sense, in addition to a lot of photographs to work with.

When the montage is made from negatives, the best results are obtained when the photographic copy is so prepared as to permit the darkroom operator to blend the images without difficulty. Contrast is obtained when the sharp edges of an object in one photograph are exposed against a light background in another photograph. Soft blending of the photographs is possible when the edges of both photographs have similar tonal values.

The photo-montage may be made on a single negative which is masked except where a particular image is to be photographed. By altering the location of the opening in the mask, the same negative can be exposed to admit other images without destroying the earlier exposures.

This short explanation of the photo-darkroom

Admirably clear camera work, excellent for reproduction, in a style photograph for hairdressing. At the right, striking "arrested motion" in a three-quarter length pose for a millinery release. Below, a close-up posed to show how "scatter pins" may be worn.

method is given to aid the layout artist in understanding how he can function in the operation. As an aid to the darkroom operator, the layout artist should make a pencil sketch locating the images to be photographed in the arrangement he desires, and suggesting as well as he can where contrasts are desired and where the blending should be softened. The layout should be made on a piece of tracing paper the size the finished montage negative is to be, so that the operator can be guided in his positioning of the images by placing the layout against the ground glass of the camera when focusing for the next exposure.

When the photographs to be used in the montage have sharp contrast of tone near the edge of the print, and if these contrasts are not desired, the print should be retouched by air-brush, using a medium tone of gray. This will reduce the contrast at this point and make the blending easier to control when photographed.

Collage

This technique may involve photographs or a variety of other materials. It was invented by some of the more extreme "modern" artists in Paris. These inventive artists conceived the idea that the public could be startled by the use of art work in association with materials, such as bits of newspaper or fabrics. Once this idea got

312

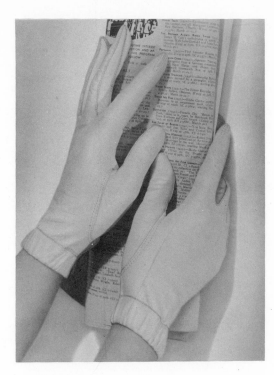

Close-up merchandise photograph of a handbag with incidental background for pictorial effect. At the right, two publicity release photographs of styles in gloves, with particular attention to detail in the lower example.

started there seemed to be no limit to its possibilities, and "collage" became a recognized technique.

Like any other form of art work, a collage should be well designed. The assortment of materials may include art work, photography, and any number of actual materials. In the collage layout, "Plan for Living" (made as a class-room demonstration), several photographs were used, as well as a piece of an actual blueprint, and a transparent acetate ruler.

Collage, as practiced by the extreme modern artists, may go far beyond ordinary understanding and hence beyond any usefulness in this book. But, if the technique confines itself to bringing into art things that make sense, things that have a real and vital bearing on what the designer is trying to say, then collage is another exciting technique to experiment with, whether you are an artist or a photographer or both.

The Photogram

The magazine *Modern Advertising* provides us with a good working definition of this unusual term. "In crudest terms, the photogram is a

Luxury merchandise excellently photographed in terms of lighting, to show metallic finished leather, and with high fidelity of detail for reproduction.

photographic image made without the use of a camera," it states. In an article on the subject, Gyorgy Kepes explains further the method involved.

Says Mr. Kepes, "The photogram is produced by recording the shadow and opacity of everyday objects, such as leaves, mechanical objects, paper shapes, by placing them on photosensitive paper, and then exposing them to the light. By the proper manipulation of light, natural forms such as flowers, feathers and insect wings, or mechanically made objects such as wire netting, textiles, prisms, lenses, etc., are translated into interesting shadow patterns. These shadow patterns often embody novel and unexpected accidental effects which have high attention values.

"For advertising purposes, the photogram can be combined with realistic photographs, diagrams, drawings, maps, type and other graphic elements to produce a wealth of effective new arrangements."

The origin of the photogram is an interesting example of how the most abstract of ideas, seemingly remote from commercial realities, can lead to new developments of practical value. It appears that a number of European artists studied photography in the search for a medium of graphic expression suitable for a world of mechanisms. Given light, natural objects, and sensitized paper, the artist could employ his organizing intelligence, instead of the camera, to manipulate light and arrange objects into interesting patterns. He can literally design with light.

Photography as a Profession

If you are inclined toward photography as a profession, it may be because you are interested chiefly in some one of the various branches of the field. You may find your urge directing you toward the photographing of fashions, or portraits, or marine studies. As in art work, most professional photographers are specialists.

To make a career of photography does not mean that your objective is solely to submit prints for salon exhibitions. A few career photographers have done distinguished work by tak-

314

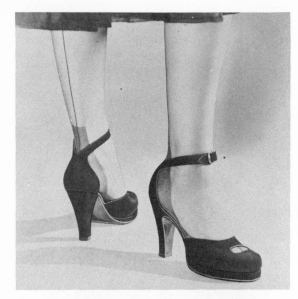

Close-up fashion photography posed to show the design and detail of footwear. To the right, two striking fashion photographs posed to show handbags, the lower dramatized and demonstrated by the model.

ing extensive series of attractive views of a city or region for publication in book form.

Miss Beth Murray, of Providence, Rhode Island, is one of these interpreters of the passing scene, whose interesting photographs of Newport and Providence are the subjects of two recent books. It is through her kindness one of the views from her book, *This is Newport,* appears in this chapter.

In an interview with Miss Murray, the purpose of which was to learn how one progresses from the status of an amateur photographer to that of a professional, the point was left unsettled. The progress is gradual, based on practice and experience, and directed by aptitude and ambition. In Miss Murray's case, it was a little different, as her mother was a photographer. It can be imagined that she practically grew up in the darkroom.

Specialization

To engage in photography professionally, it is necessary to have a working studio and considerable equipment, including a darkroom, enlarging camera, lights, and appurtenances necessary for posing models. It would not be possible in a book of this kind to pursue the subject further. Training in a commercial studio will be most valuable to any aspirant in this field. It is enough

315

Student design for a menu cover based on the technique of cutting photographs to significant shapes.

Examples of student work in the integration of photography and artwork. "Furniture of Today" was hand-lettered by the student while the dates and location were set in type. The two-page layouts were developed from fashion photographs.

"Planned photography"—
When a layout is planned to include a specially taken photograph, the photographer is given a photostat or tracing of the art department layout as his guide in arranging the merchandise or model as required by the art director.

to have pointed out the direct bearing an art training has on the quality of a photographer's output, and to have stressed the value of design as an important element in making pictures.

Preparation of Photographs for Reproduction

One of the first assignments of a young artist in an art department concerns the preparation of photographs for the engraver. This involves two operations: cropping and sizing.

Photographs may have extraneous matter not needed for the particular job in hand; this material is eliminated by showing the engraver what portion of the photograph you wish to have reproduced. Cropping is done by marking with a greasy pencil along the margins of the print the limitations of the picture when reproduced. The greasy pencil is necessary because of the highly glazed surface of most photographic prints made for reproduction purposes.

Sizing indicates for the engraver the size he is to make the reproduction, using the crop marks as the points of measurement.

"Trick Photography" is often accomplished by the taking of separate photographs and assembling them in montage, as in this example by John Muller (Muller-King Studios). The worried man coming out from behind the 8-ball illustrated, photographically, the theme of the advertising copy.

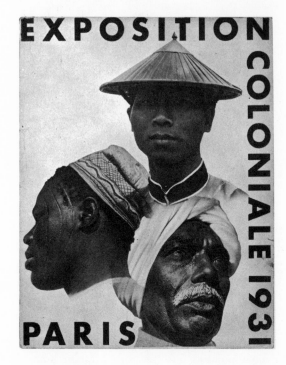

A strikingly composed montage of distinguished photographs "designed" this program cover. The photography was printed in black gravure and the type in dark red.

A montage consisting of photography, lettering, and typography. Students have shown marked ingenuity in assembling varied material in this essentially modern technique.

"Photo-editing" used to isolate and emphasize subject. This technique consists largely of painting out all, or part, of a background. The photograph before treatment is shown for comparison.

A montage consisting of photography, an old Godey fashion plate, typography, and typographic stars—the whole planned, with dummy text, for a full-page fashion layout.

An elaborate collage made for the French Line by the designer Halicka, of Paris. Partly drawn and partly composed of fabrics and other materials, the ensemble is photographed with uniquely interesting result.

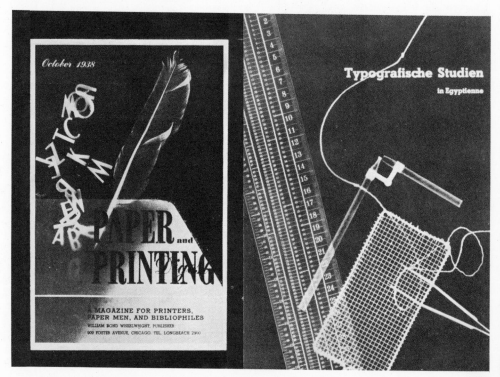

Collage, as distinguished from montage, involves not only the combination of photography, artwork, and often typography, but also the incorporation of such actual materials as the piece of blueprint and the transparent acetate ruler seen in this example.

Examples of photograms, the creation of striking effects by the simple technique of arranging opaque objects on sensitized photographic printing paper and allowing light to "print" negatives of the objects so placed.

EXERCISES IN PHOTOGRAPHY

Since the subject of photography was introduced into this book only to illustrate and suggest certain uses of photography, the following exercises have been selected accordingly. The most practical experience a student can receive at this stage of his training is the preparation of photographs for reproduction. This is part of an art department's everyday routine. Therefore, let us review this practice with the following demonstrations.

One of the first assignments of a young artist in an art department concerns the preparation of photographs for the engraver. This involves two operations: cropping and sizing.

Photographs may have extraneous matter not needed for the particular job in hand; this material is eliminated by showing the engraver what portion of the photograph you wish to have reproduced. Cropping is done by marking with a greasy pencil along the margins of the print the limitations of the picture when reproduced. The greasy pencil is necessary because of the highly glazed surface of most photographic prints made for reproduction purposes.

Sizing indicates for the engraver the size he is to make the reproduction, using the crop marks as the points of measurement.

Photographs at the upper right show architectural subjects. The first depicts the wing of a house with a pool in the foreground. Too much is shown of the blank wall at the left and a little too much of the pool in the foreground. If the entire photograph were being used, the white negative numbers would have to be retouched so they would not show. The ruled lines on the print suggest how the picture could be cropped suitable for reproduction.

The next picture, the entrance of a large country house, would need no cropping at the top or at the right-hand side. Both compose well with the house. At the left, however, the edge of the photograph cuts the triple windows at the edge, an unfortunate situation. The dotted crop marks, C-D, would be equally bad, but the solid line, running through the middle of the center window seems less objectionable. It is good practice to avoid placing any important feature in a picture exactly on the edge.

In cropping the foreground, of which there is a little too much in relation to the rest of the picture, the solid crop mark would be preferable to the dotted one because the latter would destroy the pleasing curve that marks the turf border of the drive.

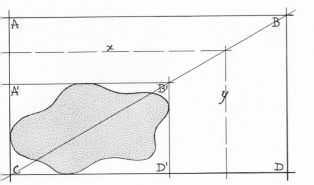

Now, try cropping some pictures by yourself, starting with the Coral Gables street scene on page 322, and then the Colonial house. When you have gained some experience with architectural subjects, study the cropping of pictures where figures are featured. Observe the studied lighting effect where the girl's shadow is cast on the wall behind her. This picture hardly needs cropping, but it would serve as an experiment to try various cropping effects just to see how damaging it can be to crop a picture which already is complete in itself. In the photograph where the girl is seated in a chair, it is possible that the photographer was attempting an unusual placement of the figure in the rectangle. For most editorial purposes, this picture would be cropped as shown, if for no other reason than to gain size for the figure by eliminating much of the excess area.

PROPORTIONAL REDUCTION

When you put the size and crop marks on the photograph, you should know what the dimensions of the final reproduction will be—both height (sometimes called depth) and width. The simplest method of determining the new dimensions is shown in the accompanying diagram.

Suppose the rectangle A B C D represents the photograph, and you wish to reduce its width to the dimension C D'. The dimension B' D' will be the height you are trying to find. Similarly, you can find the proportion of any other rectangle, based on the original size, as x-y.

In figuring the two dimensions of any irregular shape, such as an amoeba or a silhouette, you need only place tracing paper over the shape, draw a rectangle which encloses it exactly, and proceed with a diagonal as in the rectangle diagram mentioned above.

For enlargement instead of reduction, the diagonal method is worked in reverse. The diagonal of the small rectangle is extended beyond the limits of the picture until the parallel sides are of the desired dimension.

CONCERNING SHAPES

The panel containing the various reproductions of the classic head of Athena is shown to illustrate the great change in appearance that results from varying the shapes and treatments of the same subject. These are only a few possible treatments which might be used to alter the appearance of a rectangular photograph.

Not all photographs may be improved by such changes in shape or treatment. Many might be spoiled. Photographs having good design and interesting pattern quality can hardly be enhanced by altering. Cropping and special treatments are desirable only when the pictorial qualities of the photograph would be improved.

These questions are settled by your picture sense, your design sense, and good taste.

On page 325 are two special treatments in preparing a photograph for different layout requirements. The same photograph is shown as it would be treated for the layout at its right, which calls for an "amoeba" shape. This shape is painted on the photograph with opaque retouch white paint, as shown. Before sending it to the engraver, it would be marked for size, in accordance with the size required by the layout.

Next is shown the treatment called "part silhouette," which means that you retain a part of the background and silhouette a part of the figure. Above, you will notice several part-silhouette treatments of the head of Athena, and also (5) a total silhouette, in which none of the background is retained.

Try cropping the photograph of the girl standing by the doorway, and under a sign.

As further exercises, practice cropping any snapshots you may have.

For the next problem, try your hand at some combinations of art work and photography. The idea is to create a background, or setting, in art work which will contrast with the photograph and, at the same time, supplement it. Select some photograph you may have or cut a reproduction of one from some current magazine. Compose this grouping for a magazine advertisement.

The fashion photograph shown on the accompanying page was made with the understanding that it would be cropped for use. The same photograph is shown cropped for better pictorial composition, with the required size indicated. The size marks are shown with arrows touching the crop marks. Sizing may be made for either height or width, although if the fitting of the picture to space is such that no allowance can safely be made for error in proportion, it is wiser to size using the larger dimension. This observation will be appreciated when the student practices the proportioning of pictures. In the accompanying example, the cropped photograph is marked for height.

Here, too, you will see the pictorial effect of cropping a photograph of an architectural subject. In addition to making a better composition, cropping also gives a larger size to the main subject of the picture by deleting a certain amount of unnecessary or uninteresting area.

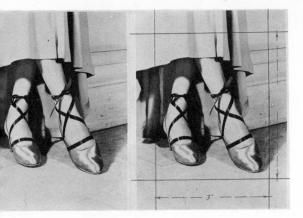

CREATE A PHOTO-MONTAGE

As your next exercise, design a photo-montage, using reproductions of pictures if photographs are not available. Think of the theme first, then collect your material so that each picture will bear some relationship to the others. Then compose the arrangement giving thought to establishing a dominant feature as a center of interest.

Your last exercise should be the designing of a collage. In this you will combine photography with art work and with materials of various kinds. From the very nature of a collage, rules can hardly be intelligently formulated. The process is essentially creative, calling for imagination and ingenuity. Only your own innate sense of design and good taste can guide you in such an exercise. The practice may be stimulating as it may open the way to a new approach in layout work.

If you are an amateur photographer, you can extend these exercises by making your own pictures. Planned photography is an excellent exercise in visualized advertising. You might pose a model for a photograph illustrating an idea or a product that you could carry further through the layout process to simulate an actual advertising problem. If your photographs are too small, any photo service can make enlargements for you to the size your layout requires.

Amateur photographers may also possess the facilities necessary to experiment with the photogram, which, like the collage, is a technique requiring creative thinking and considerable imagination.

Many photographs are given an added effect in layout by part-silhouetting. Our example is shown before treatment, after treatment, and finally as it might appear in a layout.

HOW WOULD YOU CROP THIS PHOTOGRAPH?

Package design today has been developed to the high point illustrated by this gift "beauty kit" by Du Barry which contains seven individually packaged Du Barry products. Demonstration by the model further dramatizes the promotion.

Three unusual package designs are seen in this illustration. The publishers Simon & Schuster put out a set of miniature books for children in a sliding case with cellophane window. Lentheric sponsored the playing card design, with informal script for a perfume set, and Kurt Volk, the noted typographer, created a package design entirely with type.

CHAPTER 6

Packaging

Designing packages is a professional field practiced largely by industrial designers who are usually engaged through an advertising agency to study a problem and submit designs. Some promising designs have been produced by students in professional art schools, but student designers need post-graduate practical experience which can be gained best through apprenticeship with professional industrial designers before their work is salable. This is because a package must be not only designed well but planned for practical manufacture. The cost factor is important. When many thousands are being made, a saving of a small fraction of a cent on each package multiplies to a significant figure.

It is possible for anyone to have an idea for a package and to make a colored rendering or a dummy of it. A package dummy is a complete made-up model of the package, correct to size and looking as the package would look if it were actually manufactured. But packaging is usually a part of a broad advertising program entrusted to some advertising agency or contracted for through a manufacturer of packages. Such manu-

facturers specialize in many different kinds of containers, whether made of paper, glass, metals, plastics, or other materials. The industrial designer is well aware of materials, costs, and machine processes (all packages being a mass-production proposition) so that he is able to handle the entire project from start to completion. It is because of this that the student will profit most by working with a professional designer.

Many designs involve two or more manufacturing processes, as in the case of a glass bottle with a plastic cap, called a "closure," and a printed label. Each of these would be produced by a different manufacturer, though created by one designer.

A "functional" package design might involve a novel mechanical feature for which the designer would have to prepare technical working drawings.

Prospects for success as a designer of packages depend chiefly on the natural inventiveness of the designer. He has to understand the psychological factors in display advertising in order to make his design work. His design must attract

Plastic "second use" container for LaVall nail coloring kit. The knob and legs are of metal—the kind of container now largely created by industrial designers.

attention; it must be functional. He must employ his knowledge of color as related to merchandising. But, most of all, the design must be practical, from the viewpoints of both use and the cost of production.

Your Aptitudes

If your interest in this field comes from strong design aptitudes, combined with interest in solving practical design problems, your interest would be a direction worth following.

The proportions in which art and merchandising exist in any packaging problem would vary with different situations. Generally speaking, much of the character of a package is determined by advertising executives before the creation of its finished appearance is assigned to an artist. So, for psychological appeal as well as in its practical details, most package design is a collaborative product of advertising and art.

Many new package designs today are the work of industrial designers not only because the industrial designer is trained to think of functional design but because he also thinks in terms of mass production and the costs of materials and processes of manufacture. Artists trained only toward the creation of a visual appearance lack this important background.

In package design, as in other fields, color sense is partly a natural gift and partly a sense which can be developed through training. Anyone who has studied color theory will have sensed that certain colors have certain effects on the majority of people, and that these psychological reactions are definitely a part of any designer's thinking when he is designing a package.

Nor can the cost factor ever be ignored in package design. Regardless of how attractive your package design might be in *appearance*, it would never be accepted for production without exact estimates on its cost.

So far as self-training is concerned, the active-minded designer in any field is constantly re-designing, mentally, the things he sees. He is both observant and critical. When he sees a poorly designed package, he asks himself: "What would *I* do with this, if I were asked to re-design it?"

Fundamental Principles

It is difficult to define "rules" that can govern creative design. It is much safer to state certain principles that designers recognize as having a certain sense of rightness about them. The following suggestions are offered as a guide in creating the package of a consumer product:

1. Design the package for attractive appearance without destroying its value as a container.
2. As the package itself is the first place users look for guidance in the use of the product, make instructions clear, simple, concise, and print them on the sides if possible. If instructions include a parts list, diagrams, etc., enclose a separate sheet, and print an "Instructions Inside" notice prominently on the outside of the container. Make the product easy to use.

328

In approaching a packaging problem there are two courses a designer may follow. His choice will probably be directed by the instructions of the client or the advertising agency. If the design is to be radically different in appearance from any other package for similar products, the designer will have an almost unlimited use of his imagination. However, if the design is to conform in a general way with the appearance of other packages for similar products, the designer's work begins by making a careful study of all existing packages. Then he prepares a design which is similar but has a distinctive appearance.

In some ways, the problem of making a design which conforms to others in the field, yet is different in appearance, is more difficult than to start fresh with no conditions imposed. E. E. Calkins, one of the outstanding figures in the advertising profession once said:

"If you want to design a really original package for any such product as tea, coffee, sugar, crackers or cigarettes, you should begin by forcing your mind to imagine that such products had never before been put up in packages. You would be starting with a clean slate. Your thinking would not be cluttered up with all of the things that had been done before."

Conformity has stamped many fields of packaging. Cigars make a case in point. Cigar manufacturers have not changed the nature or styling of the old cigar box since cigars were first put on sale. It is true that some modern cigar boxes have been made of cardboard instead of the traditional cedar wood, but the appearance has been kept the same, even to the use of wood-grained paper to resemble the original wooden boxes.

Materials and Their Cost

A great many products can be put up in almost any kind of material, while others require special materials or special linings. Some products can be preserved without special precaution; others react to temperature changes and require specially designed containers. When a designer starts on a problem where he is unfamiliar with the costs of the materials and their manufacture, he checks with the manufacturer of an existing package similar to the one he plans to design, and talks over the aspects of manufacture. A rough estimate of costs also helps keep the design practical.

329

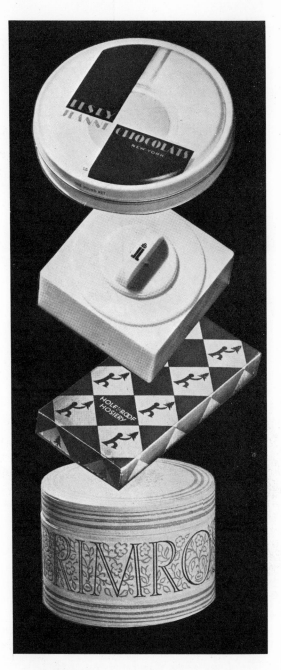

A group of attractive package designs in metal, plastic, and paper—each expressive of its material.

Appearance

Appearance of a package is of utmost importance in the display of the product. In fact, the container frequently takes the place of the product in importance. The appeal of the package "conditions" a customer's desire for the product.

Styling the product usually entails a long, careful analysis of the market's receptiveness to the container. Experimental dummies are shown

A distinguished group of packages designed for general consistency of styling.

A group of European-designed packages. Many European countries were years ahead of us in realizing the commercial importance of attractively designed packages.

Smart styling in Du Barry gift packages for Christmas. The striping is pink and gold; the products rest on puffs of cool green satin.

to public groups to register the instant response to them. The public's reaction to color, its reaction to the functioning of the design, and its resistance or acceptance to a novel idea are studied before a design is put into mass production.

Packages on a retailer's shelf should be designed so that one single, unified idea on the label will be seen without difficulty from the customer's position a few feet away. Small details blend into one another at a little distance, and form is lost. Fancy lettering is not easily legible. Units of the design should be treated broadly, and in flat, simple areas.

The package designer needs enough perception to consider whether the design should appeal to women or to men, or whether it should have general public appeal. From the appearance of successful containers now on display in stores, it would seem that to have a general appeal the design can be neither too bold or too "feminine," and the color should be gay. Articles for personal use seem to require more restrained

containers; garishness offends keener sensibilities.

Shape and Size

Some package design is conditioned in both shape and size by the customary selling units, or by the size of the product, as might be the case with a cake of soap. The size of a package is governed by the method of distribution selected to reach a certain market. A package so small that no identifying feature could be used on its label sufficient to attract a customer would have to be re-styled to hold enough of the product to afford a suitable identification. This is why products which are small in bulk must be packaged in quantity.

A pound of coffee, ground and ready for use, makes a sizable package and therefore can be sold on a single pound basis. Razor blades would be dangerous to sell singly unless they were

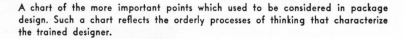

·OUTLINE for the STUDY of PACKAGE DESIGN·

A PACKAGE DESIGN SHOULD {
BE DEFINITE
HAVE RECOGNITION VALUE.
MEMORY VALUE.
BE DISTINCTIVE.

1. Consider the Nature of the Product... has it an idea which can be expressed by means of:

2. DESIGN . . . . {
a. SHAPE
b. COLOR SCHEME
c. LETTERING

3. Consider SHAPE and DIMENSIONS as conditioned or required by nature of product or by selling unit.

4. Consider DESIGN as related . . . . {
a...to SHAPE - [and SHAPE as related to DESIGN].
b...to nature of product, IDEA, Etc.
c...to other packages (if any) in series

5. Consider COLOR . . . . {
a... by itself, on intrinsic effectiveness.
b... as related to nature of product, Etc.
c... as related to other packages (if any) in series.

6. Consider LETTERING . . . . {
a... as related to total design character—and product.
b... as related to general advertising style for product.
c... as related to other packages (if any) in series.

7. Consider definite VISUALIZATION . . . . . {
a.... in advertising layouts [magazine pages, posters, Etc.]
b.... in the store, on the shelf, counter displays, window, Etc.
c.... in USE, from consumer angle.

8. Consider PRACTICAL angles . . . . . {
a... function, if package is also a dispenser. ["how does it work?]
b... material, as related to total design, nature of product, Etc.
c.... manufacture, COST estimate, packing and shipping.

A chart of the more important points which used to be considered in package design. Such a chart reflects the orderly processes of thinking that characterize the trained designer.

Three package designs, made up in three-dimensional form, by students in advertising design. The well-made "dummy" would help to sell a design.

wrapped in cardboard for safety reasons. Even then, it would take a quantity of them to make a package of sufficient size to carry a distinctive appearance. New packaging devices are appearing which offer convenient and safe handling of the blades without individual wrappings.

Other products, such as cigarettes and carbonated beverages, are affected in the packaging by trade requirements and public acceptance.

More About Color

Color in package design might be determined by the designer's preference and color sense, or dictated by the nature of the contents of the package. Packages that are to be displayed in artificial light should not be designed with light blue as a chief color. It will appear grayish and weak under the lights used in most stores.

Decoration

Most modern packages do not display much ornament or decoration. There are exceptions,

332

such as Whitman's *Sampler* candy-box and the attractive Early American "Old Spice" cosmetic series, where the nostalgic note is conveyed by old Colonial motifs. When decoration is used in packaging, the material should be treated in silhouette, and in simple masses rather than in line.

Lettering for Packaging

Lettering is suggested sometimes by the form and character of the trade-mark, as on the "Rinso" package. With a new product, the designer may have the opportunity of creating a distinctive and original style of letter.

Originality in lettering is considered important to an advertiser. A group of package designs by students were requested by the B. T. Babbitt Soap Company, which was planning to merchandise a soap flake, similar to "Ivory Flakes." While the package was to be similar in form to the "Ivory" product, an original name and style of lettering was being sought.

Lettering, drawn specially for packages, is not subject to the same rigid conditions which govern its use in booklets where it should harmonize with type matter. Most packaging designs offer opportunity for a free development of lettering. But legibility is a major requisite; the anatomy of the letters must be unmistakable.

When directions for the use of the product are to be printed, the type face should be open and easy to read in a small size.

Functional Angles

In designing a container, the economic factor of making the product accessible to the user is sometimes overlooked. For instance, a jar for cold cream should not be designed with a shoulder, no matter how attractive it might be. A certain amount of the cream will remain lodged on the inside of the shoulder where it cannot be removed.

All containers which are also "dispensers" should be given every possible test to make certain that they will function easily and effectively.

Packaging Designs by Students

An interesting package design by an inexperienced art-school student illustrates the possibility of anyone with a well-directed imagination

Made some years ago, this package for a proposed new brand of soap flakes is here illustrated to show the creative side of package design, evidenced in the work of an art student.

conceiving a good idea for a packaging problem. The product for packaging was a cake of tar soap.

Tar soap, in itself, is not particularly attractive unless you happen to like the smell of pine tar. The girl who developed this presentation, shown above on this page, started with the thought that tar soap is largely used for washing children's hair. Children do not, as a rule, like to have their hair washed. So the student thought it would be a good idea to make the soap attractive to children.

She started by modelling, in brown plasticene, a cake of the proposed soap, featuring on the cake, in low relief, a funny little figure of a sailor. Here some real cleverness and imagination entered the project. This funny little sailor is, of course, a "tar," and besides, he is also a Brownie. So here was not only a close tie-up between the name and the trade-mark personality of the little sailor, but also a tie-up with the product in both its nature and its color. It was a perfect name—"Brownie Tar Soap."

Our student designer next created a soap wrapper for the cake. It was a simple two-color design—"sailor-suit" blue, and brown for the Brownie tar's face, hands and feet. Then she designed an attractive box to contain six cakes, for a counter display.

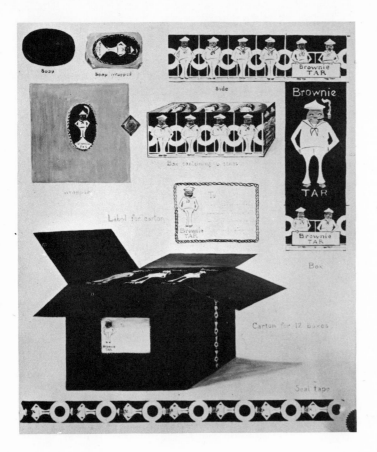

More evidence of a student's creative ability in originating and planning a packaging project. Although the work was done some years ago, the thinking which created the designs is as good as ever. They could be worked up and developed for packaging today.

Carrying the project still further, a shipping carton was designed with a special label (the Brownie tar and a coil of rope), and a gummed paper tape to seal the carton, the tape printed in blue and brown and repeating the design of the Brownie tar.

Another instance, also the work of a student, was the designing of an appealing little animal as an idea for a competition sponsored by the Babbitt Company, for soap flakes. The animal was somewhat like a rabbit but nothing known to zoology. It was given the name of "Fluff," and the slogan on the package read: "Make Friends with Fluff." The name was presented in a good, easily readable letter which could have been trade-marked. A functional feature of the package was a built-in string which would tear open one corner of the box.

Sales-minded as well as package-minded, the designer of "Fluff" proposed the idea of manufacturing a little soft toy animal, as shown on the package, and offering it as a toy for children, for 10 or 12 box tops sent in. She even went so far as to look up a manufacturer of such toys to get a cost figure on "Fluff" in thousand lots.

(This design long preceded a current product now on the market under the name of Fluff.)

No other special field within the total field of advertising design calls for greater ability, both creative and technical, than package design—and at the same time, package design offers unique opportunities for the exercise of taste and originality.

Your most comprehensive study material is to be found in the windows, show-cases and shelves of stores where packages of all kinds are displayed, and if you are realistically interested in this field of design you will look at every package you see with a professionally critical eye.

Your Career as a Package Designer

If you have a strong aptitude for creating ideas and if you can prepare a number of attractive and convincing drawings of these ideas, you should try to associate yourself with an industrial designer in some apprentice capacity. Only through direct contact with some such designing organization can a student hope to receive the

334

Another "before and after" in package design. The old package was a confused and over-decorated one and very badly lettered as to both style and legibility. The styling and color scheme of the new package were considered so attractive that all other "Aristocrat" containers, as well as signs and trucks, were similarly treated.

An example of the complete re-designing of an old package of a well-known product. Notice, particularly, the simplification and re-styling of the lettering, and also the retention of the old trademark and slogan: "Hasn't scratched yet."

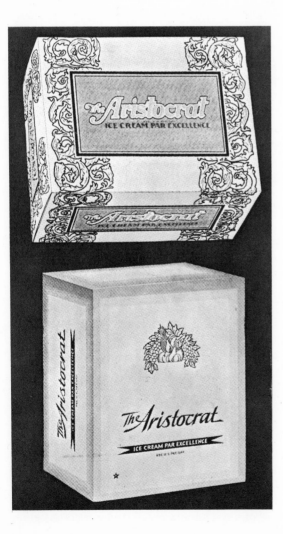

opportunities which exist in the package design field.

Experience in all phases of the work should precede any attempt on the part of the student to approach advertising agencies or clients directly. A reputation gained as the designer of a specific packaging program will carry much needed weight when the student attempts to set himself up as a professional designer.

As an aid in training, practice studying every package you see with a keenly critical eye. Ask yourself if it has been designed well, considering the product it contains. Does it appeal to the market for which the product is chiefly manufactured? Has it good recognition value and good memory value?

Suggested Exercises

As an initial exercise, select a product found on the counters of a drug store or in a general food market, and create a complete campaign for the packaging of the product. Begin by working in small studies, remembering that you are free to model your design as well as draw it.

When you have the general idea of presentation thought out, design the container for the product as your next exercise. Design this container with a view to display on the retailers' shelves. The container may need a "silent salesman" counter display.

As a further development, design the label. Carry this part of the design into careful drawings suitable for reproduction.

When you have the complete presentation ready to submit to a "make-believe" client, look up a manufacturer of box cartons (if they are needed to carry your idea into production) and discuss the manufacturing angles. Manufacturers are rather generous of their time in giving advice to young designers who have problems that fall in the general nature of their business. To learn how a design should be prepared so as to take full advantage of the manufacturing processes available is an important phase of these exercises. Knowledge of these processes will count heavily in the favor of any student who seeks employment with an industrial designer.

If the type of package selected in the above exercise was rectangular, repeat the exercises, using a cylindrical form. The problems differ, especially in the display of the label, because of the curved surface of the cylinder. Less of the label surface should be used for the important factors of the design. Only one-third of the cylindrical surface can be used for the label, and only the center half of that area should be devoted to the identification of the product.

In these four "quality" package designs, the current trend toward fine, expressive lettering is apparent. "Vision," a hosiery box, has ribbon script in two tones of gray on pink. "Chintz," a stationery box, has a distinctive italic letter in green on pink. The Lord & Taylor and Bonwit Teller boxes have informal script and formal condensed Roman in gold on white.

Contemporary furniture—usually called "Modern"—is largely the work of industrial designers. With the exception of "custombuilt" furniture, the problem is essentially one of materials, tool processes, and mass production. (Bookcase and table by Westport Design Group.)

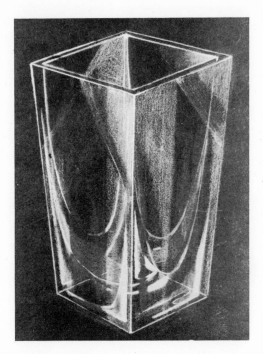

Glassware design by an industrial design student. The presentation sketch is made with white crayon on black paper, creating an effective illusion by graphic means.

CHAPTER 7

Industrial Design

Art critics, writing about the machine age, have said that the "artist of the future is the industrial designer." This may be so. It is evident that the industrial designer must be one of the most alert and best-informed artists of our present age.

Not long ago, an exhibition held in New York's A. D. Gallery (The Composing Room) featured the work of Alvin Lustig, a young industrial designer. The outstanding impression given by the exhibition was the breadth of interest shown by this designer and the variety of things which he undertakes to do. Items exhibited included:

Fabric and wall-pa-
  per designs
Magazine advertise-
  ments
Book jackets
Catalog cover
Bar in an apartment
Magazine covers
An apartment house
A helicopter

Interior of women's
  specialty shop
A modern school
  building
An entire book
Trade-mark for a
  brand of ice cream
Wall sculpture
A folder

Industrial art is not an art for the few—a special luxury like a painting or piece of sculpture, of which there is only the original and possibly a few reproductions. The people who have a vital stake in industrial art comprise practically everybody. They are artist-designers, manufacturers and sellers on the one hand, and, on the other, the purchasers and users of silverware, furniture, floor and wall coverings, textiles of all kinds, lamps, lighting fixtures, automobiles, radios, houses—hundreds of things which may be designed well or poorly.

The question of art appreciation, as it affects industrial art, is three-fold. First, there is the appreciation of the importance and necessity of training good designers. Second, it calls for an appreciation on the part of those who are responsible for approving and buying designs for manufactured products. And lastly, it depends on the appreciation by everybody who buys manufactured products when they appear on the market.

Much that appears in the preceding chapter about packaging applies to this larger field of industrial design. A student who is interested in

Examples of professional work by a young industrial designer. At the top, a model for a volt meter; next, china and silverware; and third, scale model for a prefabricated house, its design based on the use of standard plywood panels.

this work should develop his ideas in an attractive presentation, on the basis of which he might be able to get an assignment in a design studio or in the office of an established industrial designer. The field is so broad and its techniques so varied that it would be impractical to attempt to present a step-by-step procedure in a book of this kind.

It has been the privilege of Mr. Price to know personally a number of leaders in the field of industrial design. Of these, the late Donald R. Dohner stands out, as not only a designer but as a profound thinker. Shortly before his death he gave Mr. Price a rough draft for a book he planned to write. The pages were so full of sound wisdom and helpful definition that a number of paragraphs are quoted with a view to publishing some of the best thought that has been expressed by anyone on this subject.

When Noah Webster wrote his dictionary, no mention of "design" appeared in connection with his definition of "art." It had not occurred to anybody that there was some relationship between the two. Now, any modern idea of art sees design as the essence of all art effort. On this point, Mr. Dohner's text on industrial design, is illuminating.

"Industrial design is a very misleading term as used today, largely because of the breadth of its scope. The word 'industrial,' coming from 'industry,' covers a wide field . . . while 'design' has been given countless interpretations since the very beginning of man's attempts at any kind of art. The artist and, to a large extent, the layman, has always thought of design as pattern and color —the decorative treatment of a surface. To the engineer, on the other hand, design means structure, with emphasis divided among function, materials, production techniques and costs.

"Industrial design demands more than creative imagination. It demands a search for, and a collection of, all available information, after which this information must be studied and sifted until the designer begins to see what it means in relation to the design problem on which he is working.

"Industrial design, as it is recognized today, deals with the appearance factor of products made in mass by machinery. Obviously mass production cannot exist without mass acceptance. Experience teaches us that, whatever the reason, great numbers of people like the same things.

340

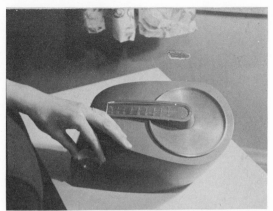

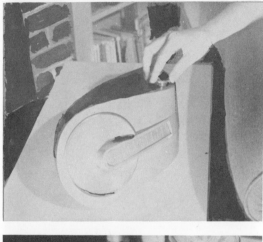

Further work of the same designer, again as typically varied as the profession itself; drawing of a pressure cooker and a model of a table radio, photographed in three positions.

That simple fact is the basis of successful mass production and mass distribution.

"Industrial design calls for a fully developed design before any process of manufacturing begins, fully developed, not only as it relates to human needs, function, materials, machine-production techniques, and costs, but also the kind of design-art that controls its appearance—distinction, timeliness and appeal. It is in this respect that industrial design differs essentially from handicraft design which is, by its very nature, one of improvisation as the work progresses. Handicraft design concerns itself with limited production, and is characterized by irregular and individual treatment often quite personal in nature, and therefore, relatively high in cost. Industrial design, in contrast, is characterized by precision and uniformity, and is consequently comparatively low in cost, and impersonal in quality.

"There are five principal 'conditioning factors' in industrial design, and these are not new. The hand-craftsman, through the ages, encountered them, whether at the potter's wheel, bench, lathe or loom; the architect or structural builder has had always these conditions to deal with in designing.

"The five conditioning factors are:

1. Environment—where and how people live.
2. Function—how things work.
3. Materials—what materials are available, and how easily or effectively they can be worked.
4. Tools—the physical means by which all things are made.

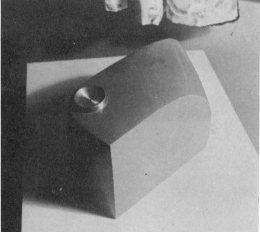

5. Economic factor—what costs are involved, in both materials used and the means of working them.

"Design itself, like art, cannot be divorced from the total influence of human living. It is an integral part of man's daily life, not something to be brought out and considered on special occasions. All honest and vital design, again like art, grows

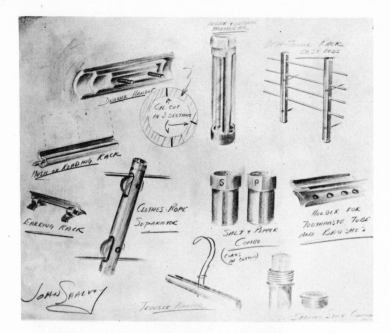

Rough sketches on a special problem, by an industrial design student. He was asked to think up things which might be made by a manufacturer who had on hand a quantity of leftover material from a larger project.

The complete training of an industrial designer should include typography. Printing, actually, is mass production, and typography is a specialized field of design. These two paste-ups were made by an industrial design student.

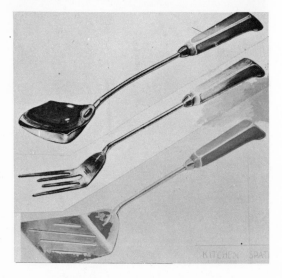

A young designer's presentation drawing of his idea for three functional kitchen implements of stainless steel with colored handles.

out of and is related to peoples' needs, environment, and a great many conditioning factors."

At this point it might be well to mention the doctrine of "right making"—the insistence that anything worth making at all should be made honestly. The designer or craftsman who plans the cheap, inferior imitation of anything, the designer who figures on inferior substitute materials or on poor techniques of making is betraying the whole great tradition of craftsmanship built up through the ages by true and honest workmen. As in most other human activities, the course you take depends on the kind of person you want to be. The true and honest course isn't always the easiest. Fortunately, however, its rewards are infinitely greater.

Mr. Dohner emphasized this point in his manuscript. He wrote:

"The hand-workman, in the days prior to the coming of the machine, took a very personal attitude toward his work; his reputation as a master craftsman stood or fell by it. He had to study and modify his designs, constantly setting a higher goal for himself. He took into consideration the function of what he was designing, and the possibilities and limitations of his materials and tools. Except in a very few instances, he used his

342

tools honestly and directly. Within him was the inherent desire to create not only a good and useful article, but one pleasing to the senses of sight and touch. And such pleasure is not dependent upon chance; consciously or unconsciously, there must be reason behind it, and this the good craftsman at his bench was able to supply. Thus, with things which he created for use, he very often endowed also with those enduring qualities of art, and we see them treasured in our museums today.

The Advent of the Machine Age

"All this was changed by the machine. Rapid, impersonal, and performing its work with precision and uniformity, the machine is, in a word, efficient. People became so entranced by this efficiency that they completely lost sight of the essential fact that the machine is merely another tool with which to work. It cannot think, nor plan, nor modify; it merely accomplishes whatever mechanical function it is designed to accomplish—nothing more, nothing less. And the creation of a work of art is not a matter of the tools employed, but of the human agency which employs them—of delicate perceptions, strong convictions, taste, and the talent to control the principles of design so as to achieve unity through organization."

Machines Cannot Design

The machine, even in an age more highly mechanized than this, cannot do everything. However ingeniously man may devise machines to reproduce, duplicate and multiply things (and his ingenuity in this almost passes belief) he cannot devise a machine that will design. Here is the last stronghold of the human being as a productive creature in a machine-dominated age.

Picture a vast plant covering acres and filled with machinery, powered with limitless energy to set those machines in motion, to start a great activity of wheels, of cams and shafts, of dies, of rollers, of lathes or presses. Picture it waiting, silent, inert, not a wheel turning, not a shaft driving. What is it waiting for? Man, perhaps one man.

Strange as it may seem, that man is not a great captain of industry, nor a great engineer or mechanical technician. The man that all this idle machinery is waiting for is an artist, a designer who will make the pattern that is to be put on

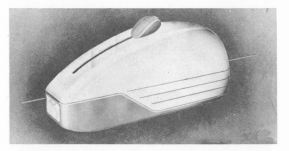

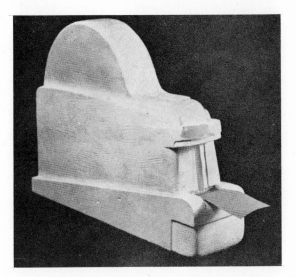

Two industrial design student renderings and an actual-size plaster model for a gummed tape dispenser.

the machine before it can function in the production of anything. Only then will it issue any quantity of furniture, of textiles, of printed matter, or whatever else.

The machine dominates production, dominates the business that grows out of production, but it exists only as a dream until products are given form by the creative art genius of man and the skilled human hand of man.

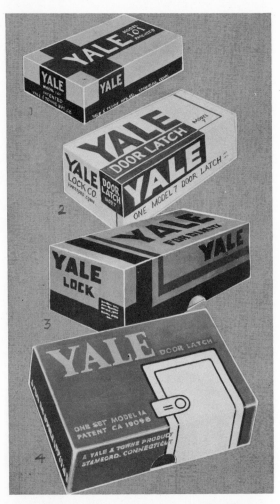

Since industrial designers today are often called upon for package design, a problem in this field —a display box for Yale locks—was given to a class of industrial design students. This photograph shows four of the designs submitted: 1, Black and Yellow; 2, Dark Blue and a light. Blue-Gray; 3, Black and Orange; 4, Light Brown letter, Dark Brown background, White door.

To some extent, it was at the suggestion of the advertising agencies that manufacturers began to consider attractiveness in their products. It became apparent that a great deal of time, money and talent was being spent on the visual presentation of many advertised products, and in these presentations the picture or rendering was stronger in appeal than the product itself.

Finally it occurred to someone that a little of this talent, put to work on the product, might not only improve it greatly, but would facilitate its advertisement and sale. This was done, and thus was opened a new field of product design, gigantic in scope, ranging from toothbrushes and tiny clocks to huge electrical generators and railroad cars and locomotives.

Now, the industrial executive has learned that art qualities are not to be found within picture frames only, but may be present in all products made by man. He has learned also that these qualities of art have universal appeal. Nor are they inconsistent with mechanical considerations; fine appearance and mechanical efficiency go hand in hand, each calling for a closer co-ordination and relationship of parts, resulting in simplicity and greater economy.

The difference between distinctive and fine-appearing products with universal appeal and those of mediocrity does not lie in the degree to which they are useful, nor yet, in most instances, in the quality of materials from which they are made. Rather, it is found in the measure of the artistic concept which created them and guided their production.

The opportunities opened up by the tremendous capacity of the machine, with its parallel necessity of distribution, caused the intelligent, creative artist to consider and study the whole nature of design. He discovered that all products made by mechanical means were not necessarily unattractive, for here was beauty in abstract forms, beauty in sheer surfaces, beauty in precision and in the logic of good engineering.

In this, you have the philosophy of modern art, or at least an important angle of it. It is modern thinking, machine age thinking, applied to creative design.

Materials

Materials have always exerted an influence and control over design—its character, scale, texture and color. A certain material is specified because of some one outstanding characteristic, such as the strength of steel, the lightness of aluminum, the transparency of glass, the plasticity of clay. We may find other favorable qualities present, such as easy workability, freedom from corrosion, attractiveness of finish, or low cost.

From the production standpoint, the designer is concerned with a few of the outstanding characteristics of a material—its strength, workability and cost. From the standpoint of appearance and appeal, he is interested primarily in its color, texture, warmth or coolness, pattern (if any), possible applied finishes, and character or imprint of the tool or process.

Student design for a glass fruit squeezer, rendered with white crayon on black paper.

Student design for a heavy glass flower holder. So far, nothing has been found to render glass more effectively than white crayon on black paper.

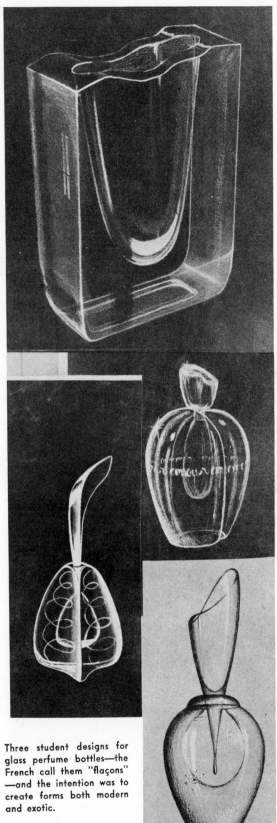

Three student designs for glass perfume bottles—the French call them "flaçons" —and the intention was to create forms both modern and exotic.

Tools and Tool Processes

Materials in the raw accomplish nothing, so we must devise methods of working or fashioning them. Tools and tool processes comprise another conditioning factor in design and exert a realistic control over the designer's work. Tools can do only what they are designed and built to do. If a product is to have beauty, integrity, and authority and still maintain the necessary balance of the other factors, notably cost, it must be so designed that the tools and processes naturally and honestly leave their imprint and character in the material.

Cost Factors

Economic control over design compels clear, far-reaching, ingenious and resourceful thinking and planning. Almost anything can be engineered and produced in this world if all regard for cost is ignored. Because of our colossal industrial set-up, geared to large-scale production and distribution, the big problem is to hold production costs within the range which the market can support, without sacrificing other equally important qualities, and so develop a product with a wide and ever-expanding market.

It is axiomatic that good design is economical design. It would seem to follow then that economic design is good design. For economical design will be simple, direct and honest. It will make wise use of materials, will take into con-

345

Silverware design by a student, the rendering made with opaque gray paint on black paper, the detail put in with pen.

Student project for a model kitchen. Practically all our fine new modern equipment is the work of industrial designers—concerned, as they are, with both function and appearance.

sideration available manufacturing processes, and will take full advantage of the production and distribution facilities. However, it may not work both ways. The element of fine appearance must also be considered an important ingredient.

Fine Appearance

This term is one which industrial design students should always associate with the teaching of the late Donald Dohner. To quote from his manuscript again:

"Fine appearance is no mysterious or occult quality to the trained artist. It depends upon the artist's taste, upon his concept, understanding and manipulation of the principles of visual design. He applies these principles to the elements with which he has to work, whether these are lines, planes, solids, colors or textures. He achieves the essentials of fine appearance, namely, an orderly and directed movement which possess relationship, balance and unity.

"There is something in our race history which makes us prefer orderly movement to agitated movement; elements that are balanced to those that are unbalanced. In the final analysis, we unconsciously prefer those things whose elements have been so carefully studied and expertly organized as to maintain that delicate balance between variety and unity, with the proper amount of emphasis rightly placed and always under control.

Mass Acceptance

"It cannot be stressed too strongly that mass production can exist only where there is mass acceptance. This problem did not confront the

346

A student watercolor sketch in which he shows his furniture designs as they would appear in an interior.

hand-craftsman of yesterday; he produced for himself or for a few consumers whose needs and likes he knew. But our present-day, large-scale producers are faced with the disquieting necessity of discovering in advance of production just what design is most likely to be needed and accepted by this large and scattered consumer public."

Presenting the Design

Industrial designs must be explained in fullest detail before production is considered. Drawings tell only a little of what the finished product is going to be, but this doesn't mean that one begins with a model. A model comes much later. The designer begins with sketches. When he has reached a comprehensive explanation of the idea with sketches, he proceeds with drawings made to scale. Then, if the design is of the kind called "plastic," he models it in plasticene. From this the professional designer has several plaster casts made. These he refines with sandpaper and carving until every contour, every part of the form has been developed as far as possible.

When this has been done, and every smallest detail of the design has been studied and restudied, the designer may make a model, which resembles as closely as possible the finished manufactured article. The model is not a step in the

A project given to one group of industrial design students was the modernization of a historic period chair (Hepplewhite) for mass production.

development of the design. It is a presentation for the client—a preview of the finished product —and it is made only after every aspect of the design has been checked carefully.

A fireside ensemble and a s‐
ple dining-room set in a ple
ing version of modern desi
These pieces, with the "kno
down" cabinet, are the w
of the Westport Design Gro

Parts of the cabinet shown below, "knocked down" for easy shipment and designed for assembly by the purchaser.

The "knocked-down" parts illustrated above are here shown assembled as a two-piece cabinet and shelves. This, definitely, is industrial design.

In large design projects, such as automobiles, the industrial designer makes what is called a "mock-up," after his design is completely developed and checked. A "mock-up" is an actual size model, made of whatever materials will most nearly resemble the finished article. It is evident that an undertaking of this kind is beyond the scope of the student or amateur.

Rendering the Finished Drawing

Sketches and drawings of industrial designs fall within the scope of a student's activity. Techniques are acquired early for indicating materials in effective ways. Glassware, for instance, is usually drawn with white crayon on black paper, examples of which are shown on accompanying pages. This gives the illusion of glassware better than drawings made in other media.

Plastics, wood and metals may be shown in transparent or opaque water color or in pastel. Sometimes a combination of two or more of these media is used. It all depends on what you are trying to show.

Industrial designers know that while many clients are agreeably impressed by bright, colored drawings, these drawings may be deceptive. They may fail to give a true picture of the design. The designer knows also that in all three-dimensional work, the only realistic presentation is a three-dimensional model.

348

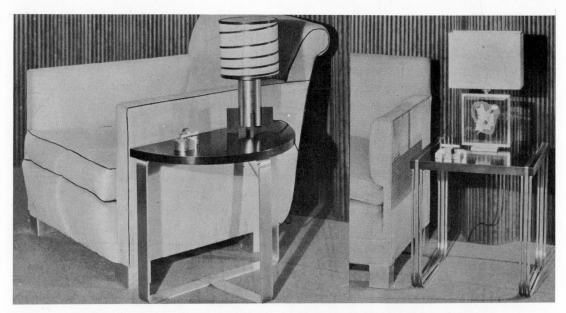
Table designs in heavy black glass and chrome steel, by a contemporary industrial designer.

Judging Your Prospects for Success

From the foregoing discussion of this subject, it is obvious that any direct suggestion to a student concerning his prospects of success are virtually impossible. Opportunities in the field are numerous and a new generation of designers will be necessary to meet the demands of an increasing market.

Two important traits which any prospective industrial designer should have are constant observation and constant curiosity about how things are made, what they are made of, and how they work. Only in this way can a student ever reach a point where he might think of better ways of making things, more economical, or with more attractive materials, and with more efficient functioning.

Your prospects for success can be determined better by self-analysis. Only you can appraise the qualities necessary for success in this field. They comprise all the attributes of an artist blended with the introspective sagacity of a businessman and the clear thinking of an engineer. Ask yourself these questions:

1. Are you creative, observant, and alert to the new things happening in the world?
2. Do shapes, colors, materials and textures mean anything to you?
3. Are you interested in processes of manufacture by machine methods?
4. Are you cost conscious when you set out on a design problem, or are you carried away, so to

speak, with the illusory aspects of the problem?
5. Are you interested in how things work?
6. Are you interested in how and why people buy things?
7. Do you think of improvements in appearance or in the functioning of things?

Because of the special and exacting nature of industrial design, a professional industrial designer was asked to prepare an aptitude test for you, based on his own extensive experience. Although some of the questions are similar to those posed above, they are nevertheless included as they bring out additional points of great importance. They are:

1. What is the principal aptitude an industrial designer should have?
2. Must an industrial designer have a basic working knowledge of materials and production processes?
3. Does an industrial designer need to know how to read engineer's blueprints?
4. Are ideas alone enough, or must the industrial designer be able to illustrate his ideas for other people?
5. Is the industrial designer's main concern that his designs will work well, look well, or sell cheaply?
6. Does the industrial designer invent new products?
7. Can every industrial design problem be solved on the drawing board in the office?

350

8. How much industrial design consists of new product design? How much of re-designing existing products?
9. Do you distinguish between two-dimensional and three-dimensional design in your think-ing about the work of an industrial designer?
10. As a beginning free-lance designer, how much of your total time would you be spend-ing in actual design work?

Aptitude Test Answers

1. The ability to organize, analyze and put to-gether a collection of *seemingly* unrelated pieces of data on basic facts. These might be set down or developed by another person, or you might be starting "from the ground up" on your own data: this is the over-all aptitude. Specific aptitudes:
   a. Curiosity—about almost anything. The "what, how and why."
   b. Observation—the ability to keep your eyes open, to be receptive to all kinds of stimuli.
   c. Perception—the ability to interpret your observations correctly; to see the *mean-ings* of things.
   d. Analysis—the ability to get to basic facts, to separate the important from the un-important.
   e. Interest—in the design of everyday things—and in *how people react* to them.
2. Yes. Everything you design should be capable of being *made*—and unless your designs can be made, their design is a failure. As you learn from this chapter, *materials* and *production processes* are "conditioning factors" which affect and influence every design.
3. Definitely, yes. Sometimes the rendering (pic-ture) is followed by a mechanical drawing from which a "mock-up" (model) will be made. The last step between the approved design and factory work is usually a detailed working blueprint. Sometimes the designer works directly from a mechanical drawing *only*, as in cases where a product has been fully engineered on paper, but not built.
4. You must be able to illustrate your ideas. An idea "in a vacuum"—existing only in the de-signer's head, cannot be seen by the client—and until it *is* seen, it cannot be approved for production.
5. The designer's main concern is that the prod-uct will *look well*, will have that all-important "fine appearance." The engineer is usually responsible for mechanism and function. The ultimate selling price *does* influence the de-sign, but is seldom the main concern of the designer. (This does not minimize the im-portance of cost, but cost might be called a "relative" rather than an "absolute" considera-tion.)
6. As stated in 5 above, "fine appearance" is most often the industrial designer's chief con-cern. He may be called on to develop a radi-cally new product, but more often the thing he is designing is more of a by-product oc-curring during the course of designing. A distinction should be made in every designer's mind between something "different" and not particularly good and something different *and* good. This is quality!
7. No. Often the final solution can be arrived at only by going into a three-dimensional model. Further, it may be necessary to go into a manu-facturing plant to observe and study a par-ticular machine or process. After this, it may still be necessary to have long conferences and considerable mutual effort between de-signer and engineer.
8. While no figures are available, I would say that more than 80% of a typical designer's work is re-design of already existing products. New product design lies in the 20% minority —or less.
9. The majority of product design (and always the proper approach) is three-dimensional. That is, you are concerned with the front, ends, top, back—and often the bottom and inside. A weakness of too many students—and even of some professional designers—is the thinking of only *two* dimensions—design-ing only from the *front view*, then only the *end* view, and so on. You must at all times consider the *over-all appearance*. How does this hole in the front affect the *back*? What happens to this chrome strip when it goes from the bottom over the end and across the top? A three-dimensional model quickly re-

veals the weakness of a design which has been incompletely thought through—a "paper design." (At times a designer works in three dimensions, making a plasticene or wood model when he realizes that lines on paper will not fully show or reveal *form*, or in cases where he is actually seeking a design idea from working with tool or shape.)

10. The beginning designer may often start by drafting up the ideas of other and more experienced designers. Or, he may be assigned to making models or renderings for other men in the office, drawing graphs or perhaps doing "consumer research" surveys in stores to check up on buying habits, etc. The beginner would be most unlikely to be started as a full-time designer until he had proved himself on a variety of minor assignments.

Suggested Exercises

(These were prepared by a professional industrial designer who is also an instructor in this field. In agreement with the author, he wrote as an introductory note: "Home study in this field is difficult because of the wide range of talents and knowledge needed—for which reason a student should try, if at all possible, to get some formal training. The student who is thinking of home study must be ambitious, very interested in his subject, and must be ready to devote a great deal of attention and study to it.")

The following approaches should be considered:

1. Study of books and articles on industrial design and related subjects. (Incidentally, every chapter in this book would add to an industrial designer's knowledge.)
2. a. A job in an allied field—engineering, drafting, advertising, etc. The objective here is to acquire some part of the knowledge you need with the possibility that some day you might be able to try the product-design end of your job.
   b. Visits to factories of many kinds making various kinds of products.

Lessons: Group I. Drawing for Industrial Design

Make perspective drawings, rendered, of three-dimensional pieces, such as electrical appliances, etc. Start in line only, using a graphite pencil. Gradually add shading, then color. Strive for accuracy, in both form and detail. Think always of the physical *structure* of the object you are drawing, remembering at the same time that drawing is actually only a tool, a means of visualization and that the main thing is learning to *think* and to develop the kind of thinking that analyzes and solves industrial design problems.

Practice drawing with graphite pencil, colored (wax) pencils, pastel (Nu-pastel), transparent and opaque water color. Try both quick, rough sketches and detailed, finished renderings. Some of your drawings should cover the paper with the media you are using; in others, let the paper (white or colored) be a part of the rendering. Check your work against advertising illustrations of products in magazines and circulars.

Group II. Mechanical Drawing (Model and Production Drawings)

a. Start with a standard drafting textbook (such as French & Swenson), nearly all of which are organized on a sequence from simple to more complex problems. Do a number of the exercises, or similar ones of your own choosing.

b. As soon as you feel any sense of mastery of mechanical drawing, pick some actual object corresponding in difficulty to the drawing lesson just finished—and make an accurate mechanical drawing of it.

c. Select one of the rendered drawings which you made under Group I, above, and make a detailed mechanical drawing of it.

d. If possible, secure a technical blueprint of a product and, "reading" the blueprint, and working *from* it, make a rendering in perspective, light, and shade, etc.

Group III.

a. After the preparatory work suggested in Group I and Group II, you could learn a great deal from trying your hand at re-designing some common object.

Select a small and easily available object such as an ash-tray, bookend or inkwell. Note its good and bad points. Ask yourself questions such as: "Does it work well?" "Is it convenient

352

Apartment house desk and magazine shelves in black glass and chrome steel.

to handle?—to keep clean?" Get other people's reactions; notice how they use and handle it; they may suggest some angle that you have overlooked. Notice how the thing is made; give its manufacture as much study as you can. Could it be made more economically? You could at least make some intelligent guesses on this angle.

b. Now, with your "findings" in front of you, analyze and evaluate all the facts and observations you have assembled. Decide which of the object's present features you would retain and which of its present features you believe could be improved. Since you are very much concerned with *appearance*, ask yourself questions such as: "Does it *look* efficient?" "Should it look light, or heavy; tall and slim, or low and long?"; "How about the colors used? Do they enhance and help to explain, or do they tend to confuse the form?" "To whom should such an article make its greatest appeal?" And there are many other such questions, each of which, and the sum total of them all, make you realize how much you should know about anything you mean to design, how much careful analytical *thinking* you need to do. The kind of "finding out" and the kind of thinking practiced by the industrial designer is the same, no matter on what problem he is engaged—from an ash-tray to a diesel locomotive.

c. Returning to your exercise problem. After the steps suggested in b., above, start making rough sketches of ideas which might improve the product. Eliminate whatever you believe to be disadvantages in the present model you have been analyzing. Seek always a better solution, making ten, twenty, thirty sketches—or more. You should never be satisfied with your first solution unless it emerges from many other sketches as definitely the best.

The procedure outlined above can, of course, be carried on into the study and re-design of much more complex articles. The more complex the thing you are designing, the more angles demand careful and thorough analysis, observation, comparison and trial.

Decorative painted panels are the dominant feature of this dining room,
the total effect of which is keyed to them.

This copy of a decorative painted panel is characteristic of much similar work of the eighteenth century in France and also in Holland. Interior decorators often commission artists to copy similar works in museums.

CHAPTER 8

Decorative Painting

Like photography, decorative painting offers an activity to talented amateurs that can develop readily into a profitable occupation. Many who have found pleasure ornamenting furniture and household incidentals have turned this hobby into a small business by filling orders for local gift shops.

No extensive art training is necessary for the appreciation of decorative painting, which was originated largely by people untrained in formal art. It is a particularly attractive field because the techniques are not difficult, the materials are not prohibitively expensive, and the results are gratifying, not only to the craftsman himself but to many who see them.

Anyone who is a designer by nature, possesses a good sense of color and is interested in the history of traditional decorative motifs should be able to produce attractive examples of decorative art. The key to success in this field is restraint in applying ornament. When planning a decoration, it is just as important to know when to stop as it is where to decorate.

In addition to an understanding of the above principles, the person pursuing this kind of work should have a craftsman's patience and an interest in the effects of various paints and varnishes.

Origin in the "Folk Arts"

Most decorative painting derives from the folk arts of the peasant decorators of Europe. That which we describe today as Early American "folk art" came directly from European sources. Typical of this is the work of the Pennsylvania Dutch. Peter Hunt, the outstanding practitioner of this work in the country today, describes and illustrates many inspirational ideas in his *Work Book*. There are many books on "folk art" which contain decorative motifs and technical instruction in the processes of stencil cutting and painting. For the amateur who cannot originate designs or make adaptations from historic examples, there are available packets of actual size designs from which to make stencils.

About Peter Hunt

Peter Hunt has restored and decorated antiquated furniture, picture frames, and many other things which are usually carted off by a junk dealer. With the increasing high prices of furniture and household articles, this kind of "decorative salvage" becomes more important.

355

This painted decorative panel, in the finest manner of eighteenth century France, is in the Metropolitan Museum in New York.

This painted over-door panel is typical of similar decorative treatments in eighteenth century France. The same idea may be carried out in modern treatments by contemporary decorators.

A few illustrations of Peter Hunt's work, which are shown on accompanying pages, have been loaned with the kind permission of the publishers of his book. According to Maude Basserman, in an article about Mr. Hunt which appeared in *Everywoman's Magazine*, "—he makes old horrors into charming, useful pieces, and he believes that the decorating should be informal, gay and suitable for the use of the piece as well as for the individual for whom it is planned. As examples, he uses angels and hearts and flowers on a Victorian dressing table for a young girl, but his angels are original and carry mirrors and brushes, or stockings and handkerchiefs! He likes pirates and ships and maps, and such on pieces designed for boys, and he feels that all children like best the furniture that has stories painted on it. He's all for the appropriate. 'Wheat is more fitting for a bread board, than tulips or roses or horses.'"

Practicing Decorative Painting

A progressive practice in decorative painting could be laid out in this sequence:

1. Trays, metal flower-pot holders, book-ends and other metal household articles.
2. Picture-frames, mirror frames, furniture.
3. Folding standing screens, panels, doors.
4. Decorative schemes for entire rooms.

Refinishing Picture Frames

Painters are interested in finding frames which harmonize with their paintings, and frequently they buy old frames which they decorate or refinish. This craft may be developed easily by any interested amateur. Many an old ornate picture frame can be painted attractively, fitted with a mirror, and made the decorative feature of a room.

Unfinished Furniture

During recent years there has been an increasing output of unfinished furniture by manufacturers. Such pieces can be found in practically any department store that carries furniture and in the mail-order houses. Fortunately, the makers of unfinished furniture have confined their designs to simple, unpretentious pieces, any of

356

Watercolor rendering by a student for a decorative painting project for a room in Chinese style.

which can be made attractive with either plain color or with painted decoration on plain color backgrounds.

Some caution should be given a beginner about this kind of work. The following article by Hubbard Cobb, which appeared in the *Providence Journal*, December 4, 1949, has a few suggestions that should be heeded. Writing on the subject of unfinished furniture, he says:

"This sort of furniture is sold for a great deal less than the finished article for two reasons. One, because it is unfinished, and two, because it is often made out of cheap grades of wood.

"A great many persons buy some of this stuff under the impression that with a little hard work they can finish it off to match some expensive items they have around. Well, it's going to take more than hard·work. It is practically impossible for anyone other than an experienced craftsman to match a finish exactly, even when he is working with the same type of wood. When the wood is a completely different breed, it's impossible.

"Your best bet is to buy unfinished furniture with the idea that it is what it is—inexpensive stuff that can never be made into museum pieces. Finish it in a simple manner, and let it go at that.

"If you get pieces made out of the better grades

of wood, a stain followed by varnish or shellac as a finish will do nicely. If the wood itself has nothing in the way of grain or coloring to recommend it, forget about a natural finish and use an enamel or lacquer."

Any amateur paint or stain job on furniture is greatly aided by several coats of wax, each rubbed well. The same treatment improves stain finishes also.

The Importance of Craftsmanship

Craftsmanship is one of the most important factors in decorative painting. The designing of decorative work is the function of the artist-designer; the execution, the actual painting and finishing, is the work of the craftsman. Craftsmanship means careful, patient workmanship. Every craft technique should be learned thoroughly, and this is done only through practice and experience.

Craftsmanship gives quality to anything you do, no matter in which field of art you may be working. This quality is quickly recognized, understood and respected, even by people who know little about art. It shows the mark of the

Two decorative screens, here illustrated to suggest style and motifs for decorative painting—not only for screens, but for doors or panels.

Decoupage

Gift shops have displayed for many years an assortment of household items such as trays, waste-baskets, screens, lamp shades, and telephone book covers decorated with pictorial prints, maps and other printed matter, antique or current. These articles, a simple form of decorative art, can be made by a person with limited art experience and training. The materials are easily obtainable, and the tools needed include little more than scissors and glue.

This hobby, with possibilities of development into a profitable occupation, had its origin in Holland during the early part of the 19th century. It was developed to popular favor in France, where it was called "decoupage." Translated freely, it means "the art of cutting" or "cutting out." Material obtained from many sources, and especially from early copper-engraved fashion plates, figures and heads, was cut out carefully, then assembled in amazingly intricate compositions and glued to trays, screens, and even to furniture. The completed decoupage was then given several coats of varnish which not only preserved it but gave to it a peculiar decorative richness.

The decalcomania is a modern version of pictorial material transferred to glass, porcelain or furniture for decorative purposes.

In addition to scissors and glue, all that one needs to practice decoupage is a considerable amount of illustrations taken from magazines, especially colored reproductions of works of art. The second-hand bookstore where all kinds of old prints may be found will offer a rich source for decoupage material.

The real investment comes in the necessity of buying such things as undecorated trays, waste-baskets, and unpainted furniture. A local carpenter can make folding screens with ¾" plywood at a moderate cost. When decorated, these screens might bring a substantial retail price.

Other decorative material which can be effectively used is wallpaper, especially the pictorial kind. While many of these designs would be found expensive if used to paper an entire room, small units of the design, sufficient to decorate waste-baskets and screens are inexpensive. Wallpaper designs may also provide motifs for painted decoration.

professional. Sloppy workmanship can defeat utterly the effect of a good design.

Good workmanship cannot be acquired in a hurry. Most work involving skills passes through a seemingly endless phase of trial and error, a great deal of experimentation and practice before it reaches professional standards. But, the attainment of the skill of the master-craftsman is a satisfaction and source of pride that makes the period of training seem of little moment.

This piece of furniture, conventionally decorated and "antiqued," suggests unlimited possibilities in this kind of work. Many uninteresting old pieces may be given new life through color and decoration.

In choosing an adhesive, avoid rubber cement which dries out eventually and sometimes stains the printed material. For lasting results, use a thin glue spread evenly over the entire surface of the material to be mounted.

Photo-montage for Decoration

Photographs offer effective material for decoration of this character. The technique of photomontage, described in the chapter on Photography, is used extensively by interior decorators for photo murals, covering entire wall areas. Professional photographers are equipped with large enlarging apparatus in which the paper used for printing the negative is the height of a room. The print is made in sections and is stripped together like wallpaper rolls when mounted into position on the walls.

Photo enlargements of various sizes may be used for decorating lamps, screens, or other articles to be used in a modern interior. The technique is the same as in decoupage work.

An important technical point in all paper work of this kind is the dampening of the paper before gluing it to the article you are decorating. This allows the paper to adhere closely and to follow whatever shape you mount it on. You should not attempt to glue paper on raw (unfinished) wood. Raw wood must be sized with a glue-size or with

shellac before you mount any kind of paper on it.

Allow the glue used for mounting to become perfectly dry before varnishing the montage. If an antique effect is desired, a thin coat of orange shellac will make the newest paper look ancient, and a little rubbing of Vandyke brown oil paint will antique it still further. These "aging" effects should be made before the finishing protective coats of varnish are applied.

For varnishing, it is a good idea to begin with a thin coat of clear shellac, which will prevent the paper from pulling loose. Then cover with clear Valspar for at least two coats. If additional coats are desired, be sure that each coat is thoroughly dry before applying the next.

The varnish should be applied with a broad sable or badger brush of as good a quality as can be obtained. When an occasional hair comes out in the varnish, it should be removed at once with a pin. It is difficult to remove these shed hairs once the varnish has dried. It is also recommended that varnishing be done in a room as nearly dust-free as possible.

Painted Relief Carving

Painting of low-relief carved panels of heavy linoleum is an effective decorative technique. These may be designed for use in chests and boxes, both large and small, furniture screens,

"Before and after" transformation magic by Peter Hunt, who has cleverly shown how taste, imagination — and decorative painting—may make a delightful piece of furniture out of something as unpromising as the piece shown below.

and panels of doors. The advantages of linoleum over wood are the ease with which it may be carved and its low cost as compared with hardwood panels.

After the linoleum carving has been completed, it should be carefully smoothed down with fine sandpaper before it is painted. Paint, enamel, or lacquer and gilding may be used for finishing. A rubbed coat of wax not only improves the appearance but also will protect and preserve the carving.

This kind of decoration dates back to the Italian Renaissance when ornament was first used in flat-painted panels upon pilasters, as in the well-known work of Raphael in the Loggia of the Vatican.

There is no greater mistake than for anyone to imagine that his early attempts at relief carving will be satisfying as works of art. It will require study and practice to approximate the products of professionals or amateurs of advanced skill.

360

Again, Peter Hunt's decorative talent transforms an old "melodeon" into a gay and amusing piece of furniture. The photographs on these two pages are from Peter Hunt's Workbook, courtesy of Ziff-Davis Co.

Do Not Be Discouraged

Resolve to keep trying. When something goes wrong and the effect is not what you had hoped it would be, it is quite possible that you did something, or more likely, you failed to do something, that made the difference. With standards set by expert craftsmen, ancient and modern, you can feel assured that the result you desire can be achieved.

It does not make sense to expect success with the first attempt. Even if this did happen, the chances are that you would not know how you had attained it, and would have to repeat the operation successfully many times in order to be sure that you knew what was happening. To experience failure emphasizes the reason for the failure far more readily than success will tell its secret. Experience with failures makes a knowing workman, so do not be discouraged.

The Great Reward

In this age, in which so much is done for us, we are inclined to lose, perhaps never to experience at all, the deep sense of satisfaction of doing things with our own hands. Even if we merely executed an old design in carving or painting, the joy of a piece of work well done is not to be compared with the feeling we may have about something produced on a machine. Craftsmanship is the last stronghold of the individual in our present age of machine-made things.

Three decoratively painted wastebaskets, available in plain metal. These examples are decorated by Jane Zook.

Four typical decoratively painted trays. The first is an authentic reproduction of an old Chippendale tray; the second, the Early American "cut corner" style; the third, a replica of an old Queen Anne tray; and the fourth is derived from a Victorian model.

As it requires considerable knowledge and research to develop authentic designs for painted trays, actual size patterns have been made available. This one and the tray illustrations opposite are from Jane Zook.

Typical small gift pieces, available, unpainted, for decoration. (Courtesy of Jane Zook.)

An illustration of découpage treatment for a tray and a wastebasket. Many decorative-minded amateurs have found découpage a diverting hobby.

Well-designed wallpapers, especially replicas of old historic examples, provide a wide range of motifs either for painted decoration or for découpage.

The decorative painter who is not content with copying will find library research work very rewarding. There are a great many early works on architecture and decoration which contain hundreds of plates like this, which shows the corner of a baroque ceiling treatment as it would appear looking up at it.

Suggested Exercises

Since the technique of decoupage consists mainly of manual operations, such as cutting out paper illustrations, mounting them, and varnishing the combination, experience in this can be obtained only through following the instructions given in the preceding pages. Creative art work is the objective of this book, and therefore the following exercises are suggested for those who desire to apply their talents in the broader field of decorative painting.

Starting with a problem concerning the decorations of a youth's room, select material illustrating a sea motif. Prepare designs suitable for continuous border treatment, and medallions for single unit decorations on furniture, the face of a waste-basket, and the panel of a closet door.

The idea for the continuous border might be a wave motif, shell forms, or a suggestion of rope, like that used for a ship's rigging. The single feature design might be an old sailing vessel, coming head on, and in profile view, or it might be some piece of nautical equipment. In the selection of the various motifs, keep in mind that the youth is fond of sea stories, of fishing yarns, and adventure.

Repeat this exercise for a young girl's room. The girl is fascinated with the legends of Camelot, the mythical kingdom of King Arthur in western England. The center motif might be the sword Excalibur, or a scene of the castle rising in a plain. Streamers, like those that trailed from the heads of lances, twisted in rope formation, might suggest the motif for a continuous border. If you are not familiar with the story,, get the book and read it. It will supply ideas for many motifs that might be adapted for decoration.

In the treatment of these decorations, keep the design simple and background areas in flat color. Do not paint miniatures in full detail, but add such detail as is needed to suggest the subject.

Begin by studying the designs on tracing paper, full size, and perfect them by laying another sheet of tracing paper over the rough sketches and improve the contours of the shapes. This is designing. When the illustration is complete to your satisfaction, transfer it to the surface of the thing to be decorated. Then paint it.

Full-rigged ships and ancient galleons suggest effective motifs for decorative painting. This striking example is from a linoleum cut by Sidney Bagshaw.

HOUSE BEAUTIFUL

OCTOBER 1939   COMBINED WITH HOME & FIELD   PRICE 35 CENTS

★

Fall Decorating Number

This cover design of House Beautiful provides
an excellent illustration of the interior designer's
"maquette"—a miniature three-dimensional
model of a room, carefully worked out to scale.

A student planning the modern interior in the most effective way—which is to make a complete scale model of it.

CHAPTER 9

Interior Design and Window Display

This field of design is also known as interior decoration. Many people believe it can be practiced by anyone having a good sense of color, an endowment of artistic judgment known as "taste," and a liking for nice things. Actually it calls for a specialized training whether it is to be practiced as a business, a profession, or a hobby.

Each of these occupations has its own particular approach.

Interior Design as a Business

In some ways, this is similar to the practice of architecture. It differs mainly in that decorators either sell decorative merchandise directly, as in a store, or, acting as expert professional buyers, take a commission on the decorative material with which they create an interior design, or which they advise their clients to buy. Selling of merchandise, or the acceptance of commissions resulting from such sales, is contrary to the standards of professional practice in architecture.

The decorator with a shop needs considerable capital for the operation of his business. He must maintain a well-located and expensive establishment, must pay salaries to a number of people, and must buy and carry in stock a quantity of furniture and all kinds of decorative materials

371

and objects worth thousands of dollars. While this organization would include a competent design staff, the business would be one of interior decoration rather than interior design.

A student or beginner might be able to get employment in an apprentice capacity with a large-scale decorator and, in such a job, he would learn how to handle large decorative contracts.

Interior Design as a Profession

This practice of interior design differs from that of the decorator with a store chiefly in that contacts with clients are likely to be more personal, and that no attempt would be made to operate a large decorative establishment full of stock. The professional would, however, need a certain amount of capital to cover his cost of doing business, which would involve some sort of studio or office, a secretary, telephone, and also a small drafting staff.

His work would consist of presenting colored sketches of proposed interior designs, advising on the purchase of everything included in the design, and supervising the installation of all work.

The professional interior designer needs to have as much technical training and knowledge of interior materials and construction as an archi-

Two-room models made by high school students in Kilbourn Jr. Trade School, Milwaukee, Wis.—an excellent method of creative study. (Courtesy of Design Magazine.)

Aptitudes, training and information which would help you to get a good position with an established decorating or interior designing firm include:

1. (a) Style knowledge and style sense
   (b) Color sense
   (c) Taste and tact
2. Knowledge of decorative merchandise sources and costs
   (a) Fabrics
       drapery and covering ⎫
       workshop costs   ⎬ trade contacts
       in making up   ⎭ trade recognition
   (b) Furniture   (credit)
   (c) All decorative   trade connections
       accessories
3. Ability to
   (a) Measure—to make accurate field notes
   (b) Do drafting, in making working drawings to scale
   (c) Render elevations, color schemes, water color perspectives
   (d) Make maquettes

Style Knowledge

Style knowledge may be gained through a study of the history of architectural styles and period designs of furniture and fabrics. In this study it will aid the student if he remembers that the architectural treatment of interiors was governed by methods of construction prevalent at the time. The spirit of a particular style may be recaptured, however, by observing the proper scale of the material selected for use and its fitness to the aesthetic "climate" sought by the designer.

Color

You may be fortunate in having a natural tendency to compose colors harmoniously. If your color sense is not reliable, it may be improved by proper information and training.

In historic styles, certain colors were accepted as the fashion and have been associated with their respective periods by practitioners in the profession. These colors were made part of an interior ensemble by the designers and architects who created the originals which we now refer to for inspiration.

Light yellow satin suggests the period of Charles I, of England, setting the high note of gaiety and affluence that contributed to the unhappy end of the monarch. Deep wine-red seems

tect; he must also know where to get all kinds of materials and workmen necessary; and he must be able to make out accurate specifications and cost estimates. As all work is done, he must supervise it and approve it. His compensation may be a flat fee or commissions on the things he buys.

Since this type of interior designer is very definitely a trained professional, a beginner could hardly practice at his level, but might possibly work for him and learn some of the many things that interior design demands.

Before studying the approaches to interior design as an art, or as a hobby, let us review some of the qualifications needed for success.

to symbolize the tone of the Italian Renaissance, just as blue and gold suggest the glories of the French Bourbon kings.

Taste and Tact

This subject was treated rather fully in the section on *Appreciation, Judgment and Taste,* in Chapter 2, of Part I. Taste operates not only in the color, design and selection of things in this profession, but can influence your appreciation of the other person's point of view. In short, it has a lot to do concerning the tact you show in your dealings with clients. In designing interiors, you are working not only to please people other than yourself, but you are designing, intimately, the rooms in which they are to live. You need to like people and to get along well with them; you need to understand *their* tastes and personalities before you can bring *your* taste and personality into the design of their interiors.

If the taste of your client is unschooled or undeveloped, it will take all the tact at your command to gain approval of your plans and recommendations.

The Social Angle

Most people who engage a professional designer to improve the appearance of their homes are in the upper income tax brackets. A wide circle of influential friends is a tremendous asset to any decorator who expects to practice as an individual. As in the case of the young architect starting his own practice, the first few clients are the hardest to get. Social connections furnish a perfect "grapevine" for tomorrow's clients. Although sound technical knowledge and long experience are important factors in building a professional reputation, nevertheless success or failure will depend on getting the business. Technical skills may be hired as needed, but the person who controls the contacts for the business is the one who "writes his own salary figure."

Sources of Materials

The practicing interior designer needs to know what decorative materials are to be had, from what sources, and on what terms. Various "cost ranges" have to be considered. There is a big difference between the mass-production furniture lines of the average department store and expensive custom-made pieces.

It is important for the student of interior design to study actual source material wherever possible, as in the American Wing of the Metropolitan Museum.

Historic replica. The scholarly architect or decorator is capable of re-creating this kind of interior in the Colonial manner. This one was part of a historic project in Philadelphia.

373

Historic design is an important consideration in selecting lighting fixtures and other decorative accessories. (From a drawing by Miriam Bartlett, made for the New York Herald Tribune.)

Information about trade practices and sources of supply can be obtained from the trade magazines, and from the confidential price-lists provided only to the trade by the manufacturers.

Workshop Costs

Workshop costs for making up curtains and slipcovers can be learned only through practice, through estimates on actual orders, and through discussion with the contractors about the requirements of the various jobs.

The cost of a pair of curtains, for instance, would begin with the wholesale and retail cost of the material, plus the workshop cost of making it up, to which would be added the cost of whatever hardware or fixtures might be necessary. To this the decorator adds his profit. The percentage of profit to be determined should be based on a knowledge of the cost of doing business over a certain length of time, taking into consideration the average gross business handled during that time.

Each decorator's business will vary in the amount of overhead expense he entails that will have to be included in the percentage of profit

he adds to the material costs of each contract. A reputation for fair price depends upon the consistency of price levels established by the decorator. Your profit figure should not be arrived at through guessing. You can lose money that way. It is also a poor policy to attempt to charge "all the traffic can bear" if clients are to feel they are treated fairly.

Accurate Measuring

In order to present your plans to your clients and to the dealers and workers who are to provide the materials and labor needed to carry out the design, you must begin with accurate measuring of the space involved. This work is usually given to an apprentice as one of his early "fitness tests." Accurate measurements of a room, or of an entire apartment or house, together with information of the size of openings, such as windows and doors, are needed to estimate correct quantities of materials.

Scale Drawings

From these measurements you prepare accurate scale drawings. These would consist, for a

An ensemble drawing of a dining room in the eighteenth century English style of Hepplewhite, from a line and wash drawing by Miriam Bartlett.

single room, of the floor plan and all four walls, called "elevations," showing exact locations of all doors, windows, and any other features. These drawings are the basis for both "working drawings" for contractors and for the presentation drawings you will have to prepare to show to your client the design you propose.

Scale drawings are similar to those made by an architect. These are not the drawings you show your client; they are the working drawings on which you figure quantities and get cost estimates.

Perspectives and Water Color Drawings

From these scale working drawings you make perspective drawings showing the appearance of the various rooms in water color renderings. Those visualizations are easy for a client to understand, whereas he might find reading the technical working drawings too difficult.

Making of perspective drawings from working plans was discussed in Chapter 3, Part I. Those who have not acquired sufficient skill to make the drawing by this method may obtain blank perspective charts from art supply stores, with the aid of which perspectives of interiors can be laid out easily.

When using color for the rendering, remember that the quality of light indoors is cool compared with that out-of-doors. Save the washes of warm sunlight for the rays slanting through the windows.

The "Maquette"

The *maquette* is a form of presentation developed by interior designers to give the client the best possible "preview" of the design being proposed. A well-made *maquette* is simply an assembly of the scale drawings (elevations) of the four walls mounted on the floor plan in the form

A decorator's grouping of pieces which go together harmoniously, the style note being that of the "Neo-Grec" Directoire period in France, immediately preceding the Napoleonic Empire style.

A manner of interior design called "Neo-Classic," since it combines some feeling of Classic precedent with modern overtones.

 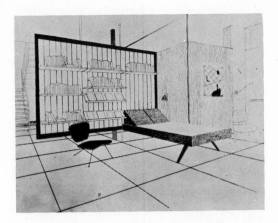

Two modern interior designs by students working under an instructor whose background is European and whose ideas depart radically from the historic styles.

of a box. The elevations are rendered in watercolor to simulate the effect of the finished work.

The *maquette* may be developed to any degree of elaboration, including scale cardboard models of the furniture. It shows the client what the scheme looks like, and serves the designer also in his study of the problem. It is a kind of model and, with the aid of light effects and transparent color "theatrical" mediums, can create the tone of the setting better than is possible with a flat drawing.

How to Obtain Experience

There are two possible courses to take in seeking training and experience in the field of interior design:

1. A position in the furniture and decorating department of a department store.
2. A position on the staff of an established decorator.

For preliminary apprenticeship, the student should work under the direction of an experienced man. Whether in a department store or in a decorator's establishment, the training to be gained by measuring customer's rooms, figuring quantities, learning from experienced people who estimate costs, will be varied and helpful. Here the beginner can learn the sources and price ranges of various grades of merchandise, and here he will become acquainted with the trade practices and the popular tastes of a clientele.

Entering business on one's own resources should follow only a thorough experience in the

Today's students of interior design not only create essentially modern interiors but present them in new techniques of rendering.

A few American manufacturers are creating handsome furniture for modern interiors and are avoiding the more extreme types which may soon seem out-of-date. (Photograph courtesy of Dunbar for Modern.)

employ of a well-established firm, and the acquiring of sufficient capital and social connections to offer a good chance for success.

Interior Design as a Hobby

Many women practice interior decoration more or less as a hobby, beginning with the planning and execution of schemes for their own homes. If their friends admire the result, they are apt to ask advice on color schemes, furniture, floor-coverings, wallpapers, and antiques. With this encouragement many women, with an honest flair and aptitude for the work, might build up a small amateur practice. Often they permit themselves to believe that a big professional practice is right around the corner.

One difficulty in "hobby" decorating is found in the "pay" angle. It is not easy to charge professional fees for non-professional work or advice, even though such work or advice may have definite value. Also, non-professional interior de-

signers or decorators will find it difficult, if not impossible, to receive trade discounts from manufacturers if they have no business or professional standing, and no credit rating.

Many women, however, have become recognized as "professional shoppers" and as such they have been able to make arrangements with local stores for commissions on retail purchases. These commissions are not as great as those offered by wholesalers, yet, if you consider interior design as little more than a hobby, local store commissions could add up to a profitable sum.

How to Get Started

Regardless of the approach you desire to make toward a practice of interior design, certain basic considerations will apply to all. First, study the person for whom you are asked to propose a decorative scheme. Learn to define his likes and dislikes. List them as far as it is practical. The list might read like this:

An attractive and practical feature of some of the better-designed modern furniture is the interchangeable unit—a variety of pieces which may be used in many different arrangements. (Photograph courtesy of Dunbar for Modern.)

He likes	*He dislikes*

He likes

Green and yellows
Mountain scenery
Flowers
Autumn foliage
Distant vistas
The smell of wood burning
Brocades
A strong melodic line in music
The sound of woodland streams
Orderliness

He dislikes

Reds and orange colors
Seashore
Big crowds
Cheap domestic carpets
Sense of confinement
Exotic perfumes
Silks and satins
Dissonance in music
Factory noises
Confusion

As a result of these findings, you have many basic convictions to guide you in a broad selection of color, style and treatment of any room you design for him to live in. Further discussion with your client might reveal his preferences in reading. If he is fond of biographies and historical matter, you know that he will probably approve designs which follow traditional lines. If he favors modern social studies and essays on sociological lines, he may be receptive to the modern treatment involving simple areas and a feeling of space. There is a relationship between the things people like, and just as definite a relationship between the things they don't like. Learning these things about your client is "getting on the beam."

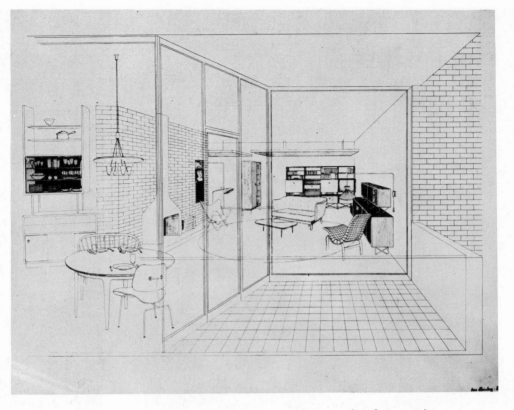

A student's modern rendering of a modern interior. This type of rendering requires a precise kind of draftsmanship which has become the "style" for modern interior designers.

Build Around a Feature

Every home, even every room, has some feature in its design which offers the interior designer a focal point for his planning. It may be a large picture window or a fireplace, a bay window, or a staircase. In some small rooms, it may be no more than a large blank area of wall space that can challenge the designer for an unusual and attractive treatment. If nothing distinctive presents itself, the designer has to create a focal point. The room, like any art effort, should be organized in its design with some one center of interest dominating the composition.

A picture can become such a center of interest. It can be selected with full appreciation of the client's likes and dislikes, and made an integral part of the room's color scheme. Large color reproductions of works by famous artists are available at reasonable prices. The quality of these prints will please anyone familiar with the original work of the artists. Among the painters whose pictures are available are the old masters Rembrandt, Gainsborough, Constable, Reynolds, and Vermeer. In addition to these are the post-Impressionist painters Van Gogh, Degas, Monet, Cézanne and Gauguin. Modern American art is represented by Grant Wood, Thomas Benton, Georgia O'Keeffe, and Frederick Waugh.

Consider the Architectural Factors

If you are asked to decorate rooms in a Cape Cod cottage, you would have to recognize the dominating spirit of the style and would have to preserve a feeling of unity throughout the treatment of the rooms. Chintz draperies, homespun upholstering, pewter and colored glass accessories would come to mind, to harmonize with pine, cherry, and maple furniture.

Student design and rendering for a modern bookstore. The project involved not only an interior visible from the street but complete drawings of every feature of the interior.

Rooms less distinctive in character, with possibly a group of windows opening on an interesting vista, may offer the opportunity of a color scheme that will harmonize with the elements in the scene beyond the window. Most houses being built today lack the traditional styles that would stamp a definite character on the rooms, and would cause the designer to adhere to some copy-book pattern. For most rooms, the designer can supply the theme, but he should begin by determining the character he wishes to establish and create his design to be consistent with this idea.

A room should have personality which conveys to some degree the kind of person who lives in it. In determining this you will have to ask yourself:

Should the room be restrained in tone, or bright and gay?

Should it be formal or informal, simple and friendly or conservative and dignified?

Should it be modern in treatment or follow some traditional style?

Should it be unique, imaginative, and possibly feature some idiosyncrasy of the occupant?

When you have settled this question, look for some article which will serve as a keynote in the scheme. It may be something your client already possesses. If not, begin by proposing a suitable object and start your color studies, using the featured article as a key for the complementary and analogous arrangement of the color scheme.

Measured Drawings

In both interior design and display work, information is acquired through measured drawings. In making measured drawings, the process is the reverse of making scale drawings. In making scale drawings you show whatever is to be built in a small scale so that it can be executed in actual size. In making measured drawings

(1) First, a freehand sketch of the interior feature of which a measured drawing is to be made.

With this equipment and a number of sheets of drawing paper, fastened to a small drawing board with thumb tacks, you make a rough sketch of the detail you wish to record—a mantel, for instance, as in the pen sketch reproduced.

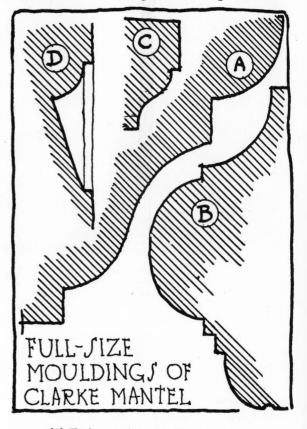

FULL-SIZE MOULDINGS OF CLARKE MANTEL

(3) Third, actual-size profiles of all the mouldings, keyed to the "field sketch" by letters.

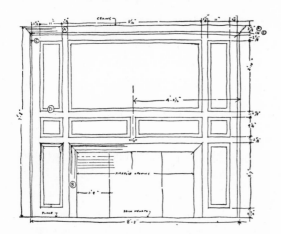

(2) Second, a rough "field sketch" of the same, with all essential measurements accurately made and noted.

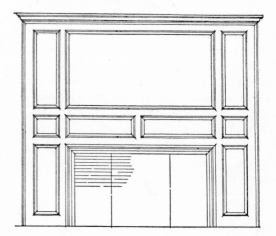

(4) Finally, an accurate scale drawing of the mantel. With this drawing, together with the drawing of the mouldings, an exact copy of mantel could be made.

you work from something that is already built and reduce it to scale in your drawing.

Let us assume that you have access to an old early Colonial house in which there are panelled interiors and fine old mantelpieces, and you wish to make an accurate architectural drawing of some of these details. The equipment for making a measured drawing includes a tape measure or a long folding rule, a screw-driver and a strip of lead about $\frac{1}{32}$ of an inch thick. Leadfoil is too thin for this purpose.

A fashion window keyed to the time of return to college. For this sort of work, imagination, together with an interior designer's training, is indispensable. (McCreery's College Shop.)

Your "field sketch" will be a rough one which shows how you note all the essential measurements and also how you "key" all the mouldings with letters.

To record the mouldings, take the strip of lead and the screw-driver and press the lead into every contour of the moulding, after which you carefully remove it and lay it on a sheet of paper. A pencil outline is then made, following the form in which the strip of lead has been bent, and this "profile" is keyed or located on the general sketch by means of letters, A, B, C, and so forth, as shown.

Reproduced here also is a drawing of the mouldings, at actual size, as taken by the lead. After transferring a moulding profile to the drawing paper, the lead is flattened out and other mouldings are recorded similarly. If there is any carving, this should be carefully drawn, full size, with notations as to the depth or height of the carving. These records complete your "field notes" for that particular mantelpiece, and the same method is used for any other details, for the complete measuring and recording of a whole room, or for the exterior of a building.

The measured sketches are then taken home and careful, finished drawings are made from them, as shown in the fourth illustration. The full-size moulding profiles, and, if possible, a

A small display unit in "high style," based on the rococo Style Louis XV.

The work of the creator of window displays, like that of the interior decorator, is essentially "designing with merchandise." This display was created by a student in a German art school.

photograph of the mantelpiece, should be incorporated with the scale drawings to make a complete record.

This technique in obtaining accurate information about an enclosure for which a design is to be prepared will be found useful whether the design concerns an interior of a room or the space allotted to a display of merchandise.

Use of Color in Interior Design

The majority of color schemes used in interior design are based on two colors, one a warm color and the other cool. Endless combinations are available; apricot and apple-green, delphinium-blue and daffodil-yellow, coral and chartreuse, grey and wine-red, pale-yellow and light French grey, and tan with French blue. Tints and shades of one color should be used for the larger areas, the other color, used in full strength, should appear only in small amounts for accents.

In introducing some red into a green room where the red might be used in full strength on one chair and the green alternating with a white stripe on a sofa, some small amount of the red should be used in the design of the fabric for the sofa to help associate the two colors.

When a third color is used in a room scheme, it is usually analogous to one of the other colors and it is used sparingly.

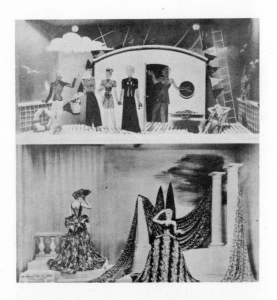

Two modern French window display ideas from the French publication Étalages, by Manera.

An "idea" window for a "Beach Shop" in a large department store. Ingenuity in construction and in the use of materials is important in this kind of design. (Abraham & Straus.)

Color can play an important part in your interior design. Dark walls will make a room seem smaller; light ones, larger. As light penetrates into a room, it is either absorbed by dark walls or reflected by light walls. A tint of yellow will allow the greatest amount of light rays to be reflected; all other colors will reflect less.

When selecting fabrics for a room, or choosing the color for walls and ceiling, match your color in the room where it is to be used. The quality of light differs in rooms where sunlight enters from rooms having a northern exposure.

Treatments for Wall Design

The proportions of a room can be affected by the treatment of the wall design. A pattern of vertical stripes will make the room seen higher; horizontal stripes will have a reverse effect. Large units of design will make rooms seem smaller; small units give the effect of greater space. This is why small, flowered wallpapers are suitable for the small bedrooms in cottages.

When a room is poorly proportioned, its length too great for its width, the long walls should be painted a solid color and the end walls accented with a heavily patterned paper.

A ceiling can be made to look higher if it is painted with a tint lighter than the side walls; it will seem lower if painted darker than the side walls.

Windows Are Important

Curtains and draperies play a big part in the feeling of space in a room. Small rooms require less accent at the windows. Strong contrast between the draperies and the general color tone of the room will make the room seem more crowded.

Curtains and draperies should not be arranged to prevent light from entering. It is not necessary to regard the shape of the window as dic-

A beautifully designed window display composition, dramatic in its simplicity and "high style". (B. Altman & Co.)
(The windows for McCreery, Abraham & Straus, and B. Altman & Co. are from Cora Scovil's Lady's Book, a privately printed publication by Cora Scovil, creator of the mannequins appearing in the windows.)

Two window designs in which the display of merchandise plays an important part.

in the following manner, with draperies only, or with casement curtains only, or with draperies and glass curtains. Tapes on Venetian blinds may match the color of the blinds or contrast with them.

When draperies and curtains are used they should be fastened back at the same level on each side. Drape tie-back curtains loosely.

Valances and boxed cornices are used to give the window a more finished appearance. Where the soffit of the window opening is lower than the ceiling height, keep the valance above the opening so that it will not reduce the amount of light the window can provide. If the window opening extends as high as the ceiling, or near to it, the valance will have to be reduced to a thin strip or abandoned.

Valances may be made of the same material as the draperies, or of a contrasting material. The valance may be a plain color if the draperies are figured.

A Word About Furniture

No book endeavoring to cover the broad scope of a preliminary art study can hope to include specialized fields, each demanding much concentrated study. The study of furniture is one of these. Any attempt to discuss it in this book would result in a sketchy outline that could lead to false impressions instead of general knowledge.

Styles and their appropriate uses should be studied from books specializing in this field. The same might be said of the design of textiles and their use in upholstery. The study of both furniture and textiles is fascinating and romantic, involving personalities associated with the great historic periods of decoration.

The Art of Window Display

Creating window displays may be considered a field of design allied to the practice of interior design. It is much more than just "window dressing." It calls for imagination and a keen awareness of the things people are interested in seeing.

Taste, a sense of color, an intelligent selection of merchandise and accessories, and an appreciation of construction problems—all of the attributes of a finished artist are drawn upon for

tating the shape of the drapery arrangement. Design the wall on which the windows occur, ignoring the outlines of the windows. Outlining poorly located windows with a decorative treatment would make a badly designed wall.

Shades and Venetian blinds may be used correctly in many types of rooms. Shades control light easily and are less difficult to keep clean. Venetian blinds are better at large windows where the exposure is sunny. They may be used

the modern window design. Because window presentations involve a great variety of articles and a minimum of space, they must depend for their effect on the inventiveness of the designer.

Display work in a store is generally a store job since the "display man" must be constantly in close contact with department heads, and must know all the merchandise in the store as well as understand the problems of the "construction crew" which installs the display.

In the smaller stores where window display work would not be a full-time job, an artist capable of presenting ideas for window displays might interest the store proprietor in giving him the opportunity to carry out an assignment.

Selecting Material for a Display

According to A. S. Hurst, a specialist in this field, and author of *Displaying Merchandise for Profit,* "Merchandise display space consists not only of the show windows of a store, but also of the interior and exterior show cases, counters, aisle tables, floor stands, display niches, ledges and other areas."

Sound art principles are set forth in his further statements:

"The most effective windows are those which exhibit a dominant thought. Singleness of purpose drives home the merchandising idea . . . the display man, in arranging a 'trim' should keep it so unified that it makes but one distinct impression.

"In a tabulation of opinions of experts, twelve points were given as the most important points of advantage for a window display. Arranged in the order of the number of votes received for each item, there are:

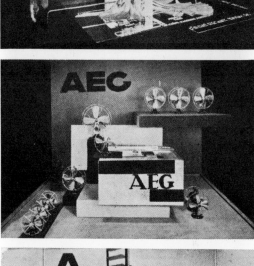

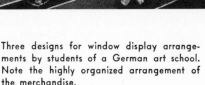

Three designs for window display arrangements by students of a German art school. Note the highly organized arrangement of the merchandise.

1. Power of Attraction
2. Color Harmony
3. Selling Power of the Display
4. The Merchandise Exhibited
5. Arrangement
6. Balance
7. Lighting
8. Uncrowded Appearance
9. Cleanliness
10. Timeliness
11. Originality
12. Window Cards

It is interesting to see the factor of "Originality" so far down on the list, and the item, "Uncrowded Appearance" in eighth place instead of among the first four. The list is valuable, never-

theless, and students should keep these factors in mind whenever they are engaged in a problem of this kind.

As a further note, Mr. Hurst reminds us that "fashion, or style, now enters into the construction of many lines of merchandise aside from garments, and good displays feature information concerning styles in color, and other qualities that may increase the urge to possess."

Not only must the designer of window displays consider the most effective selection and dramatization of the merchandise involved, but like a stage designer, he must also give careful thought to lighting.

Suggested Exercises

Your first suggested exercise might as well be on one of the basic things in interior design—one of the first things you would most likely be expected to do if you were to get a job with any kind of a decorator.

This is *measuring*.

As recommended elsewhere in the text, put down on paper your best guesses on a few dimensions. How long and how wide is the room you are now in? What are the dimensions of the doors?—of the windows? How high is the window above the floor? How high is the ceiling? What are the dimensions of a picture or a mirror hanging on the wall?

With all these guesses put on paper, now check up to see how good you are at this very important accomplishment of guessing measurements. For this kind of measuring your best instrument is a six foot folding rule; a foot rule is inaccurate and also laborious to use.

If your guesses are a foot or more "off", how could you expect to be anywhere near right if, on visiting a client's home, you were asked if a certain sofa would be low enough to come below the window sill, or if a certain desk would fit a space between two windows?

Measured Drawings

Your next Lesson should be a measured drawing of the room you are in. This should be drawn to scale, as explained on page 374, and should consist of a floor plan and all four elevations (that is, a direct "pattern" of each wall, with doors and windows figured.) All the dimensions should be neatly noted on these drawings, with lines and arrows.

No matter how extensive or elaborate an entire apartment or house might be, your procedure would be the same. Such measured drawings are the first thing needed by any decorator in order to figure quantities on curtain materials, wall paper and floor coverings, as well as to plan the placement of furniture.

A Practical Experiment

From this elementary exercise in making measured drawings, you should, through permission, gain access to an interior in which there is a detailed mantel piece, doorway, stair rail or other feature from which to make measured drawings as explained on pages 382-383.

Sketching

Anyone who thinks of going into interior design or decoration will find it a serious handicap to be unable to sketch easily, quickly and with reasonable accuracy. Such sketching might well make a "sale," if done on the spot, while discussing an interior scheme with a client.

Make a number of practice sketches of any interior and, also, make *many* sketches of furniture. You should be able to sketch a piece of furniture as easily as you write your name.

Make a Scrap Book

It is never too soon to start a scrap book of clippings from home furnishing magazines, or any other source. Most decorators have had the scrap book habit over a period of years, and, supplementing clippings with sketches, notes on color schemes, illustrations of lamps and many other accessories, in the course of time they have a collection of invaluable reference material. This sort of material, since it consists of things which you have chosen yourself, will have particular significance. Wherever possible, sources, costs and prices should be noted in such scrap books. Very often the Sunday papers contain illustrations of interesting current interiors, and such illustrations are usually accompanied by notes on color schemes, etc. Such attention to current ideas and trends, supplemented by following the consumer and trade magazines in the field, is a matter of course with practicing interior decorators and designers.

Color Schemes

It is impossible, here, to go into any detailed discussion of color. You have "color sense" (like an "ear for music") or you haven't. If you have good color sense you won't need instruction. You will know good color schemes when you see them and (if you're wise) you will make a note of them. And you will have no serious difficulties in creating color schemes of your own.

If you haven't a reliable color sense, I can only hope that a lot of study of books and texts on color will help you to develop in this important phase of interior design. A stern advisor might even say that if you really have no color sense you wouldn't be very wise to go into this field at all. Many people imagine that the creation of attractive color schemes is the most important part of interior design and decoration—but while color unquestionably *is* important, there's a lot more than that to be learned, understood and known. Remember that a decorator, like an architect, is assuming the responsibility for the spending of someone else's money and is therefore expected to have *authority*, along with many specific requirements.

The Maquette

As a final exercise, you might try out your creative ability—and also your craftsmanship—on making a complete maquette, as illustrated on page 370 and described on page 375.

Sometimes, in a maquette, the furniture is merely drawn on the elevations of the walls and indicated, for placement, on the floor. In other cases, the furniture is made to scale, from cardboard, and colored to resemble the real thing, as in the student maquettes on page 372. This, of course, is the best way to study, as well as to present a room—three dimensionally and complete in miniature in its actual appearance. But you must remember the vital essential of keeping *everything* as accurately *in scale* as you possibly can.

Two drawings by art school fashion students. The drawing at the left done mostly in opaque; the other, a brush drawing rendered in water-color, partly dry-brush.

Fashion sketch by a high school student in Oak Park, Ill. An entry in Scholastic Awards.

CHAPTER 10

Fashion

The field of fashion is an attractive one, particularly for women because of their innate sense of appropriateness in wearing apparel. Whether the branch of the business chosen is fashion illustrating, styling, serving as a buyer of clothing and accessories, or manufacturing, the outstanding aptitude required is a "style sense."

Jobs in the fashion field demand a knowledge and "flair" for style. The highest salaries are paid to those whose style sense is keen. Because modes and fashion change, the accomplished person in the business will intuitively see the potentialities in the latest designs.

Quoting a former art editor of *Vogue* magazine:

"A 'sense of elegance,' or 'fashion point of view,' or a 'feeling for chic' is one of those qualities which it is very difficult to define precisely, but which is of tremendous importance to all fashion editors and stylists."

It may be well to define the important difference between the terms "style," "fashion," and "mode." Modes change frequently, depending on the reaction to them by the general public. Smartness is the chief attribute of a mode; it may be based on some event current in the popular fancy. There is nothing of permanence in it.

Fashion is also transitory, but it gains and holds favor by its newness. Change is the life blood of fashion because it appeals to the human desire for change.

Style, on the other hand, is a permanent quality, an innate loveliness that endures through the ages. Certain styles are associated with historic periods but it is not the form of the art which endures but rather the highest expression of thought that the period represents which denotes its permanent value in art.

Frequently, these terms are used as though they were synonyms, and one hears the expression "out of style" when "out of fashion" or "out of date" is intended.

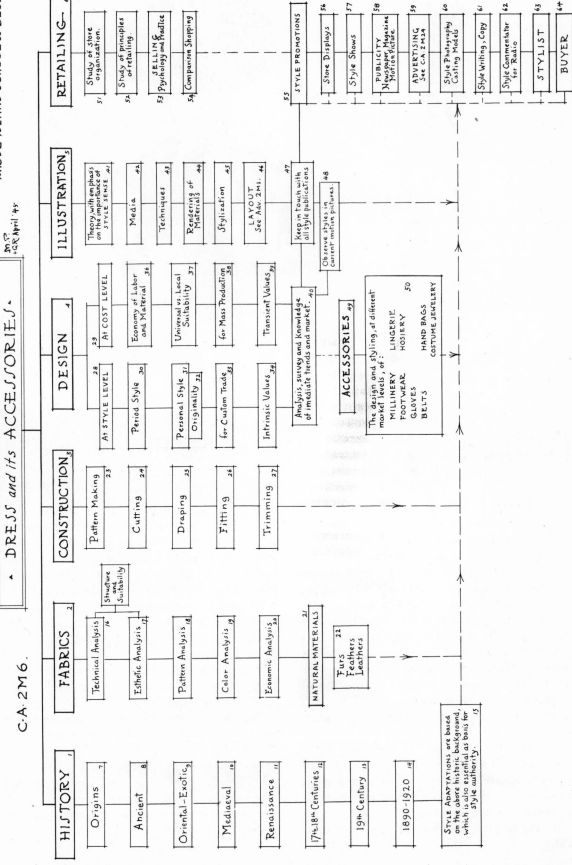

Fashion pen drawing by an art school student. Great care was taken here in the indication of the patterned fabric.

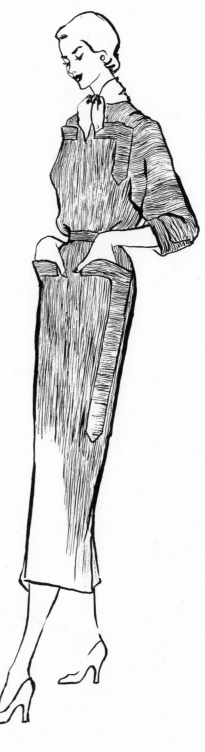

Fashion pen drawing by an art school student. This drawing was given additional accent by touches of bold brush-work, and the pen rendering aims to show texture in the material.

Quick line sketch of a pose, done by the same student. Literally hundreds of sketches like this should be made by any beginner entering this field.

To present graphically the field of fashion and its many branches of activity, a chart is reproduced on an accompanying page titled Dress and its Accessories, and listing the topics History, Fabrics, Construction, Design, Illustration, and Retailing, which will be treated separately in the following pages. From this survey, a student may decide where he or she feels the prospects for success are best.

Regarding for the moment the activities numbered 55 to 64, appearing at the extreme right-hand side of the chart, it will be seen that it is important to be considered a style authority. As in any professional field, authority is to be attained only through co-ordination of knowledge and experience.

Although we are concerned only with fashion illustration and fashion photography as the activity of an artist, we will discuss all factors as they represent the sum total of knowledge which would lead a student eventually to the higher levels in the field.

Numbers are used to help identify the topics as they are discussed. They read downward, and from left to right.

Strong evidence of ability in fashion illustration is seen in this quick outline sketch by an art school fashion student.

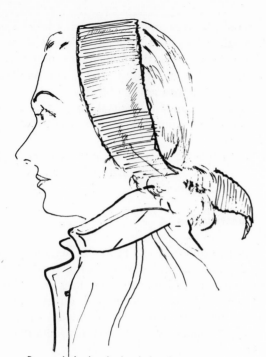

Pen and dry-brush sketch by the same student who made all four of the drawings on these two pages.

1. History

Like most background material, the history of costume can be learned from book and museum study. Information concerning the evolution of fashions in dress, for men, women, and children, is important to the designer and the illustrator. Beyond its use to the theatrical costumer, it offers a vast reservoir of inspiration. Many new frills in fashion have an ancient ancestry, and to know the "newest fad" in its original form is part of a fashion stylist's education.

Historic fashion is recalled frequently because of a personality with which it is associated. When the fashion reappears, even in its modified form for present day usage, it remains identified with its historic patron. Thus we associate the great lace ruff with Queen Elizabeth, the feathered hat with King Charles, the falsely broad shoulders with King Henry VIII, the open collar with Lord Byron.

2. Fabrics

From numbers 16 to 21 are listed five things the student should learn about fabrics:

16. Technical Analysis, meaning a study of ma-

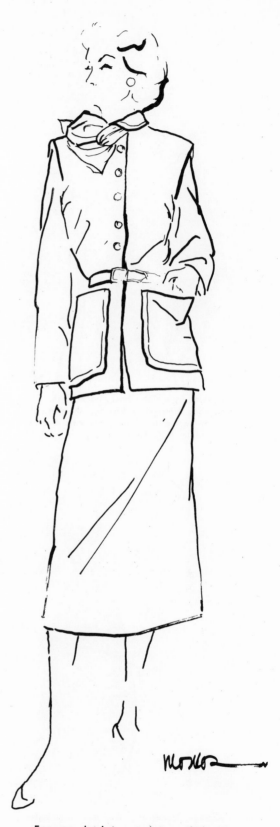
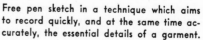

Free pen sketch in a technique which aims to record quickly, and at the same time accurately, the essential details of a garment.

Drawing by a high school student of the kind called a "dressmaker drawing," showing style of the back of the dress. (Scholastic Awards: Scarsdale, N.Y., High School.)

Another Scholastic Awards "dressmaker drawing" by a high school student. A sample of the fabric to be used usually accompanies this kind of fashion drawing. (Cass Technical High School, Detroit, Michigan.)

terials, weaves and manufacturing processes.

17. Aesthetic Analysis, meaning a study of, and familiarity with, the appearance of fabrics.

18 and 19. Pattern Analysis and Color Analysis cover the appearance of fabrics.

20. Economic Analysis covers the important question of the comparative costs of all costume fabrics.

21. With specific items listed in 22 covers what are called "natural" materials used by costume designers.

3. Construction

The five divisions (23 to 27) under the heading of "Construction" pertain to the actual work of dressmaking. Since these activities are technical, they are best learned through direct apprenticeship or in the costume department of a well-equipped school where expert instruction may be had.

4. Design

This activity is engaged in professionally at two levels, one concerned with style, the other with cost (28 and 29). Most designers do not attempt to design for both levels. They specialize in one or the other, but in either case the expression of style in their work is of central importance.

The style level is aimed at the more expensive "custom" trade, and the cost level is directed at the low-priced "mass production" type of garments for nationwide distribution. The differences may be compared in the notations 30 to 34, and 36 to 39, and both should be affected by the notations 40, 47 and 48.

"Intrinsic Values" (34) mean the qualities of a costume design that should retain its style longer than the qualities of the "Transient" (39) design which is made for a short-lived moment of fashion.

Many designers have specialized successfully in the creation of accessories of dress, listed 49 and 50. Every artist who is working in the fashion field should be able to make attractive reproduction drawings of accessory merchandise. This consists of experimenting with various techniques and media that will reproduce materials, such as black calfskin or alligator-skin for hand bags, polished metals, and the textures of various weaves of fabrics.

5. Fashion Illustration

The attribute most important to a fashion illustrator is "style sense." This inner feeling for style should be apparent in all of his illustrations. Any dress or other garment or accessory drawn must look at least as smart and attractive as the merchandise itself, whether it is rendered from a photograph or from a dress on a model.

A clever fashion artist usually makes the drawing look a little smarter and a little more attractive than the actual merchandise, but too great an exaggeration could lead to dissatisfied customers.

Style Sense

Style sense is one of those intangible things, like an ear for music or an eye for color, which certain people possess to a greater degree than others. However, a feeling for style may develop from (1) a desire to know as much about fashions as can be gained through study, and (2) patient application to this study. Style sense involves a technical understanding of dressmaking and materials, plus an ability to produce smart effects with them on the human figure.

Good proportions in clothing have accounted for those styles we are more likely to recall as distinguished or beautiful than those where the elements comprising the costume were not arranged harmoniously. Aesthetic influences have been at work for centuries and it may be instructive to observe the principles which have directed the trends of fashion for some time.

The major divisions of the human figure for costume purposes are: a line below the knee, whether of skirt or breeches; a line at the middle, whether of girdle or waistcoat; a line in the center of the breast, whether of bodice or vest. Although these lines do not indicate that which is most important in the proportions of the human figure, they furnish a method of representing proportion which the costumer has recognized quite consistently.

Media (42) and Technique (43)

Fashion illustration is usually done in line, wash, or a combination of the two. The line can be executed with a pen or a brush, and the wash

Informal brush drawing entered in Scholastic Awards by a high school fashion student. (Washington Irving High School, New York City.)

Fashion photograph, with informal script lettering, incorporated in a layout for Scholastic Awards. (Lane Technical High School, Chicago, Ill.)

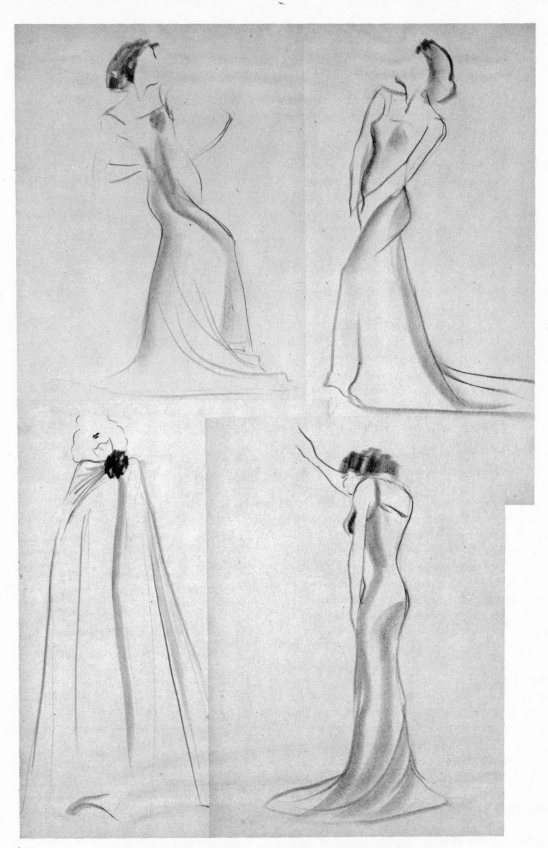

Well-trained students of fashion illustration are required to make a great many quick sketches in which the aim is to record action and pose in the least possible time.

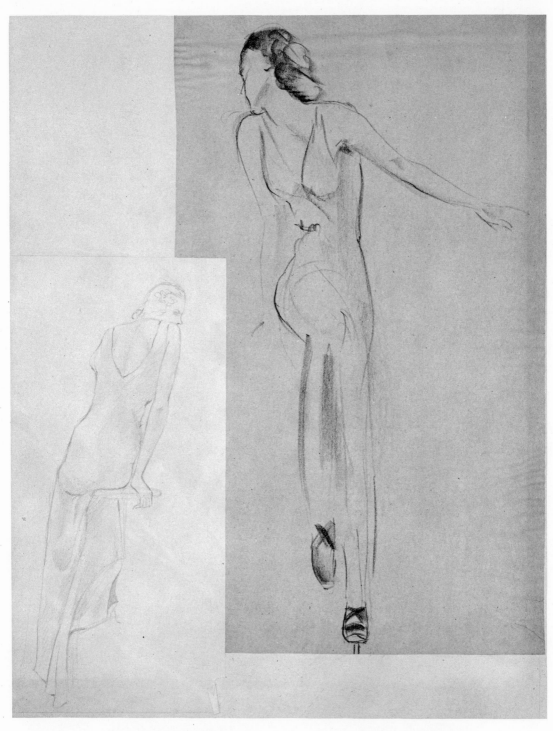

These quick fashion sketches were aimed mostly at registering the model's pose, usually in less than a minute.

The soft-pencil sketch at upper left was made in thirty seconds. The medium used in the sketch at lower left was sanguine conté crayon; the technique of the sketch at lower right, free brush.

Action and pose, with few lines and with the utmost speed. Many, many
sketches like these are required of fashion students drawing from a model.

A fashion photograph, from which a fashion
artist shows three drawings.

The first drawing is a pencil outline, which
would be your starting point, capturing the
pose and accurately showing the garment.

The second rendering, suitable for newspaper reproduction, is in dry-brush technique, in this case effective in suggesting the softness of the material.

The third drawing is in line and wash, two tones and blade, with a few touches of dry-brush to give softness.

Millinery publicity release photograph from which a professional fashion artist shows us three renderings. The first, a pencil outline, which would be the first stage of any rendering.

The second rendering is in wash, with a minimum use of line (adaptable for newspaper reproduction), and the third a line and dry-brush rendering which would be suitable for newspaper use.

Here the fashion artist is called upon by an advertising agency art director to apply fashion illustration styling to a window display ensemble.

done in black and white. Dorothy Hood, famous for her illustrations for Lord and Taylor's advertisements, uses wash exclusively. Dora De Vries, who has produced many masterful drawings for Saks Fifth Avenue, works with pen and ink with a restrained used of the brush with ink. Jacqueline E. Lindner, also well-known for her Saks Fifth Avenue drawings, confines herself to pen and ink with limited use of black areas.

Students who are interested in rendering fashions and accessories usually start by copying the methods, as far as they are able, of artists prominent in the field. This is natural, but it is not healthy for the growth of the individual's talent. The student should make an effort to develop his own style as he gains experience.

Merchandising has two objectives which the artist must regard when he prepares a drawing. The material or article advertised must be either described factually or suggested abstractly. In the case of a choice detail of the garment, a careful indication is necessary to put across this unusual feature; this could hardly be handled vaguely or abstractly. However, where the en-

A detail illustration of one of a small display unit which could be used with the arrangement above or, singly, as a counter display card.

405

Professional fashion illustration from a retail selling promotion in loose-leaf form. (Lord & Taylor.)

of an observer may be stirred by the sweep of the garment's main lines, and curiosity aroused by the fascinating detail shown on a lace collar. The competent artist will put both of these points across without losing the feeling of unity in the drawing.

Stylization (45)

The present trend is away from the over-stylization of 20 years ago. The poses are more natural, the faces more realistic, and the human proportions more nearly normal. Some years ago, all instruction in fashion illustration was predicated on the assumption that the fashion figure should be shown nine heads tall, whereas the normal height of the average woman is seven heads.

There is charm today in the well-drawn figures, the varied, unconventional poses, and the personality which is suggested as the model. No longer is the field of fashion the haven for those who couldn't make the grade in life class. Fashion illustration demands the finest draftsmen.

Layout (46)

Fashion artists who work in art departments of department stores either work from a layout made by the art director, or they may be so engaged as to propose their own layouts. Frequently, an art director selects an artist because it seems that the idea visualized in the conference between the art director and the buyer for the department can be developed by that artist better than by any other. The artist then plays an important part in the working up of the idea in layout form.

When such an assignment is given, the artist needs to know many things about the conditions concerning newspaper space or magazine space —how it is ordered, and what specifications are necessary for the engraver.

Newspaper space is based on columns wide and inches deep. Columns are figured as two inches wide, and newspaper lines average in depth 14 to the inch. Space ordered for a layout as "112 lines on three columns" would mean six inches wide and eight inches deep. Usually the art director or "layout man" gives the artist a pencil "rough" sketch on tracing paper as a guide.

semble is distinctive because of qualities other than its details—such as its silhouette, or an unusual sweep of line—a presentation of it can be suggestive of these qualities rather than by a careful drawing of less important parts.

Study should be given, therefore, to both phases of fashion illustration. Both factors may be introduced into the same drawing, depending upon the material being illustrated. The emotions

Getting the "Okay"

Approvals on fashion illustrations must come not only from the art director (if you are working with one) but from the buyer or head of whatever department is conducting the sale of the merchandise appearing in the advertisement. While the art director may be concerned with the technique and value of the drawing as a piece of art work, the buyer or department head is more concerned with the selling power of your drawing, and will okay it or not on that basis. The buyer will check every detail carefully and insist that the drawing be an accurate portrayal of the merchandise.

Items 40, 47 and 48

If you are earning your income as a fashion illustrator, you should follow every activity where fashion is of paramount importance. Attend the fashion style shows, keep abreast of the new ideas from abroad through the fashion magazines, and note the latest designs worn by film stars in the most recent motion pictures.

Retailing (6)

For this topic we must branch off from the direct art course, but we face an alluring career field in which the future fashion illustrator can learn many lessons. Probably the retail selling field is the most direct way for a student to become familiar with merchandise, the various textures, and the selling factors in a design. Even though he or she may aim at the high level careers, such as stylist and buyer, the student has much to learn from the place behind the counter.

All of the special designations (55 to 64) are positions for which an art training in the fashion field is essential. Yet without the experience to be acquired in a selling capacity, these positions might be beyond the reach of the person trained solely in art techniques.

One of the most outstanding examples of a career which began with selling is that of Miss Dorothy Shaver, president of Lord and Taylor's, who worked through the various positions of buyer, stylist, vice-president in charge of merchandising, and finally to the top executive position of the organization.

This style of fashion illustration represents the best in the field. It will be noticed that the artist shows thorough understanding of style and materials. (Lord & Taylor.)

If you are thinking of training for the fashion field, remember that it represents not one but a number of specialized areas. You should consider carefully which branch of fashion work appeals to you most and in which you would be most likely to succeed. Few career fields related to art or design have so constant a "turnover" as the fashion field; few have such a continuous demand for new designs, and for new people with something worthwhile to offer.

Several steps in fashion illustration are here shown, in this case developed from a publicity photograph, not from the actual merchandise. The first drawing shows a pencil outline, the second a wash rendering, the third a combination of line and dry-brush.

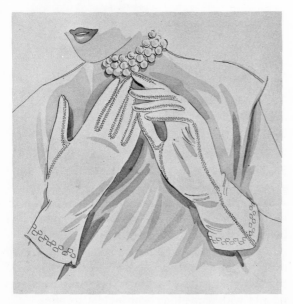

 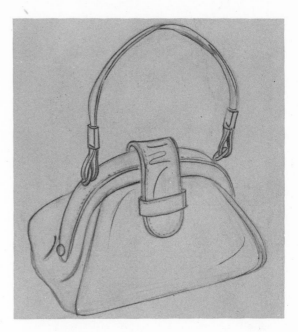

A similar sequence is illustrated here in a professional fashion artist's rendering of a handbag. First, a pencil outline drawing, then a wash drawing, then a dry-brush rendering. Indication of the kind of material is essential in this merchandise rendering.

Fashion photograph of a dramatic evening dress in black
velvet.

Two fashion photographs skillfully taken to
show detail. A student would do well to use
these for studies in draping.

A pose arranged to feature the handbag in an effective close-up.

Well-posed fashion photograph to show an evening cape. The fashion artist may learn much from the outstanding fashion photography done today.

Both handbag and costume necklace are emphasized by the posing of this striking fashion photograph.

These two pages show progressive states in male fashion illustration—one a hat close-up, the other a full figure.

Quite apart from the style angle and the artist's portrayal of "the well-dressed man," the type of man is very important. (These two pages courtesy of W. T. Foster.)

Typical "high style" male fashion illustration from the consistently excellent advertising of Lord & Taylor.

"The Very Latest Thing"

Style sense applies as much to fashion photography as to fashion illustration. In a book of this kind, it is impractical to offer illustrations that would suggest "the very latest thing." By the time a book can be published, most fashion material would be out of date. For the most advanced fashions no book could hope to compete with the specially posed photographs which can be studied currently in *Vogue, Harper's Bazaar, Mademoiselle,* and other magazines in this field.

Suggested Exercises

There are a number of exercises you can practice that will help develop your facility for illustrating fashions. First, study the fashion magazines, *Vogue, Harper's Bazaar, Mademoiselle,* and *Glamour,* and cut from them illustrations which will set standards for you in various methods of presentation. Collecting a file of photographs for permanent use will prove unsatisfactory because of the constant change in mode. Work from photographic copy while it is still current.

Learn to sketch the costumed figure quickly. Set a time limit for each sketch. Start by allowing yourself 10 minutes, then reduce the time as your facility improves until you can put down the major outlines of the figure in good proportion and with the salient features of the garment noted in about two minutes.

This restriction of time will force you to adopt a method of working wherein you will indicate only the broad lines and the accented features of a garment. Many students make their drawings slowly and, as a result, the drawings look labored and lacking in vivacity. Draw with spontaneity. The French call this "verve."

Have some of your friends pose for these quick sketches for which you should use a soft pencil, crayon, or Conte. Give special attention to the long sweeping line of the back, carrying the line over the hips, down the thigh to the leg. This line will determine the pose in most instances. If the figure in your drawing seems to lack grace, check up on this line. Something you may have overlooked would make the difference.

Dressmaking Details

Any fashion illustrator should be able to indicate, simply but clearly, any distinctive details of a garment, such as pleats, lapels, cuffs, and drapery. As an exercise, practice drawing such details from actual garments. A good test of your skill is to take a piece of new ribbon, two or three inches wide, tie it in a crisp, smart bow-knot, and draw it, first in pencil outline, then in pen and ink, then in pen line with tones in transparent water-color wash. If you can do this well, it should be very encouraging evidence of your aptitude for fashion illustration.

Working from Photographs

On accompanying pages are a few photographs from which a series of fashion illustrations have been made, each with a different kind of technique. Compare the different methods of working and try a series of your own from a photograph appearing either in this book or in a fashion magazine. Give special attention to the line and wash drawing technique as this kind of rendering is used in the greater quantity of fashion drawings.

As a further exercise, take your pad and pencil to the nearest department store, and sketch the costumed figures used in the window display. You will find it convenient to work fast and you will acquire speed in sketching fast out of necessity.

Supplement to Part II

The chapters in Part II have been devoted to the various fields of art in which design is used commercially, with special emphasis on advertising and the graphic arts. The scope of the work discussed has been confined to the general level of art activity which the average beginner will most likely experience.

Each of the subjects treated is a specialty about which many books have been written. Should a student desire to pursue further study in any particular field, a bibliography will be found in the back of this book where the titles and authors of standard works are listed under general headings.

If this book has encouraged you to explore further one of the fields of art, with a view toward a profession or a hobby, then it has been of value. For an appraisal of your own progress, the following exercises are presented. The material covered in these exercises is limited to the subjects touched on in the chapters of Part II.

Exercise No. 1

Design a poster for a Red Cross drive. Proportion the design for use as a three-sheet lithographic poster. (Sizes are given in Chapter 2.) The illustration may be either a photograph or a drawing. The copy to be used is:

"The life you help save someday may be your own. GIVE!"

Be sure to include the Red Cross symbol, and give particular attention to the display quality of the lettering.

Exercise No. 2

Design a letterhead, using for copy the names of two persons (as in a partnership), the subject of their business, address and telephone number. Prepare the design for the regular 8½" x 11" size. Make a layout of the design with pen and ink to simulate type. Consult your type styles before beginning this problem.

Exercise No. 3

Design a book jacket for a murder mystery story. Select your own copy, and make the lettering by hand. Prepare a dummy for this book jacket, designing the front and back covers, together with the backbone, as one unit. (The backbone is the narrow binding edge of the book —its thickness.)

Exercise No. 4

Design a title page for an edition of *The Miscellaneous Work of Oliver Goldsmith,* with a trim page size of 5" x 7½". The type area of the page is to be 19 x 32½ picas. (Information about printers' measure can be found in Chapter 4.) The full text for the title page is:

The Miscellaneous Works of Oliver Goldsmith
London: Simpkin, Marshall, Hamilton,
Kent and Co., Ltd.
New York: Charles Scribner's Sons

Exercise No. 5

Design a new package for table salt. This design can include any new idea for dispensing salt. Remember that salt cakes when unprotected against moisture. Design the package so that the salt can be poured easily into salt cellars. Select a name for the salt as part of the assignment.

Exercise No. 6

Design a novelty perfume bottle and holder. Here your imagination may have plenty of latitude. The problem should be approached from both the utilitarian angle and the fashion angle. Almost any shape that is practical for manufacture or use can be given consideration.

Exercise No. 7

Design the decorations for a tea room where the theme requested is based on Lewis Carroll's *Through the Looking Glass.* Consider a high wainscot around the room with a space above for decoration. Give consideration also to the ceiling, the table linen and menu cards. Suggest a design for the front of the tea room and sign embodying the same theme. The interior of the tea room is approximately 20 feet by 50 feet. Prepare the sketches at a scale of one-half inch to the foot.

Exercise No. 8

Design a parchment lampshade using tropical birds as a decorative theme. Look up material on these birds at the library and draw the design on tracing paper first. When satisfied with the arrangement, transfer the drawing to the parchment, and execute the work with outline pen and ink and color. Oil colors used thinly will give an interesting effect when light passes through them.

Exercise No. 9

Design a folder advertising a sale of spring suits for women. Make the folder six pages so that with two parallel folds it will be 3½″ x 6″ and suitable for mailing with monthly statements on charge accounts. Prepare the dummy for the folder, sketching roughly the garments shown on models, and make the presentation suitable for submission to one of the dress shops in your town. You may be able to interest someone in such a folder. The contact should result in a discussion that would yield helpful criticism.

Exercise No. 10

Prepare a fashion illustration for a newspaper advertisement full column depth by five columns wide (approximately 9¾″ x 21¼″) and include a suit for women and silk shantung blouses in the upper half of the layout, and a display of hose in the lower half, together with suitable descriptive copy for each group of articles. Suggest a novel use of the merchant's trade name in the advertisement.

Render the illustrations with crayon and wash, with sufficient accents to hold well in a coarse-screen reproduction.

Bibliography

HISTORY AND APPRECIATION

Art Through the Ages by Helen Gardner, Harcourt, Brace & Company, Inc., New York, N. Y.
> One of the most reliable standard art histories you can study. Each of the historic periods into which Miss Gardner divides the development of world art is studied as a unit of culture. 900 illustrations, including 5 color plates.

Art in the Western World by Robb and Garrison, Harper Brothers, New York, N. Y.
> The material is so arranged that the three great arts, painting, sculpture, and architecture, are presented separately, enabling the student to grasp the main principles of a single art at a time. Nearly 400 illustrations.

Understanding the Arts by Helen Gardner, Harcourt, Brace & Company, Inc., New York, N. Y.
> The best examples of the arts of building, landscape gardening, city planning, sculpture, painting, bookmaking, weaving, and pottery are viewed in their historical and social settings.

A World History of Art by Sheldon Cheney, Viking Press, New York, N. Y.
> This important book gathers, in one comprehensive volume, the immense cultural fund that has accumulated through the ages. Close to 500 masterpieces are reproduced, and they have been chosen not only to illustrate the text, but also for the pleasure which they afford in themselves.

The Story of Modern Art by Sheldon Cheney, The Viking Press, New York, N. Y.
> This book tells the story of modern art from 1791 to 1941. 373 reproductions, including whole blocks of plates for such key artists as Daumier, Whistler, Cézanne, Gauguin, Seurat, Van Gogh, and many others.

Modern Art: The Men, The Movements, The Meanings by Thomas Craven, Simon & Schuster, New York, N. Y.
> One of the most helpful of all books in developing an understanding of modern art in terms of the personalities who have made it.

An Illustrated Handbook of Art History by Frank J. Roos, The Macmillan Company, New York, N. Y.
> A collection of 2014 reproductions and photographs of the world's art masterpieces, this is a picture encyclopedia designed to answer the questions: what is it, who made it, when, where, and what does it look like.

The Art of Enjoying Art by A. Philip McMahon, McGraw-Hill Book Co., Inc., New York, N. Y.
> One of the best texts on art appreciation. Professor McMahon conducts the student through the three levels of art: sensation, technique, and form. The book contains a color chart, 96 full pages of pictures, including 150 reproductions, covering painting, sculpture, architecture, drawings, prints, ceramics, textiles, furniture arms and armor, etc., from prehistoric to modern times.

Art Is for Everyone by Martha Simpson, McGraw-Hill Book Co., Inc., New York, N. Y.
> Tells in everyday language what goes into a masterpiece from the points of view of both the creator and the spectator.

DESIGN

The Art of Color and Design by Maitland Graves, McGraw-Hill Book Co., Inc., New York, N. Y.
> Shows you how to create perfect color combinations for painting, designing and decorating and how to deal with areas and values in problems of design and composition.

Design and Decoration by Paul Carlyle and Guy Oring, McGraw-Hill Book Co., Inc., New York, N. Y.
> This practical book shows the artist how to *create* or *adapt* designs. More than 100 designs of varied style and character.

Decorative Art Reference Material
> An interesting variety of decorative reference material, mostly in loose-leaf form is available from School Arts, Worcester, Mass. Among the subjects covered are:
>> *21 Plates for Lettering Lessons, A History of Costume Design, Instructions for Block Printing,* Packets of Designs of *Birds in Art* and *Trees in Art, Ships in Decoration, Landscape in Decoration; Pen and Ink Drawing for Beginners; Simplified Modern Art; Figure Drawing; How to Draw the Human Head; Symbolism for Artists; The Art Ages* (Visual History of Art Material) *Mexico: Arts and Crafts; Indian Arts; Old World Decorative Designs*

Styles of Ornament by Alexander Spelz, Grosset & Dunlap, New York, N. Y.
Artists, designers and students find this an indispensable reference book for every type of decorative design and ornament of all periods and styles. More than 2000 examples.

Meyer's Handbook of Ornament by F. S. Meyer
A source book of design throughout the ages, shown in 3000 illustrations with annotations as to source, period, and significance.

Design by Charles H. Howard
This modern handbook of design has 25 chapters and 200 drawings illustrating the principles and requirements of good design.

Discovering Design by Marion Downer, Lothrop, Lee & Shepard Co., New York, N. Y.
An unusual book which shows you that ideas and motifs for design may be found by the trained eye in many unexpected places.

You Can Design by Winold Reiss and A. C. Schweizer, McGraw-Hill Book Co., Inc., New York, N. Y.
This is a book to help you produce attractive designs and develop facility of expression. Examples of design planned for lampshades, book jackets, greeting cards, furniture decoration, etc.

Handbook of Designs and Devices by Clarence P. Morning, Dover Publications, Inc., New York, N. Y.
1836 design motifs for artists, draftsmen, typographers, layout men and commercial designers, offering a rich background for designing products, packages, decorations, trade-marks, etc.

Art Structure: A Textbook of Creative Design by Henry N. Rasmusen, McGraw-Hill Book Co., Inc., New York, N. Y.
Design Fundamentals by Robert Gillam Scott, McGraw-Hill Book Co., Inc., New York, N. Y.
These two books are among the most recent instructive books on the theory and practice of design.

A Manual of Design by Janet K. Smith, Reinhold Publishing Corporation, New York, N. Y.
A clear, practical textbook which teaches modern design and the application of methods and materials to the art and commercial products of today. Excellent for beginners as well as for the more advanced.

An Introduction to Functional Design by Richard A. Rathbone, McGraw-Hill Book Co., Inc., New York, N. Y.
A unique treatise in which the author unites the three aspects of Idea, Technique and Function, with particular emphasis on the importance of design composition. Simple diagrams.

ADVERTISING

Effective Advertising by Harry W. Hepner, McGraw-Hill Book Co., Inc., New York, N. Y.
One of the best basic texts on advertising for those who are thinking of advertising as a career.

The Technique of Advertising Production by Thomas Blaine Stanley, Prentice-Hall, New York, N. Y.
A comprehensive book for the prospective advertising artist or production man. Covers Visualization, Layout, Illustration, Color, Photo-engraving, Lithography, Typography, Paper and Planning Printed Matter.

Introduction to Advertising by Arthur Judson Brewster, McGraw-Hill Book Co., Inc., New York, N. Y.
The fundamental principles of advertising for beginning students, and how these principles apply in writing copy, choosing illustrations, and placing advertising in various media. Includes chapters on Layout, Printing Processes, Radio Advertising, Media Selection, Testing Advertisements, and Typography.

LAYOUT

Commercial Art and Layout (A Complete Course in Self-Instruction), Illustrated Editions Company, New York, N. Y.
This book is planned for training at home. Chapters deal with Layout; Lettering; Engraving; Fashion; Book Jackets and Displays; Alphabets, Monograms and Vignettes.

Advertising and Editorial Layout by Matlack Price, McGraw-Hill Book Co., Inc., New York, N. Y.
This comprehensive book is based on the author's long experience in creating layouts and in teaching layout in professional art schools. Illustrations include suggestions for "home work" in practice layout problems, and exceptional layouts by students.

101 Roughs by Don May, Frederick J. Drake & Co., Chicago, Ill.
This small book is recommended to anyone wishing to develop skill in layout work. Teaches the technique of making quick rough "visuals."

Advertising Layout: The Projection of an Idea by Richard S. Chenault, Heck-Cattell Publishing Co., Inc., New York, N. Y.
This book presents the study of layout in such a way as to help the student (or even the professional) learn how to design better, more compelling layouts. Profusely illustrated, including original layouts of actual advertisements reproduced directly from the designers' drawing board. Includes lettering and typography.

Layouts and Letterheads by Carlyle, Oring and Richland, McGraw-Hill Book Co., Inc., New York, N. Y.
In addition to discussions of layouts and the layout man's work, there are more than 200 layouts for advertisements, letterheads and many other purposes, and many suggestions for creative work.

POSTERS

The Art and Use of the Poster by Chuck Thorndike, Dover Publications, New York, N. Y.
(One of "The House of Little Books" series)
See also: Chapter on "Color and the Poster" in *Commercial Art*, by C. E. Wallace, McGraw-Hill

Poster Design by J. I. Biegeleisen, Greenberg: Publisher, New York, N. Y.
This book tells you what it takes to break into the profession, lists the materials needed, describes the complete procedure for making a poster and the best techniques.

Poster Design by Matlack Price, G. W. Bricka, New York
This richly illustrated book has long been an authoritative text.

PRODUCTION

Commercial Art by C. E. Wallace, McGraw-Hill Book Co., Inc., New York, N. Y.
A practical guide to the fundamentals of design and the techniques of art for commercial reproduction. Chapters on Essentials of Graphic Design, Representative Drawing, Lettering, Pen and Line and Wash Drawings, Color and the Poster, Layout in Advertising, and Processes of Reproduction. Many exercises and lesson plates.

Advertising Production by Ben Dalgin, McGraw-Hill Book Co., Inc., New York, N. Y.
This practical manual describes techniques applicable to each phase of reproducing art and printing material. It traces the handling of a production job from start to finish—covering the mechanics of setting type, making engravings, rotogravure work, etc.

Handbook of Advertising and Printing by Carl R. Greer, Tudor Publishing Co., New York, N. Y.
An encyclopedic volume which explains every step in printing and advertising production from conception to publication. Analyzes all the processes of reproduction, the selection of papers, and other essential production details.

PRINTING AND TYPOGRAPHY

Your Career in Printing published by New York Employing Printers and New York City Board of Education
A splendidly illustrated booklet which answers all the vocational questions you might ask. All the copy, text and pictures were critically checked by practical printers.

Printing and Promotion Handbook by Daniel Melcher and Nancy Larrick, McGraw-Hill Book Co., Inc., New York.
A deskbook which shows how to produce, buy and use printing, advertising and direct mail.

Printing Primer by Hartley E. Jackson, Stanford University, Stanford, California
A laboratory manual for the principal operations of letterpress printing. It enables the student to proceed directly with typesetting, press lockup, simple presswork and related procedures.

The following handbooks are listed by the Manual Arts Press, Peoria, Illinois:
Practical Typography, McClellan
Elementary Platen Presswork, Polk
The Practice of Printing, Polk
Type Charts for Printers and Designers, Polk
Printing for Apprentices and Journeymen, Witt

The Book by Douglas C. McMurtrie, Oxford University Press, New York, N. Y.
The best book you can read for a good background of the history of printing and typographic development.

The Moods of Type by Clayton Whitehill, Barnes & Noble, New York, N. Y.
This is the best book so far written on the *style* of type. The author sees type as something with which to design and to express varied moods.
See also: Chapter 5 in *Advertising and Editorial Layout* by Matlack Price, McGraw-Hill

Type for Books and Advertising by E. M. Ettenberg, D. Van Nostrand Company, New York, N. Y.
From the basic mechanical details of typesetting and type construction to the elements of design and layout, this book covers every important aspect of type.

Using Type Correctly by Kurt H. Volk, New York, N. Y.
A practical and not too mechanical workbook written by one of the most prominent typographers and printers in New York.

Type Specimens by William Longyear, Watson-Guptill Publications, Inc., New York, N. Y.
Proofreading marks, explanations of the point system, definitions of printing terms, and other helpful information on type and its uses are discussed. A selection of 145 specimens of type faces in common use today.

Books and Printing edited by Paul A. Bennett, World Publishing Co., New York and Cleveland.
A collection of unusually informative articles by many authorities dealing with a wide range of topics.

LETTERING

An Alphabet Source Book by Oscar Ogg, Dover Publications, Inc., New York, N. Y.
 The author's approach is inspirational as well as practical, and the historic material on the *how* and *why* of lettering presents a basic philosophy of lettering. Covers the choice of pens and paper, method for ruling guide-lines, method for laying in, etc. Illustrated sections show the relationship between letter styles, decorative initials, pictures and typography.

Lettering, Its History, Principles and Practice by Matlack Price, New York Graphic Society, Greenwich, Conn.
 This is a book specially prepared for the beginning student. The text is brief and the illustrations carefully selected or drawn for the book. Typical alphabets in the principal styles are reproduced as large as possible.

A Handbook of Lettering by J. Albert Cavanaugh, Dover Publications, Inc., New York, N. Y.
 This workbook contains hundreds of complete hand-lettered alphabets now in use in the advertising field, including a variety of formal and informal scripts. Suggestions on combining lettering styles to fit the advertised item.

Learning to Letter by Carlyle, Oring and Richland, McGraw-Hill Book Company, Inc., New York, N. Y.
 An authoritative textbook providing a tested method of learning lettering.

Letters and Lettering by Paul Carlyle and Guy Oring, McGraw-Hill Book Company, Inc., New York, N. Y.
 A graphic treatment of advertising and commercial lettering combining specimens of many types of lettering with practical instructions in how to draw and apply them.

A B C of Lettering by J. I. Biegeleisen, Harper Brothers, New York, N. Y.
 An introduction to the development of skill in free-hand lettering, with suggested exercises, analysis of letter forms, and many complete alphabets for copying and reference. More than 100 plates.

Lettering: The History and Technique of Lettering as Design by Alexander Nesbitt, Prentice-Hall, Inc., New York, N. Y.
 Part I, History of Letters; Part II, A Practical Course in Lettering. Full Page Plates. This is a book of distinction—a standard, definitive text.

Lettering from A to Z by Clarence Horning, Ziff-Davis, Publishers, Chicago, Ill.
 For the student who wishes to go further in his style training in lettering, this is an excellent book. The many fine alphabets illustrated make it a valuable reference book, as well as a stimulus to creative thinking in letter design.

Applied Lettering and Design by Rand Holub, Watson-Guptill Publications, New York, N. Y.
 An excellent workbook. Following a demonstration of media and methods, it offers a variety of specimen alphabets, including basic styles from the past, up-to-the-minute scripts and cartoon letters. Covers lettering in advertisements, letterheads, logotypes, book jackets, etc.

How to Letter by Maxwell L. Heller, Bridgman Publishers, Pelham, N. Y.
 A manual of practical examples, showing how to use a pen, when to use it and when to use a brush. Over 100 illustrations of forms and hand lettering.

Lettering by Higgins Ink Co., Inc., Brooklyn, N. Y.
 One of the Higgins monographs, compiled for students and professionals, showing 32 distinctive script alphabets with an analysis of each. There is a section devoted to engrossing and another dealing with type faces.

SPECIALTIES IN LETTERING

Elements of Lettering (*Second Edition*) by Benson & Carey, McGraw-Hill Book Company, Inc., New York, N. Y.
 A little advanced for the beginner, but no one who plans to become a calligrapher should fail to become familiar with it.

Calligraphic Lettering with Pen and Brush by Ralph Douglass, Watson-Guptill Publications, Inc., New York, N. Y.
 This book should be of practical help to the many people who want to develop the calligrapher's skill.

Manuscript Writing by Jean Corser, Harter Publishing Company, Cleveland, Ohio
 A good introduction to calligraphy, particularly prepared for school use, with 12 plates calligraphically written by Miss Corser.

The Script Letter by Tommy Thompson, Studio Publications, New York, N. Y.
 The author shows how each letter of the alphabet should be constructed and drawn, as well as how it may most effectively be applied to lettering projects.

Diploma Engrossing by Ralph A. Loomis, Charles A. Bennet Co., Peoria, Illinois
 The author shows you the range of strokes that must be mastered for "Old English" lettering. Examples of finished diplomas and scrolls, applying flourishes and variations of style that can be developed from basic strokes. Equipment and materials are described and illustrated.

Practical Sign Painting by Robert E. Owen, Bruce Publishing Co., Milwaukee, Wisc.
 A thorough guide to the field for the man who wants to set up his own sign painting business and for anyone who wishes to learn the trade. Fundamental techniques of lettering and methods of producing signs are clearly explained and illustrated.

How to Design Monograms and Symbols by Curtiss Sprague, Bridgman Publishers, Pelham, N. Y.
  Monograms have become important in the merchandising of hand-bags, stationery, toilet sets, etc. This book has helpful suggestions and drawings for anyone interested in designing monograms or symbols.

Simplified Show Card Writing by C. R. Havighorst, Greenberg: Publisher, New York, N. Y.
  An excellent self-training workbook on this profitable branch of lettering. Covers the basic alphabets, the planning, designing, and "tricks of the trade." More than 100 illustrations.

PHOTOGRAPHY

Elementary Photography (new edition) by Guilford G. Quares, McGraw-Hill Book Co., Inc., New York, N. Y.
  This well-known text provides a treatment of photography of both elementary and advanced nature. The student is brought very quickly to the actual making of photographs.

Photography: Its Principles and Practice by C. B. Neblette, D. Van Nostrand Co., New York, N. Y.
  Practical and scientific information on all phases of photography, cameras and lenses; exposure, development and printing; special printing process. Hundreds of illustrations.

Photography is a Language by John R. Whiting, Ziff-Davis Co., Chicago, Ill.
  A book of picture methods, non-technical instruction, ideas in pictures. Directs the amateur in the application of photography to advertising.

See also: "Taking Fashion Photographs," Chapter 18 of *Keys to a Fashion Career* edited by Bernice G. Chambers; McGraw-Hill, New York, N. Y.

Fun with Your Camera by Jacob Deschin, McGraw-Hill Book Co., Inc., New York, N. Y.
  Both the novice and the more advanced amateur will find here hundreds of profitable suggestions on how to get better results with pictures. Line drawings and 50 photographs.

This is Photography by T. H. Miller and W. Brummit, Garden City Books (Doubleday), New York, N. Y.
  A well-written, profusely illustrated book which is just as delightful to read as it is valuable as an instruction book.

Make your Pictures Sing by P. L. Hexter, Camera Craft, New York, N. Y.
  An inspiring guide for the advanced amateur on the creative possibilities of photography, showing how to make the camera record a subject in an expressive manner.

The Fun of Photography by Mario and Mabel Scacheri, Harcourt-Brace Company, New York, N. Y.
  A most enjoyable introduction to photography for anyone who wants to have fun making pictures and at the same time learn the fundamental principles of photography.

How to Take Industrial Photographs by M. H. Zielke and F. G. Beezley, McGraw-Hill Book Co., Inc., New York, N. Y.
  This is a book for career photographers, written by two experts—one on photography, the other on advertising and public relations. Outlined in concise text and illustrated with over 100 samples is the knowledge you need in order to tell an industrial story clearly and effectively with your camera.

A Guide to Better Photography by Berenice Abbott, Crown Publishers, New York, N. Y.
  A new book of expert information and instruction on all phases of the fine art of photography, illustrated with 80 photographs.

Say it with your Camera by Jacob Deschin, McGraw-Hill Book Co., Inc., New York, N. Y.
  This book tells how to achieve meaning with the camera; how to interpret subject matter through personal feeling and understanding.

Making your Photographs Effective by J. A. Lucas, McGraw-Hill Book Co., Inc., New York, N. Y.
  A handy working manual of everyday photography for the professional and amateur alike. Covers fundamental photographic operations from the practical rather than the theoretical side.

Fun with your Camera by Jacob Deschin, McGraw-Hill Book Co., Inc., New York, N. Y.
  Hundreds of profitable suggestions and instructions on how to get better results with pictures.

New Ways in Photography by Jacob Deschin, McGraw-Hill Book Co., Inc., New York, N. Y.
  A discussion of the methods used in obtaining good photographs of all kinds of subjects under all conditions. Includes "trick" photography, night and indoor work, flashlights, the candid camera, double exposures, long-range photography, photo-murals, transparencies and retouching.

Finding New Subjects for your Camera by Jacob Deschin, McGraw-Hill Book Co., Inc., New York, N. Y.
  A practical manual which points out the picture possibilities in the many everyday subjects that exist all around us.

Handbook of Photography edited by Keith Henney and Beverly Dudley, McGraw-Hill Book Co., Inc., New York, N. Y.
  This book presents a fundamental *why* and *how* approach to all subjects, so that all photographers can find in it information of their level of work.

No field of art is better served by helpful books than photography. Look through a subject file in your public library and you will find a long list of titles ranging from the general introductory books described here to books dealing specifically with lenses, lighting, color photography, developing, printing, enlarging.

The Eastman Kodak Company, Rochester, N. Y., publishes an extensive series of booklets on various phases of photography.

Ziff-Davis Company, Chicago, Ill., publishes a series of helpful books on photography.

Greenberg: Publisher, New York, N. Y., has an excellent list of books on various phases of photography as well as "The Modern Camera Guide Series," manuals for operating "name" cameras.

The Mortensen Books: These books, well known to all advanced photographers, are published by Camera Craft. There are nine books, in all, including one called *Command to Look,* dealing particularly with *pictorial composition.*

Most camera stores carry the leading books on photography as well as the stimulating monthly magazines, such as *Photography.*

PACKAGING

The Art of Packaging by D. E. A. Charlton, Studio Publications, New York, N. Y.'
A recognized authority describes methods of designing and producing effective labels, boxes, and containers of all sorts. Information on materials and equipment, as well as hundreds of illustrations.

Developing Marketable Products and their Packaging by Ben Nash, McGraw-Hill Book Co., Inc., New York, N. Y.
This book touches on all the technical details of consumer needs and use, habits and preferences. Not for beginners.

See also *You Can Design* by Weiss and Schweizer, McGraw-Hill Book Co., Inc., New York, N. Y.
Design and Decoration by Carlyle and Oring, McGraw-Hill Book Co., Inc., New York, N. Y.

Packaging Design Considerations by A. and C. Heythum, Syracuse University Press, Syracuse, N. Y.
A fresh and effective approach to packaging design discussed through "case histories" and experimental laboratory procedures. Types of containers, appropriate materials, labels, lettering and layouts are covered.

INDUSTRIAL DESIGN

Industrial Design: A Practical Guide by Harold Van Doren, McGraw-Hill Book Co., Inc., New York, N. Y.
This book shows the importance of industrial design in business and answers your questions on the skills and training required, remuneration, and how to break into the field. Instruction is given for the complete procedure of product styling.

Design for Business by J. Gordon Lippincott, Paul Theobold, Chicago, Ill.
A candid discussion of the fundamentals of industrial design. 300 illustrations, from fountain pens to airplanes.

Design in the Industrial Arts by Charles B. Bradley, Manual Arts Press, Peoria, Ill.
A thought-provoking text on the study of industrial design.
The first part deals with the factors of art and practical use that go into the production of furniture and mechanical devices. The second part takes up design in particular crafts. More than 100 photographs and many drawings.

Modern Furniture: Its Design and Construction by Mario Dal Fabbro, Reinhold Publishing Co., New York, N. Y.
The author gives, in drawings and photographs, a comprehensive view of current design trends in furniture and equipment. Recommended for the amateur hobby craftsman.

U. S. Industrial Design 1951
The second issue of an annual publication. Over 500 illustrations with explanatory text shows how mass-produced things of all kinds have been redesigned for greater efficiency, better looks, and at lower cost. Also included are store design, displays and packaging.

Working with Plastics by Arthur Dunham, McGraw-Hill Book Co., Inc., New York, N. Y.
Practical information on how to work with Lucite and Plexiglas, and how to create useful objects with them.

DECORATIVE PAINTING

Peter Hunt's Workbook by Peter Hunt, Ziff-Davis Company, Chicago, Ill.
As described by Maude Basserman in *Everywoman's Magazine,* "Peter Hunt's Workbook has 100 pages. It's crammed with before and after photographs, has some five color plates, minute instructions on how to restore furniture the Peter Hunt way and a delightful text. . . ."

How to Use Color and Decorative Designs in the Home by Howard Ketcham, The Greystone Press, New York, N. Y.
A wide variety of decorative paint projects, both inside and outside the house, including many of the quaint Pennsylvania Dutch motifs. Many practical illustrations.

Painting Patterns for Home Decorators by R. W. Spears, Barrows & Company, New York, N. Y.
The amateur decorative craftsman is here offered actual size patterns for dozens of designs, directions for altering old furniture and making new pieces, for preparing surfaces and mixing paints.

Revive your Old Furniture by Louise Sloane, Studio Publications, Inc., New York, N. Y.
A practical manual on how to convert old furniture into new, and ugly pieces into useful decorative ones. Upholstery, carpentry, repairs and refinishing are completely covered and fully illustrated.

A Handbook of Designs and How to Use Them by Gordon de Lemos, Educational Materials, Inc., New York, N. Y.
120 large pages crowded with attractive motifs based on flowers, birds, animals, figures, ships and landscapes—over 300 new designs. Suitable for use in all types of handicrafts.

Decorative Arts of Sweden by Iona Plath, Charles Scribners' Sons, New York, N. Y.
   A comprehensive treatment of the traditional and modern arts and crafts of Sweden, including textiles, ceramics, decorative painting, etc.

Pennsylvania Dutch American Folk Art by Henry Kauffmann, Studio Books
   A survey of early Pennsylvania folk art, with hundreds of illustrations in halftone and color.

Flowers in Nature and Design by Fritzi Brod, Stephen Daye Press, New York, N. Y.
   A unique collection of designs based on the wild flowers of Europe and America for the craftsman, designer and decorative painter, brilliantly executed by a distinguished artist.

50 Pennsylvania Dutch Patterns for Trays, With Full Instructions
50 Early American Tray Patterns With Instructions by Jane Zook, Lancaster, Pa.
   Portfolios of actual size patterns, ready to use on standard sizes and types of trays, for the beginner who lacks design ability.

How to Paint Trays by Roberta Ray Blanchard, Charles T. Branford, Boston, Mass.
   An excellent practical book of Early American designs (including 12 large-scale plates), and how to adapt them for boxes, chests and trays.

You Can Design by Reiss and Schweizer (described in Reference Books under "Design" Chapter 1, Part II)

Picture Framing by Edward Landon, Tudor Publishing Co., New York, N. Y.
   Describes every phase of picture framing, from mounting to finishing, information on tools, materials and sources of supply, with 257 helpful illustrations.

Folk Art Designs by Julienne Hallen, Home-Crafts, New York, N. Y.
   Oriental, European and American designs, easy to trace, stencil or paint—a helpful collection for decorative craftsmen or hobbyists.

Transformagic by Dupont
   A booklet produced by the lacquer manufacturers. It is in full color and illustrates the art of making old things look new with paint and brush. Most of the designs are by Peter Hunt.

Decorative Design by Fritzi Brod, Pitman Publishing Corporation, New York, N. Y.
   A book of fundamental ideas for decorative design. All types of design are included: stylized flowers, plant life, snow crystals, fruits, vegetables, birds, fish, sea life, animals—real and imaginary.

INTERIOR DESIGN

Harmony in Interiors by Vernita Seeley, McGraw-Hill Book Co., Inc., New York, N. Y.
   A well-illustrated handbook covering the fundamental principles of taste and decoration. Contains a wealth of ideas for solving decorating problems regardless of the amount of money to be spent.

Home Planning and Furnishing by Anna Hong Rutt, John Wiley & Sons, Inc., New York, N. Y.
   A straightforward explanation of the elements of art and the principles of design, plus many practical ideas for putting these ideas to work. All types of furnishing problems are discussed—country, suburban and city houses; modern, cottage, ranch and traditional styles, as well as apartments.

Fashions in Furnishing by Lee and Bolender, McGraw-Hill Book Co., Inc., New York, N. Y.
   More than 350 illustrations and five full color plates show the tools and techniques needed to create an attractive and comfortable home—whether it is a one-room apartment or a Georgian country house.

Refurbishing the Home by Carl G. B. Knauff, McGraw-Hill Book Co., Inc., New York, N. Y.
   This stimulating book discusses the application of principles of good taste to the choice of color and design, fabrics and rugs, furniture and pictures. Includes useful sample plans and budgets.

MAGAZINES: *Interiors, House & Garden, House Beautiful, Better Homes & Gardens.*

For display students: *Display World*, Display Publishing Co., 1209 Sycamore St., Cincinnati, Ohio
   NOTE: The designer of window displays needs the same aptitudes, training and taste as the designer of interiors.

Window Display Manual by J. T. Chord, Display Publishing Co., Cincinnati, Ohio

Fundamentals of Window Display by C. Ellison, International Textbook Co., Scranton, Pa.

Principles of Window Display by J. H. Pickens, McGraw-Hill Book Co., Inc., New York, N. Y.

Displaying Merchandise for Profit by A. E. Hurst, Prentice-Hall, Inc., New York, N. Y.

Art of Window Display by H. A. Down, Pitman Publishing Co., New York, N. Y.

Contemporary Art Applied to the Store and its Display by F. Kiesler, Brentano's, New York, N. Y.

Selling Through the Window by H. Trethowan, Studio Publications, New York, N. Y.

Display Animation by I. L. Cochrane, Reeder-Morton Publications, Inc., New York, N. Y.

FASHION

Elementary Costume Illustration by Ruth Austin, McGraw-Hill Book Co., Inc., New York, N. Y.
   For the student without extensive art training who wants to express ideas pertaining to clothing. Emphasis placed upon costume detail.

Fundamentals of Dress by Marietta Kettunen, McGraw-Hill Book Co., Inc., New York, N. Y.
   A complete survey of the field of dress, both historical and contemporary, including accessories.

Keys to a Fashion Career edited by Bernice G. Chambers, McGraw-Hill Book Co., Inc., New York, N. Y.
   For the young man or woman who plans to enter any phase of fashion work. Covers the procedure followed by professionals in retailing, styling, designing, advertising, manufacturing, magazine editorial work, merchandising, display, promotion and publicity.

How you Look and Dress by Byrta Carson, McGraw-Hill Book Co., Inc., New York, N. Y.
   A basic book written especially to meet the needs of anyone taking a course in the varied angles involved in clothing.

Fashion Illustration by Christine Schmuck and Virginia Jewel, McGraw-Hill Book Co., Inc., New York, N. Y.
   A practical treatment of fashion illustration, describing vocational opportunities and requirements.

Costume Design by Kay Hardy, McGraw-Hill Book Co., Inc., New York, N. Y.
   Presents a complete costume-design course.

Fashion Drawing: How to do it by Hazel R. Doten and Constance Boulard, Harper & Brothers, New York, N. Y.
   One of the most comprehensive books to be found in the field of fashion work.

Fashion Fundamentals by Bernice G. Chambers, Prentice-Hall, Inc., New York, N. Y.
   A good technical book which deals with fashion illustration, accessories, and retailing.

Fashion is our Business by Beryl Williams, J. B. Lippincott Company, Philadelphia, Pa.
   A stimulating career book which tells the success stories of twelve prominent designers and how they reached the top.

Fashion Advertising Layout and Illustration by Charlotte H. Young, Walter T. Foster, Laguna Beach, California.
   This is one of the helpful books in the Foster series. Simple, direct and practical.

DRAWING

Fun with a Pencil by Andrew Loomis, Viking Press, New York, N. Y.
   The author, a successful artist, uses an amusing approach to teaching facility in drawing. The face, figure in action, perspective, interiors, light and shadow, are some of the subjects treated. Hundreds of two-color illustrations.

Freehand Drawing Self-Taught by Arthur L. Guptill, Harper & Brothers, New York, N. Y.
   An inclusive one-volume text on drawing in all media which takes account of the known needs of students, both beginning and advanced.

Practical Course in Memory Drawing by E. G. Lutz, Charles Scribners' Sons, New York, N. Y.
   A series of clear and detailed lessons in landscape and figure drawing, illustrated with drawings and diagrams.

Drawing Without Drudgery by M. C. Cuzner, Pitman Publishing Corp., New York, N. Y.
   A small, compact manual containing, among other essentials which a beginner needs to know, an excellent simple introduction to perspective.

How to Draw by Edward B. Kaminski, McGraw-Hill Book Co., Inc., New York, N. Y.
   Beginning with five basic shapes Mr. Kaminski shows the artist how to give form and depth to his drawings. Simple perspective, the human figure, draperies and clothing, textures, glass, and metal, materials and techniques are all covered.

Drawing for Fun by Walter Willoughby, Bridgman Publishers, Pelham, N. Y.
   Covers every phase of drawing and includes chapters on the proper selection of materials, Technique, Perspective, Landscape, Action Drawing, The Human Body, Composition, and Commercial Drawing.

How to Draw the Human Figure by Arthur Black, McGraw-Hill Book Co., Inc., New York, N. Y.
   A simplified, step-by-step method of learning to draw the human figure without a model, and also how to draw from the model.

Drawing for Beginners by Dorothy Furniss, Bridgman Publishers, Pelham, N. Y.
   This book is written in non-technical, simple language, and the objects chosen to be drawn are those found in the ordinary household. More than 75 halftones.

Drawing Made Easy by Charles Lederer, Bridgman Publishers, Pelham, N. Y.
   Contains over 1000 illustrations; chapters on Clay Modelling, Paper Cutting, Action Figure Drawings, Comics and Cartooning, Animals, Principles of Composition, Nature Drawing, Charcoal, Pencil, Pen and Ink, Lettering, Water Colors, etc.

Foster Art Service, Inc., Laguna Beach, California
   The Foster books for beginners, with solid pages of illustration, include several excellent ones on figure drawing and on heads.
      Drawing Simplified
      How to Draw
      Drawing the Figure
      How to Draw the Head
      Figures from Life (Charcoal)

Heads from Life (Charcoal)
How to Draw Children
101 Heads

Anyone Can Draw by Arthur Zaidenberg, Illustrated Editions Company, Inc., New York, N. Y.
Not only the figure as a whole, but heads, features, arms, hands and feet are shown in sketch as well as finished forms. Sketching and drawing of animals are covered, as well as figure composition and the design organization of pictures.

Principles of Figure Drawing by Alexander Dobkin, The World Publishing Co., Cleveland and New York, N. Y.
Every phase of the construction and delineation of the human figure is fully discussed and illustrated. Over 500 well-chosen illustrations.

The Simplified Human Figure by Adolfo Best-Mangard, Alfred Knopf, New York, N. Y.
Teaches you how to draw the human figure in any imaginable position and explains the basic forms and proportions.

Natural Figure Drawings: A New and Easy Method by Anton Refregier, Tudor Publishing Co., New York, N. Y.
Among other subjects treated are: The Clothed Figure, Drawing Materials, Light and Shade, Anatomy, Drawing and Sketching Exercises from Models, Work of Non-Professionals.

Anatomy and Construction of the Human Figure by C. Earl Bradbury, McGraw-Hill Book Co., Inc., New York, N. Y.
Based on the author's own representations of human anatomical structure, this inclusive study of the *structure of the figure* in combination with *methods of constructing the forms* is unique in the field. 150 charcoal drawings, 26 color drawings.

About George B. Bridgman: For many years he was the "maestro" of the famous Art Students' League in New York, one of the great masters of figure drawing of our time. Every art student interested in anatomy and better drawing of the human figure will have available an authoritative approach to the human body in its motions and its details in all or any of the books by Mr. Bridgman, all published by Bridgman Publishers, Pelham, New York.
The Human Machine
Constructive Anatomy
Bridgman's Life Drawing
Heads, Features and Faces
The Book of a Hundred Hands
The Book of One Hundred Figure Drawings (Selected by Mr. Bridgman)

Other excellent standard books on varied aspects of figure drawing and rendering on the Bridgman list are here listed:
How to Draw the Head in Light and Shade, by Edward Renggli
Figures, Faces and Folds, by Adolphe A. Braun
Figure Construction, by Alon Bement
Figure Composition, by Paul G. Braun
Anatomy and Figure Construction, by Sloan Andrews
Human Form, by Adolphe A. Braun
Figure Drawing for Fashion and Costume Designers, by Louis A. Eisele

How to Draw Children and *Figure Sketching* by Bernice Oehler, Bridgman Publishers, Pelham, N. Y.
In *How to Draw Children* this artist has selected over 100 drawings from her sketchbook and prepared a helpful book on this specialty.
Figure Sketching is an equally helpful book, full of direct advice on techniques.

The Human Figure by John H. Vanderpoel, Bridgman Publishers, Pelham, New York
A very famous book on figure drawing. If you wish to draw any part of the human figure, or the figure as a whole, this book contains helpful progressive drawings which have never been equalled.

Hands and their Construction by Victor Perard, Pitman Publishing Corporation, New York, N. Y.
Of all details which need to be drawn correctly, *hands* are among the most important. This book, in 216 illustrations, presents more than 1000 drawings of hands in action and at rest, their anatomy, character and expression. A valuable source-book for any artist.

Figure Drawing for All It's Worth by Andrew Loomis, The Viking Press, New York, N. Y.
This is both a primer and an advanced work on figure drawing. Definitely instructive.

Drawing Figures by George Giusti, Studio Publications, Inc., New York, N. Y.
A modern approach to the art of drawing figures, with emphasis on design and expressiveness. Completely illustrated.

Drawing People for Fun by R. W. Vernam, Harper Brothers, New York, N. Y.
Offers practical instruction by a successful artist on drawing and sketching people at home, at work, at play.

ANIMAL DRAWING

Animal Drawing and Painting by Walter J. Wilwerding, Watson-Guptill Publications, New York, N. Y.
The author explains the proper procedure in studying and drawing animals. The illustrations, from Wilwerdings own paintings and drawings, include progressive stages in animal sketching. Animals of every description, plus a few birds and fishes, are presented.

Animal Anatomy and Psychology by Charles R. Knight, McGraw-Hill Book Co., Inc., New York, N. Y.
Birds, fish and reptiles are included, as well as a wide range of animals. Many of the animal drawings show multisided views, with the muscle and bone structure highlighted.

Foster Books on Animal Drawing, Foster Art Service, Laguna Beach, California
Like the entire list of books by this author-publisher, the books on animal drawing are planned for the beginner, with Foster's usual helpful progressive sketches and comments.
How to Draw Animals
How to Draw Horses
How to Draw Dogs

36 pages of "how to do it" animal drawings in *Anyone Can Draw* by Arthur Zaidenberg, Illustrated Editions Company, Inc., New York, N. Y.

Animal Drawing by J. Skeaping, Studio Publications, Inc., New York, N. Y.
An original approach to the drawing of animals, stressing design and character in a free interpretation of natural forms. Illustrated in line and color.

The Art of Animal Drawing by Ken Hultgren, McGraw-Hill Book Co., Inc., New York, N. Y.
By studying a simplified skeleton of the animal's figure, analyzing its appearance in action, and by accenting its outstanding characteristics through caricature, the student will find himself able to draw a variety of contrasting types. Special emphasis is given to animal grouping. Hundreds of drawings.

SKETCHING

Sketching as a Hobby by Arthur L. Guptill, Harper & Brothers, New York, N. Y.
Here is specific help in text and illustrations, on:
The Elementary Steps—choice and use of equipment, layout, tone and shading, proportion, etc.; Technique for Different Media—pencil, water color, crayon, charcoal, wash, pen, etc., Techniques for Different Types of Art Work—still life, portraiture, figures "funnies," etc.

Outdoor Sketching by Ernest W. Watson, Watson-Guptill Publications, New York, N. Y.
Subject matter includes landscape, trees, skies, and old buildings. The techniques: pen and ink, brush and ink, pencil, pen, charcoal, pastel, and water color.

Color in Sketching and Rendering by Arthur L. Guptill, Reinhold Publishing Corporation, New York, N. Y.
This is a standard book on representational painting and rendering in water color and related media. Covers materials and equipment, pigment acquaintance exercises, color facts vs. color theories, color harmony, indoor and outdoor sketching in color, treatment of reflections.

Sketching and Rendering in Pencil by Arthur L. Guptill, Reinhold Publishing Corporation, N. Y.
A thorough treatise on the subject of pencil drawing. Many illustrative sketches by the author and other well-known artists.

Landscape Sketching by Arthur Black, McGraw-Hill Book Co., Inc., New York, N. Y.
A step-by-step approach to the subject of landscape sketching, illustrated by nearly 60 highlight halftones.

PERSPECTIVE

Practical Perspective Drawing by Philip J. Lawson, McGraw-Hill Book Co., Inc., New York, N. Y.
This book provides student and practicing artists in the fields of advertising, industrial design, production, and fiction illustration with perspective drawing methods to improve their skill.

Perspective Charts: (Set of 8, 21″ x 24″) by Philip J. Lawson, Reinhold Publishing Corporation, New York, N. Y.
The accurate construction of instrumental perspective drawings of architecture, furniture, pieces of merchandise etc. often requires so much drudgery that many designers will welcome these labor-saving charts. One merely lays tracing paper over a chart and traces such lines or utilizes such measurements as his problem demands.

Elementary Freehand Perspective by Dora M. Norton, Bridgman Publishers, Inc., Pelham, N. Y.
A particularly good text for beginners because it offers a wide range of simple examples and demonstrations to provide a working knowledge of the representation of objects. 250 drawings, sketches and diagrams.

Perspective by Arthur Bridgman Clark, Bridgman Publishers, Pelham, N. Y.
Among other important points, this comprehensive book covers Interiors, Shades and Shadows, Horizons, and Sizes of Human Figures and Their Value in giving "Scale" to a landscape.

Perspective Made Easy by Ernest K. Norling, The Macmillan Co., New York, N. Y.
Ernest Norling knows how to teach, fully explaining each step as he goes along. Anyone can easily follow his instructions and soon learn to produce drawings with correct perspective.

PAINTING

Oil Painting for the Beginner by Frederic Taubes, Watson-Guptill Publications, New York, N. Y.
With the mixing and the application of colors as a start, the step-by-step text introduces the treatment of still life, flowers, landscapes, and portraits.

Week-End Painter by Laurence V. Burton, Whittlesey House (McGraw-Hill), New York, N. Y.
For those who want to make oil painting their hobby. Offers easy-to-understand advice on equipment and materials; how to find one's way in color; paints and how to use them; painting mediums (thinners and driers); mixing colors; brush work; choosing the subject; the care of paints and brushes.

Painting for Enjoyment by Doris Lee and Arnold Blanch, Tudor Publishing Co., New York, N. Y.
Covers figure, portrait, still life, and landscape painting, describes materials necessary, tells where to buy them, and, in some cases, how to make them at home. Many illustrations, showing paintings in various stages of completion.

Painting as a Hobby by Stephen D. Thack, Harper & Brothers, New York, N. Y.
Fundamental facts about the necessary equipment and materials and their proper use; how to mix colors, how to organize subject matter, how to obtain proper proportions and perspective, how to get different effects of tone and form with oils and water colors.

Anyone Can Paint by Arthur Zaidenberg, Crown Publishers, New York, N. Y.
How to paint in oils, water colors, tempera, etc., and how to make etchings, lithographs, woodcuts, and linoleum blocks.

Technique of Oil Painting by Leonard Richmond, Pitman Publishing Corporation, New York, N. Y.
Problems of technique in the actual handling of oil colors in painting are discussed in detail. 47 color illustrations.

Painting in Oils by Bertram Nichols, Studio Publications, Inc., New York, N. Y.
Instructions for making oil paintings, including a description of materials and their preparation.

Portrait Painting by Michel Jacobs, Pitman Publishing Corporation, New York, N. Y.
A thorough treatise on the technique of portrait painting, including drawing, anatomy of the head, composition, under-painting, color for the portrait painter, brush work, lighting, drapery, facial expressions.

The Painter's Craft by Ralph Mayer, D. Van Nostrand Company, Inc., New York, N. Y.
Unique information on the control of a professional quality in paint and on the development of an expert handling of materials. 74 clear action photographs, and an ingenious color plate which demonstrates the behavior of pigments.

The Simplified Essentials of Oil Painting by Charles X. Carlson
Water Color Painting by Charles X. Carlson, Dover Publications, New York, N. Y.
These are two of "The House of Little Books" series for beginners.

Making Water-Color Behave
Making the Brush Behave
Water-Color Fares Forth by Eliot O'Hara, G. P. Putnam's Sons, New York, N. Y.
Water-Color Fares Forth consists of 18 experiments, illustrated with charts and reproductions of paintings by O'Hara and other noted water-colorists.
In the other two books, the author discusses Shadows on Local Colors, Neutralized Palette, Keyed Color, Limited Hues, Water Color on Smooth Paper, Colored Areas on White Paper, Restraint, Abstraction, Non-Objective Painting, Light Paint on Dark Paper, Quick Impressions, Focus in Confused Subjects, Water Color by Brushing and Scraping, Calligraphy, and Rhythm.

On the Mastery of Water Color Painting by Adrian Hill, Pitman Publishing Corporation, New York, N. Y.
Deals with choice and use of materials. Among the phases explained and illustrated are composition, the rough sketch, clouds and skies, individuality in technique, and interior rendering.

Making a Water Color by George P. Ennis, Studio Publications, Inc., New York, N. Y.
One of the most popular how-to-do-it books by a famous American water-colorist. Stage-by-stage instructions are given, and a series of 16 color plates show different techniques which are analyzed.

Water-Color Demonstrated by Ernest W. Watson and Norman Kent, Watson-Guptill Publications, New York, N. Y.
This book describes and illustrates the working methods of 10 American water-colorists, showing the whys and hows of working in this fascinating medium. 8 color plates, many line drawings.

Water-Color Painting is Fun by Frank A. Staples, McGraw-Hill Book Co., Inc., New York, N. Y.
Here are the basic facts about landscape water-color painting, presented step-by-step in nontechnical terms, and illustrated by the author.

Water-Color Painting for the Beginner by Jacob Getlar Smith, Watson-Guptill Publications, New York, N. Y.
Covers all the needed equipment, customary technical procedures, and how to apply them.

Technique of Flower Painting by Esther B. Johnson, Pitman Publishing Corporation, New York, N. Y.
This book presents the techniques of a successful artist in dealing with materials, color and light, composition and methods of training and approach. Many examples of the author's work in water-color, oil and pastel.
Excellent progressive illustrations of flower painting, in demonstration form, by Nell Walker Warner, composition sketch approaches and the simply instructive text should prove most helpful to beginners.

Water Color Painting by Walter T. Foster
Oil Painting by Walter T. Foster, Foster Art Service, Inc., Laguna Beach, California
These can be found at most art supply stores.

Technique of Still-Life Painting by Leonard Richmond, Pitman Publishing Corporation, New York, N. Y.
A practical guide, with 18 color plates and other illustrations, on the design and composition of the still life, and instruction in the handling of oil paint.

Technique of Water-Color Painting by Leonard Richmond and J. Littlejohns, Pitman Publishing Corporation, New York, N. Y.
The making of a water color in progressive stages, with clear directions and illustrations in line and 49 in color which show processes of applying the medium.

Painting a Portrait by De Lazlo, Studio Publications, New York, N. Y.
A world-famous portrait painter describes simply, with illustrations, his methods and techniques from the preliminary drawings to the finished portrait.

Figure Painting by Walter Klett, Watson-Guptill Publications, Inc., New York, N. Y.
A complete home study course by a famous illustrator. Well illustrated.

The Art of Doing Portraits by Tommy Beere, Dover Publications, New York, N. Y.
One of "The House of Little Books" series for beginners.

Elementary Principles of Landscape Painting by John F. Carlson, N. A., Bridgman Publishers, Pelham, N. Y.
This excellent elementary book covers the theory of angles and consequent values, design, light and the unity of values, aerial perspective, color graduation, linear perspective, color and its emotional value in painting, trees, clouds, composition, the expressive qualities of line and mass, line, pure mechanicalities with a glossary of technical terms.

TECHNIQUES

Pen, Brush and Ink by Henry Pitz, Watson-Guptill Publications, New York, N. Y.
This book describes the tools of the trade—pens, inks, brushes, papers, erasers—and tells how to use them for drawing, in a wide variety of line and tone, practically everything under the sun. Hundreds of illustrations of the work of outstanding professionals.

Pencil Drawing Step-by-Step by Arthur L. Guptill, Reinhold Publishing Corporation, New York, N. Y.
This volume leads by easy stages through construction of subjects, outline drawing, light and shade, texture representation, composition, etc. Over a dozen comparative techniques are fully presented, and every common type of subject matter is considered.

El Dorado Pencil Techniques by Ernest W. Watson
Pencil Drawing by Ernest W. Watson, Watson-Guptill Publications, New York, N. Y.
Both the above are recommended to the student who wishes to develop sureness and professional skill in the handling of pencil as a medium.

Art of the Pencil by Borough Johnson, Pitman Publishing Corporation, New York, N. Y.
A detailed account of how an expert draftsman and artist uses the pencil. Contains a wealth of practical information on the technical methods best suited for a wide range of subjects.

The Simplified Essentials of Charcoal Drawing by Charles X. Carlson
Simplified Ink, Pen and Brush Drawing by Charles X. Carlson, Dover Publications, New York, N. Y.
Two of *The House of Little Books* series for beginners.

The Second Stencil Book by Emmy Zweybruck, The American Crayon Company, Sandusky, Ohio
In her *Second Stencil Book* the artist gives you her special stenciling process in detail. Many illustrations, some in full color.
Another good hobby book, by Emmy Zweybruck, also published by American Crayon, is *Hands at Work*. It covers a variety of home crafts which you can enjoy as hobbies and might well develop into profitable occupations.

There are several good books on techniques published by Bridgman Publishers, Pelham, N. Y.
Pencil Drawing by Frank M. Rines
Drawing in Lead Pencil by Frank M. Rines
Design and Construction in Tree Drawing by Frank M. Rines

Drawing with Pen and Ink by Arthur L. Guptill, Reinhold Publishing Corporation, New York, N. Y.
Discusses the basic principles of composition, life drawing, rendering buildings and interiors, etc. Hundreds of drawings by the author and other leading illustrators.

Pencil Pictures by Theodore Kautzty, Reinhold Publishing Corporation, New York, N. Y.
Landscapes of the seashore, farming country, mountains and woodlands are illustrated and analyzed. Examples of the author's drawings are reproduced in gravure.

Pencil Broadsides by Theodore Kautzty, Reinhold Publishing Corporation, New York, N. Y.
A manual of broad-stroke technique consisting of 12 lessons ranging from fundamental strokes to composition pointers with applications noted to the expression of architectural and landscape forms and textures commonly encountered. Includes 24 plates by the author.

Techniques by Higgins Ink Co., Inc., Brooklyn, New York

Every technique involving the use of ink, whether black or colored, is discussed. Examples of the work of prominent artist-illustrators are included.

SPECIALTIES

Scratchboard Drawing by Meritt Cutler, Watson-Guptill Publications, Inc., New York, N. Y.

In this book, an outstanding scratchboard artist tells how you can accomplish such work.

Airbrush Illustration by Ben Torj Harris, Chas. A. Bennett Co., Peoria, Ill.

Gives inside "know how" in selection, care, and operation of the airbrush, how to plan, develop, and finish work in black-and-white or color. Illustrated procedures, including a section on photo retouching.

Airbrush Techniques by J. Zellers Allen, Graphicart Publications, Ferndale, Michigan

An excellent practical handbook by an expert. Fully illustrated with examples of various treatments.

ILLUSTRATION

The Practice of Illustration by Henry C. Pitz, Watson-Guptill Publications, Inc., New York, N. Y.

Media, methods, composition, technique, and the preparation of drawings for reproduction are discussed as well as the business side of illustration.

40 Illustrators and How They Work from American Artist Magazine (Introduction by Ernest W. Watson) Watson-Guptill Publications, Inc., New York, N. Y.

A most helpful book, showing how artists actually work. There are reproductions of the various stages through which illustrations are developed by professional illustrators.

Creative Illustration by Andrew Loomis, Viking Press, New York, N. Y.

This book shows how to proceed from merely drawing a figure to telling a story or selling a product. The illustration field as a market is given practical treatment. Hundreds of Loomis drawings and 22 pages of illustrations in full color.

How to Illustrate for Money by Sid Hydeman, Harper & Brothers, New York, N. Y.

Detailed and helpful advice from a prominent art editor on the best ways to sell commercial illustrations.

Illustration: Composition, Helpful material in *Anyone can* Draw by Arthur Zaidenberg, Illustrated Editions Company, Inc., New York

A Complete Guide to Drawing, Illustration, Cartooning and Painting edited by Gene Byrnes, with the editorial assistance of A. Thornton Bishop, Simon & Schuster, New York, N. Y.

This comprehensive book contains an extensive section on magazine and book illustration, and gives a remarkable survey of the varied fields of the illustrative arts.

CARTOONING

Introduction to Cartooning by Richard Taylor, Watson-Guptill Publications, New York, N. Y.

Sound and practical instruction by a famous cartoonist who takes up the beginner's problems. There are chapters on supplies, drawing for reproduction, selling, etc.

A Complete Guide to Drawing, Illustration, Cartooning and Painting edited by Gene Byrnes, with the editorial assistance of A. Thornton Bishop, Simon & Schuster, New York, N. Y.

Contains an extensive section on comic drawing, with illustrations by successful artists in the cartooning field. There are many sequence drawings to show their methods.

Cartooning for Everybody by Lawrence Lariar, Crown Publishers, New York, N. Y.

Virtually a "home course" in cartooning and comic illustration.

Cartooning for Fun and for Profit by Lois Fisher, Wilcox and Follett Co., Chicago, Ill.

This completely illustrated book for beginners tells how to go about learning cartooning, what tools to use, what exercises to practice, and what techniques and "tricks of the trade" to employ.

Caricature by Nerman, Studio Publications, Inc., New York, N. Y.

The author presents a stimulating picture book, as well as a technical guide to the art of making caricatures.

Walter T. Foster, How to Draw Library, Foster Art Service, Inc., Box 456, Laguna Beach, Calif.
Modern Cartoons
Animated Cartoons
How to Draw Funnies

How to Draw Comics and Commercial Art by Gene Byrnes, Bridgman Publishers, Pelham, New York

Instructions for drawing features, faces, heads, and "match-stick" figures, the "cylinder" figure in action, and the grouping of figures and composition. 800 Illustrations.

Editorial Cartooning by Dick Spencer, Iowa State College Press, Ames, Iowa

This book deals particularly with news and political cartooning. It tells how to go about analyzing news events and making analogies for cartoon ideas using generally known fables, proverbs, etc. Covers various techniques and symbols.

SCULPTURE, MODELLING, AND CASTING

Plaster Casting for the Student Sculptor by V. A. Wager, Chas. A. Bennett Co., Peoria, Ill.
Detailed instructions for casting from clay, plasticene or wax, casting from life, and making papier mâchés. Fully illustrated.

The Sculptor's Way by Brenda Putnam, Watson-Guptill Publications, New York, N. Y.
This book has been rightly called "the best in its field." The section on comparative anatomy is excellent. Modelling, casting, treatment of drapery, enlarging or reducing, and ceramic sculpture are also discussed.

Modelling by Petrie, Chas. A. Bennett Co., Peoria, Ill.
Designing and modelling of figures from clay, with a brief coverage of ceramics to explain how to make the figures permanent. Many photographs of finished work by young artists.

Fundamentals of Clay Modelling by R. R. Fiore, Dover Publications, New York, N. Y.
One of *The House of Little Books* series.

Sculpture by Henry Liou, Foster Art Service, Laguna Beach, California
For its condensed scope, this presents a remarkably clear introduction to the sculptor's art and to his working technique. Pages of excellent photographs show the progressive steps in creating a piece of sculpture.

For explicit instructions on casting plaster of paris, and also for the relief carving and coloring of wood, see *Arts and Crafts Projects,* published by Higgins Ink Co., Brooklyn, N. Y.

Soap Sculpture by Lester Gaba, Studio Publications, Inc., New York, N. Y.
An excellent instructional book. Every project is illustrated photographically as well as by simple working diagrams.

The Home Workshop by William W. Klenke, Chas. A. Bennett, Peoria, Ill.
This book tells you how to select tools and machines, how to arrange the equipment of your home shop, how to operate and care for such small motor-driven machines as circular saw, band saw, jointer, and sander. Includes plans for making workshop benches, tool cabinets, etc.; also chapters on joint making, use of glue, assembling, and finishing, and charts about nails, screws, etc.
The publishers also offer 12 workbooks by the author, covering a variety of woodworking techniques and things to make.

You can Whittle and Carve by Franklin Gottshall and Amanda Hellum, Bruce Publishing Co., Milwaukee, Wisc.
Shows how to carve quaint wooden animals, figures, wall plaques, etc. Illustrated.

Modern Furniture Making and Design by R. Hooper, Chas. A. Bennett Co., Peoria, Ill.
This book presents drawings and construction methods for furniture in simple modern styles for home and garden.

See also *Creative Design in Furniture* by Varnum, Manual Arts Press.

More Ben Hunt Whittlings by W. Ben Hunt, Bruce Publishing Co., Milwaukee, Wisc.
Advanced projects for whittling are presented, including colorful birds and unusual animal poses, as well as human figures and original character studies.

Chip Carving, Brown Book of Carving Designs, Fellowcrafters, Inc., Oliver St., Boston, Mass.
Chip carving is the beginner's introduction to more advanced wood-carving, particularly relief carving.

Woodcarving as a Hobby by Herbert W. Faulkener, Harper & Brothers, New York, N. Y.
An exceedingly helpful manual containing step-by-step instructions. The author's supplementary manual, *Designs for Woodcarving*, contains a hundred plates of designs.

Design and Figure Carving by E. J. Tangerman, McGraw-Hill Book Co., Inc., New York, N. Y.
An encyclopedia of designs and applications for whittlers and woodcarvers. More than 1,200 illustrations.

Whittling and Woodcarving by E. J. Tangerman, McGraw-Hill Book Co., Inc., New York, N. Y.
From simple whittling through rustic, chain, and fan carving to models, ships-in-bottles, chip carving, surface decorations, and applications of woodcarving in interior decoration. Selection and care of woodcarving tools and knives; wood characteristics, how to carve soap, ivory, fruit pits, etc. Many sketches and photographs.

The following books for craftsmen are listed by the Craftsman Wood Service Co., Chicago 8, Ill.:
Woodfinishing by F. N. Vanderwalter
Furniture Finishing by A. B. Pattou
Furniture Finishing, Decoration and Patching by A. B. Pattou and C. L. Vaughn
50 Popular Wood-Working Projects by Joseph J. Lukowitz
It's Fun to Build Modern Furniture by Clifford K. Lush (Complete drawings and directions)
Woodcarving Made Easy by J. L. Sowers
Forty Pieces of Fine Furniture by Herman Hijorth
Woodworking for Everybody by Shee and Wagner

It's Fun to Make Things by W. T. R. Price, Crown Publishers, New York, N. Y.
For people who may possess no technical skills, nor any tools beyond a hammer and saw. Practical instructions and sketches covering bookshelves, window seats, screens, closet fittings and many simple pieces of furniture.

How to do Woodcarving (one of the popular Foster books)

New Ideas in Woodcraft by John T. Lemos, Bridgman Publishers, Pelham, N. Y .
 Among matters explained and illustrated are: the best woods for various handicrafts, useful and inexpensive wood-craft outfits, sawing, carving and tooling, finishing wood objects, color schemes.
 Making or decorating a variety of objects, such as book ends, door stops, desk sets, bracelets, wooden plates and bowls, etc.

The following practical handbooks are listed by Chas. A. Bennett Co., Peoria, Ill.:

Creative Crafts in Wood—Dank	*Essentials of Woodworking*—Griffith
Wooden Toymaking—Horton	*Selected Furniture Drawings*—Klenke
Chip Carving—Moore	*Coloring, Finishing and Painting Wood*—Newell
The Art of Whittling—Faurot	*Wood and Lumber*—Newell
Woodwork for Beginners—Griffith	*Woodworking Manual for Students*—Nichols
Furniture Projects—Bryant	*Design and Construction in Wood*—Noyes
Workshop Notebook—Greene	*Elementary Woodworking Projects*—Wise
Carpentry—Griffith	

Index

435